JEANNETTE VEATCH, Ph.D., New York University, is Professor of Education at Jersey City State College. She previously taught at The Pennsylvania State University, University of Illinois, Goucher College and New York University, and was Director of The Program Development Division of the Girl Scouts of The United States of America. Dr. Veatch is active in the National Council of the Teachers of English, and the Association for Supervision and Curriculum Development.

PHILIP ACINAPURO, Ed.D., Teachers College, Columbia University, is Principal of the East Memorial School in Farmingdale, New York. He previously taught at the Oak Lane Country Day School of Temple University and was Supervisor of Reading in the Farmingdale Public School System.

READING IN THE
ELEMENTARY SCHOOL

JEANNETTE VEATCH
Jersey City State College

With the Assistance of
Philip J. Acinapuro
East Memorial School
Farmingdale, New York

THE RONALD PRESS COMPANY • NEW YORK

Library of Congress Card Catalog Number: 66–16854

PRINTED IN THE UNITED STATES OF AMERICA

PREFACE

There has been little change in approaches to instruction in reading for many decades. If there is anything wrong with the way American children are taught reading, it must be traceable to traditional practices.

This textbook is intended for teachers at the pre-service and in-service level. A combination of approaches is provided that together add up to new ways of teaching reading, even though each part of the process has been used, in some form or other, in previous years.

The content might be concisely described by citing Sylvia Ashton-Warner's concept of *key vocabulary,* coupled with what has come to be known as the *language experience* approach. Furthermore, this text weaves the contributions of linguistic science into instructional patterns, particularly the usefulness of the alphabet and spontaneous speech of the learners. The ways in which good literature can be used when children have achieved some modicum of reading ability are presented on a self-choice basis. This latter practice has gained the name of "individualized reading" and has been written about extensively by the author of the present book, as well as others in the field.

From a classroom management sense, this book suggests meeting individual differences by ways other than the usual ability groupings and other homogeneous patterns. It further suggests a sequence of teaching that differs from the common Directed Reading Lesson. Thus, as children are truly different, their instruction must take these differences into account. Teachers need to be trained to teach children to read no matter what book or piece of material they bring for their instruction. The acceptance of individual differences in children means that teaching must be on a one-to-one basis at fairly regular intervals, while grouping must be such as to support such a philosophy.

This book is intended to help teachers with ordinary-sized classrooms, with average budgetary support, and therefore presents nothing that should require unique situations or people. It is hoped that this material will aid instructors who are training teachers at the pre-service college level, teachers in service, and administrators who wish to encourage the growth of their teachers. Nor can those single teachers be ignored who, sometimes heroically, wish to find new paths when no one around them is interested.

This book presents a point of view that differs from past practice, but this view is by no means impractical. Most of all the author wishes to re-personalize the teaching of reading and, more than in the past, base instruction on the human interaction between child and teacher.

JEANNETTE VEATCH

Jersey City, New Jersey
February, 1966

ACKNOWLEDGMENT

Among those who helped in the crystallization of the ideas presented in this book, the most important are the classroom teachers all over the nation who have worked to use, in part or whole, the concepts included here. The graciousness of those teachers who let the author come, watch, and even teach, is greatly appreciated. They will never know how much encouragement they engendered. Nor, for that matter, which of the ideas they fertilized in my mind.

Most important of all, of course, was the invaluable assistance of my friend, Dr. Philip J. Acinapuro. It was his thinking and first hand experiences in the early stages of the manuscript that were so helpful. He provided much needed clarification at frequent intervals. Without his support and interest this book would have been long delayed, and certainly would have appeared with some differences from its present form.

In addition, the author is indebted to Dr. Carl Sailer, friend and colleague, whose detailed help in the final stages of the manuscript was most constructive. Also John Burks, Jr., whose pictorial and graphic representations must be mentioned in grateful appreciation and Judge Lester Kahan, who contributed several photographs.

Grants from the research funds of the Pennsylvania State University considerably aided the initial exploration of the author into the patterns of teaching letter sounds using the alphabet and children's own words. It is a comforting example of how small money grants may explore original fields, and, hopefully, contribute to new growth in exhausted areas.

Finally, this author is no different from any other in her appreciation of the many friends who provided a kind of intellectual mirror into which we all must look. Francis Bacon may not have been thinking of the teaching of reading when he wrote the following words, but he was, nevertheless, encapsulating the message between these covers.

Reading maketh a full man, conference a ready man, and writing an exact man.

The point is, after all, not that children *can* read, but that they do read. Herein lies all of our greatest hopes.

J.V.

CONTENTS

Part III: PROGRESSION AND DEVELOPMENT

I

INTRODUCTION AND BACKGROUND

1

THE READING PROGRAM

Herein is presented a way of teaching reading that has certain major characteristics that set it off from current practice. The first is that of the prime use of children's own language in learning to read. The second is that of pupil self-selection—i.e., every child should be taught to read with books that he himself chooses. He may and probably will be asked to justify his choices, but these are his instructional materials nevertheless. The third is the individual conference. Every child must have a frequent, private individual conference with his teacher wherein his own unique needs are assessed and steps taken to improve his whole reading performance. The fourth element of this text's approach to reading instruction is that of specific needs grouping, or grouping for tasks. Based upon the observations and records of the teacher during the individual conference, children are grouped, as necessary, upon certain and highly specific needs, tasks, projects, and difficulties that coincide with two or more members of the class.

That children do read is a mark of their desire to read. There are, of course, many people who can read, but only do so when escape from reality, usually a boring reality, is necessary. We are concerned here, as is everyone who has been interested in the teaching of reading, with a program that will produce eager readers, omnivorous readers, book readers, as well as those who devour the many newspapers and magazines now available.

What is suggested within these pages is really a new philosophy of reading. As is usually so, it is a combination of several old ideas. Many adherents of present practice will exclaim "We believe this, too!" This may well be so, but at this writing, the actual prevalent patterns of reading practice are based upon totally opposite philosophical bases.

Where this text urges self-selection of instructional materials, basal reader systems insist that the teacher give the children books with which they are taught to read. There is no self-choice. Where this text describes grouping on the basis of tasks to be accomplished in highly specific terms, prevalent patterns segregate pupils into groups based upon generalized ability. Where this text insists that there is enough motivation for reading in the highly personal act of choosing a book, basal systems proceed through what is known as the "directed reading lesson," the first step of which is "developing interest" or motivating the pupil to be interested in what is to be read. Where this text shows that the gradation of reading materials from easy to more difficult can be within the act of free choice by the pupil, conventional patterns require that a planned sequential set of books be given children in a regularized order.

READING IS READING IS READING

Teachers who read through this text will find patterns of instruction that have, at one time or another, been labeled "individualized reading" or "language-experience approach" or "personalized" or by some other term. As none of these labels serves to describe the total practice presented, the author proposes to proceed without benefit of label, and discuss "READING," for such is the topic of this book.

There are some distinguishing features, however, that set this presentation apart from any other now in print. The basic assumptions upon which recommendations are made are the benchmarks that will distinguish these patterns from any other.

BASIC ASSUMPTIONS

Reading instruction depends centrally upon:

A variety of materials with literary merit.

The use of children's own speech, in various ways, at all age levels.

The incentive factor of pupil-selected material.

The teacher-pupil conference on a one-to-one basis.

Groups organized on specific items must be based upon a set of assumptions that will not hold for those traditional patterns that depend centrally upon: a series of books with carefully controlled vocabularies to be used according to manuals; classroom groups organized upon generalized ability levels, with planned sequential steps from grade to grade as outlined in manuals, and intended for use in all schools in the entire nation.

If the approach that this text presents has merit, it rests upon some important assumptions that are unique at this present time.

1. Reading must be taught as part of all of the other language arts.
2. Spelling is as important in learning to read as it is in learning to write.
3. Reading and spelling are but two sides of the same coin.
4. Children learn to read better and faster when they are free to pace their own growth, seeking help when necessary.
5. The act of reading must center upon the child, with the materials used of secondary importance.
6. Children's own language is a valuable source material for reading instruction.
7. Individual differences are met by teaching individuals one by one.
8. Classroom efficiency is enhanced when groups are organized upon an identified need, problem, difficulty, or interest.
9. There is no established rank order of reading materials.
10. There is a series of progressions or developmental stages that can be recognized and provided for with a variety of materials.
11. Reading growth results when a pupil commits himself to a piece of material.
12. As reading is a personal act, the choice of material is an expression of self.
13. The human factor of personal commitment of the pupil will enhance reading growth when matched by the ability of the teacher to change and adapt procedures on the spot.
14. Not all skills need be taught to every child, nor in identical sequence to more than one child.
15. Progress may be steadily cumulative, but it may also be apparent in great leaps and bounds.
16. Skills are gained during the act of reading and not before it.
17. There is no clearly established sequence of skills for all children.
18. There is no single piece of material that meets the needs of every pupil in any given class.
19. While silent reading is central, oral reading is placed in a prominent position with a purpose.
20. The love of books and reading is encouraged when loved books are read.

Look these over carefully. They contain the essence of the profoundly revolutionary character of the instructional program presented in this text. These may have roots in the past, but, if so, such have been in desultory practice and some theory. The practice we are proposing is, in its total pattern, quite new. Much of it will be familiar to some. Some of it will be familiar to many. But few will have put together the sweep, the panorama of reading instruction in these terms. Let us proceed to describe briefly what we propose.

Talking to explore spontaneous language patterns.

One key feature of the practices advocated in this text is that children's *own* language is used to teach a myriad of reading skills—particularly those that are needed to get reading started. This "language experience" approach is not a new practice, having been used by most teachers in the elementary grades for years. However, the glaciating action of commercial systems pushing their materials has served to reduce, materially, teachers' use of children's own language in reading instruction. Although most teachers do use experience charts frequently in beginning reading, it is the rare one who sees such as a dominant pattern of her work. Even more rare is the use of children's own language to develop skills necessary at more advanced levels.[1]

Another key feature is the importance of classroom management during the reading period, as differentiated from "method." "Method" is that which happens to children actually being instructed. "Method" is what happens after a teacher has the children with him. "Method" is what a teacher does in order to teach, regardless of who are there

[1] D. M. Lee and R. Van Allen, *Learning to Read Through Experience* (rev. ed.), New York: Appleton-Century-Crofts, Inc., 1963, and printed with the kind permission of Appleton-Century-Crofts, Inc.; Mildred Dawson, *Language Teaching in Grades 1 and 2* (rev. ed.), New York: Harcourt, Brace & World, Inc., 1949; *Use of Charts in the Primary Grades,* pamphlet, Madison, Wis., Public Schools, 1947.

to be taught and how they got there. Instruction can vary under any manner of management, basal or otherwise.

"Classroom Management," on the other hand, is what the teacher does to get ready to instruct. How are the children asked to move? Where are the books? What books are there? Where does the teacher place himself? How is it decided which children shall be taught when? How are the pupils managed as they go about the business of being taught to read?

In this text a pattern is proposed that we feel makes for the optimum conditions of learning to read. We say "optimum" because children are being taught to learn to read by means of materials they themselves select. Failure can certainly occur. But when children choose their own books, meet their teacher in a situation that is geared to their individual needs, and face their problems and diffi-

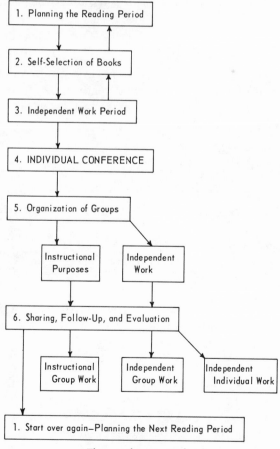

The reading period.

culties openly under manageable conditions, success is not an accident.

There are certain procedures that must occur or our basic assumptions are not followed. Yet within these there are infinite possibilities of variety. The differences between teachers are almost limitless. The flow chart on page 7 indicates how these principles can be applied. However, this chart presents classroom management only. What happens within the individual conference, or within a group, is described elsewhere. This is a complete picture, perhaps in oversimplified form, of a succession of reading periods over weeks of time. It is intended to be used with a total class, rather than just a part of a class. Notice the direction of the arrows.

Taking each block on this chart, let us briefly describe how such a pattern of instruction will proceed. The reader will find footnotes referring him to chapters where the discussion of the same topic is in greater detail.

Planning the Reading Period

As can be seen, there are arrows going in both directions between the activities of planning for the total reading period, and the self-selection of books. Each child is trained to choose his own reading material on two criteria:

1. He likes it.
2. He can read it.

This is self-selection. Each child must decide further:

1. Shall I prepare this book for my individual conference with my teacher?
2. Shall I just read it by myself?
3. What will I do when I am finished reading?
4. Where do I get help I need?

This is planning the whole reading period. All plans must be made with the knowledge and approval of the teacher. He gives clearance.

Self-Selection of Books[2]

As the criteria for book selection are that the child likes the book, and is able to read it, he may need help in finding suitable material. The supply of books, of course, must be ample to meet all ranges of interests and abilities. Usually three to five titles per child is an

2 See pages 197–98, 299–300.

adequate supply. The teacher's help and advice do not necessarily mean a child loses his right of choice. Even though the teacher says, in effect, "Read"—that directive is broad indeed.

The Independent Work Period[3]

The first item on every child's independent work period is the silent reading of his own material. He may change his book if he wishes, even though the teacher might want to ask why, but he settles down to become lost in the world of literature. When he is "read out," so to speak, he proceeds with whatever plan he has made. It might be intensive study of a story to present to his teacher in an upcoming conference or it might be developing a report to present to the class on certain materials or experiments during sharing time. It might be polishing a skill from another curriculum area—handwriting, spelling, or written composition. There are limitless possibilities. But whatever he does, he is quiet and independently occupied, alone or in a group.

The Individual Conference[4]

The peak, the summit, the climax of the reading instructional program must lie in the intensive individual sessions, on a one-to-one basis, with the teacher. In such a situation the teacher can make or break a reading program. The more a teacher knows about reading skills, the more can be taught. The more a teacher demands high standards of performance, and asks helpful questions to facilitate high standards, the more children will accept and follow and learn.

The teacher does not attempt to check on everything a child reads, but concentrates on a portion of the child's reading that *he has selected and prepared* for presentation. Similarly, not every child can read privately with his teacher every day, but the teacher who perfects his conference skills neglects no one, not even the gifted.

The teacher keeps detailed records of each conference of each child. These records give clues for later instruction.

Organization of Groups[5]

The teacher plans for group-teaching from the records and impressions gained during his conference and from other work with each pupil. When two or more children show the same need, or the

[3] See Chapter 4.
[4] See Chapter 6.
[5] See Chapter 7.

same interest, or the same purpose in their reading, a group is obviously called for. Thus groups are organized on bases other than the traditional slow, middle, and fast abilities.

GROUPS FOR INSTRUCTIONAL PURPOSES. When groups are organized with specific clear-cut needs, they will probably require the direct attention of the teacher. They probably will need the kind of help that cannot be left to an independent situation. They, thus, will meet with the teacher in succession—often during one-half of the reading period.

GROUPS FOR INDEPENDENT WORK. When groups are organized on a single purpose that does not require the continuing and intensive work of the teacher, they can meet simultaneously and work independently. In such a case, the teacher can move from group to group, checking to see that the purpose for which they were organized is being served.

These two types of groups may meet during the reading period, but in that case must observe the need for quiet so that the teacher can work in single conferences or teach directly one of the groups.

Sharing, Follow-Up, and Evaluation[6]

Sharing or telling about one's book seems to have become a regular feature of personalized reading programs. It seems that children, having chosen a book of their own, wish the chance to "brag" about it. Many studies reflect this phenomenon. It is often better that such sharing take place outside of the usual reading period. It is wonderful on Friday afternoon!

Follow-up allows for the wise use of workbooks and other similar types of semiprogrammed materials. These are best used not in the traditional pattern, the way the publishers and authors intended, but on a pick-and-choose basis of fitting a given page to a given child or group that has need of that particular lesson. These materials can be time- and teacher-savers in spite of their too frequently grotesque, ugly, and uncreative format.

Evaluation is an on-going process and is based best upon well-kept records. The one-to-one conference allows for an immediately available evaluative activity between the child and teacher—but even so, the teacher's records would show what was accomplished. With such a wealth of information, teachers find report cards, parents' conferences, and supervisors' and administrators' questions no problem at all.

[6] See Chapter 12.

SUMMARY

Thus we come the full circle and are ready to start over again—even though some children might not have proceeded at the same pace as the rest. Page 384, then, is the "map" of how an individualized program proceeds through the days and weeks.

2

NEW PATTERNS:
PRELIMINARY STEPS

This chapter is addressed to those teachers who wish step-by-step help in moving from the traditional reading programs dependent upon basal materials to those dependent upon, initially, children's own language and later upon a variety of books and other materials used upon a self-choice basis. Here the author presents an overview. Details are left for later chapters. How can a teacher get started? What does happen first? Where are the books kept? Which children are involved if the whole class is not? Where does one secure enough books? How does one proceed once a beginning is made?

GENERAL DIRECTIONS

There are several operations that are necessary for the teacher to get ready. A teacher's mind must carry mental photographs that get him started. These are a starting point, often incomplete and undeveloped, even though they become more clear from day to day. The dangers in beginning with a new approach are not so much in lack of information, although information is certainly needed, but in the biting off of more than one can chew. It is better to begin on a small scale and work to larger operations, than to begin large and be forced to reduce to a smaller scale.

Whatever else may be said, the patterns presented in this book are not DIFFICULT, but they are most sharply DIFFERENT. The whole philosophy of teaching runs counter to the traditional three-ability grouped, planned sequential materials of the current practice. A teacher must be prepared for the cold bath, as well as the heady excitement of discovery of new and effective methods of teaching.

Several preparatory steps seem important. Their order represents a rationale, but certainly this should not be viewed as mandatory.

If skipping around will work better for one person, he should skip around.

Preliminary Steps

1. Make up your own mind.
2. Consult, as necessary, parents and school authorities.
3. Observe one or more teachers who have been working along the desired lines.
4. Read as many references as possible.
5. Get all of the supplies possible, books, and other materials.
6. Arrange your classroom for the best productive effort. Draw a sketch if it will help.
7. Fix a notebook for keeping records.
8. Plan necessary routines.

Each of these steps needs special discussion to make sure that it is understood in the context of a changing pattern. We will take them one by one.

1. Make Up Your Own Mind

Teachers who wish to try these patterns of reading instruction must make up their own minds that this is what they want to do. How a teacher would arrive at such a decision is a personal matter. Some teachers may be so angry with traditional practice that they will try anything for a change. Some may wish to try new ideas because they are unutterably bored with what they are doing. Others with the genuine spirit of exploration, with a joy of breaking new paths, will try a new way of doing things.

Whatever the reason, teachers must *want* to try these patterns for personal reasons. Administrators would do well to encourage, to support, to help, to provide necessary books, but not to mandate. It won't work, either with reading or with any other portion of the curriculum.

The age of the teacher has nothing to do with a desire for change. It is his state of mind. Inspirational supervision has much to do with such a state of mind. To lead is not to exert one's status. Most people love a good leader. Bringing about a desire to change is a true administrative skill. One thing is certain: Teachers will do most anything if they are convinced that a different way of working will make

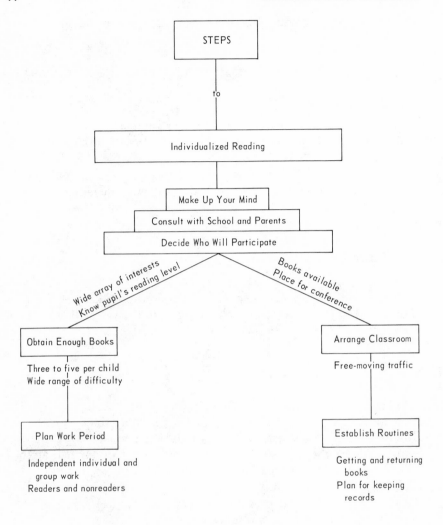

You're on your way!

One way to teach reading. (Courtesy of Joanne Fratti.)

their life in the classroom more satisfying. The quiet rebellion and resistance against change that so many administrators feel in teachers come not from lack of desire but from bitter disappointment in those changes suggested in the past that did not fulfill an early promise. For glory is in teaching, as many know. It holds the most satisfying of human emotions. But satisfaction does not come by

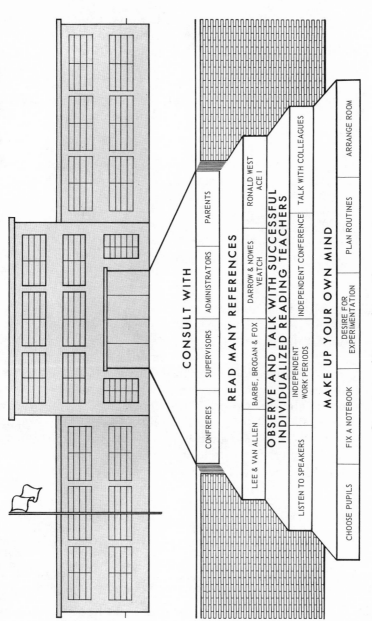

Steps to teaching reading with new patterns.

edict. It comes through the teacher's discovery, exploration, and experimentation of new patterns, or at least those new to him.

The research findings[1] that are clear at this writing might be useful to a teacher who would like to move into new patterns. There are three clearly established results from studies of programs involving self-selection and an individual conference. Regardless of what else was noted, or the design of the study, the following are noteworthy:

1. Choosing one's own book for instruction sharply improves attitudes toward reading (and in some cases a reduction of discipline problems was reported).
2. The quantity and quality of reading increase markedly when children choose their own reading material and have an individual conference with their teacher.[2]
3. Children are uniformly enthusiastic about reading alone to their teacher.[3]

There is a fourth finding that needs to be mentioned. It is the increase in achievement. Some studies in which the "halo" effect is obvious report dramatic improvement in reading. Other studies, more tightly drawn, report improvement or no worsening of achievement when a self-selection program is pursued. The authors would guess that achievement will be dramatically improved when teachers' diagnostic abilities are better developed for the individual conference. The matter of teaching skills for skills' sake has corrupted reading methods. The mere fact of allowing a child to read alone to his teacher has already proved beneficial. Once teachers are more clear as to methodology in that conference, greater improvement can be expected than is now evident.

[1] As we go to press, a new important and comprehensive study has been released. The Lakeshore Curriculum Study Council of Milwaukee, Wisconsin, experimented in a three-year longitudinal study comparing classrooms under an individualized program (conforming in description to points made in this book) to those under a basal program. Among several of the findings one stands out. Children in individualized reading programs show significantly better reading achievement than children in basal programs. Records of 361 children from 29 classrooms were in the final tabulation. Lakeshore Curriculum Study Council, *Three Year Longitudinal Study Comparing Individualized and Basal Reading Program at the Primary Level: An Interim Report.*

[2] This was true only of first and second grades in Lakeshore Curriculum Study Council report, as far as quantity of reading only is concerned. Measurement of quality is not reported to date, and, indeed, is rare in any research report.

[3] This has been established as far as children in the elementary grades are concerned. The author suspects that at the secondary level individual conferences held in the same room with a peer group will not be so successful. There is no research one way or the other on this point. The element of privacy is probably vital to adolescents.

2. Consult, as Necessary, Parents and School Authorities

Parents have a right to know what is going on. Parents can be informed of developments, but should not be asked to make professional decisions. They should know that a new program in reading is being started that will extend the literary horizons of children beyond the drabnesses of Alices and Jerrys.

There is much that parents can understand about the technicalities of reading instruction. For example, parents will not be surprised to know that teachers know what parents have always known—that children are speaking in sentences that contain dependent clauses, independent clauses, all kinds of prepositional phrases, past, present, and future verbs, singular and plural number, and thousands and thousands of words, by the time they are FIVE years old.

Thus, why restrict change to material predominantly comprised of repetitive exclamations and simple sentences? Suggested change in teaching pattern simply uses this knowledge and puts it into practice. Parents are naturally concerned about what happens to their children. They should be. They are impatient when they see that progress is being limited. They are delighted when they see progress bounding ahead. So teachers must work with parents and help them to see what is going on. They need to be invited to school so often that they truly feel welcome.

If parents are worried, teachers can allay any fears by assuring them that:

1. Their children will learn to read from books.
2. Their children will be taught phonics.
3. As the program is based on good literature, the best books available will be used in the instructional program.
4. The technical problems of doing all of this for each individual child have been solved. We know HOW.
5. Their youngsters will become as fine human beings as possible, and very good readers to boot.

Inasmuch as the principal has ultimate authority over a school building, he must know what is going on. His authority must be accepted. In the experience of the authors, it is the rare principal who denies an excited teacher the right to try new things if that teacher is clear about what he would like to do. So often teachers complain about principals, "They won't let me do anything"; and principals complain, "If only my teachers would try something new."

Once his mind is made up, the teacher must think through what is to be done and explore the barriers and the aids that would be available. But, in all events, superiors must be informed of any change to come in educational procedure. It is discourteous and non-professional not to do so.

Most teachers are well aware of the situation they face as far as status figures are concerned. They are aware of limits. They are aware of possibilities. Knowing these things, and inquiring about that which they do not know, is the preliminary step to making the necessary plans for what is to come. Everyone must know where he stands.

If a teacher is in a situation where he is forbidden to try any of the patterns herein suggested, or to try ANY idea that is new to him, he has at least one recommended step that can be followed: He can seek a position in another school system. All colleges and universities maintain placement services for those who wish better positions. There are also private, professional employment agencies. (The National Association of Teachers Agencies maintains a list of such agencies in the various states. This list is available from most colleges and universities that maintain a teacher placement service. The Association enforces a rigid code of ethics and all must subscribe and practice these or lose their listing.)

3. Observe Other Teachers Who Have Been Working Along the Lines Desired

Most school systems provide "visiting" days for their teachers. Teachers find someone who is doing something they would like to see. A substitute is hired so that the teacher's class is covered. He loses no salary, and he sees a different classroom for that day. Seeing another teacher teach is one of the best in-service training practices; even when there is some question about the observed practice, teachers learn what NOT to do, as well as what to do.

There are several types of observations that could be arranged for teachers who would like to see another do some of the following patterns: For example, a teacher could watch:

1. The taking of children's dictation in the first week of school.
2. The taking of dictation, editing it, and recording it for later use in instruction.
3. The use of dictation at upper-grade levels for such projects as a class newspaper, planning a dramatic effort, etc.
4. The independent work period started with silent reading of books chosen by each pupil himself.

5. The individual conference in any or all its phases.
6. Planning for groups when general achievement is not the consideration, while learning some specific skill is.
7. Watching the record-keeping of the teacher, as well as those kept by the children.
8. Observing classroom routines in various classrooms.
9. The guidance role of the teacher in helping children choose books wisely.
10. The teaching of groups that have been organized on the basis of records taken during the reading conference.

These are but some of the general suggestions of activities that would be helpful to teachers who wish to move in new and different directions. Perhaps a supervisor could assist a teacher in deciding what to concentrate upon, or better yet, go along!

However, teachers get ideas from watching each other. It is easy for them to identify with another teacher in action.

Of course, if there are no such classrooms available, there are films. Watching films is another way of watching another teacher. A list of good ones can be found in Chapter 14.

4. Read as Many References as Possible

There are literally hundreds of articles now available in which teachers have written of their experiences with these approaches. In part, much is quite old. There is a list in Chapter 14 for those who are interested, with comments upon each entry.

Below are some important writings on the approach presented in this text, but these should not be expected to be in total agreement with everything herein offered. This list is made up of books that TEND in the same direction. The reader or teacher must pick and choose, as usual, from all that is available. However, the following materials can be cited as among the most useful:

Language Experience Approach

Burrows, A. T., *et al. They All Want To Write* (3d ed.). New York: Holt, Rinehart & Winston, Inc., 1964.

Lee, D. M., and Van Allen, R. *Learning to Read Through Experience* (revised ed.). New York: Appleton-Century-Crofts, Inc., 1963.

Herrick, V. E., and Nerbovig, M. *Using Experience Charts*. Columbus, Ohio: Charles E. Merrill Books, Inc., 1960.

Self-Selection Practices

Association for Childhood Education, International, *Individualized Education*. Washington, D. C.: 1964.

Barbe, W. *An Educator's Guide to Personalized Reading*. Englewood Cliffs, N. J.: Prentice-Hall, Inc., 1961.

Board of Education of the City of New York. *A Practical Guide to Individualized Reading*. New York: Bureau of Educational Research Publication #40, 1961.

Brogan, P., and Fox, L. *Helping Children Read*. New York: Holt, Rinehart & Winston, Inc., 1961.

Darrow, H. F., and Howes, V. M. *Approaches to Individualized Reading*. New York: Appleton-Century-Crofts, Inc., 1961.

Veatch, Jeanette. *How To Teach Reading with Children's Books*. New York: Teachers College, Columbia University, 1964.

Veatch, Jeanette. *Individualized Reading for Success in the Classroom*. New London, Conn.: Arthur C. Croft Publications, Educational Trend No. 654, 1954.

Veatch, Jeanette. *Individualizing Your Reading Program*. New York: G. P. Putnam's Sons, Inc., 1959.

Phonics, Linguistics, and Phonetics

Dolch, E. W. *Teaching of Sounding*. Pamphlet. Champaign, Ill.: Garrard Publishing Co., 1962.

Durrell, D., and Murphy, H. *Developing Word Power*. New York: Harcourt, Brace & World, Inc., 1945.

Russell, K. V., Murphy, H., and Durrell, D. *Developing Spelling Power*. New York: Harcourt, Brace & World, Inc., 1957.

5. Collect the Books and Other Necessary Supplies

To begin a self-selection program in any classroom, the book supply should exceed the number of pupils by about three to five times. But just quantity of books is not the point. A teacher needs to do a kind of "interest census" of the class. He would ask:

1. What kind of books do you like?
2. If I can't get books on all of these topics, which are the most important?

These kinds of probing questions are really the beginning of motivation or incentive to read. If a boy who has previously been bored with reading finds that his great interest in baseball will produce several books on the subject, he will look upon reading much more favorably than before.

In any event, the teacher needs to do the best he can to find books that have an appeal to his class, as well as fitting the relative achievement levels of each child. For example, first-grade teachers will need books for children with abilities ranging from nonreaders to third- and fourth-grade levels. Picture books, beginner books of all kinds, more advanced trade books, and certainly a smattering of basal readers, co-basal readers, and multiple basal would be in order. Swapping a few books from many sets has helped many a teacher get started.

Similarly, intermediate-grade teachers would want to select books that their pupils are interested in, and perhaps have some that go a grade or two below the lowest score on the reading achievement test, and two or three grades above for the more able reader.

The following is a brief list of book sources. See also Chapter 14 for many more.

1. Enlist the school librarian's aid.
2. Seek out public library supplies.
3. Use bookmobiles.
4. Use personal library cards, child and adult.
5. Use the regular book order.
6. Book fairs for new and used books.
7. Teacher representation on school budget committees.
8. Swap basal and supplementary readers.
9. Find paperbacks.

Such wide-ranging possibilities are necessary in order to guarantee that each pupil has a genuine free choice of material. Upon that foundation of choice is the best reading program built. Teachers will find surprising ranges of difficulty in a class supposedly of one grade level. Even those who are convinced that children can be grouped homogeneously in a useful fashion must admit that great differences exist within such a supposedly uniform group, yet such ranges are quite normal and in a self-selection program cause no problem.

Providing for ability ranges of five, six, or seven years takes a bit of doing but is far from an overwhelming task. Getting boxes of books from libraries, joining paperback book clubs, setting up book fairs, trading of a few copies of basals and their supplementary books between teachers in the same building, and having children bring books from home are all possible. Enough books should be found to allow a teacher to begin a self-choice program.

6. Arrange Your Classroom

Arranging the seats and supplies and children is a management problem. Every inch of floor space should be used to best advantage. If a table takes up too much room, swap it for a bookcase! If single rows of seats use up all the floor space—and they usually do—double up the rows. If seating children in a large sweeping half moon of triple rows leaves more room than any other arrangement, that is what should be done.

While the reading period must consist of quiet activities (the activity period allows children to pound and hammer and saw), children need to have a working spot for themselves that is as non-distracting as possible. Often the traditional rows of seats are the best way to provide that. But children can shift their movable seats so that they are not distracted if they happen to look up. Children also need places for independent group work. These may be tables, or circles of seats, or something similar.

As the reading program centers upon quantities of books, where should these be put? Out of traffic—where children can take their time to look over the supply and make their choice.

Many teachers like to draw a map of their room. It helps one think through coming events. The element of privacy is important for the teacher-pupil conference. It is also important for independent individual work. The conference should be heard as little as possible by the rest of the class.

Here are some necessary points to be included in room arrangement:

1. Single seats (rows or otherwise) for individual concentrated work.
2. Tables of circles for quiet independent group work.
3. Floor space for partners or trios to pull their seats off to the side for planning and execution of projects.
4. A special spot, out of ear shot and eyeshot, for the individual and group conference.
5. As much room as possible (considering everything) for traffic to and from supply centers and areas for conferences.

Below is one way in which a teacher arranged his room. There are more on page 77.

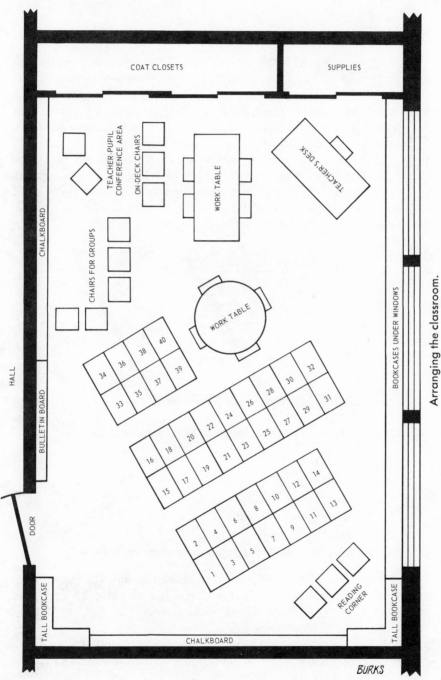

Arranging the classroom.

7. Fix a Notebook for Record-Keeping

A program that includes an individual conference permits the teacher to take running notes for his records. Group-teaching, unfortunately, does not permit this, as the teacher is too busy to write as he is teaching a group. Counselors of all kinds know this and often use the conference as a time to make notes on what is being said.

Teachers getting ready to move away from traditional patterns should prepare a notebook in which there is a page set aside for every child. A three-ring dimestore notebook is good because pages can be put in and taken out as necessary. A full double-page spread can be used as illustrated in the following diagram with the pupil's name recorded on the upper left-hand sheet, as follows:

Briefly, teachers need to note, for each child's conference:

1. The book read.
2. Problems, interests, encountered.
3. Dates of conferences.
4. Individual or group assignments.

8. Plan Necessary Routines Including Independent Work Period

Teachers and children alike need to think through the managerial aspects of a reading period. It should run like clockwork. There are many things to think about. Try these as a checklist:

1. Are all the supplies available and in sufficient quantity?
2. Do children know how to get supplies without interfering with the major work of the period, i.e. reading?
3. Are the notebooks for keeping records in proper order?

4. Are the books arranged for the children to peruse them with as little confusion as possible?
5. Do children know how to get new books and change old ones?
6. Is provision made for those difficulties that might arise, such as helpers for those pupils who need to know words in their reading or writing?
7. Do children understand that the teacher is not to be interrupted— except in the most drastic of circumstances—once the individual and group conferences start?
8. Are all normal classroom routines planned so that children move around as little as possible, and with as little confusion as possible?
9. Is the independent work period planned?
10. Do the children understand how they are to work with the teacher, either in groups or singly?

Now you are ready to begin the actual reading period. You should be ready for most anything that happens. From a physical point of view the room is prepared and the human beings in it are set. The framework for a self-selection program at any grade level is laid.

READY TO BEGIN

Once such mechanical details as have just been discussed are taken care of, the actual process of instruction can begin. The extent of change depends a great deal upon the grade level involved. For example, a first-grade teacher would not be as concerned about the mechanics of an individual conference as an intermediate-grade teacher. And the latter would not be as concerned about developing his skills of taking dictation as would a first-grade teacher. Whatever decision has been arrived at by the teacher should be rather unique for his own class and classroom. The new shoe should fit the foot, so to speak.

Let us repeat the major characteristics of a good reading program.

1. It is based centrally upon children's literature, especially trade-books.
2. It is strengthened, particularly in the beginning levels, by the prime use of children's own speech.
3. It allows all children to make choices of reading material by which they are taught to read.
4. Individual differences are met head on by self-choice of material on individual conferences.
5. Groups are set up when teachers isolate what needs to be taught to which children.

3

THE PRIMARY GRADES

The major job of the teacher in the very beginning stages is to help as many pupils see, as soon as possible, that the language they speak is the same[1] as that which appears in books. The teacher must build this bridge between the symbols in writing and those in speaking. When the learner makes the discovery that speech and writing are symbols for one and the same thing, he is on his way to learning to read. Needless to say, this is true whether the learner be an illiterate adult or a retarded reader of any school level, assuming psychological blocks are taken into account.

FIRST STEPS WITH BEGINNING READERS

A teacher must know how to proceed, what materials to obtain, and how to use them from the very first day of the first grade. "But are they READY to read?" would be a common question from those teachers familiar with the basal reading programs. This question is understandable, even if unnecessary. It matters little if a child is ready or not. There is so much that needs to be done and *can* be done without "being ready," i.e., using the reading readiness materials of basal programs.

As one first-grade teacher said, "You mean I don't have to take each child through every set of pictures in the reading readiness

---

[1] It is true that we use different sets of language, just as we use different wardrobes for different occasions. There is the informal language of the home, of one's peer group. There is the more formal language that is spoken in school, church, and the like. There is the still more formal language that is written down for purposes of writing or reading. Even within all of these categories are variations that are so taken for granted that it is a problem to bring them to the conscious level, for both the child and for the teacher. The reader of this text may be helped to realize these different types of language patterns if he thinks of the startling difference he may have noticed when he has read a transcription of something he has said as compared to that which he has written. Or, for that matter, the differences between the language of humor and that spoken in lesson assignment.

book?" That is exactly what we mean. The so-called "necessities" of vocabulary drill, workbooks, tests, and their accompanying materials are more classroom time-killers than educational devices.

WHICH CHILDREN WILL PARTICIPATE?

A first-grade teacher will need to decide which pupils are to participate in any departure from the recommended procedures in the basal manual. It may be easier for teachers to conduct talking sessions (that get recorded in some manner) with the entire class.

Other teachers may not feel comfortable with such a large group, and find that holding the attention of everyone is too hard at first. In any case, the teacher would choose a group of children for some reason. There may be a group of children who are exceedingly quiet. They need *help* in expression. Maybe they must draw pictures first and then ask that their pictures be labeled or described, or in some other way identified as an act of expression. Similarly, there may be a group of children who are so vocal that they dominate any class discussion. Such children need to be dealt with in a small group or even singly.

Children react differently to various classroom operations. Some find such security in having a seat that is their very own that they don't wish to leave it immediately. They shouldn't. What should the teacher do? Some kind of activity can be started in which all do not need to leave their seats. The pupils talk from there. Gradually, through playing games requiring response, showing various items, books, animals, and conducting various activities, all the children will eventually feel comfortable leaving their seats and coming to the place in the room where talking can be more easily carried on together.

When the teacher is able to sort out those children who show specific needs of various kinds, then grouping to meet *those* specific needs follows easily. (See Chapter 7.)

GRADUAL STEPS AT THE PRIMARY LEVEL

For those teachers who are wary of trying something totally new, there are many intermediate steps that can be suggested. Whatever a teacher does must be sensible to him or her or the results are awkward and possibly unhappy. Teacher security is as important as child security. In fact, it is more important, as children must depend upon teachers.

Some teachers will want to move a step at a time, keeping a foot on whatever might be considered their *terra firma* before exploring unknown land beyond.

What are some of these intermediate steps? There is no rigid order. Each teacher can start where he wants to.

1. A teacher, not sure of beginning steps, may take her children through all the reading readiness materials and activities as she has always done. But once children are reading somewhat independently, THEN the teacher can experiment with having those children choose their own books, come up for individual conferences, etc. In this way a teacher will start in a familiar manner while postponing experimentation until he is more secure in trying new patterns.

2. This same teacher, once more secure with patterns that come after children achieve some independence, can take another class, another year, and experiment with the beginning stages of using children's own language. In other words, a teacher experiments on the level or area that is not frightening, be it early or late.

3. Another teacher can look at all of the traditional methods he has been using and choose to experiment with just a portion of them. For example:

    a. The activity in the manual devoted to developing experience charts can be expanded. Most manuals, and college texts, too, have more or less help in the development of pupil dictation. A teacher can decide to double or triple the amount of time spent doing this, ignoring the rest of the program suggested in the manual or text.

    b. Using the same vocabulary as is found in one or more of the pre-primers, a teacher can make a book, or several books, using that vocabulary but based on the experiences (although not necessarily the language) of the children in that class. Teachers can listen as children talk (during sharing times or opening of the day planning) and take brief notes—then later on write out a story and print it on large paper, as one does an experience record, or duplicate it in some way so that every child has his own copy. The teacher makes the book herself and then uses it for reading instruction.

    c. Using as many of the words in the coming pre-primers as possible, a teacher can help children make their own books by helping them to write down the words they want to say about snapshots, their own drawings, or other pictures. Taking one of the several lists of words available, such as the Dolch List of 220[2] "service words," the teacher can check off each word as it ap-

[2] E. W. Dolch, *Teaching Primary Reading*, Champaign, Ill.; Garrard Publishing Co., 1950, p. 267.

pears in its natural habitat—the speech or dictation of that specific group—and so have a record of words taught.

d. Taking the Dolch List of words, or the Dale List[3]—or any other—the teacher can proceed to have children *say words of their own* beginning with the same initial letter as the ones on the list. This is practice in oral-aural discrimination—the feel of the beginning of a word on the tongue, as well as its sound in the ear. Word analysis is begun in this way, and a path is laid in the direction of visual discrimination.

These are some ideas that are intermediate in character for the teacher who does not wish to leave the security of the familiar. Let us go on to ideas that are for those who, for whatever reason, are more than eager to move into new patterns, and who do not need or desire in-between measures.

MOVING ENTIRELY INTO NEW PATTERNS AT THE PRIMARY LEVEL

In general, the procedures that follow are what has been called the Language-Experience Approach. Van Allen suggests a sequence of concept development on the child like this:

What he thinks about he can talk about.

What he can talk about can be expressed in painting, writing, or some other form.

Anything he writes can be read.

He can read what he writes and what other people write.

As he represents the sounds he makes through speech with symbols, he uses the same symbols (letters) over and over.[4]

To carry these out the teacher must know and follow patterns of instruction that change according to the given child and the topics arising in the day's discussion. The general progression is stated above, but the order may be changed according to the needs of the moment. Therefore, the teacher must know how to adopt these ideas if he is to move in new directions away from the planned sequential basal programs.

In whatever order, a number of abilities are necessary.

[3] Edgar Dale, "List of 755 Words," *Educational Research Bulletin,* Ohio State University, December, 1931.

[4] D. M. Lee and R. Van Allen, *Learning to Read Through Experience* (rev. ed.), New York: Appleton-Century-Crofts, Inc., 1963.

1. Perfecting the children's ability to hear and speak and *then* to identify any letter of the alphabet as heard and enunciated in the beginning of any word.

2. Perfecting the children's ability to record ideas in any medium (paint, crayons, movement, patterns in space), or verbally with whatever assistance is necessary to make the record.

3. Developing the children's ability to give dictation on his own ideas to whatever degree, even if only a one-word caption or title.

4. Developing the children's ability to talk on different ideas and to keep to their own topic.

5. Developing the child's ability to copy dictation, first his own, then that of others.

6. Developing the child's ability to straighten out his expressed ideas in terms of his own sequence, waiting for maturity as necessary.

7. Developing the ability to recognize *by sight* his own ideas in smaller and smaller units, waiting for maturation as necessary.

8. Helping the child to read what he has written and to write what he can read.

9. Combining all these skills of speaking, listening, and seeing to facilitate the recognition of ideas in sentences, phrases, words, and finally letters in the words recorded.

10. Helping children to transfer recognition of their own ideas in whatever form—sentences, phrases, pictures, and the like—to recognition of similar ideas in whatever form in published materials.

Thus children learn to read by reading. Rather than drilling to learn words before they read, they dictate and learn those words after they have read. There is little need, as Vorontosov[5] discovered, for repetitive drill when an idea expressed in a word or phrase is a caption of a large emotional feeling in children. Children will learn to read more rapidly, and with infinitely greater fluency, when they are reading those ideas that they were bursting to express. The more exciting the idea, the better for teaching.

MOVING TOWARD BOOKS

The gifted teacher seizes upon an interest and builds it into learning. Thus the child who has a book and shows by his attitude that he wants to know more about it, who tags around after his teacher with this question and that question, and who will not be put off, is the child who should begin to participate in a self-selection program. Children have ways of letting you know when they are ready for

[5] Sylvia Ashton-Warner, *The Spinster*, New York: Simon & Schuster, Inc., 1957.

learning. When such indications are strong in a child, he has the right to go ahead. He chooses his book, and the teacher takes it from there. He can't read it? Well, let him find one that he can read! Can he read the story we wrote this morning? Can he find some of those words in some other books? Let him do it. Have an individual conference with him on the newly chosen book or other matters.[6]

The display of books in a prominent place is the magnet of the reading program. Writing and reading develop sight vocabulary, as well as ability to identify letter sounds, and thus are part of the process.

Many first-grade teachers prefer books that have many simple stories in them, rather than books with single stories that might swamp the insecure. Luckily the publishers are turning out more and more good books of simple material. There is no reason to eliminate the pre-primers as *books,* as these often provide much satisfaction to the child whose very first step in the direction of independent reading can be with anything within his range.

Progression from Charts to Books

There seems to be a kind of progression or transition that occurs. Check your class against this, or various children in your class if you wish. These steps are:

1. Short and long experience charts largely of the children's own words.
2. Short and long experience charts of teacher-edited experience stories.
3. Short and long pages in a book.
4. Short and long stories in a book.[7]

How children pace themselves through these progressions is not known. Perhaps it is quite different with different children. But in any event, whether or not children benefit most from reading a book selection of their own at an easy level such as *Go, Dog, Go,*[8] from *The Little Owls,* or from teacher suggestion and assistance in reading from a pre-primer, is not as clear as it should be. What is known is that children—once the ability to read with little help is attained— clearly prefer to choose their own reading material.

[6] Teachers of beginning readers are finding help from the many titles in the *Little Owls* series, New York: Holt, Rinehart, & Winston, Inc. They are designed for this kind of use.

[7] From unpublished notes of observations and discussions with first-grade teachers.

[8] Phil. D. Eastman, *Go, Dog, Go,* New York: Random House, Inc., 1960.

Some children will give early signals of reading. They will haunt the "Library Corner," asking interminable questions—not to get attention, but truly trying to decipher the hentracks that adults call sentences and words. These are children who will pretend to read, and who will carry on great conversations with themselves and others about the content of the books that they are "reading." The teacher who notices these symptoms does not need a reading readiness test. Such children are ready to go!

Eventually, when a child can read alone, he must be allowed to do so. If he and a friend, or two or three friends, can and wish to read together, that, too, can be set up. Stendler describes such a first-grade situation as follows:

Teacher A in a first grade composed of 26 children had a period set aside during the day for individual and small group activities. In November, when the class was observed during this period, many different kinds of activities were going on. Half of the class were working on games related to reading or on booklets, or were looking at books at the library table. The rest of the class was organized into small reading groups, three and four to a group, scattered in various parts of the room. These were friendship groups, rather than ability groups, made up of children who were congenial and who worked well together. Pat had the first turn in group I and he proceeded to read, with gusto, ten pages in a pre-primer, going to Teacher A for help on words he didn't know. Mary followed him. She was not yet reading from a pre-primer but had a booklet with stories about a dog she had dictated to the teacher and illustrated herself. She read one of these to the group:

Faith chews.
Faith chews candy.
Faith chews gum.
Coconut chews.
Coconut chews rugs.
Coconut chews shoes.
Coconut chews everything.

The others were delighted with the story and had her repeat it. Then all three children looked at the script and tried to pick out words they knew. The teacher who had been moving about from group to group joined them at this point and did some work on beginning sounds with them, writing words other than chews" but beginning with the "ch" sound on the board as the children suggested them. Then Larry, who had not yet had a turn to read, showed a picture of his dog doing a trick, and dictated his story to the teacher, who wrote it on the board. Following this she moved on to another group, leaving Larry to read his story from the board with Pat and Mary helping. All three children had two more turns apiece, then went back to their seats for individual activities and another group took their place.[9]

[9] Celia B. Stendler, "Ritual of Primary Reading," *Elementary English*, 25:153–60, March, 1948.

Thus those teachers who want to base their beginning reading program upon children's own spoken language will say something like this to themselves.

Once the children have a degree of ability to read even if still at the level of "reading" pictures, the matter of classroom management to promote as much reading in as easy and compact a way as possible becomes important. Individual conferences, partnerships, group sessions all come into their own.

The Child as an Author

Perhaps the best way to induct children into reading is to help them make booklets of their own using their own language. Children can copy words ad infinitum without damaging their perception of words as a whole (unless their attention is sharply drawn to the separate letters). Children see words as wholes, just as they see a friend as a whole body. But to point out that whole words have parts called letters is no different from pointing out that the child's friend has two arms, two legs, a head, and so forth.

A
SCIENCE
BOOK
by
ME

Mike brought some bulbs so the bulbs can grow
they need water. they need sun.
they grew it to flower.

Glenn brought a telescope.
it has a special glass.
it has a tri-pod.
We look at it.

Nancy brought a potato
it has grown big.
it is in a bowl
there is water in the bowl.

First-Grade "Book."

Strickland[10] noted on a trip to England that at least one educator felt that no child should be exposed to a printed book until he has lived through the experience of making one himself. The sheer act of making such a booklet teaches a child many skills of reading—such as front to back, left to right, line by line, let alone sequences of plots, of words within a sentence, and perhaps of letters within a word.

How does a teacher proceed to make a child an author? There are many ways. Here are some:

1. Take a snapshot of every child. Have him write a booklet about himself, his home, his pets, his family, and anything else he so desires. The words he needs in writing would come from the experience stories hung around the room, from a picture dictionary, from a friend, from the teacher, or even a visiting mama!

2. Decide upon a topic that a child would want to illustrate, such as "Our School," or "The Block Where I Live," or "My Daddy's Work," or "Our Postman" (or policeman, or custodian, etc.) The booklet can be any number of pages, and the writing will tell about each drawing. The teacher through the regular class activity of developing oral-aural discrimination will, as much as possible, help children to make the transfer of what is in their minds to the writing they are putting on a page.

3. These booklets can range from those done by the teacher herself after taking dictation from children, to those in which just the writing is done by the teacher and the illustration by the children, to those booklets that the children make independently, seeking help only when needed.

The Teacher Reads Aloud

By all rights the teacher should be the best oral reader in the room. No day should go by without the teacher reading, in the most fluent and interesting manner possible, selections from good children's books. Setting such an example for children teaches many necessary reading skills. Hearing a teacher read delights most girls and boys—as most parents know. In the classroom it is not a waste of instruction time, and teachers who feel guilty in spending time reading aloud miss the point. Good literature is a gift. Who can give it better than the best reader in the room? Is it not instructional to expose children to the finest writing available? We believe it is and feel that more of it needs to be done.

[10] Ruth C. Strickland, *Reading in Its Setting,* language monograph, Boston: D. C. Heath & Co., 1960, p. 2.

Encouraging class discussion.

Writing down what they say.

Reading back what was said.

A pupil-dictated and -illustrated story.

Helping each find a book of his own choice.

Transition Into Books

By one or all of these methods, children will acquire a substantial ability to read and write, both sentences and words. At *some* time the teacher begins the "nudging" of the children toward the book supply that has always been available. All along the teacher has been reading aloud from good books. The pupils know where they are. They should be somewhat aware of names of authors and illustrators of their favorite books. Thus the teacher says:

Some of you don't realize that all of these words we have written for our whole class, and that you have written for yourself, can be found in those books in our library. Why don't you hunt for some sometime? See what you can find. When you do find something exciting, bring it to me—you know that I will be interested. Did you know that you will learn to read real printed books faster when you can find your own words in them? Go ahead and try.

Soon, of course, many children will do just that. Then as they come with books, the teacher must figure out a way to hear each one read what he has found. Maybe a group would be the best way to start, or, during a quiet work period, the teacher might call for one after another of those children who have let her know they have something. Maybe a "buddy" system might work well, with two children reading to each other. Later each chooses something to bring to read aloud to their teacher.

These are some ways in which teachers can move children into books. The whole progression of talking, writing talk down, reading it back, moves in the direction of reading print.

SUMMARY

This chapter describes, in brief, some ways in which teachers of primary grades can move children from the language that they speak into the language they are to read in books. Helping teachers edit what is to be written down from the extensive oral expression of children, as well as suggestions in the area of classroom management, is mentioned. There is steady progression from ideas to talk, to writing own words, to reading own words, to reading others' words, to reading in books. Later chapters will deal with these areas in much greater detail. This chapter is intended as a quick once-over for busy teachers.

4

CHANGING TO NEW PATTERNS IN THE LATER GRADES

As the major job of the primary-grade teacher is to help pupils see that their own language could be used to learn to read books, the major job of the teacher of the middle grades is to bring all pupils to the state of rapid, meaningful reading of quantities of good books. There should be no necessity for reading periods, as such, above the fifth grade. Mechanical details of word recognition can be handled mainly in the writing or spelling period. The content of social studies, science, and mathematics can be dealt with as knowledge in and of itself and not as lessons in reading. Detailed word breakdown must be replaced by broad, sweeping, page-devouring eye movements of the reader who has passed through the analytical stage into the totality of whole perception stage. He again sees wholes—on a greatly expanded scale—just as he did when he began to learn to read. He needs to analyze words, as do most adults, only when they are unusual in form or meaning.

To bring this rapid reading about, after the mechanical details listed in the beginning of this chapter have been resolved, the teacher needs to decide first steps.

FIRST STEPS WITH MIDDLE-GRADE CLASSES

Let us say there are enough books. A notebook has been prepared so that it doesn't matter who comes first for an individual conference. The classroom has been arranged so that pupils may come and go, without disturbance.

Now, a first decision:

1. "WHICH CHILDREN SHALL I START WITH?" A teacher has many choices and can begin with

CHOICE A $\left\{ \begin{array}{l} \text{One pupil} \\ \text{or} \\ \text{Two pupils} \\ \text{or} \\ \text{Three pupils} \end{array} \right.$

or

CHOICE B

One regular reading group
or
Two regular reading groups

or

CHOICE C   The whole class

The next decision is:

2. "HOW MUCH CHOICE WILL I GIVE MY PUPILS, AND IN WHAT BOOKS?" You may want to decide about how much self-selection you will allow before you decide the pupils who will participate. The important thing to remember is that you should change your way of teaching only as far as you are sure of yourself. That is why we made such a point in the beginning "MAKE UP YOUR OWN MIND."

Our ultimate goal is an instructional program in which every child is learning to read with materials of his own choosing, and is benefiting from an individual period with his teacher, and is not subjected to the practice of ability grouping. For many teachers this goal is far off indeed. For some it is merely a matter of organization and so is easily accomplished within days or weeks. In any case, there are many intermediate steps. Let us describe some.

INTERMEDIATE STEPS TO NEW PATTERNS IN THE MIDDLE GRADES

There is no regular order in these. Find a place to start, take a big breath and begin!

CHOICE A—Individual Children

One Child Chooses His Material

There is often one child who stands out in a group for one reason or another. He fits nowhere. He may be such an excellent reader that he puts all others to shame if he is put in a group with them. On the other hand, he may be a very slow reader and therefore cannot keep up with any of his peers in any group in the class. Take such a child and help him to choose a book that he likes and can read. Show him how to get it ready for a conference with you. When he is ready, set aside a time when the rest of the class is busy and proceed. The guide on pages 155–58 will help you.

Two Children Choose Their Material

Sometimes there are two children that do not fit with the rest of the class in the usual groups. Or maybe the success you had with the single child above was so satisfying that you are now ready to try your wings with another.

Helping Children Choose Books

Ask each child to find a book he likes and can read. One way to help him do this is to sharpen his ability to find material at his level. Try this:

Look over all the books. Pick out one that interests you. Riffle the pages and stop on one page in the middle of the book. Start to read it to yourself. If you come to a word that you don't know, put your thumb on the table. If you come to another word you don't know, put down your first finger. Another unknown word, another finger, and so on. *If you use up all your fingers,* that book is too hard for you. Put it down and find another.

If you find a book that has no unknown words, it is probably too easy for you. Save it for a free time, and choose another book to bring to me for your conference.

Thus each is shown how to prepare to read his self-chosen piece for you in a private conference. Keep a weather eye out to make sure both are on the right track and make room for them on your schedule as soon as they are ready. You might want to experiment with different ways of having one or more children come to you at the same time, each with his own book. It is one way to save classroom time, although a child can be shortchanged in his reading instruction if you are not careful.

Two Children Working Together as Partners

Two children can work together as partners in many different kinds of arrangements. For example, during the recreational reading period, the teacher could say: "All of you who would like to find a partner and read your stories to each other may do so. I will be glad to help you with words, or with anything else you need." So the pupils may all choose a partner and sit around in pairs reading first silently and then aloud to each other. The teacher can move around from pair to pair, helping, advising, listening, and making notes, mental or otherwise, about what needs to be taught another time.

Perhaps only part of the class wishes to read aloud with partners. The rest can read their material silently while the teacher moves around as necessary. Those reading alone can be helped as well as those with their buddies! However, whatever material is chosen must be of such a level that the teacher can keep up with any demands for word help, or for assisting in finding another book "just as good as this one" or whatever.

Partners in a Reading Group

Some teachers can change to new patterns by asking pupils to choose a buddy in their regular reading group. In this way the general pattern of grouping in a class stays the same (not forever, we hope!) but as the Robins or Redbirds come up with their usual basal reader, you might say something like this:

Today I would like to have you choose each other in partners. (If there is an odd number, you can be my partner.) Choose any story (or specify a story) and read it to yourself. I will help with words that you don't know. When you are finished, look up and see who else is finished. Get together and take turns reading aloud to each other. I will be listening to you all so do your best. Soon I will ask some of you to read aloud to everybody.

This pattern has been successful: Pupils are encouraged to choose partners or buddies to work with after they have finished their silent reading of their reader. The teacher might say something like this:

I want you to read on ahead in your reader. You take the next story, or even the next two stories. But when you are through reading to yourself, look up and see who else is also through. Then change seats so that you are together and read and talk about the story you have read.

You may have noticed that when partners were together during the recreational reading time, the teacher was walking around— going то the children. In the reading group on the other hand, teachers tend more to stay put, and let the children come to them. The difference lies in the amount of confusion that might occur in either case. Follow the pattern that is the easier to handle.

Of course, there are matters of instruction that will need to be taken care of in some way. If recreational reading is the only time children choose their own reading material, some teachers feel that the regular, unchanged basal reading programs at some other time of the school day meets all instructional problems.

Three Children Choose Their Material

In the same way that two children were asked to choose their reading material, a third child is asked to do likewise. The reasons for asking any of these children to start such a pattern is not important. It really doesn't matter which child is chosen first. The reason that we suggest one, or two, or three children first is to show that these first steps can be very simple ones. It is really no trick at all to have three children come and read to you, singly or together, while the rest of the class is busy with some kind of independent work. If the thought of having ALL your class reading different books at the same time is overwhelming, then begin with one or two or three.

Once a teacher arrives at a stage of being able to handle three children at a time, together or in succession, he is ready for a group. The practice of helping children choose books, conducting individual conferences, and managing the rest of the class while so doing leaves no real reason to delay changing over a whole group of children—does it?

CHOICE B—Groups

One Group Changeover

Some teachers feel more secure if they branch out into new practice from a firm base of their regular reading groups. What is the simplest first step in such a case?

One that works for some teachers is to keep the regular reading group the same, but have each child choose his own story (even in the basal) or book and read silently in the group. Later he can come up beside you to read alone.

With the rest of the class doing some kind of independent seatwork, the Bushytails would come up as was their wont. The teacher might say something like this:

FINISHING THE READER, GETTING ANOTHER BOOK.

Today I want you to take the next story in your reader, and read alone silently. Ask for help if you need it. Read on ahead. Don't wait for anyone else. If you finish the book you may go and choose another one from our library. As I see that you have all finished the next story, I may stop you so we can talk about it.

CONFERENCES ON THE BASAL READER.

Today I want you to read on ahead in your reader. Ask for help if you need it. When you are through with the book, go back and choose one of the stories you liked best. Read it again and be sure you know it well, and can read it aloud just as if you were talking. One by one I want you to come up beside me and talk and read the story you chose. We won't bother with the rest of the stories, unless there is one you like so well you want to read it very much. But when you choose just ONE story it must be your favorite in the book.

As a child finishes the basal text (or has obviously lost interest in it) invite him to take another book from the room supply. By the end of a week or ten days, all children will be either in a different book or on a different page of his reader. Then you are all set to teach each child individually.

Partners Read Aloud to the Teacher

Another way to use partners was suggested by Stendler[1] in the same article we quoted before:

. . . Teacher B in the third Grade [had] twenty odd children . . . reading from library books, working on reports illustrating stories, listening to record-ings of stories and the like. Miss B was busy with a dozen more pupils in a reading circle. These children worked in pairs with each child taking turns reading to his teammate. At the same time one such team of two pupils, sitting on either side of the teacher, took turns reading to her. When they had finished, another team took their place so that the teacher could hear every child in the group read. Since she was sitting next to the pupil reading to her, it was quite possible for her to hear despite the fact that five other children were reading at the same time. The children read from a variety of materials, including readers of different grade levels and library books. . . .

How might Miss B set it up so that she could have these teams or pairs of children read to her during a regular reading period? She might have said something like this: "While everyone is busy, I want you to come to me in groups that I choose. Will you and you (point-ing to a dozen children) come up to the circle?"

The children come with their library books. Then Miss B. would give directions like this:

You know who your partners are. Sit beside them and read to each other. Before we are through, I want each team to come and sit beside me (pointing to the chair on each side of her) and read to me. If you get stuck on a word, and neither of you know what it is, I will not be too busy to help. But be sure neither of you know it. Now I won't have enough time to hear you read a lot. But we will change teams every so often.

Another way a teacher might use partners or the buddy system is to ask the pupils to choose a buddy with whom they want to read.

[1] Celia Stendler, "The Ritual of Primary Reading," *Elementary English*, 25:153–60, March, 1948.

Have the buddies sit together, choose the story they want to read—either the same one or two different ones—and begin reading silently and then to each other. Help them organize their activity something like this.

Before you start to read to yourselves, decide how much you will read, or how long you will read, or what you will read, and plan it so that you both will be through at the same time. Then when you are done, read together or to each other, or in some way swap the ideas of what you have read. If you want to, you can begin to plan a project about what you have read—if it is that kind of material.

For that matter, even three children could read together in this same way. The teacher will need to decide WHERE they will do that reading. Shall it be at their seats? Shall it be in the front of the room in the circle? Whatever the place, the teacher should know why he makes the decision. Perhaps the group themselves can decide and then explain how they made up their minds. Such simple decision-making produces more independence of a useful, healthy nature.

Extending Silent Reading

In these ways, the silent reading portion of the regular reading period is extended to shift the pupils from reading a single basal text to reading different books without needing to change the grouping organization in any way. It is no trick at all to let children read on ahead! They want to, anyway, and, according to research reports, like reading much better when they are allowed to go on ahead. Certainly it is more sensible than stopping those who are good readers to wait for the rest to catch up. This common practice is truly prevention of learning. Those children who must wait are being held back in their education.

Combining Self-Selection and Basal Reading Programs

Another way to move gradually into new patterns of instruction is to combine the usual traditional reading groups for half of the day, say in the morning, with the self-selection and individual conference in the afternoon. Teachers seem to feel more comfortable and thus are more relaxed when they feel they can cover the "skills" in the basal period in the morning. Even though there is little research basis for this faith in such teachings, if it provides the teacher with a sense of security, then that is what must be done.

Two-Group Changeover

Once you have mastered the way of handling one reading group as suggested above, the next logical step is to move into two reading groups.

Set up the independent work period as usual. When the class is settled and busy, ask the group you want to work with first to come to the place you meet with them. The first group might be the one that is already reading "on ahead" and so are a bit more experienced in new patterns. Probably you will have more trouble adjusting than the children—don't be surprised if this happens.

On the other hand, if you want to work with another group that has not departed its basal ways, call them up. After they are all seated with their books in hand, proceed just as you did before when you started a group. Perhaps something like this might be said: "Maybe you have noticed that your friends in the _____ group have been reading on ahead in their readers. They have liked doing this so much that I thought that maybe you might like to do the same thing."

If necessary, with one or two children, you might say this: "If you want to read in your reader, that will be all right. I want you to choose the book that you like best. You see, I am making this change to see if you would like to read better, and will become better readers when you choose the books for your reading time."

Once you are sure that everyone knows what to do, ask them to read on ahead in their readers, or, as with the first group, encourage them to go to the library corner and choose a tradebook for their reading period. Having had experience changing over one group, you are in a position to put into practice those ideas that worked best *for you*. Remember there is a great deal of difference between teachers and that which works for someone else might not be the best thing in another situation. For that matter, the fun of experimenting is in not knowing QUITE what to expect. Again, be sure that one foot is on your *terra firma*, and what you want to have happen will happen.

If you can change two groups of your class, you are now ready to change over the whole class. Maybe you don't think you are ready yet. If this worries you, then proceed with your third, or, if you have one, your fourth group, and handle them just as we have described the second group. The key to the whole matter lies in the independent work. When children are absorbed in worthwhile activity, rather than busy work, their teacher is free to work with whomever he wishes.

Independent Seat Work

As this matter of seat work is so important, now might be the time to look at the attitude of pupils. Ask yourself these questions:

Do I need to keep insisting that some children keep busy? If so, my seat work jobs are not good enough.

Do children work quietly alone, moving from one job to another without being told? If so, my seat work jobs are good ones. They fascinate the youngsters. They don't need to be helped to change activities.

Are my children obviously proud of what they have done by themselves? This is another good sign.

Does my class groan when the seat work is assigned? Watch out for I am in trouble! Look over Chapter 5 and see what I can do to improve matters.

If you are satisfied that your room organization is reasonably smooth running, you are ready to make the biggest leap of all— changing your whole class to new patterns all at the same time.

CHOICE C—Whole Class

The Whole-Class Changeover

How do we go about changing over a whole class? To change a whole class to new patterns in any part of the curriculum is an undertaking that overwhelms some teachers and challenges and excites others. The approach to reading described in this book is not so difficult as it is nontraditional. Try to visualize what your room will be like with no ability groups—no Bushytails, no Red Birds, no Green Birds. Try to see in your mind's eye every child reading from a different book at the same time. Ask yourself if you really need to teach EVERY step in the basal manual. Haven't you noticed that some children were simply far beyond those lessons anyway? Many teachers have moved into new patterns bit by bit. But many of them, once they were all changed, wished they had done the whole class at the same time. It is really not as hard as it seems.

Here are some steps to follow—and as usual, skip around if necessary. What follows really comes under the heading of "Planning Classroom Routines."

Describe to the class what is expected, such as:

1. GETTING READY.

Girls and boys, today we are going to go about our reading differently. I will ask you to choose any book of your own from our supply over there (point to it), that you can read and that you like very much. Then I want you to read it to yourself. While you are reading, you will choose some of that story or book to bring to me. You and I will work ALL ALONE with what you bring to me. I will help you become a better reader with any book you choose. Now let us practice how to do all of this so you will know what to expect.

2. DRY RUN. Have the class walk through, or watch a group walk through, the steps of choosing a book, changing books, coming up for the individual conference, moving to a new activity after they are finished reading silently. Have them use this kind of role-playing to practice how they will get help when they need it, how they will get supplies when needed and do all of the various kinds of things that must happen in a classroom.

3. PLAN SEATWORK. Be sure each child has thought out a worthwhile activity that will follow his silent reading. There is no seat work as such. Instead, children read self-selected books and do related jobs as letter writing, dioramas, and other projects.

4. GET READY FOR CONFERENCES. When all is quiet on the seatwork front, retire to the spot you have fixed for the conferences, notebook in hand, and wait for all comers.

The adjustment of children to such new classroom organization is no problem. Within a matter of minutes a quiet, working classroom is possible. The secret, of course, lies in the silent reading of a self-chosen book as the first item on the independent work-period agenda. Such an activity practically guarantees an absorbed and concentrating class, assuming, as always, that there are adequate supplies of books from which children may find one that will hold their attention for a reasonable length of time.

If you are worried that children might not choose their material wisely, make more of a point of such selection as you are doing the "dry run" of the reading period. If this still does not work, you will be able to pick up the deficiency during the individual conference of each child. You must, of course, plan for that conference as soon as possible.

When you are reasonably satisfied that everyone understands what is to happen, let them get their books. Walk around among them as they do so, commenting here, helping there, suggesting changes to another one. When the class settles down, and peace descends upon a busy, gratified, and contented room, go to your conference corner. The individual conferences may now begin. You will no longer need the slow, middle, and fast ability groups. They are no longer necessary. You can teach every single skill in reading, and MORE reading than ever before.

THE INDIVIDUAL CONFERENCE

Because a one-to-one conference has been such a rarity in classroom practice the writer feels it important to present a boiled-down version of the entire chapter on this topic. It is designed to give you in the shortest possible way all of the important considerations of this crucial activity.

Once the children have each chosen a book that keeps them absorbed, the teacher can sit somewhere in the room where he can see all and yet not be in the direct line of vision of pupils. There those children who have signed up for the individual conference will come to their teacher. Together they will proceed to work together to improve reading. The two should sit side by side rather than face to face, as it is better, psychologically and educationally, to work side

A conference with two at a time.

by side on something that is in front of the two. Face to face really means in opposition, and is thus harder for the teacher to establish the essential feeling of unity—of we-are-working-together—than if they sit opposing each other.

Conducting the Individual Conference

There are several things that need to be done during the individual conference. The teacher needs to perfect his skills in analyzing the reading performance of the child in this close, intimate situation. Teachers should not get discouraged if it takes several weeks to work smoothly and rapidly through a set of criteria of analysis. Usually teachers find themselves taking a long time as they first try individual conferences, mostly because the pleasure of both teacher and pupil in this personal, interactive situation makes time pass so rapidly. Suddenly fifteen minutes have gone by! But this seems to be quite normal. As long as the teacher consciously works to speed up things in order to get to every child at frequent intervals, there is nothing to worry about. If, however, the teacher continues to have such lengthy conferences after a couple of months, many children will not have the amount of individual instruction that is necessary for their optimum growth.

Areas of Exploration in the Individual Conference

Usually four areas should be explored in the individual conference:

1. The sheer mechanical ability of the child to read, silently
   Does he stumble over words that have no contextual clues?
   Does he show ability to use substitution when he is stuck on a word?
   Has he understood all of the more difficult words in his material?
2. The ability to read critically
   Does he clearly understand the overall sense of the story?
   Can he read "between the lines?"
   Can he analyze the author's purposes?
   Does he catch the central thought of the material?
3. The personal involvement of the child
   Why does a child prefer what he has chosen?
   Does he have friends with the same preferences?
   Will he recommend this story to others? To whom? Why?
   How does this story relate to the child's personality development?
4. The ability of the child to hold an audience when reading aloud
   Do all within earshot stop what they are doing to listen?

Does the child like to "ham it up" when reading aloud?

Does the child like to prepare a story to read during sharing time—
or to another grade?

What questions are to be asked? They vary with each child and each book. Each one of these areas has literally hundreds of possibilities within it. For example:

1. Area of Mechanical Skills
   Teacher: What words did you have trouble with?

   or

   Here are two words that look very much alike. Tell me how you know the difference?

   or

   Let me point to several words in your story. Tell me what they are and what they mean?

2. Area of Critical Reading
   Teacher: What kind of a story is this? Real? Or—?
   Could this story have happened? Why? Or why not?
   Tell me the story rapidly.
   If this character did so and so, would you think he would get in trouble?
   At the time this story was supposed to have happened, what was going on in our country that was very important?

3. Area of Personal Involvement
   Teacher: Why did you choose this story?
   Do you know anyone else in this class that would like it also?
   Why do you think you are more interested in this kind of story than others in this class?
   Would you like to be this character? Why?

4. Area of Oral Reading
   Teacher: Which part of the book have you chosen to read to me aloud?
   Tell me what has happened up to this point.
   Remember to read so well that you will have people in the rest of the room stopping what they are doing to listen.
   Make your voice go up and down.
   Make your voice spooky, or scarey, or sad, or mean, or whatever the story calls for.

These are suggested questions that will start the teacher out as he begins individual conferences. Now many of these questions can be asked—and be WISE questions—whether or not the teachers have read the particular book the child has brought to the conference. Of course, teachers will do a better job of questioning when they know each book. But with the hundreds of books available, to expect each teacher to have read each book in the room is impractical. Besides, experience shows that the teacher can skim each book during each conference, and, as things proceed, listen to the child *tell the story.* We know that teachers' knowledge of children's literature expands prodigiously in such a program.

Word Analysis During the Individual Conference

As we grow in the practice of having individual conferences, there is one observation that needs to be made. Children will rarely reveal their SPECIFIC needs in word analysis as they read. Teachers worry about this, and rightly so. But teachers have also worried about the blockage to reading that occurs as children get stuck on several words, one after another, even when they are reading material well within their level of ability.

Word analysis is best taught during the writing time—in the first grade—and in the formal spelling time from that point on. When word analysis is applied to spelling and writing, the transfer of training to the reading situation is easy and less painful than if word analysis is taught only in reading. Spelling is for writing, of course. But spelling *requires* that words be broken up in parts, in letters, in syllables. One is supposed to do that in spelling. Not so in reading. There words are supposed to be seen as wholes and only broken up when they are unknown to the reader. To teach word analysis during reading violates the whole operation of reading, which is flash-type recognition.

This is not to say that word analysis is never taught in reading. It is, but it is taught initially, more strenuously, and more comprehensively during writing and spelling skill-development periods. Then those skills are transferred to the particular reading situation requiring their use.

Use of Commercial Materials

When commercial materials are so made that they cannot be used on a pick-and-choose basis, they block those teachers who desire to fit materials into their instruction. Yet, a good look at many commercial phonics systems, text manuals, and workbooks will show that there are lots of ways to skip around in the various lessons or suggestions. Perhaps the future will bring more and more such publications that tend to encourage teachers to hunt for that lesson needed on *that* day for *that* group's problem.

An example of this could be shown by reference to the "New Reading Skill Text Series."[2]

Using the following items for investigation, a teacher would have some excellent methods of procedure whether or not he was following the "Reading Skill Text" or a book selected on a self-choice basis and brought up for an individual conference.

The following items[3] suggest many questions for the conferences or follow-up group sessions on such activities as word analysis in written or oral language sessions. In short, these items have a richness which certainly beckons beyond the narrower limits of their intended setting.

Locating Pertinent Information:

. . . Pupils are asked to complete statement of facts, to answer questions about details in the story, and to name, list, or describe specific facts in the story.

Recognizing Main Ideas:

. . . Pupils are trained to recognize main ideas and to interpret specific story details correctly. . . .

Organizing Information:

. . . Pupils learn to organize information from the story in a variety of ways . . . arrange related ideas in sequence, to classify details from the story, to group facts and to summarize paragraphs, to outline stories and parts of stories, and to choose key words that would help them find more information about a topic.

Making Sound Judgments:

. . . Pupils develop the ability to analyze stories so as to draw sound conclusions, to understand fooling or mood, to evaluate character, to make generalizations, to support personal opinions, and to relate the story to their own personal experience.

Studying Words:

. . . the meanings of key words in the story are developed. Pupils study synonyms, antonyms, homonyms, descriptive phrases, parts of speech, and many

[2] "New Reading Skill Text Series." Used with the kind permission of the publishers, Charles E. Merrill Books, Inc., Columbus, Ohio.
[3] *Ibid.*

other types of word relationship and function. They learn to analyze the structure of words through the recognition of roots, prefixes, and suffixes, compound words, contractions and singular and plural forms. They learn how to attack new words phonetically, how to use diacritical markings as an aid to pronunciation and how to use a dictionary.

Record-Keeping in the Individual Conference

No teacher should begin any conference unless he is ready. As noted before, a notebook is essential. Here is a sample page of records kept by a teacher.

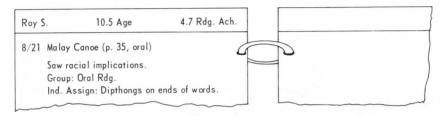

| Roy S. | 10.5 Age | 4.7 Rdg. Ach. |

8/21 Malay Canoe (p. 35, oral)

Saw racial implications.
Group: Oral Rdg.
Ind. Assign: Dipthongs on ends of words.

With these notes the teacher can plan the following day's reading period. Roy will work with a group of children who do not read well aloud. Personally, he has trouble with words that have "ph" in them, not recognizing that the sound of those two letters is that of an "f." The teacher has several choices:

1. Wait a few days and see if several children have same problem. Group and teach.
2. Watch for general disability in written composition on same problem and use this phoneme as basis for a set of the class list of spelling words (as photo, telephone, etc.).
3. Set aside an individual time with child during some free period when the rest of the class is busy and teach him alone, following up with a page in a workbook.

This is a single sample of how a teacher can find out what children do not know and then arrange the class work so that the difficulty can be met and resolved. We are ready then to describe grouping in general.

GROUPING IS ESSENTIAL

The final concern in our discussion of changeover patterns is that of grouping. There is, of course, a whole chapter (Chapter 7) devoted to the details of matters of grouping; thus only a brief description is needed here.

The reason that we have placed grouping as a final concern is because it is the last thing that a teacher is concerned with after individual conferences have been held. Group sessions are a result of diagnoses made by teachers during the individual conference and from other sources during the school day. Contrary to the usual practice of grouping, this writer insists that an instructional group be formed ONLY when a teacher has identified a single fact that needs to be taught to two or more children.

Put another way, we can say that several children are put together upon the basis of something they need to know or need to do that no one else needs to know or needs to do at that time. Groups save teachers' time. They are an efficient way to teach several children the same thing at the same time. But they cannot be justified if they are organized on a generalized, indefinite basis. That is the case when the traditional patterns of grouping depend upon the nonspecific findings of standardized reading tests, or intelligence tests—nonspecific, that is, in terms of diagnostic value to the average teacher. Even when items on such tests are specific, the findings are probably obsolete within a few weeks, or even days. There is little or no research on the obsolescence of tests as to their daily practical use in the classroom.

What then, does a teacher do to know how to group his pupils?

The key is his ability to keep and use good records. After the school day is done, he can look over the notes he made while having his conferences and from written work. Taking a fresh sheet of paper, he can list those children that have common difficulties, problems, interests, projects. This sheet might look something like this:

Electromagnets		Word Analysis; Hearing Vowels		
Joe Z.		Suzy T.		
Bill M.		Bill A.		
Larry		Ralph M.		
Old West Diorama		Ability To Hold an Audience		
Mary B.		Good	Fair	Poor
June C.		Karen	Philip	Carl
Martha A.		Lynne	Andrew	
Jerky Oral Reading		Theresa	Cindy	
Sandra B.	Jane O.			
Matt N.	Wendy F.			
Barney G.	Paul V.			

There are many small details that add up to overall reading achievement. In addition to those above, it might be helpful to list several more, so that teachers who are not familiar with this type of analysis can get a feel of what is meant.

"Other Types of Groups"

Groups might be formed upon such topics as these, which would be revealed during the individual conference:

Inability to hear final letters of spoken words.

Inability to use the technique of substitution in the beginning, or latter part of words.

Inability to use voice inflection to indicate questions.

Needs help to find a book that holds interest.

Needs help to find a book at reading level.

Needs far more challenging material.

Needs help to see that word analysis in spelling carries over into word analysis in reading.

Wants someone to join them in project on snakes (or turtles, or alligators).

Needs more books on horses (or farm animals, or rain, etc.).

These, as can be seen, are highly specific. Using these and other topics of the same type, a teacher can organize his reading period to strike these several irons while they are hot.

Teaching the Unknown

The important thing is to realize that children should be taught only what they don't know. Rather than being made to sit through lessons while less able peers learn skills and work on other matters, each child can proceed at his own pace, either reading silently to himself, aloud to his teacher, or working with others with the same needs. No one's time is wasted.

How Long Is the Reading Period?

The amount of time needed for the reading period varies from the usual hour of the traditional basal program to a whole half-day. After a teacher has changed over from a basal series, the experience of the writer has found that many teachers accomplish all that is necessary in about a 90-minute period. In the beginning of the term, the individual conferences take the longest part of the period. Later on, periods seem to be split about half and half between individual conferences and group sessions. Nor is it unusual for a teacher to organize the school day so that reading of all types, group sessions, and whole class sessions on all subjects keep unrolling. There is planning, but the necessity to run on a strict schedule seems to disappear in many cases. As children become absorbed in their work, their dependency on the teacher lessens. This frees the teacher to work more concentratedly on matters at hand. When one thing flows into another, and yet everything that is important gets accomplished, the classroom is well run. The human beings in it work harder in a more relaxed fashion. As one sixth-grade girl wrote to her teacher: "I never learned so much in such an easy way."

SUMMARY

The authors have designed this chapter to help those teachers who want step-by-step hints in changing their patterns of reading instruction. At least seven major considerations were given. These included:

1. Making the decision to change.
2. Consulting with school authorities and parents.
3. Deciding who will participate.
4. Obtaining books and materials.
5. Arranging the classroom.
6. Planning the independent work period.
7. Establishing routines.

The two fundamental methods of changeover from a basal ability-grouped program into one that is individualized were described. First, the transition can be evolutionary—that is, changing over part of the class or one group at a time. Second, a revolutionary method, changing the entire class at one time, was also described. Modifications of these two basic ways for transition into the improved reading pattern in the primary and intermediate grades were described in detail.

The reader should think over the ideas, situations, etc., as he advances through the pages of this book. He should make up his mind whether he would like to try this different pattern of teaching. He should be sure that it is something that he really wants to do before he starts.

II

CLASSROOM
MANAGEMENT

5

THE INDEPENDENT WORK PERIOD

CRITERIA FOR ACTIVITIES

The independent work period, or "seatwork," that we are concerned with in this chapter contains activities that:

1. Absorb pupils so that there is little need for them to interrupt themselves or to interrupt the teacher while he works with individuals and groups.
2. Are open-ended in the sense that they need not all start or finish at the same time.
3. Have a strong element of self-education and self-assignment.
4. Require little formal checking and much informal teacher-approval through planning and time.
5. Are notable for encouraging the unique use of ordinary materials through the initiative, originality, creativity, and inventiveness of each pupil.
6. Are regarded by children with enthusiasm, as opposed to being considered a chore, even when the activity might normally be so considered.

There are, of course, other work periods during the school day. But these are not our concern here simply because they are not primarily related to the reading program. There are several excellent references available for those readers that would like a full treatment of independent work periods per se.[1]

[1] The reader is referred to the following for many helpful and sound curriculum ideas: H. F. Darrow and R. Van Allen, *Independent Activities for Creative Learning*; Board of Education of the City of New York, *Practical Guide to Individualized Reading*, pp. 46 ff; Association for Childhood Education, International, *Children Can Work Independently*, pamphlet; Board of Education, City of New York, *Skillful Teaching Practices*, Series 1961–62, No. 12; D. M. Lee and R. Van Allen, *Learning to Read Through Experience* (rev. ed.), New York: Appleton-Century-Crofts, Inc., 1963.

A glance at the flow chart of the reading period (page 7) will show that the bulk of the time is spent upon individual conferences and group sessions. At the beginning of the year the individual conferences tend to be longer and more frequent than later on when a teacher can save much time and effort by grouping children on those items they do not know and upon which they need instruction.

Working independently.

When a reading period is so used, obviously those not being taught need to be well occupied so that the teacher will not be interrupted in his major effort of the period. Thus, here we are concentrating on the type of work that will keep the class busy and quiet. For the purposes of this chapter, this is a salient characteristic of this work period. At another time of the day, sawing and hammering, for example, would be quite appropriate. Not so during the reading period. Whatever the seatwork activity might be, it must allow the teacher to teach with full concentration. Only in a case of real emergency should this direct teaching stop. The matter rests upon the ability of the teacher to manage a classroom so that those working independently and those working with him do not interfere with each other.

INDEPENDENT WORK ALLOWS TIME

One great advantage of the independent work period is that it allows time for unhurried thought and activity. With its lack of emphasis upon chore-type learning, and its encouragement of exploration and contemplation, the element of open-ended work should be attractive.

EDUCATION DURING THE WORK PERIOD

But just keeping children busy so that a teacher may teach is not the whole story. The author felt that a chapter devoted to the work period was imperative for the reason that reading instruction *requires* a follow-through after direct instruction has taken place. Teachers cannot teach the whole class all the time and meet the ever present differences between individual pupils.

Although the phrase "no man is an island" is most certainly true, there are times when a man must be an island to pursue his own thoughts, work out his own problems, seek his own answers, and plan his own plans. The "seatwork" (and we put this term in quotation marks because the activity involved may or may not be in "seats") stands or falls on its *educativeness*. "Exercises" of the usual work-book type teach very little[2] when used without specific application to certain children on a page-by-page basis. The misuse of such material has many critics other than the authors of this text.[3] When such is the assignment, serving mostly to kill time, it does not educate. Activities that serve only to pass the hours are tragically lost opportunities for learning and are evidence that teachers either don't know what else to do or don't care to do anything else.

[2] J. Schunert, "The Association of Mathematical Achievement with Certain Factors Resident in the Teacher, in the Teaching, and in the School," *Journal of Experimental Education*, 19:219–38, 1951.

[3] George Spache, *Towards Better Reading*, Champaign, Ill.: Garrard Publishing Co., 1963, pp. 28, 29.

THE NATURE OF INDEPENDENT WORK

A mark of good teachers during the seatwork period is helping children develop activities that stand or fall upon the answer to this question:

"What will this activity teach *by itself* that I cannot teach?"

For such activity must set the feet of children upon the never-ending path of inquiry and eternal curiosity. A teacher cannot, if he would, teach everything to every pupil. There must be times when the intellectual seed germinates in the soil that has been readied by the teacher. A child must explore, discover, experiment, and find out a million things. A good teacher can start a child learning, but he cannot learn for him—a fact, no doubt, that has saved the intellectual and psychological lives of numberless children.

Independence is a major drive of all human beings. We need to be loved and accepted, but we need just as much to be able to do things for ourselves, by ourselves, and with our own ideas. A child, by the time he starts to school is largely independent, and the American mother really wants him that way. The saying "Mother, I'd rather do it MYSELF!" strikes a chord in us all. Tying shoelaces, buttoning coats, climbing on a big chair without help, going to the toilet alone are small battles in the campaign of growing up. Love and affection should come to all without asking. But just as important is the feeling "I know how to do that." Such is the sense of achievement, every bit as powerful a force in human development as any other.

The independent work period is a most important time, if not THE most important time, where achievement comes into its own. By *himself* a child finds out both the extent of his ability and the limits of his ability. When he knows what he cannot do, he will know where to start. He has a beginning point that is not damaging to him. People who suffer are those that don't know what they don't know. Such is the nature of ignorance.

How can we set up vital, absorbing, educative work periods during the daily instructional reading period?

WHICH ACTIVITY WHEN?

The presentation will insist that there is an order to independent activities. It is the following:

1. Silent reading of self-chosen books.
2. Selection and preparation of portions of that reading for:
   a. An individual conference with the teacher.
   b. A project, or presentation, for the class during sharing time.
3. Activities that stem from class activity in all curriculum areas that are independent in nature, such as:
   a. Drilling on some already taught skill, recognized as needed by the pupil, even though at the insistence of the teacher, as in handwriting.
   b. Pursuing of knowledge in an area, such as science, to develop a project of interest to the individual pupil.
   c. Some highly personal, yet educative endeavor, such as a diary, creative story, or letter-writing that lends itself to the climate of such an activity period.
   d. The application of the pupil to an assigned task by the teacher for instructional purposes.

WRITING

Sarah Asmuth   May 1, 19—

s s s s s s s s s s s s s s s s s s s s s s s

w w w w w w w w w w w w w w w w w w w w w w w

sweet   sweep

swing   swell

I wish you were here.

I love you and you?

A child assigns herself a task to improve her hearing of the blend "sw." This was not asked for by the teacher.

This sequence holds within it all of the necessary activity for any teacher, if he could and would, to keep a large class busy, not only during the reading period, but the entire school day.

SELF-ASSIGNED TASKS MAKE THE BEST INDEPENDENT WORK

Some teachers are scared at the thought of each child's pursuing his own way, more or less, during an independent work period. Still other teachers are grateful that children are resourceful and inventive and so encourage them. They even conduct a campaign in the beginning of the year designed to improve the abilities of pupils to be resourceful. These teachers know that self-winders and self-propelled pupils work harder, longer, and accomplish more. These—both the pupil and the motivation—work when nobody, including the teacher, is looking or checking up. How do they do this?

TRAINING CHILDREN TO WORK INDEPENDENTLY

Every teacher has his own ways of proceeding but common elements can be observed in such a campaign. First, the teacher makes sure that there are work centers. The teacher sees that they are ready for use. But this is not all. There is much that can be done that is not related to any of the centers, or if related, uses them as a supply base at the most.

Second, the teacher lists on the board several ideas that children might consider once they have finished their silent reading. Such a list might be:

Make something about a story you have read.
Write a story of your own.
Keep a diary—or write in your diary today.
Finish a job you have started.
Get ready for a sharing time.
Write a letter to a friend.
Write a letter to someone in your family.
Write a letter to someone who should know what you think.

This list can be so extensive that it could be changed each day. The point is that the teacher helps children plan *before* the reading period starts. In addition to a list such as that above, the teacher might also write on the chalkboard, or at least make these points orally, something about the MANNER in which children are expected to go about their independent business. This might be:

What do you do if:

Q. You break your pencil? Need more paper?
A. Pupils respond in terms of the way that classroom operates.
Q. You need to spell a word, or can't read a word?
A. Pupils respond that they ask the "word helper" or a neighbor or whatever other person is the one that has been decided upon.
Q. The supply you want has run out?
A. Pupils respond in terms of what is to be done if, for example, it is paint that has been used up, or if the paper pile is gone, or whatever.

Q. You are told that you are too noisy for the teacher to work with other children at the reading center?

A. Pupils respond that they will stop the noisemaking and re-organize their activity to prevent the noise from arising again.

Etc.

ROLE-PLAYING TO ANTICIPATE PROBLEMS

Once the teacher has set up the problems that might arise, he can organize what can technically be called a "role-playing" session. This is just a term that describes the way people can run through some act in a practice kind of session. By acting out what is to be done when pencils break, or words are unknown, pupils can see, in a rather dramatic fashion—which is the value of role-playing—what they are supposed to do when they are not to ask for direct attention from the teacher. There can be the trial runs for any possible need that might arise while the teacher is busy with reading instruction of individuals and groups and cannot be interrupted.

So it goes. The children must be made well aware of all consequences that would result under a variety of situations. Children can be trained to do almost anything. There is no valid reason why they cannot be trained to keep themselves busy with worthwhile activities for at least an hour. The proof, of course, is in the pudding. It is not really difficult for a teacher to encourage independent activity to such a degree that all children are busy on their own all day long, only stopping for such periods as music and physical education or for handwriting or something else that needs everyone to work together at one time. Better yet, these whole-class activities are fodder for the NEXT day's independent work.

For example, a teacher may introduce the spelling words for the week. Let us hope and assume that these are not randomly selected words, but have some common element that is discoverable and would further spelling power in writing situations—the only excuse for spelling anyway. During the whole-class session, the children discover that all of the words contain a short "a." Using any or all of the words they could write their own sentences, or follow some procedure that will stamp the words in their minds, or they could take these words and see how many other words they can figure out because they know that particular set. If children know that "can" has a short "a"—they can figure out many other words. The family of "can, man, fan," etc., of course, immediately comes to mind. But that is the most obvious of independent thinking of this kind. If a child knows "can," he could also figure out something like "canned, canning, cannot, candy," and perhaps a dozen other words. In this way such a teacher would be encouraging an operation that would teach far more about the use of word bases than he could in a whole-class session. Each child could work at his own level—and the puzzle-like character of this activity would egg him on as would teacher pressure. The fire would be within, and the answer to the question "What will this activity teach by itself that cannot be taught well otherwise?" is answered in the delight in the child's eyes when he shows the list of words—or whatever—that HE HIMSELF made.

Surely the skill of the teacher in training children to work well independently lies in the *ability* of the teacher to work out the logistics of the activities. If the teacher has cut his umbilical cord to the basal manual, so to speak, he has made the first major step. Once the work centers are set up and stocked, the children trained through a series of practice sessions on the many possible activities, that classroom is truly ready for its independent work period.

THE TIME OF THE INDEPENDENT WORK PERIOD

We have mentioned the advantages of having a long period of time available for children to accomplish tasks oriented around their own self-recognized needs. At the same time we have referred to "work periods" as a specific part of the day, with a definite beginning and ending time to which the entire class must conform. There may seem to be a contradiction between these two ideas. The difference lies not in our philosophy, but in the nature of the state of classroom practice at this writing.

The author prefers that the work period have no definite beginning or end; that children work at certain jobs, under the supervisory eye of the teacher, without regard to time limit, but only in regard to the quality of the job. If a time limit interferes with the excellence of the work, then there must be no time limit. If a time limit improves the quality of the job (and there are certainly many possibilities that this might be so), then there must be a time limit. But the accent is not on the *amount* of time, but on how much the work teaches.

In this context the experience of the teachers in San Diego, under the leadership of R. Van Allen,[4] is notable. He reports:

Some of us who worked to develop . . . this program had hoped that at least half of the children would be well advanced enough in reading skills that

---

[4] R. Van Allen, *The Language Experience Approach in Reading Instruction*, paper presented to The Conference on Beginning Reading Instruction, Office of Education, Washington, D. C., November 14–16, 1962.

they would not require daily, systematic instruction after the third year. To our surprise, many of the children reach that point in the second year. The time once spent in the endless round of reading circles is now spent by the children in actual reading situations where there is information to be located, problems to be solved, horizons to be lifted. There is time for creative self-expression in many media. Children are not only spending more time with mathematics, they are writing their own problems. They are not only studying *about* science, they have the skills and attitudes necessary for engaging in problem solving with a scientific attitude. . . .

When teachers understand how to run their classrooms without the need of bells—symbolic or otherwise—they will be in a better position to help children pursue learning, as everyone must eventually, on their own. Again we repeat the question which pierces the heart of the matter.

"WHAT WILL THIS ACTIVITY TEACH BY ITSELF THAT CANNOT BE TAUGHT OTHERWISE?"

This is the major question for the teacher during the independent work period.

OBTAINING THE NECESSARY SUPPLIES

Obviously, with the preceding lengthy—yet still incomplete—list of centers of activity, the more equipment a classroom has, the easier is the task of the teacher. But equipment can be expensive, and space may be at a premium. What does the teacher do when the administration will not put in movable furniture, sinks, worktables, counter space, storage space for all of the supplies needed? What does the teacher do? Quit? Some do—either by changing jobs or by refusing to "make do" with makeshift substitute materials.

Again we are at the point where a teacher must make up his own mind how important a piece of equipment might be. For example:

> *Problem:* Want to work with clay? No table? No clay jar? The dime store has oil cloth. It spreads on floors as easily as tables and can be washed and picked up at the end of the day. Antique shops, hardware stores, second-hand stores, and again the blessed dime stores, have jars. Failing that, they have PAILS! No money? Does the principal have petty cash? Does the parents' association have spending money for school needs? (Not that we recommend they should spend it that way. The Board of Education should do that.) Can money be raised by some kind of a sale? If the items have small cost, can the teacher dig into his own pocket? (Not that we recommend that either, but such is tax-deductible, and sometimes it is the only way.)
>
> *Problem:* Need a place for large-sized paper? Make a rack like this:

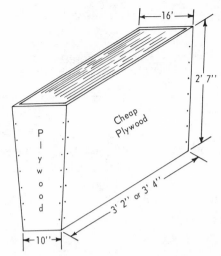

Space saver for large paper art work or charts. Can fit against the teacher's desk or against the wall or other out-of-the-way place.

So goes one way that a teacher might look over his situation and proceed in the light of what is needed. The teacher with initiative and a small amount of imagination can improvise. We urge such improvisation. It is good for the soul of the teacher and marvelous for getting children started on the path to independent learning. There are wonderful stories of the handicaps teachers have overcome since education began. There will always be a need for invention, improvisation, initiative, indeed, creativity in surmounting the endless obstacles put in the way of teachers by the society that wants their services.

BEGINNING THE INDEPENDENT WORK PERIOD

Planning the Activities

Planning has two faces. One can be the eager anticipation of those problems, goals, undreamed of heights revealed to teachers and children to stretch far beyond the first glimpse of possibility. The second face is that of the ugly, laborious, step-by-step plodding through slow-paced demands for "order and system" and a maniacal insistence that such action lead to perfection. No. The first face of planning carries the soul. One is sure when one has a vision.

Elriede Abbe,[5] a famous sculptor, when asked what happened if she took off too many chips, replied:

[5] E. Carving Abbe, "From the Mind's Eye to Reality," *Realm Magazine*, October, 1963, p. 87.

A sculptural concept is conceived in the mental vision of its creator. . . . The action toward this end must be sure, decisive, unquestioning. Too many chips lost through uncertainty—ruin. A strong conviction and a sure hand— triumph. The sculptor who attacks his material directly plays to win. . . .

And so it is with teaching. The sure teacher plays to win. Playing his own hunches as to what will succeed. "Playing by ear"[6] is a great advantage to a teacher. Great teaching consists of instant, wise, intuitive adjustment to the moment. Planning as a fetish will wring the juice out of learning if handled by the compulsive demander.

Planning for variety.

But the teacher who dares to trust himself with broad outlines of what is expected, with a looseness and open-endedness that brings inspiration *because* it allows infinite variety of learning is truly a teacher, and a master one at that. A large amount of unpremeditation mixed with a goodly measure of predictability is what we need. Planning, yes. But not taken as something that is "good" for you, like medicine. Planning is a freedom-making operation.

[6] The authors are not alone in this opinion. The reader is referred to Elliott Eisner, "Qualitative Intelligence and the Act of Teaching," *The Elementary School Journal*, Vol. 63, No. 2, pp. 299 ff, March, 1963.

Planning must get things started. It must include second and third steps that are changeable when necessary. It must anticipate possible trouble areas—lack of supplies, lack of time, lack of an absorbing and sustaining job for every pupil. But above all, it must not strangle nor inhibit. Planning is really a promotional activity. It motivates. It moves along. It intices. It sets the stage. It gets the show on the road. It frees minds, hearts, and spirits of both teacher and child, in the direction of self-imposed education.

How does the planning work for such a period as we are describing? As our major purpose deals with the reading program, the planning of the work period must be geared to that end. Thus the first item on the agenda is reading—silent reading of self-selected books.

The First Order of Business—Independent Reading

Whatever else children might plan to do during this time, the first thing that they must do is "read themselves out," so to speak, with material that they themselves have chosen. The whole reading program depends upon this independent reading. It is crucial, and it is essential. With the prospect of a long block of time with no other assigned requirements to deal with, a child can relax with a book of his choice and get on with his reading—which is the reason for our whole effort.

As we have explained elsewhere, children select that which they like and that which they can read. Let us listen to what a third-grade teacher might say:

> As you know, the first thing you must do is to find a book that you like well enough to stick with and that you can read with very little help. Remember that you need to get ready to read alone with me. You know I will ask you many questions about your book. You know that I will try and stump you about your book—not to be mean to you—but to see what I need to do to make you a better reader. Remember that reading a book to yourself is easier than reading one aloud. If you choose one to bring to your conference with me, be sure you know what to do. I want your best reading, not your second best. Let me check around the class quickly to see what you have chosen or what you would like to choose.

How To Get Books Chosen

A more detailed planning in anticipation of the needs of the coming block of time is illustrated in the following quotes:

A teacher might say something like this: "It is time to get ready for the day. First of all, how many need to go to the Book Center to get new books?" Several children so indicate. The teacher con-

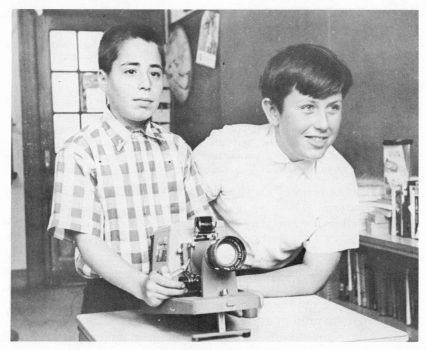

Organizing the period.

tinues: "How many of you will need to change their books within a short time after our work period starts?" A few children so indicate. The teacher says:

It would work better if you got your books right now. There are not enough of you to make a traffic jam there around the books. So if you do not think you are ready yet, it will be all right to wait. But you know my reasons for asking this. I cannot stop for any confusion at the book center while I am working with those in conference.

Another way for a teacher to begin is by enticing the class with books that he may have found since the day before. Maybe a book order came through. Maybe the librarian had sent a new supply. Maybe there are other kinds of reading material—childrens' weekly papers, such as the "Junior Scholastic," the "Young Citizen," the "Weekly Reader"—that have arrived and are ready for distribution. Maybe a child has prevailed upon his parents to bring books from his home library. All these can be piled temptingly before the group. So the teacher holds up some of the items.

Here is a book about the jungle. I read it when I was your age. I loved it, especially when it tells how the animals came to have their present shapes. You will need to decide whether these stories are true or not. But that is the fun of it. Who would like this?

Here is a book that tells about a boy who has so many hats that he doesn't know what to do. Who would like to find out more about his problem?

Here is a book about dinosaurs. If you have been wondering what these creatures were like, here is your chance. It is not easy reading for some of you, so be sure that you want it badly enough to work at it. Who wants this?

Here are our weekly papers. Who would like to read them and then be a part of our news discussion later on? You might like to compare what several papers deal with this week, and also, remembering what happened last week in our local papers, decide if these papers are really helping classes like ours know what is going on in the world. Who wants them?

So the teacher exposes his charges to the world of books and other printed material. They are offered as desirable, attractive, enticing by not forcing them on anyone. The choice lies with each child. He knows he must choose—but the variety makes his task simple. He also knows that if he has exhausted the supply he can so indicate— through regularly organized classroom channels. But each child knows that he must settle down with something and work with it— read it, make a note of it, make a report on it, DO something with it, or prepare to present it to his teacher in a conference.

The first responsibility of the teacher in planning the day with his pupils is to make sure that each is settled with a book or two of his own choice. This is not unlike the traditional library period where each pupil searched the shelves and subsided in pleasure into a library chair and peace descended upon them all. Each day a teacher works his charges toward this self-assignment that becomes a kind of temporary oblivion found in the pages of a book. The only thing different is that the setting is the classroom, not the library. The teacher is *teaching*, not watching. We are *not* describing "Recreational Reading."

Before moving into what's to be done when this silent reading is over, there are a few matters that need to be presented to insure that the work period runs smoothly. These might seem petty, and perhaps they are. But they cannot be ignored.

A Smooth-Running Work Period

One of the goals of education is the development in all children of a sense of mutual respect for materials, for one's fellow workers, for the general good of the group. In a usual class of twenty-five to forty pupils, there are bound to arise dozens of needs or difficulties that, if not taken care of on the spot, will wreck the best planned independent work. For example, these questions need to be considered:

Who helps a child with a word he does not know?

Who explains, *again*, what the directions were to him who has forgotten—or didn't really hear in the first place?

What happens if certain supplies run out, or a needed implement is missing?

What happens if the activity planned is simply not as suitable as it seemed to be when planned?

What do we do about broken pencils, or illegible duplicated assignments, or insufficient copies of a desired book needed right away?

These are everyday problems to the experienced teacher. But they must be planned for. They must be met. What to do? Several things are possible.

HELPING EACH OTHER. Pupils can help each other in a systematized and structured way, or in a most informal fashion, and still not upset the serenity of the reading period. What is needed would probably dictate how the need was met. Take the matter of helping children with words they do not know. This is an important need during a reading period. There are many ways to work this problem out. For example:

The teacher may choose five or six pupils each day to whom anyone may go and ask for help. There is danger in having the same children act in this role too many times, as favoritism can become rampant—rapidly spoiling the morale of a class. To offset this, new word-helpers can be picked each day, or the teacher can ask the class for suggestions as to who should take such responsibility each day. For that matter, the teacher can avoid favoritism by picking no one, instead suggesting that those who need help turn to a neighbor who might have the necessary answer. In asking for help with a word, a child can point to it without saying anything and wait for the response.

The forgotten set of directions produces a similar kind of solution. There may be those specially appointed, or can encourage the quiet request of a neighbor. In any event children can help each other resolve their needs during this work period without interrupting the teacher. Should an emergency arise, in the sense that the wheels completely stop *unless* a new package of paper or a new box of powder paint is found, or whatever cataclysmic event might have occurred, then the teacher will needs be interrupted. But such is the nature of teaching, and most teachers get used to it, and, as we are urging, take all steps possible to avoid that interference that is truly unnecessary.

ANTICIPATING NEEDS. The best planning will anticipate that if certain supplies are low, children are quite capable of meeting the problem. Certainly children can check their readiness for work by making sure of sharp pencils, pens, adequate paper (that can be kept in a desk without spoiling its enticing whiteness), and other supplementary supplies that can be labeled "In Case of—" as one fifth-grade teacher described them. In case of what? In case of a brainstorm that might occur without being anticipated.

Good planning will also involve housekeeping chores for individual desks and for supply depots in various places around the room. Once children know—and even help in deciding where various things are kept—they easily fall into patterns of desirable orderliness. Thus desks should be organized, first on a specific schedule, and later when the pupil sees the need. Taking responsibility for this is very much the part of education. Teachers must work for the self-recognition that "My desk is a mess. I will clean it today" rather than "This is Friday afternoon. We will clean our desks at 2:30 p.m."

A classroom is a microcosm of society itself. An easy, mutually helpful, relaxed yet busy atmosphere is the goal we should be seeking. In fact, one test that teachers can apply to their work is that of the decreasing difficulties. "Do I have more trouble now than I did at the beginning of the term?" Obviously, things should ease off as the weeks progress. If not, the teacher is terribly wrong about the way he is working.

We have not yet discussed or mentioned or listed specific activities for a teacher to follow. These lists are available from several excellent sources. We have already cited Darrow and Van Allen's *Independent Activities for Creative Learning* and the Board of Education of the City of New York's fine *Practical Guide to Individualized Reading*. In addition, teachers will find many excellent suggestions in Amy Jensen's[7] article to help children share their books with each other. (See also Chapter 13.)

In the preceding pages we have tried to indicate centers of interest that will stir children's imagination in such a way that there will be no necessity of all doing the same assignment. On the contrary, our hope is that teachers will maneuver their classes in such a way that they become beseiged with requests for permission—to do what? To pursue educationally valid—self-assigned individually or in groups— tasks, recognized by the pupils themselves as something that needs to be known.

For example, one first grader described how he had tried to write a story on the chalkboard about "snow." He had left out the "N." When his teacher's roving eye caught the error and through asking

    [7] Amy Jensen, "Helping Children Share Books," *Elementary English*, Vol. 33, No. 2, pp. 33–39, October, 1956.

him to say "snow" established that he was quite capable of *hearing* that blend, he told her, "I won't make that mistake again." When the visitor arrived the next day, this boy had covered a large part of the board with "snow-snow-snow"—*ad infinitum*. He had recognized what he did not know, and went to it to correct it.

Another child in fourth grade could not make the more difficult capital letters of the alphabet. The teacher said over and over; "When you realize that there is something that you cannot do, go to work on it. Ask for help if you need to—but YOU are the one that must learn these things. I cannot do it for you."

Is the Room Ready?

Although the burden of the seatwork will largely be individual, there will be many activities that will occupy two or more children at the same time. Because some children must work alone and others in groups, the room must be so arranged. All supplies and work space must be designed to allow free access by all pupils. Traffic problems around any center are a signal to the teacher that he has not properly trained his charges, nor has he arranged his room to the best advantage for an independent period. The setting of classroom routines, discussed in the preceding chapter, is essential to the smooth operation of children working by themselves while the teacher is occupied with specifics of individual conferences and the like. Traffic problems would constitute an interruption to the instruction, and so cannot be tolerated. Quite simply, a teacher puts his foot down. Again let us repeat that only emergency interruptions are permissible. If the room is set up right, if the planning has been adequate, the problem of interruption will be minimal.

The implications of these needs for smooth operation are reflected, of course, in the room arrangement. There are literally hundreds of ways in which rooms can be arranged and rearranged.[8] The most suitable use of space depends on many factors: number of children; amount of floor space; placement of windows, closets, built-in book cases, sinks, and the like, as well as such furniture as desks and tables. The diagram on page 23 is suggestive in that it allows for the free access to all centers of activity, including the teacher, and yet is organized and lends itself to noninterruptive routines. Yet it is only one of a hundred ways to arrange a classroom to advantage.

[8] One of the best discussions of arranging seats, activity centers, and the like is to be found in Robert H. Lane, *The Teacher in the Elementary School*, Boston: Houghton Mifflin Co., 1941, pp. 118 ff.

Centers Suitable for Independent Work
During the Reading Period

1. The Book Center—i.e., where ALL books are kept, trade books, text books, reference books, etc.
2. The Writing Center—where supplies and writing space are available, as well as a typewriter (with its table and rules of use prominently displayed). Chalkboard use is vital. Complaint box.
3. The Art Center—or centers, as follows:
   a. *Wet color*—easels, powder paint, show card paint, water color, brushes, and paper for these media.
   b. *Dry color*—crayons, chalk, and paper to match.
   c. *Clay table* (also used for fingerpaint)—covered with oilcloth or plastic, with covered jar underneath.
4. A Science Center—terrarium, aquarium, and such materials as magnets, magnifying glass, scales, tables for collections, exhibits, and experiments, demonstration materials.
5. Dramatic Center—social studies unit dramatizations or playhouse for younger children, puppet stages (assuming the teacher can control these while running the reading period).
6. Manipulative Materials Center—creative toys and playthings—large blocks, small construction type materials, cuisenaire and others, mathematics materials.
7. Follow-Up Drill Materials—a place for supplies of work books and other similar type of follow-up exercises.

WHAT CENTERS ARE BEST FOR THE READING PERIOD?

As we stated before, the seatwork activity of those pupils not working with their teacher during the reading period must be the type that will not interfere with the teaching. Therefore, noisy activities are out. Whenever the noise level rises above the point where children working with the teacher are distracted, it must be stopped. Absolute silence seems a bit silly, as no child is absolutely silent unless sick, asleep, or under too rigid control. The teacher must find his own level of comfort with the noise of those working independently. The thing to prevent is interference with the instruction. When teacher or pupils are distracted, it is time to calm things down.

With this in mind, those centers that are intended for pounding or loud talking (as a puppet stage, etc.) are not the best for the reading period. If the teacher can control the decibel level, a puppet stage going full blast is all right. In the same way, blocks are all right if they can be used in such a way that they do not clatter and bang. But there are many things other than dramatizations and blocks that can be done, involving a great deal of learning and a small bit of racket, that would seem more suitable especially for those teachers just starting new practices. The following list includes some of these centers we feel appropriate for the reading period.

Those centers not listed are those that seem not to lend themselves easily to the necessities of the reading period. Of course, work benches, games, musical instruments, and blocks are all fine in their place. But our sole purpose here is to make it possible for the teacher to teach. Hammers and nails, xylophones, etc., must be relegated to some other portion of the daily schedule.

Let us take each center and describe briefly how it will be set up and how it will be used.

THE BOOK CENTER

There are two major book centers for every teacher. The first is that of the central library in the building, and the second is the classroom book supply. Of course, the community library is important too. One of the finest activities carried on by a classroom teacher is to take his charges to this local library, where they learn how to secure books of their own when they are not in school. These libraries and their staffs make a great contribution to the reading of our citizens. Our purposes here, however, are with that book supply that is directly connected with schools.

At this point we must bring the school librarian[9] into the discussion. The school library is, of course, and properly so, the center for all books that are not text books, in a given school building. The school librarian is a central resource figure to teachers and children alike. In fact, in the darkest days of the complete dominance of reading programs by the planned sequential basal systems, it was the librarian, more often than not, who fought for the right of children to read trade books. It was the librarians, singly and in groups, who welcomed that break in the horizon called "individualized reading" and gleefully helped teachers secure the necessary books for use in such a program. These are the librarians who have proved over the years to be some of our finest teachers of reading.

But, of course, they are not teachers and their spot in the administrational structure of the school is that of resource person. In all

---

[9] For more details see J. Veatch, "Clarify Teacher-Librarian Roles," *School Librarian*, Vol. 8, No. 1, p. 21, September, 1961.

ways possible they bring their considerable expertize on books to bear to close the gap between children and books. Unfortunately, there have been a group of school librarians who have felt threatened by the existence of classroom libraries, or book centers. This attitude is not only incomprehensible from an educational point of view, it is intolerable. It must not affect book operations.

The school librarian helps in book selection.

What does the school librarian do? She helps teachers select, from the multitude of book lists available, suitable books for a reading program that fits the needs of the pupils in the classroom involved. She organizes the considerable task of keeping library books moving from room to room. She sets up and counsels pupil advisory boards to the school library—an application of a youth agency technique that pays off in better libraries, better child attitude toward books and the library, not to mention the early practice in a skill essential in a democratic society. Librarians do all within their power to advertise and promote the school library and its use. They move heaven and earth to increase the usually paltry budget allocations to this essential part of the reading program. They help mobilize public opinion to spend money on trade books.

As for the operation of the school library itself, a suggestion might help. The Dewey Decimal System, we suppose, is essential. But it must be recognized that when it is applied to arrange books on shelves in ways that segregate easy and hard books, it is being used to perpetuate a system that discourages reading, particularly on the part of the overage reader who is ashamed to be seen near the "baby books." It is on this point that librarians sometimes act as teachers and not as resource people. Properly they offer suggestions of possible book choices to children, but they may not insist—as we have heard librarians insist—"Oh, these books are too hard for you. Go over there" It is, to put it bluntly, none of the *librarian's* business what book a child chooses. It is the teacher's.

In the same vein, it is not the librarian's job to discipline the children in the school library. That is the responsibility of the teacher.

But the arrangement of books can have a real effect on the increased desire to read. We would suggest that easy AND hard books be placed together—regardless of their card catalogue number—in highly specific topics. For example "Space" is a topic. But such books are better arranged and their shelves labeled as:

Space Ships
Astronauts
Space Science Fiction
Space Stations
The Moon
Voyages to the Stars
Etc.

Then children of all grades would search through the book supply, being trained to reject the too easy and find a good book for them, not the too hard. They would not be embarrassed to select a large picture book, that, while resembling the kind read only by very small children, is, in fact, pegged at a much older difficulty and interest level.

To sum it all up, the school librarian is the helpmeet of the teacher. Her or his role is unique and vital. It has been traditionally the librarian who has fought for the right to read books of one's own choice. The right to read is part of the right to citizenship. It carries strong civil rights overtones, as demonstrations in many American cities are currently attesting. In the school library, slightly different in role from the community library, the one in charge has a great deal to do with helping children to love to read, simply because one is reading what one loves. Librarians understand this. All honor is due their efforts.[10]

The Classroom Book Center

Here is the place where all the books in the room are kept. There will be no such thing as "work-type" books, or "recreational" (i.e., trade- or "library") books. Books are books. To set some aside as something unpleasant to be taken in the morning only when one feels strong, or to be taken in doses as one does medicine, finds no sympathy in the philosophy of this text. We disapprove of such approach to reading. One learns to read from all books selected to be read. Therefore, books must be categorized as to their contents—not as to how they are to be used.

Just as in the building library, the way books are arranged facilitates their use. Book arrangements, particularly in the classroom library, are for the children, not the teacher or the librarian. Books should be clumped—without regard to difficulty level—in topics that will attract. For example, these titles will pull readers:

Frogs, Snakes, and Lizards
Prehistoric Man
Prehistoric Animals
Civil War Fiction
Civil War Nonfiction
Digging Up the Past
This Week's Books from the Community Library
Reference Books
Etc.

There are no limits to titles. The important thing is that there should be no shelf that advertises its wares as being only for the slow readers. This is death to the incentive to read—and too many such massacres occur daily in our nation's schools and libraries.

If the furniture for such a corner is some kind of shelving, these should be built to child-sized specifications. The books on them should be get-at-able. The kind of square set up in three sides (and

[10] It could even be said with some truth that without the help and encouragement of many librarians in the early and middle 1950's this book might not now be written.

perhaps part of the fourth) with book shelves, and organized in some kind of way for easy and tempting browsing, will pull the children to find a book to which they can devote their energies. Within that square can be several chairs. We have seen a child-size rocking chair that was such an object of desire to so many that signing up for turns was necessary. We have seen a 9 x 12 rug with children belly-whopping or sitting cross-legged upon it. But these unfortunately are unusual, at least at the present time. We have also seen a davenport in a classroom. It was designated a place for reading and needed a signing-up slip, too.

Making the Book Supply a Magnet

The common classroom chair and table are what most teachers must make do with. These have their advantages, too. Tables can be used to spread the books around so that the front covers show face up! Book jackets are designed to enhance the attractiveness of the book. DON'T take them off. Let them fall off with wear! It is fascinating to watch children work their way through a large supply of colorful books. They might take two at a time because the decision as to which is the best is impossible to make on the spot.

In an instructional program dependent upon such highly personal book choices, everything possible must be done to increase the attractiveness of the book supply. Their arrangement upon tables or shelves serves a true motivational end.

Yet the book center is not a place of instruction—in the sense that the teacher directly teaches there—it is a place for browsing, for looking over books, for selecting those desired, for the quiet contemplation of the bountiful world of books. Pupils may or may not sit there to read, but they most certainly go there to find reading material. As a magnet pulls iron filings, so should books pull children (and adults, too) of all ages. The point is that a classroom cannot be a school library.

The Room Library

If a teacher is lucky, he may lay in a supply of around 200 books. Many more than 300 can present unwanted management problems. However, there is always a way to involve children in taking care of the books. A committee could cull out those that need to be returned to their owners. Another committee could make decisions about how to arrange them on shelves or tables. A child librarian or a committee could take care of the chore of keeping track of who has which book.

For the purposes here, however, our description of the way a room library should be set up is pertinent. This center is the place where all the books are kept. Whatever gets in the way of smooth exchanging of books must be eliminated. Literature must always be a magnet.

ONE WAY TO ALPHABETIZE. One teacher of a first and second grade taught alphabetizing by disregarding the content of the books, having each child look at the first letter of the title of the book he was using. Then around on the window sills were placed enough wooden blocks (not in use) as props for books. The letters of the alphabet were thumbtacked onto them so that the books that began with "A" were placed just after the block that said "A." The books that began with "B" after "B" and so on. Although it was true that her book supply was meager, her children had no trouble finding a book they wanted when they wanted it. (In passing, it might be noted that she did an exceptionally good job of teaching initial letter sounds.)

The window-sill library shelf.

Using the Book Center

As the first time on the agenda of the independent work period is that of silent reading, planning for use of the book center begins the reading period. With the exception of the early days of the first grade before children can read very much by themselves, the material at hand on the book shelves in the classroom is the prime source of activity as the children begin their instructional reading period. As we emphasize strongly, the child must have the free choice of reading material in order to prepare properly for his instruction with his teacher. It is imperative, more than anything else in the reading program, that that choice element be developed and utilized to its greatest advantage. Within the teacher's broad directive "READ!" the child furthers his skill through WHAT he reads.

After the silent reading, the moot question is always that of "What to do next?" Why can't that second activity be more silent reading? Once the child has finished his task set by the demands of his first choice—say, he gets himself ready for his individual conference with his teacher, or, perhaps, plans what he is going to do with a friend about a chosen story to present during sharing time—once he is satisfied that he is ready for what is to come, he can go to the book center and pick another book.

However, the second activity can very well be derived from books, even though a child is not using them! Of course the book center is much involved to this end.

Book-Centered Activities

Whether or not a child, or a group of children, actually takes a book away from the book center while they are working on their independent project is not as important as what is done with the book. There are so many possibilities that a list can only be suggestive. For ease of use by teachers we will divide the suggestions into two categories: (1) best for beginning learners; and (2) suitable at all levels, as the individual or group's skill, knowledge, purpose, and energy will determine how simple or complex the activity will be.

Book Activities Particularly Suitable for Beginning Learners

1. Listing titles of all books read in file or notebook.
2. Finding words in books that the child knows from his writing.
3. Contributing to the bulletin board, or class exhibit, labels, pictures, other *objets d'art*.

4. Practicing to read aloud.
5. Making an original book jacket in color.
6. Making a series of pictures of salient points of story to use in re-telling.
7. Finding words that have certain beginning letter sounds, or ending letter sounds, or sounds in the middles of words, and listing them somewhere, in some way, to be retrieved when needed.

Book Activities Suitable for Learners at Any Level

These activities are dependent upon the individual's or the group's initiative, leadership, purpose, time, skill, and energy for the degree of complexity or simplicity.

1. Finding facts for a certain topic of discussion, such as "Our Turtles" or "Fire Prevention in Our Forests."
2. Choosing a poem from many to learn with fellow poetry lovers to recite at a future sharing meeting.
3. Performing chore-type work around the book center, as:
   Dusting books.
   Alphabetizing cards.
   Making new cards.
   Keeping track of "Books in" and "Books out," etc.
4. Using books to deepen understandings in a social studies unit.
5. Locating books—or authors—on a large map with all kinds of pins, flags, and other representational objects.
6. Planning, organizing, and executing a bulletin board display, or exhibit.
7. Making rough tabletop maps to scale of local spots, as school district, or historical spots, as battlefields, using compass, stones for roads, etc. (See "orienting" a map with a compass as described in various Boy Scout and Girl Scout Manuals.)
8. Keeping records of books read, using title, author, dates taken, pertinent comments, and whatever follow-up ensued.
9. Recording hard-to-locate reference material in a notebook for use at a later time.
10. Evaluating the *way* books are arranged in the book center, improving the arrangement for easier use.
11. Planning a skit that comes from a story book.
12. Planning a puppet show on a book story using either simply made puppets of socks, potatoes, etc., or those of intricate construction.
13. Picking a book that the reader disagrees with and preparing a refutation for sharing time (as: *The Big Ball of String* could produce differing points of view as to sick-bed activities).

14. Selecting something to be read aloud for a unique purpose, as: beauty of language, excitement of the story, hilarity of story, or proving a point that had previously been at issue.

15. Making something from a story that can be used later in a dramatization, exhibit, etc., as: a homemade reproduction of the Bill of Rights.

15. Collecting books and other memorabilia for an exhibit. For example, an exhibit on birds, forest animals, sea animals, old lanterns, old newspapers.

17. Preparing an oral reading session with appropriate sound effects. For example, drums for an Indian story, Far Eastern music for *Silver from the Sea* or *Malay Canoe*, jungle noises for *The Elephant Child*, etc.

These are but a few ways in which children can use the book center in a classroom. Needless to say, the school librarian can be a superb aider and abetter for this kind of activity. We hope you will notice that in each case listed above there is a quality of:

1. Self-assignment.
2. Creative activity unique to the individual or individuals involved.
3. Open-endedness that will carry along for hours and days with only the most informal kind of supervision from the teacher.

To the question "Will these activities teach the skills?" the answer must come—what skills? In every case, the skill of choosing an appropriate book for a child is encouraged. The skill of "Reading between the lines" and thus developing critical reading faculties is notable. The skill of "Gaining central thought" is imbedded from first to last. The skills of word recognition and word analysis may or may not come into play. But these latter skills, as described later, are more subject to direct teaching action in the individual conference and during the independent *writing* period.

A WRITING CENTER

Such a center will need to hold supplies for writing with all necessary paper, pencils, and pens. Children might choose to write at a desk covered with colored construction paper in some way, or designed to attract budding authors. One sixth-grade teacher tied a ballpoint pen to a gorgeous pheasant feather (a trophy from one of the boy's father's hunting trips), and set it in a small Jugtown ceramic inkwell, next to a pile of *new* paper, put in on a colorful table, and let nature take its course. Soon rules were needed for taking such turns at *that* table. Another teacher found a short vase, pasted a label on it "IDEA Pencils Only" and put in it a dozen exquisitely pointed *soft* lead pencils, plus a pile of new shiny paper, and waited for its magnetism to exert itself. It did. The result in a very short time was a class newspaper project!

In other classrooms, some children like their own seats so well— from a need for a sense of security perhaps—that they will get whatever writing supplies are needed and bring them back to the sanctuary of their own desks.

Still other teachers like to have a large table set aside where those who choose to write together can get together and produce whatever deathless prose might be appropriate for the day.[11]

Another kind of situation is found in those classrooms blessed with much chalkboard or bulletin board space. Younger children, particularly, need and enjoy writing "big" on large wall space. One of the nicest things about a chalkboard is that one can erase mistakes. Writing on large paper, while it has its attractions, requires much more correction and proofreading than board writing.

These are but a few ideas that illustrate the possibilities of a writing center. Each teacher needs to look at his space, his equipment, and his furniture, and set up a place where children will be encouraged to write.

A typewriter on a table may not seem, at first glance, to fit into the requirement of quiet work. But it is rare that children become proficient enough to interfere with teaching going on elsewhere.

Learning the touch system is much to be desired, but we have a way to go before that becomes an actuality in most classrooms. However, children love to hunt and peck, and are marvelously patient about it. The typewriter does not clack enough to bother anyone much.

Using the Writing Center

Writing activities are legion. The young poet or author may choose his place of writing after securing the necessary supplies from the center and go to work. What might he be writing? Here are some suggestions to those who need and want them. These, too, as in the Book Center, will vary in complexity only in degree, depending upon the ability of the child or the group.

[11] For one of the best descriptions of a group or class writing activity, we refer the reader to: Natalie Cole, *The Arts in the Classroom*, New York: John Day Co., Inc., 1940. Alvina Burrows, *They All Want to Write* (3d ed.), New York: Holt, Rinehart & Winston, 1964.

1. An autobiography using snapshots or baby pictures.
2. A diary—titles could be something like "All About Myself" or "This Is What Happens to Me" or "The Fun I Have" and the like.
3. A story, real or imagined, fact or fiction.
4. A cumulative story written with co-authors.
5. Letters to sick friends, well friends, pen and pencil pals, relatives, a manager of a place to visit, the President, anyone who should have one.
6. Poetry, rhymed or blank verse.
7. The class newspaper: writing, editing, collating, organizing.
8. A report for the social studies unit.
9. Record-keeping—milk money, cafeteria lunch money, money from the cookie, cake, or candy sale.
10. Writing a new story similar in plot to one read, as "How the Dog Got a Tail" from *How the Elephant Got his Trunk.*
11. An advertisement to the rest of the class about a best-loved book.
12. Ideas for later writing times, listed on a page in a notebook.
13. Making a scrapbook on a theme to be referred to later when needed, as "Bridges," "Sea Animals," etc.
14. Compiling a list of words for "My Own Word List" for the coming week.
15. Compiling words of unusual sound or meaning for use in creative writing situations.
16. A biography of a beloved author.
17. A book report designed to intrigue a future reader.
18. Perfecting some skill in penmanship that has been previously taught.
19. Finishing a written assignment from another class, as social studies.
20. Organizing a bibliography on topics of interest to others in class. For example: "Books about Snakes," or "Books about Indians" and the like.

These are but a few activities. However, before discussing the use of the chalkboard, the reader should note that the preceding activities have one common characteristic besides that of being "writing" activities. That is, NONE of them are "make-work" or "busy-work" activities. Too often seat-work projects are founded upon ideas that have little, if any, educative value. This is such an important point that we would like to stop for a moment and describe what we mean.

Identifying "Busy Work"

1. Such a wasteful, time-consuming activity might be "Writing a Play." We take issue with anyone who says that dramatics in the elementary school should be from written scripts. Drama is emasculated and destroyed by such writing at the childhood level. For if one has a *written* play, one must learn the lines. Few teachers have enough skill at coaching dramatics from a script to bring out anything but the most awful of parrotted, dry, and dull readings. No. This is not an activity that we encourage at all, independently or otherwise.

Reading back their own questions.

2. Take another. "Put the events of the story in words." Why? What good does it do to arrange events in a story? This activity is a hangover from basal manuals' directions to teachers desperate to teach children to follow a story in which they had little or no interest. Some authorities call "teaching sequence" a reading skill. It is a sheer waste of time unless used to help children write their own

stories. Then, perhaps, some kind of a "teaching sequence" helps them, particularly in first grade, develop plots.

3. Or another—"List action words, descriptive word, etc." Why? What good will that do? The theory is that such an activity will teach a pupil those words that are action words or descriptive words. Unfortunately, there is no basis in research that this will occur. Usually it is a waste of time and serves to show that the teacher is out of ideas for good activities.

4. The desperation of teachers for FREE time during which they can teach individuals or groups has led too many to fall into patterns —of which copying exercises from the chalkboard is one of the worst —that serve non-educative functions. Look back over our series of lists. There is not one idea that is "make work" and so non-educative. All are open-ended. They do not NEED to all stop and start at the same time. No one has to do something that is exactly like that of his fellows. Everyone can use his initiative and ingenuity to the degree that he possesses those traits. It is permissible to be different from one's peers. Diversity is encouraged and yet the room work goes on smoothly and in a systematic and organized fashion.

So far we have been mainly describing seat operations. The chalkboard is too valuable a piece of equipment to be used just by the teacher. It can be used by children for all manner of reports, stories, directions, news events of the class, and myriads of other activities. Let us talk about using it in various educatively important ways.

Writing on the Chalkboard

Learning to write needs instruction. The teacher will have whole class sessions teaching children how to make the various letters, and those words in which they are found. Once a child knows how a letter is made, he can choose to go to the board and practice—on a self-assignment basis—on that and other letters.

In the beginning children need to be helped to get an orientation point. The teacher might say:

We will write from left to right. When you are practicing to make your letters better, you must go from left to right. In this room, why don't you start by seeing if you can make a straight line from the side of the board BY THE DOOR (or window, or bookcase, etc.) and go toward the window (or desk, flag, or bookshelf, etc.).

Thus the teacher needs only a quick look at any child at the board making a line (or two lines, or a dozen lines) to see that he is following the crucial principle of left to right. Once the teacher is sure of that, then she can keep a weather eye out for the same thing in the making of letters. For example, does the child make the letter "d" with the round part first? If he makes the line first, he is making the back part first and must be corrected.

"Tell me" asked a first grader of his teacher, "Is the line of the 'd' on the flag side of the circle or on the door side of the circle?"

"Where is the 'd' in the alphabet?" replied the teacher looking up at the alphabet cards above the blackboard (unlabeled pictures illustrating something that, unmistakably, had the same initial letter as the letter illustrated.) "Find it and see for yourself which side of the circle the line of the 'd' is made."

"It is on the flag side," said the boy as he turned and went to his paper to make that "d" with more sureness than he could have before.

After children have acquired enough sight vocabulary, they can write stories of their own on the board. If they make spelling mistakes, they are easily correctable—as writing on the boards is so *visible*—to everyone. As children's ability to write increases, they can proceed to use the board for reports, for daily news, for dozens of things that should be of interest to the class.

ART CENTERS

Expression in color is a most desirable activity. It is not "busy" work. Art is beauty and deserves more respect than to serve as a time killer. It is one way in which teachers can stir the juices of communication in a child who is afraid of his world. Happily, it is a most admirable independent activity for a reading period. Although it can be carried on at the pupils' desks, there is no place in the room that cannot lend itself to painting or drawing. Walls will take murals that can be planned during a group session. Floors allow large-size paper that does not fit on tables. Thus, accepting that some of the material is messy—such as clay, finger paint, and the like—the matter of an art center can be largely that of a supply center.

An easel is placed over a piece of linoleum to save extra work for the custodian—although children can and should be required to clean up the worst of a mess they might make—and in the easel's trough is placed the paint jars with brush. Or a box or carton of jars of color with brushes is available from a spot where they are available to two or more easels.

All shapes, sizes (large sizes are best in the elementary school), and colors of paper must have their place of easy access. Scissors,

Painting as independent work.

paste, crayons, colored chalk, all these, and more too, must have their spot. Should a teacher worry that supplies will be used up too fast, let this be a matter to talk over with the class. It was Carolyn Pratt who said:

We are wasteful of paper and paint and clay . . . but we try not to waste a child, or his energies, or his time. I have seen time wasted in a traditional classroom where out of 40 children one is reciting, while thirty-nine sit with empty hands, empty faces, and empty heads. I have seen a little boy with his chin in his hands and his eyes on the door, doing nothing, thinking nothing, only waiting and with dreadful resignation, for the moment when the bell would ring and the door would open and he could get out of school.[12]

As for the clay and fingerpaint table and its protective covering, hopefully calculated to keep all the goop ON the table and OFF the floor (and clothes, too, of course), it must be situated where an occasional spot or splash does no harm. A quiet corner where a child can retire and work with these media is most desirable. If the room affords a sink, this should be within easy reach for those with drippy hands who need to clean up. Without a sink, a washbasin or pail of water will serve for the needed ablutions.

Woodcarving, whittling, and soap carving all need a place, too. These are fine activities and should be encouraged.

As in everything else, pupils are trained to use the art supplies with care and yet with enjoyment. The centers themselves serve as supply depots, yes, but also as work places where children can express themselves in a chosen medium that will further their appreciations and learning.

Using the Art Centers

Suggested activities around the art centers, while centering around the promotion of academic learning, need not wreck the concept of art as beauty and as individual and unique expression. Writing and reading can be made uncreative in the same way that drawing can be reduced to conformism. "Everyone turn to the story on page 23" is the same philosophical kettle of fish as "Draw four red apples." With these philosophical points in mind, let us turn to the activities that can come from the supply center for wet color—i.e., paint, on easels or desks or tables; fingerpaint; clay table:

Suggestive Art Activities with Wet Media

1. Making a poster advertising a well-loved book—two or three dimensional.
2. Illustrating an original story, or diary, or other handmade book with paint on the cover, or fingerpaint for the end papers of the front and back covers of a book.
3. Painting a backdrop for a large real stage in the auditorium for Thanksgiving.
4. Painting the background scenery of a small diorama, as well as mixing up concoctions to make snow (salt, flour, water), or leaf color (green paint on old bread or sponge rubber), etc.

[12] Carolyn Pratt, *I Learn from Children*, New York: Simon & Schuster, Inc., 1948, p. 10.

Using the art center.

5. Drawing the salient points of a story for presentation at a sharing time.

6. Making a relief map in the sand table, or on a piece of plywood of stiff cardboard.

7. Painting a mural illustrating the era of a unit in social studies.

8. Making puppets and painting their faces, whether the bodies be of the simplest of material—paper, potatoes, rags, etc.

9. Painting backdrops of puppet stages, for various scenes of stories.

10. Using fingerpaint to express something—a mood, a feeling—i.e., not representational; as: "going over bumps in the car" or "a toothache."

11. Painting or drawing fictional or historical notables.

12. Making personages of clay and painting after drying.

13. Soap carving of figures, and other ideas needing representational treatment.

14. Painting on the easel.

15. Painting with brushes on the chalkboard dipped in water only.

Suggestive Activities with Dry Art Media

1. Drawing a portion of the story that is fun, exciting, scary, etc.

2. Drawing a salient point of a story to put on a mural or windup "movie" in a box.

3. Illustrate own creative writings.

4. Make parts of bulletin board displays and other exhibits—two or three dimensional.

5. Drawing anything in crayons or chalk that cannot, for whatever reason, be done at that time in paint.

6. Make an original book jacket to use in advertising a loved book to classmates or to another class in the school.

7. Preparing visual material that will help in running the school, such as posters of how the safety patrol does its work, where the line starts and stops in the cafeteria.

8. Decorating anything decoratable—diaries, notebooks, etc.

9. Sewing in color. Swedish embroidery on crash linen towels. Dressing figures for the dioramas for social studies. Making costumes. Making aprons.

10. Any kind of original illustrations for a story, no matter who the author.

11. Experimentation to perfect certain art skills, as the blending of one color into another with colored chalk. Or practicing the difficult art of painting with water color.

These are art activities that have an inherent artistic reason for existence. As in the previous section, there are certain activities erroneously labeled under the heading of art. Such things as: "Draw two red balls" is not an art activity. It is not even arithmetic as some might claim.[13]

Art must be preserved as a means of expression, essentially creative in its nature. To use it to teach uncreatively is to abuse it.

[13] The concept of two is hardly taught by such directions. Far better to ask the child "Draw something you know or saw that shows me you know some number between two and ten." Or "What number story can you draw today?" In these ways we do not emasculate art. Nor do we mandate the learning of number concepts by "make-work" assignments.

A SCIENCE CENTER

A table or work space where children may experiment and explore and discover is essential in a good classroom. While terrariums and aquariums and growing plants may find their places on the window sill, a place for exploration is needed for the child who would find out facts he did not know.

Such a space must be large enough for two or more to work. Probably rules will have to be made about taking turns there, too. But, in any event, as in the art centers, the source of supplies is in this spot. The magnets may be taken to an open spot of floor and various materials can be tested against their powers. In the same way, a magnifying glass can expand children's appreciation of those elements in his world that he has not looked at closely. A most absorbing activity is fixing the eye on a leaf, an insect, a piece of cloth, an onion cut crosswise—dozens of such things that can hold the child spellbound with the new dimension of his universe.

Truly, it is the expansion of a child's universe that we are seeking during the independent work period. It is the time when creative powers are used to seek answers to those problems that have arisen during the day. The teacher works best, in these cases, when he works least. "The world is so full of a number of things" said Robert Louis Stevenson and he was right. A classroom must be full of a number of things also. The child is the explorer, the inventor, the investigator. And during the independent work period he has the TIME to do so.

Using the Science Center

In the exploding market of science books for children are many ideas that are intended for children's experimentation. In fact, the measure of a book on science for children is whether or not it moves the child OUT of the book and toward the manipulation of materials to discover knowledge original with that child. We do not read *about* science in the elementary school. We must develop the habit of curiosity—for surely it is one of the most fragile of habits and needs much tender, loving care.

In the science center what can we do? First there should be much experimental material—all kinds of equipment that can be used independently. Mary Everest Boole pushes in this direction: "The typically scientific mind may be described as one which stands in a definite relation to the As-Yet-Unknown-Truth, and especially to that portion of the As-Yet-Unknown which is just below the horizon of knowledge."[14]

A Suggested List of Supplies

The independent work period must hold these opportunities to some degree for all children. There are many reference texts available. Let us select from one some of those materials and equipment that are particularly suitable for our purposes of quiet independent work.[15] This list is suggestive only, and far from complete.

Aquarium tank, 5- or 10-gallon
Baby bottle, Pyrex, 8-ounce small neck
Baby powder cans, empty and clean
Baking tin, 12 inch x 18 inch
Candles
Dry cells
Flashlights and bulbs
Iron filings
Magnets, bar, cylindrical, large and small horseshoe
Marbles
Mirrors
Needles
Paper sacks
Pipe cleaners
Plaster of Paris
Pulleys
Rubber bands
Rubber tubins
Spring balance
String
Thermometers

This pointedly incomplete list serves to illustrate the kind of material best for valid science experiments that will not interfere with the instructional reading period. Naturally, when there is much more than can be done, a great deal more material can be stocked. But

[14] "The Preparation of the Child for Science," *Collected Works* (Eleanor M. Cobham, ed.), Vol. III, La Salle, Ill.: Open Court Publishers, 1902, p. 875.

[15] For most of the science ideas that follow, we are indebted to J. B. Navarra and J. Zafforoni, *Science Today for the Elementary-School Teacher*, Evanston, Ill.: Harper & Row, 1961, p. 41.

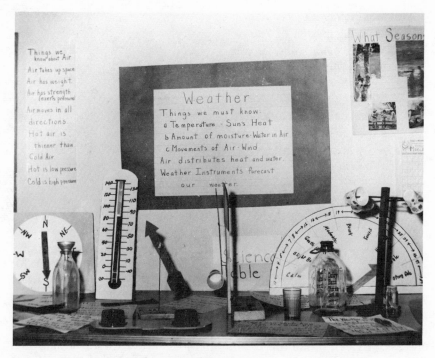

A science center.

these are some things that are uniquely usable during the reading period. This is what we are concerned with in this book.

Some Science Activities

What are some good activities?

Again, any good elementary text for teachers or children is loaded with ideas. Let us again take a sampling—a hop, skip, and a jump through a text.

1. Air has weight—air takes up space—air can be poured.
2. Weather observations:
   Measuring the wind
   Finding the dew point
   Taking indoor and outdoor temperature
   Making a barometer
3. Study of rocks:
   Growing crystals in the classroom
   Making stalactites and stalagmites
   Arranging and classifying a rock collection
   Making a relief map of the ground contours of area near school

4. Making fossil casts and prints
5. Studying inertia
6. Making models of solar system
   Rocket ship
   The moon
7. Making a sun dial
8. Making a foil electroscope
9. Experimenting with pulleys
10. Experimenting with levels:
    Wheels
    Inclined plane
11. Experimenting with steam
12. Experimenting with dry cells, electromagnets, magnets, etc.

Before we move on to the next center it should be clearly understood that these types of activities are not intended to *substitute* for the science work in an elementary classroom. They are suggested as supplementary activities. The independent work period, as has been said, is one time during the day when scheduling is not prime. A child finishes his reading and moves into another activity. This second activity can range throughout all of the areas we are suggesting. But here the child has the time to think, to be thoughtful without being hounded to finish this or that. He can experiment. He can observe to his heart's content. We include these ideas as a way to provide solid educational activity that produces the kind of school climate conducive to learning. In our opinion, science is very much a content area, and this type of project with its attendant write-ups—including spelling and rereading—is exactly the kind of practice that instructional reading requires. These are greatly superior to workbook lessons.

Later on, in the chapter on reading at upper-grade levels, there will be more discussion on this point. Reading has been mistakenly separated from the rest of the curriculum. This is one of America's more serious educational mistakes.

A PLACE FOR DRAMATIC PLAY

If the teacher feels confident that he can handle dramatic practice, puppets, choral-speaking, and the like, he can proceed to set the ground rules for such an activity in a center or corner of the room. If this is not possible, there may be a coatroom or work closet where children can go to practice those dramatics that they have planned. Often has the unit in social studies, as should all good social studies units, produced some form of construction that lends itself to dramatic play. One teacher had a dairy unit going full blast, complete with a telephone retrieved from the dump, milk cases (empty bottles, of course, but then—) in which children took milk orders, prepared them, and, in general, played "Dairy" while the rest of the class was otherwise occupied. A sixth-grade teacher, with a dietary experiment on white rats set up, enjoyed watching various children re-enacting their observations of laboratory technicians weighing out minute amounts of all kinds of substances (not the least of which was chalk dust) on the scales (grams only) while waiting for the rest of the class to finish up whatever tasks had been assigned. One first-grade group, in recapitulating their latest discovery in the neighborhood, a new trailer sales park, built and played "house" endlessly (they called it playing "trailer") as soon as they were finished with their seatwork.

Incidents like this can be recited *ad infinitum,* but not *ad nauseam,* as they hold a precious ingredient for education—the natural interest of children in their surroundings. For the purposes of the reading period, this dramatic play can occur in centers that allow a child to lose himself in another world. He becomes someone else. He practices for his later role in the grown up world. He practices living in his own world.

However, this kind of activity is not the easiest to control and interruptions that occur when the teacher needs to restore quiet can prevent instruction. If so, such activity must be relegated to other work periods. However, even then there are things that can be done without such disruption. Costumes can be sewn, stage scenery can be planned and made, individual memorizing (with expression, NOT parroting) can be done, lines of songs can be copied, and various stage "props" can be made. One sixth grader, after spending the good part of the day working on a reasonable facsimile of the Magna Carta, went home and finished it—in spite of her parents' pleas—at midnight. Similarly, the head of the horse of the "Headless Horseman" can be prepared and executed without disturbance, as can the papier mâché figures of Santa Claus, or the Seven Dwarfs, or who knows what manner of man or beast?

The point is that the TIME of the independent work period lends itself to such constructive and absorbing activities. The teacher needs only to set up a supply center that is accessible and well outfitted.

Using the Center for Dramatic Play

The activities that lend themselves well to these centers allow a child to change his place in society. He becomes a father, a scientist working with the gram scales, a doctor using the child-sized stethoscope on a colleague or doll. She becomes the mother, the teacher, the nurse, or someone else in her life.

The reading period, as far as dramatics or dramatization is concerned, cannot have the help of the teacher, or can have it very rarely, as in a group organizational session. Therefore, the kind of dramatization that works best during the reading period is that which the children can run pretty much on their own. If they enact other people, they must have observed those other people, either at home as they have played, or at school, or on trips, as they have studied various members of society and how they serve.

What follows are suggestive activities and, as before, make no pretense of being all inclusive.

Impromptu Dramatics[16]
  Pantomime
    Smelling a skunk
    Opening a box without knowing what is in it
    Smelling a lovely rose or perfume
    Holding a very young kitten
    Threading a needle
  Being Another Person
    A doctor taking temperature
    A mother with a sick baby
    A snake handler
  Dramatization of Every-Day Living
    Playing house
    Playing school
    Daddy coming home on the commuter train
    Mother cooking
    Teacher teaching
Planned Dramatics
  The scientist takes care of his experimental animals
  The laboratory technician measures out materials carefully
  The poetry lovers plan a choric-speaking presentation
  The puppet stage gets a workout
  The skit that presents certain learnings in connection with social studies

These and many more activities may or may not have play corners, doll corners, or other specially set aside portions of the classroom for such activity. There is no doubt, however, that if space makes it pos-

[16] Girl Scouts of America, *Dramatics and Ceremonies*, New York: Cat. 19–751, 1956, has many fine ideas for teachers in these areas.

sible, the teacher will have more active and productive children when they do have their own area.

MANIPULATIVE MATERIALS CENTER

The toy market has never been richer than during the current affluent years of our society. Creative toys and playthings are abundant. There are large blocks and small blocks. There are blocks that are simply blocks and can be piled without regard to which end is which way. Then there are many kinds of especially made blocks that fit together in certain ways so that playing with them can produce an amazing number of remarkably substantial constructions. These have important uses during the independent work period, particularly in the primary grades. (Nevertheless, the more complicated structures possible with these materials, the more usable they are in the middle and upper grades—either as objects illustrating something in the social studies areas, or as out-and-out recreational materials. They even have appeal to adults.)

A manipulative materials center.

As the possibilities of the use of these blocks stem directly into the creative intellectual areas of the child, and all creativity and ingenuity is to be encouraged by a democratic society in its own self-defense, the use of school time for blocks can be used to advantage by the teacher who knows what to do.

For example: A first-grade child leaves his seat and constructs a complex that is a reasonable facsimile of the interchange of the new four-lane highway near his home. The teacher, noticing this in her rounds of direct and indirect instruction, asks: "Why don't you put the signs up as they really are?" The child does, and in so doing, pushes his learning through a series of words, two of the most important being "left" and "right." In their proper meanings *at an abstract level.* Yet is it really abstract? The blocks are there. And so the child recapitulates from his larger life experience, and reproduces on a smaller scale that operation that every intelligent being must accomplish in order to mature.

MATHEMATICS MATERIALS

Other materials that could well be in this type of center are those relating to mathematics. Several companies provide commercial materials that are most helpful to children in formulating and discovering the meaning of mathematical concepts. The Cuisenaire Rods and the Catherine Stern materials are examples of this kind of class equipment.

Of course, since time immemorial teachers have invented "counters" to help a child figure out for himself his addition, subtraction, or multiplication facts. Bottle caps often come into their own *after* they are off the bottle! Thus such a center would entail learning materials that would help a child proceed—by himself and therefore quietly—along the path of mathematical understandings.

USING CREATIVE TOYS AND PLAYTHINGS

The market for creative toys has made great contributions to the play of children in the last few decades. Holgate toys, Creative Playthings, Erector Sets, Lincoln Logs, Tinker Toys, and many more come to mind when one thinks of these types of materials. All of these are very useful to promote the element of creative thinking and dramatizing what has already been emphasized for previous centers. The absorption of children in building the hundreds of objects possible with such materials is notable. Again the factor of having time to do this kind of construction is important.

But, in addition, we have many excellent manipulative materials for seat-work activity that are fairly new to classrooms of this nation. The last decade has seen the unique Cuisenaire Rods, already mentioned, as well as other kinds of blocks. Once a child has finished with his silent reading and its attendant work, he can turn to any other portion of the curriculum and proceed to other independent work. Simply because the period under discussion frees teacher for reading instruction does not mean that children must only do reading. True, the pupil's major job is with reading, to which he must be held responsible. But once that is finished he is his own master within the rules of the game.

The following is a list that suggests what children might do when they are finished with their reading.

Using materials available from creative playthings:

Playing with blocks to make reproductions of life environment.

Using manipulative materials for mathematics—Cuisenaire Rods, Stern materials, either Tower of Hanoi, beans, washers and what have you for free play or discovery of number concepts.

Building a crane from Erector set.

Building a bridge with blocks.

Building a scaffolding with Tinker Toys.

Building an electromagnet with Erector materials.

Building an Old West stockade with Lincoln Logs.

Building a church and surrounding houses with small or large blocks.

Building a community shopping center

In short, the use of these materials can be of the simplest nature for the very young child or complex enough to challenge an adult. In fact, a few years ago a whole television program was devoted to the exploration of how skillful adults could utilize children's toys of this nature.

The open-ended quality of the activities carried on with these materials is notable—in sharp contrast to a painted tin layout of an airport, or a garage, so frequently seen in shops, that allows the child to play with only one thing. Once these are set up and played with, that is the end of it. There is literally nothing else to do with such canned playthings. But with blocks—there is no limit beyond the imagination of the child. The airport one day, the Holland Tunnel the next, the Golden Gate Bridge, and so on. The activity with such open-ended materials is literally practicing for adult life.

THE SUPPLY CENTER FOR FOLLOW-UP EXERCISES

Although we feel their worth is overrated, most teachers like to use some kind of workbook exercises or teacher-made exercises in the reading program. Although the basic tenet of the necessity of the *sequence* of published exercises is unproved, most teachers need and should have material of this nature available. As the major analytical work of skill development of word recognition and remembrance[17] should be carried on in WRITING instruction rather than reading instruction, and, as such skills are best learned when writing is independent, original, and a truly individual product, it then follows that the use of work-book exercises must be done as the teacher analyzes needs. The teacher can fit the exercise to the child, the practice to

[17] Details of this idea appear in Chapter 10.

the need. The teacher must choose that exercise most appropriate to a specific child at a specific time.

Every teacher should have at his elbow a dozen workbooks and similar commercially produced materials. Most of these contain many well-constructed, and well-organized exercises that might nail down a specific learning for a child or a group in short order, once the teacher has developed the basic principle involved.

Just as important as the excellence of such selected exercises is the factor of time-saving out of the teacher's too-busy day. There is no reason for a teacher to use his free time in developing exercises when there are just as good or better ones commercially available. Teachers don't want to spend their time that way, and have said so loudly, as well as refused, in their own wonderful and unique ways, to develop original materials when their own free time was involved. There are many resources available.

In addition to the several workbooks that he prefers, each teacher needs prepared sheets that can be duplicated. We would NOT have every child have a workbook of his own. There is none that is of such proved worth that the money spent is worthwhile. It is far better to have a room supply—and at varying grade levels—so that the teacher is able to pick and choose those lessons that he wishes to use to reinforce skills on given occasions.

Workbooks and Similar Exercises

Before proceeding into describing these independent activities, a discussion of the types of exercises found in workbooks, particularly those connected to the planned sequential use of basal readers, is indicated. Teachers have been made to feel that their children will miss something important in the skills if they do not finish the prescribed—and *prescribed* is the word, page by page—set of exercises. Faith of teachers in such materials is grossly misplaced.[18] The very

[18] The following are some references on this topic: R. L. Doctor, "Reading Workbooks: Boon or Busywork?" *Elementary English*, March, 1962, 34:3:224–8; Martha Thompson, "The Purposes of Workbooks and Teachers Guides," *Materials for Reading*, Supplementary Education Monograph No. 86, Chicago: University of Chicago Press, 1957; V. Herrick, D. Gurth Anderson, and L. Pierstoff, "Basal Instruction Materials in Reading," *Development In and Through Reading* (Witty, P., ed.), Chapter X, NSSE Yearbook, LX, Part I, Chicago: University of Chicago Press, 1961, p. 177–78; J. Schunert, "The Association of Mathematical Achievement with Certain Factors Resident in the Teacher, in the Teaching, and in the School," *Journal of Experimental Education*, 19:219–38, 1951; Mary C. Austin, C. L. Bush, M. H. Huebner, *Reading Evaluation*, New York: The Ronald Press Co., 1961, pp. 116–18; Albert Gray, "Lift the Workbook Cover," *Phi Delta Kappa*, 33:286–87, 1952; Harry W. Sartain, "Do Reading Workbooks Increase Achievement?" *Elementary School Journal*, 4:157–62, December, 1961.

few studies that do examine the value of such materials in any kind of an objective fashion lend only weak support to their use. This is not to say that there are not exercises that might be very valuable to many children, for there are. But it is to say that *no* workbook, assigned day in and day out, one page following another, can be clairvoyant enough to meet the needs of *one,* or *any* child, day in and day out. This kind of use of such materials has little value.

So, too, is the common practice of teachers who put "seatwork" on the chalkboard, with the honest intent of providing a "check" or reinforcement for some skill or story assigned in the basal reader. Writing such exercises on the board, rather than giving them out in dittoed or mimeographed form, keeps children busier for a *longer* time than they would be by just filling in the blanks in a workbook. No doubt there are times when teachers are desperate to keep children occupied. But neither boardwork nor consumable workbooks offer exercises that are educational. On the other hand, if they are used in a highly specific fashion, in a pick-and-choose manner, fitting the page to the learning need of the child, their value increases. Unless teachers can learn how to single out a specific page for a certain child when he needs it, they are wasting children's time. They are, in fact, not very good teachers.

The Myth of Value of Related Planned Sequential Materials[19]

When teachers are helped to use workbooks wisely (or study-books, as one publisher calls them), these materials still leave much to be desired on an educational basis. Any honest appraisal must include such notes as the following:

1. Workbooks deny handwriting opportunities.
2. Workbooks are seriously delinquent in the area of the encouragement of creativity, art-wise and language-wise.
3. Workbooks violate most of the accepted principles of artistry in publishing.
4. Workbook purchase uses money that could be better spent upon more literary material, particularly tradebooks of merit.
5. Workbooks limit children needlessly to paper space and the resulting finger action that can be damaging.
6. The existence of workbooks provides a tacit approval by administration that teachers should follow all lessons or be guilty of wasting money.

[19] See also Agatha Townsend, "Workbooks—The Research Story," *The Reading Teacher,* Vol. 17, No. 5, February, 1964, p. 397.

7. The existence of workbooks gives tacit administration approval to a still unproved assumption that such material contains the crucial elements of learning for the age and grade level purportedly covered.

8. Workbooks contain, too frequently, lessons that are better taught orally by the teacher, with pupils using less expensive ream paper for whatever writing is necessary.

9. Workbooks sometimes provide pages that are simply bound blank paper for the necessary practice of certain activities, such as handwriting.

10. Workbooks do not keep children profitably busy for long enough periods.

Some teachers worry that reading skills will not be reinforced unless specific sequences in a workbook are followed. Others will worry if each pupil does not go through without exception, each step of the Directed Reading Lesson, whether or not a child or group needs it. Following this sequence:

1. Developing interest or setting the stage for the story
2. Introducing new words and concepts
3. Reading the selection silently
4. Reading the selection aloud
5. Talking about the selection and doing a follow-up exercise in the workbook

is a waste of time. That children have learned to read through the many decades that such practices existed is hardly adequate proof. The authors of this text strongly suspect that children have, in the main, learned to read in spite of the Directed Reading Lesson and other suspect practices, and not because of it. As with so many elements of traditional basal reading, there is no research proof of validity.

Thus, when a teacher is trying to decide which activity should be promoted or permitted during the independent work period, he can, with some confidence, ignore the need for every child to follow every step in the traditional pattern of reading sequence.

In summing up this section may we say that teachers should have available a few copies of many workbooks, and should get to know the contents within. A card file for the particular skills, interests, or what have you can be made. Then, when a child or a group of children has revealed a need, and it has been taught, a useful follow-up exercise can be assigned, not so much as a chore, but as a challenge to each child to show that he has mastered a weakness that had caused him to work with the teacher in a group.

For each child to have a copy of the same consumable workbook not only is unnecessary, but also strongly suggests the lack of training and initiative on the part of the teacher. He who does not know what else to do in the independent work period gives a mass assignment to the entire class. Teachers who know how to develop individual and independent activities do not need to resort to such misuse of materials.

Using Workbooks Wisely

Workbook exercises, especially those that are intended to be used with the planned sequential material of the basal readers, stand or fall on their ability to teach a skill, ability, or fact that the teacher has introduced previously—or failing to have introduced, can assume that these semiprogrammed materials will be taught for him. Unfortunately, there is little evidence to believe that such is the case.[20] As we have shown, there are very few studies that even pretend to present a case for the value of workbooks, either as to their whole or their items. Many people believe that there is value in such materials if they are not misused. Most of the literature, with rare exception, is in the realm of opinion.

One exception is a study by Doctor[21] that compared the effect of the use of basal workbooks and teacher-made exercises both used in connection with a total basal reading program. Not surprisingly, teachers of the second, third, and fourth grades greatly favored the former material. Significantly, the first-grade teachers did not, nor did the fifth- and sixth-grade results of the experimentation, reveal any significant findings. One portion of this report is particularly interesting. The opinions of 1,200 teachers and 80 administrators as to the value of effectiveness of workbook materials were solicited. Of fourteen areas of inquiry, weighted to bring a total score of 1,000, the heading of "Child appeal" (i.e., "arouses pleasant associations" and "attractive cover") was rated 20 and 10, respectively, with 80 the highest rating. The item "Opportunity for growth in attitude and appreciation for reading" brought a score of 20. These contrast to the reactions of the item "Previous introduction of skill before use in workbook," which rated 80, and "relationship of vocabulary of workbook to reader," also rated at 80, both the highest rating of any item. Doctor concluded:

[20] Austin, Bush, and Huebner, *op. cit.*, p. 117.
[21] Doctor, *op. cit.*, pp. 224ff.

Workbook usage has a peak of efficiency [when compared in a totally basal reading program to teacher-made exercises] in grades two, three, and four. It can also be concluded that non-workbook materials proved to be superior for the purpose of initiating the reading program during the first grade. Neither the workbook nor the non-workbook materials demonstrate a clear superiority at grades five and six . . . the reading readiness and pre-primer work books of the first grade tend to be rated somewhat lower than those of other grades.[22]

Workbook publishers, of course, maintain that a workbook is an integral part of the total basal reading program.[23] Unfortunately, little has been presented beside authors' personal opinions that workbooks teach what they are alleged to teach. It is claimed by the supporters of workbooks that the reader, the teacher's manual, and the workbook are all interdependent. This may be so, but there is no research evidence accessible in major reference works.

On the other hand, many reading authorities are highly critical of such materials—not so much for their content, but understandably for the way they are MISUSED by teachers. With this we agree. Teachers too frequently use these materials as a sort of disciplinary measure—"Keeps them out of my hair," said one. "I don't know what else to do!" said another. "I don't have to sit up half the night preparing exercises" said a third. "I can't keep the children busy LONG enough," wailed another.

All of these comments are understandable. All of them are a serious indictment of both teacher-training practices—or lack of them, as Austin[24] points out—and the in-service training of local school systems. The blame falls on many shoulders: 1) teacher educators who never taught in a classroom, or if they did, did so in the dim and distant past and have long forgotten the unique and peculiar needs of that situation; 2) the administrative and supervisory staff in school systems who either are overloaded and cannot help teacher sufficiently, are so ignorant they do not know how to help teachers, or have personality adjustments that require the expression of a power drive that prevents interaction between staff; and finally, 3) the teachers who are subjected to all of the ill practices of those who trained them and those who supervise them. For one truth about classroom teachers is that they will go to surprising extremes to make their daily school lives fruitful, exciting, and satisfying—they will, in short, violate all manner of edicts to make their life with children rewarding and pleasant. The great failure of administrative and supervisory personnel is the lack of recognition of this fact. The secret

[22] Ibid., p. 228.

[23] Albert Gray, "Lift the Workbook Cover," *Phi Delta Kappa*, 33:286–87, 1952.

[24] Mary Austin, *The Torchlighters*, Cambridge: Harvard University Press, 1961, Chap. 1.

to inspired teaching is the development of practices that inspire the child AND teacher, for it will follow as the night the day that the former will affect the latter.

Using the Supply Center for Follow-Up Exercises

To the degree that the teacher can fit the needed learning to the individual child, to that degree does this supply center come into play. A mass assignment from the same workbook is a denial of individual learning needs, as well as a sign of an ill-trained teacher. Whatever is assigned in the nature of follow-up exercises must truly BE A FOLLOW-UP—that is, a child reveals he needs to know more about "to, two, and too." Then he must show that he has learned that after a direct teaching session.

Follow-up exercises cannot be valuable, educatively, in isolation. They must be used by the pupil who knows that he needs further work in a given area. The professional literature is loaded with texts and materials that will help teachers. Unfortunately, too much of what is available is designed to be used as busy work. Desperate teachers gobble it up and foist it upon children—literally because they know not what else to do.

The following are designed to be used by a single child or a specific group upon assignment. These can be duplicated and put in the supply center.

1. Duplicate various sheets on which there are many words, among which are scattered words from a specific "family." For example: Draw a line around words that sound like "book."

cook	led	fed	took
red	look	cake	lake
fed	make	rake	book
bake	book	bed	

Or another: Pick out the words that rhyme with "night."

right	maybe	brown	owl
day	can't	swing	fright
would	sight	should	light
fight	mind	grey	

2. Duplicate lists like the following: Ask the children to copy the following words, but arrange in alphabetical order:

water	boy	hawk	home
ink	syrup	milk	mother
owl	jam	quake	nice
rain	test	zebra	hair
horn	lamb	fork	plum
bug	cake	apple	pear

3. Rewrite these words so they mean only one thing:

books	knives	thieves	trees
babies	flowers	ladies	cries
flags	knees	skies	houses

4. Make short lists of abbreviations and contractions similar to those below. Ask pupils to find as many more as they can:

Avenue	Ave.	we will	we'll
Doctor	Dr.	I am	I'm
Street	St.	you are	you're

5. Underline the two small words in these compound words:

shipwreck	armchair	footstep
landlord	blacksmith	lifeboat

6. Duplicate the following list of words. Have the children mark each "a" long or short (ā or ă):

lady	tame	lash	lamb
plant	tassel	wager	safe

7. Prefixes

  a. Write the meaning of the following prefixes. Then write as many words as you know for each prefix, using the dictionary as desired. See how many words have the same ending for the different prefixes.

trans	sub	post
con	circum	ex
in	ir	inter

  b. Look up three words each beginning with:

im	in	un

  What is alike about them?

  c. What is the difference in meaning of these two prefixes? Write two words with each prefix.

ante	anti

  d. Write the prefixes meaning one, two, three, as

  unicycle
  bicycle
  tricycle

What's the difference? Can you find more words like these?

8. Keep list of words (these can be changed daily or weekly, etc.) that have to do with:

Holiday words (Christmas, Easter, etc.)

Space words (orbit, satellite, etc.)

Words that mean the same

Words that mean the opposite

Words that tell things you see in school, home

Write names of things that are round, square, etc.

Words I would like to use in writing

Words that sound nice

Match related objects—boy-girl; knife-fork; cat-dog

9. Select and write lists of words from books according to the number of syllables they contain, a column for two-syllable words, three-syllable words. These can be alphabetized.
10. Work out as many items as they can of what various baby animals are called:
    "A baby dog is called a puppy." Etc.
11. Write months of year and abbreviations—as many as are known.
12. Write as many animals as possible and organize them as to where they live, noises they make, or some other designation.
13. Make a collection of small pictures (flowers, animals, community helpers, occupations, tools, etc.). Mount separately on cards and organize in some way.
14. Duplicate a column of words similar to the one below—leave space at right of column where the pupil is to write its opposite.

left	short	light
heavy	sweet	long
dark	right	sour

Open-Ended Activities for Critical Thinking

1. Comparing Objects and Ideas
   a. In kindergarten and primary grades comparisons are simple. These might include (oral) comparisons of:

   animals   leaves   people

   b. Of stories by the same author.
   c. Of characters, plots, settings of different stories.
   d. In research—findings on the same topic by different sources, authors, etc.
   e. Of pictures, photographs, of same subject(s)
   f. In organizing research projects around comparison. For example:
      Customs and dress in two countries
      Modes of living in two countries
      Life in water—land
      Animals—plants
2. Creative and Practical Activities
   A television, radio, or assembly program
   Outlining of research findings
   Putting things into chronological order
   Keeping records or diaries
   Making a time line of historical, classroom, etc., events
   Reporting on who, when, where, how, why of current events
   Research in social studies, science, etc.
   Writing "how to do" projects
   Reporting on field trips

Writing on such topics as:

What we see at the beach, store, etc.

How policemen, firemen, etc., help us

Foods I like best

Smells I like best

Keeping records of weather, height of children, etc.

Writing sentences telling what one can do.

Writing names of things children see in the classroom, playground, library, etc.

Writing names of as many things as children can remember that they saw on the way to school. Tell children the assignment will be repeated tomorrow—and note the difference in the results.

Writing the names of things one knows by smelling, tasting, hearing, feeling, etc.

Writing sentences telling what each of the following can do: cats, dogs, squirrels, cows, mice, etc.

Listing the names of things that are sweet, sour, hard, soft, etc.

Writing sentences telling three things made of cotton, wool, stone, etc.

3. Miscellaneous Open-Ended Exercises or Activities (The extent of these activities will be limited only by the ability, the time, and the energy, of the child) such as:

Making a rebus story

Learning to use the globe

Learning to use a map

Listing geographical elements such as island, continents, oceans, etc.

Cutting out newspapers or magazines to make an exhibit

Making an alphabetical list of something

Practicing handwriting that was taught previously

Compiling a glossary of terms on a given subject, such as all the terms one needs to know about an animal laboratory, or an airport

Doing time line or time chart

Keeping a record of collections for the various drives

Keeping attendance records

Making a calendar with original designs

Making albums on various things, such as "Our Class" or "Our Trip," etc.

Making a crossword puzzle for self and others

Making a set of directions to a certain place so that anyone can follow it

A mural: an independent activity.

Making and organizing a colored slide file using pictures from various parents and others

Making an individual dictionary, illustrated or otherwise

Writing evaluation of week to come

Making a picture file that deals with broad areas—France, Germany, other countries; New York, Pennsylvania, other states; farming, building, transportation, etc.

Listing or collecting ideas and/or pictures dealing with time—past, present, and future

Making books containing pictures of things that fly, things that crawl, farm animals, wild animals, insects, fish, community helpers, etc.

Listing things that are round, square, like a box, etc.

Making charts, graphs, and tables

Listing figures of speech

The activities listed above are but a sampling of the many, many types of profitable seat work exercises.

TEACHER-MADE MATERIAL

Teacher-made materials can occupy an important place in learning. Many teachers accumulate a stock of seat work material, much of which is more or less permanent in nature. A variety of this material insures interest and provides practice along many lines of useful activity.

Experience charts, records, stories, etc.—composed jointly by teacher and pupils—have made important contributions to children's growth in reading. Mention is made at this point, but these teacher-made materials play such an important part in the teaching of reading that much time is devoted to their use in Chapters 9 and 11.

Teachers in the primary grades have numerous means of presenting new vocabulary in repetitive ways through their "homemade" materials. Many teachers use duplicated versions of experience stories. Lee and Van Allen[25] are especially helpful on this point.

Teacher-made materials are useful at the intermediate-grade level as well. Experience records are used when materials are difficult to read, or they are scarce. In these grades, experience records may be used to summarize activities, projects, experiences, experiments, etc. Here, too, the teacher may "rewrite" difficult materials and present them to children as an experience chart. Charts may also be used in giving directions, recipes for making cakes, etc.; records of class plans; summaries of experiments; lists of committees, projects, duties, etc.; questions to be answered, etc.

In addition to this reading material, teachers can prepare practice or drill activities that can help take care of children's needs. These drill materials can be used in individual or group settings. These may be used with children who have been absent for a period of time, who are new students, who need to overcome a specific skills deficiency, or who need additional practice to "sew up" a skill. Thus, teacher-made materials have a direct relationship to a child's needs at a specific time and to other events in his school day that no commercial material can ever hope to achieve.

EVALUATION OF THE WORK PERIOD

Constant evaluation is important in the development of children's planning, for the making of intelligent decision standards is necessary. Children must know when they fail and when they succeed in carrying out what they have undertaken to do. Evaluation also means opportunity to discuss and to check on problems or questions that crop up, to check on progress, and to decide on future plans.

Evaluation of this type takes place when children and teacher meet to correct the exercises done during the work period. Seated in their small group they discuss the answers, how they were got,

[25] Lee and Van Allen, *op. cit.*, Chap. 5, p. 106.

what makes them right or wrong, steps in arriving at the correct answer, and whether additional drill is needed.

SELF-EVALUATION

The capacity for self-direction and independence necessarily involves the capacity for self-evalution. A first step in this direction is offered when the teacher (during planning sessions) helps children to see the need for more practice. Awareness of needs develops in other ways. A group of children themselves may identify the problem. "He won't give us a chance." "The material isn't in our library." "That group is doing the same thing." Teachers, during the conference or in working with groups, may point up children's needs. "I have noticed two groups working on the same problem." "You will need additional information under the section—Occupations." "You need more practice with this list of words containing this root." Sometimes problems are forestalled as new projects are initiated— the first field trip of the school year; the first time research materials in the library are used, etc. Tests of all kinds—formal, informal, standardized, teacher-made, etc.—help in the identification of weaknesses. All of these offer evidence that can be used to help children see the need for more practice.

The teacher encourages children to pass judgment upon the quality of their own work, and also to defend the standards used in arriving at their answers. Children less frequently need to ask the teacher "Is this O.K.?" "Is this what you wanted?" And the teacher with less frequency has to say, "Yes, that's right," or "That's wrong." "Use charcoal instead of pencil." Instead, he will find it better to say, "What do you think?" "Ask John to see if it says what you want it to." The pupils find that their work has to satisfy them. The result, as the year goes on, is that the teacher finds her pupils become more and more particular with what they are accomplishing.

SUMMARY

The purposes of this chapter are to present some selected ideas that will help teachers during the reading period. The following points serve as a summary. The independent work period should aim:

1. To free the teacher to teach individuals and groups.
2. To allow children to explore a classroom proposition or project in depth.

3. To allow children to develop increasing ability to think and work independently.

4. To allow children the privilege of privacy to develop personal activity of creative nature without the glare of unwanted sharing.

5. To allow children the necessary time for each to perfect a skill that has already been taught.

6. To encourage the sense of ethical behavior and concern for others. not because a teacher mandates such respect, but because it is built into the situation.

7. To encourage the development of inquiry, curiosity, and creativity in the course of the activity.

8. To promote observational skills in all possible areas.

9. To check or test children's proficiency on some aspect of a learned ability.

10. To develop the concept that learning is a highly personal act, and works best when the purpose lies within the learner.

6

THE INDIVIDUAL
CONFERENCE

"I can wait," said the nine year old, tears of disappointment standing in his eyes, "because, you see, when it is my turn, she is all mine."

"May I read to you during recess?" asked a second grader. "It is such a good book."

"Just wait," said Mark as he came into the room from home. "Just wait till you hear this book! Boy!"

In one form or another children react positively to the personal interest of their teacher in what they are doing. And teachers find themselves glowing when they see a child, with stars in his eyes about his work, demanding their attention. No part of the curriculum, no classroom activity, can begin to compare with the warmth of human relationships in a one-to-one conference. When the climate of learning has an element of personal warmth, the learning is faster, easier and more permanent.

The individual conference is the peak, the apex, the climax, the high point of the instructional reading program. Everything that comes before leads to it. Everything that comes after should be determined by what happens in it. Some teachers are quite successful in holding such conferences with two or three children at the same time, each with a different book, of course, but the writer feels that such doubling up should be an emergency measure, and used only when the need is dire. One-to-one is the best teaching situation ever devised. Now that we have mastered the classroom management techniques, now that we know what needs to be done to make individual conferences possible with even a large class, there is no good reason why this practice should not become a major feature of every reading program.

CRITERIA FOR A SUCCESSFUL CONFERENCE

Historically, as we noted in Chapter 1, teachers have always known that the best way to meet individual diffrences is to teach each child separately. But few teachers were able to figure out HOW. It has taken some time for educators to find the key that would unlock the problem of too many children for one teacher. What we are describing is really an adaptation of the tutorial system—or of Mark Hopkins' end-of-the-log technique. Two criteria help a teacher have an individual conference with every pupil, even in large classes, and still meet them frequently enough to carry on the bulk of the reading instructional program. These two criteria are ridiculously simple and managerial in nature—that is, they are not a curriculum itself. They just make good curriculum possible.

1. *The child presents only a portion of his total reading effort during the conference.*
2. *A time limitation for the conference is necessary.*

1. WHAT THE CHILD BRINGS TO THE CONFERENCE

The following diagram shows that each child brings a representative portion of his total reading—recreation and "work-type" (whatever that is)—to the individual conference. It is a *sample* of what he has read. It cannot be everything he has read, as that would prevent the teacher from moving rapidly from pupil to pupil. The diagram shows the proportion.

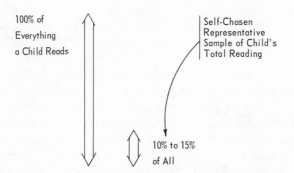

100% of Everything a Child Reads

Self-Chosen Representative Sample of Child's Total Reading

10% to 15% of All

The ten to fifteen per cent is not meant to be an arbitrary figure. It is meant to suggest that no teacher need try to check in detail everything a child has read. In the first place, such total evalution is not necessary for proper reading growth. In the second place, such a requirement makes the child feel that he has no responsibility to further his own learning. In the third place, it is impossible.

Let us go into this in greater detail.

Dangers of Too Much Checking

Checking everything a child has read is an impossible task with any class of more than ten children. In order to check everything, the teacher must, quite literally, *stop* children from reading in order to check. The teacher must have pupils wait for their turn to be checked. This is prevention of learning, and no better than the common practice of asking children not to "read on ahead," lest they lose their place! One first grader told his mother that reading meant "keeping the place."

Checking everything every child reads denies him the opportunity to perfect a major reading skill—that of reading widely to make a *personal* decision about what is important to read. To review and select from a variety of materials those ideas that mean most to an individual is an ability worthy of development. But when a teacher accepts everything that is read, to that extent, the powers of discrimination in reading are undeveloped. At no age level—from six to sixty-six—should everything be read without the reader's accepting, rejecting, verifying hunches, and in a dozen of ways perfecting his ability to choose that which is important.

Checking everything a child reads is motivated by teacher suspicion. Many teachers feel that children need to PROVE that they have read whatever they have read. Sometimes workbooks must be filled out or written work must be copied from the chalk board. Such classroom procedures are based upon the teacher's lack of confidence in children. Teachers are suspicious that no child will read, then, unless he is forced to read. And the checking thus becomes a measure of enforcement.

Checking everything a child reads denies the child the opportunity to be responsible for his own learning. He, in effect, is not considered able to share in his own reading destiny. When a child has a stake in his own learning, his enthusiasm, his eagerness, his initiative increase. Any practice that supposes children must be forced to learn is a poor practice.

To sum up, then, checking the entire amount of each child's reading is:

1. Impossible without preventing and stopping reading.
2. A denial of an opportunity to read with discrimination.
3. A coercive act based upon the need for the pupil to prove that he read.
4. A denial of a child's own responsibility for his own learning.

Checking the Child's Representative Sample

Only the best reading of which a child is capable need be checked. If the reading is less than the best, then the teacher has trouble finding the real difficulty, or the crucial difficulty. When a child does less than his best, dozens of problems will appear that really have little to do with his basic reading ability. These may well disappear with a bit of practice. One can turn to the example of the housewife who prefers company when the house is clean—not when it is dirty. Whatever major housecleaning problems she has will still show when she considers her house presentable. Others disappear in the process of cleaning.

Why else is it good to check only the best reading of a child, and a portion of it, at that?

The responsibility for the learning is placed largely upon the child's shoulders. He may seek help. But the obligation is his. From the time a child chooses his own book for his independent work, he makes a decision that, within the broad outlines of the classroom regimen, *is his own decision.* One learns to make good decisions by *making* decisions. Each one is practice for growing up.

Similarly, once such a personal commitment is made, the child will accept higher performance standards for what he has chosen than he will for other materials (unless force, coercion, or psychological conditioning is used). One first-grade child told another who was reading to him getting ready for a conference, "Joe, you ain't ready yet. You'd better practice on that some more." And he did!

Selection Is a Reading Skill

Next, the very essence of the reading act is that of going through books and materials to select that which is appropriate. Just *handling* books that one might choose produces a favorable climate toward reading.

Once a seriously retarded group of ten year olds were asked if they would like to go through the storage-room pile of discarded books. These—all boys—could barely read at a beginning level. The teacher, quite wisely, suggested this search, feeling they had everything to gain and nothing to lose. Their reading could hardly be worse, and the books were to be trucked away within a week. Result? The boys took all day. They simply refused to leave the book pile until they had satisfied themselves that they had all they wanted. They staggered up the stairs to their classroom with arms loaded, and passionately clutched worn books to their chests if someone tried to take them away. The next day one boy asked the teacher, "Would you help me read this book?" Others heard and wanted to join in. Thus one teacher, so moved she could hardly speak, set up a reading group. This was the beginning, literally, of learning to read for those boys.

Another reason for checking a sample of the child's reading is that it moves him away from closed, repetitive systems of learning. He chooses material, reads it at his own pace, and then subjects himself to intense interrogation, review, reporting by his teacher. But the variety of the choices makes differences unimportant. He waits for no man. He goes as fast as he can go. He explores areas other than the prescribed interests in the reader. His reading has no lid, no fences upon it. It is open-ended. There is no limit.

Thus, to sum up, checking a portion of the best reading of the child is good instructional practice because:

1. The basic difficulties, interests, and purposes are not obscured by other problems that could be eliminated by self-practice.
2. The child accepts responsibility for his own learning.
3. Higher standards of performance are possible with self-chosen material.
4. The process of handling books in order to select one produces favorable learning climates.
5. His reading interests and activities wait for no one.
6. What he does read has been first read silently. He brings no material "cold" to the conference.

2. THE CONFERENCE TIME LIMITATION

A suggestion of time limitation is, of course, not intended to be absolute. Yet a teacher must discipline himself rigorously, must polish his skills and abilities in conferring, IN ORDER TO ACCOMPLISH HIS GOALS in a short time. It *is* better to teach each child separately for the key activity of his reading instructional program. Therefore, time limitations must be observed rather rigorously. It might not be exactly five minutes, but it will be between three and ten minutes. What must be done, and why is it important to hold these conferences to such brief times?

Early in a term, or when a teacher is learning how to conduct a conference, these sessions run much longer than 10 minutes. This is not a serious matter unless some children are forced to wait too long for instruction. The individual conference, lest we forget, *is* an instructional period.

First, longer periods of time reduce the number of conferences for each child. Each child should see his teacher about once every three days. Although there is no illuminating research on this point, there are reports that too few conferences mean that children do not receive the special attention each needs, no matter how gifted.

Next, a teacher who is conscious of time pressure is more apt to study ways of deepening and strengthening his own skills of interviewing. The nature of the situation is such that teachers will be pushed in that direction in order to get the best out of every conference. It is easier to be conscientious when the backlog of demanding conferees is lengthy. Of course, some teachers will just throw up their hands in frustration when they get so behind in their class schedules. But these teachers could not have been ready for a full class schedule in the first place.

Teachers must practice their own skills. Perhaps this might be done first with one child, then two, then a group, and finally a whole class. There are many ways in which a conference can be conducted. The variety is endless, and this fact alone leads to the sense of freedom and "being out of a rut" reported by so many teachers. This could be the main factor that has led to the spread of individualized reading.

But whatever else may occur, a teacher must resolve for himself some of the problems he faces when he is side by side with each pupil. It is hard to ignore the personal factors when one is in a one-to-one situation. It is possible, but the human factors of being together smooth the way for the adult to work, gropingly perhaps, to find out what he needs to do to teach a particular child to read. There are books that have helps[1] to those teachers who want other

[1] See Walter B. Barbe, *Educator's Guide to Personalized Reading Instruction*, Englewood Cliffs, N.J.: Prentice-Hall, Inc., 1961; Peggy Brogan and Lorene K. Fox, *Helping Children Learn*, Yonkers-on-the-Hudson, N.Y.: World Book Co., 1955; Alvina T. Burrows, *Teaching Children in the Middle Grades*, New York: D. C. Heath & Co., 1952, pp. 165–205; Helen Fisher Darrow and Virgil Howes, *Approaches to Individualized Reading*, New York: Appleton-Century-Crofts, Inc., 1960; E. W. Dolch,

sources than this text. However, let us proceed to our discussion of such details.

Frequency of Conferences

Usually teacher and child spend between three to ten minutes in conference with the goal set for approximately five minutes. Off-hand, this does not seem to be very much time, but it equals the amount of personal time (that is, time actually spent reading with teacher) under an ability-group approach. Time devoted to the individual conference is minutes charged with intense teaching-learning, with action and reaction from child as well as teacher. No time is wasted.

Roughly one-third to one-quarter of a class should be met in these sessions each day. This must not be taken as a blanket requirement. One or two children might come to the conference every day—others will meet in these one-to-one sessions two or three times a week. There will be some children who will come to their individual sessions once a week. The need of each child determines frequency as well as the type of material to be presented. This is not to say that the teacher is unaware of these children's needs and of the methods and techniques of meeting them. The observant teacher will use the countless opportunities afforded by group and total class sessions (in addition to the individual conference) as the initial, exploratory teaching act.

A common practice of neglecting the gifted must come into this discussion. So many teachers, particularly those who have not worked out the management problems for their classrooms, feel that good readers can just go along by themselves. They most certainly can, but they do need help, too. Naturally, their abilities and skills are different in type from those of the rest of the group. They tend to read like adults. They rarely need specific help in analyzing words,

---

Individualized vs. Group Reading, Champaign, Ill.: National Council of Teachers of English; M. Lazar, M. Draper, and L. Schweitert, *A Practical Guide to Individualized Reading,* New York: Board of Education of the City of New York, pp. 27–34; Alice Meil (ed.), *Individualized Reading Practice,* New York: Bureau of Publications, Teachers College, Columbia University, 1958, p. 59; Ruth Robinson, *Why They Love to Learn,* Charlotte, N.C.: Heritage Printers; Jeanette Veatch, *Individualized Reading: For Success in the Classroom,* New London, Conn.: Arthur C. Croft Publications, Educational Trend #654, 1964; Jeanette Veatch, *Individualizing Your Reading Program,* New York: G. P. Putnam's Sons, 1959; Jeanette Veatch, *How to Teach Reading with Children's Books,* Teachers College, Columbia University, 1964, pp. 18–19; Roland West, *Individualized Reading,* Port Washington, N.Y.: Kennikat Press, pp. 84 ff.

and other kind of detail work. But they do need to be lifted to the skies in their ability to "read between the lines"—to read well orally to anybody, to perform feats of covering material quite impossible for less able readers. Thus it becomes important for the teacher to spend as much time with the gifted readers as with any other pupils in the class.

Finally in this section the experience of a fifth-grade teacher in New York City (reported in a city-wide study[2]) is of interest. With a class of very slow readers with a record of serious trouble throughout their school career, she turned to individualization in desperation. She held comprehensive individual conferences at first, in order to more adequately diagnose each child's attitude toward reading and the gaps in his skills. These conferences were often fifteen minutes in length at first, but served the purpose, in the beginning, to help get a program in motion. Although this text has made a point of conferences of three to ten minutes with hopes of being closed at five minutes, there are many occasions demanding more time. The point is that teachers must become skilled in the art of interrogating. Working under time pressure provides a kind of incentive for accomplishing that ability.

Conferences Are on a Voluntary Basis

No matter how differently each teacher has worked out the techniques and routines of his program, the individual sessions are best held on a voluntary basis. Teacher invitation, having the children come up by seating arrangement, by alphabetical, or any other order, as "pretty please" as it may be, seems to put a damper upon interest in the conference. It actually interferes with the process of incentives or motivation the child began when he chose his book for silent reading. Some teachers ask for volunteers and watch to see that all come eventually for individual attention. Other teachers make it possible for children to voluntarily "sign up" for an appointment. A calendar, a schedule, cards, chalk-board space, or a paper tacked up on the bulletin board could each serve the purpose of making a reading appointment with teacher. The chart from the teacher's notebook (page 128) is useful in helping a teacher see at a glance who is needing a conference.

This chart enables a teacher to see, at a glance, the frequency of pupil conference. This should be kept daily by teacher or a child appointed by the class. It should be posted.

[2] Lazar, Draper, and Schweitert, *op. cit.*, p. 108.

Names	Conference No.					
	1	2	3	4	5	6
1. Claude A.	9/22					
2. Isabelle C.	9/23	9/26				
3. Sadie F.	9/24	10/1				
4. Clayton F.	9/24					
5. Hilda G.	9/23	9/26				
6. Alfred K.	9/24	9/29	10/3	10/5		
7. Gerald M.	9/22					
8. Yvonne M.	9/25					
9. Marshall M.	9/23	9/26	10/3			
10. Sue R.	9/24					
11. Olga R.	9/24	9/26				
12. Ross S.	9/26					
13. Margaret S.	9/23					
14. Becky S.	9/22	10/1				
15. Joel T.	9/23					
16. Mabel V.	9/22					
17. Warren V.	9/25	9/29				
18. Marietta W.	9/24					
19. Kathryn W.	9/24	10/1	10/5			
20. Alex W.	9/24					

Checksheet for dates of individual conferences.

"No-Show" Children

Of course, teachers would occasionally insist upon a particular child coming up for a reading session. Any competent teacher should be able to ask, "Where have you been?" to an errant conferee and expect a responsible answer. It is certainly within the prerogative of any teacher to ask for justification for such lack of appearance. But that is just the point. A teacher in asking a child to justify any portion of his behavior, whatever it might be, is showing interest and understanding in that child. The teacher may or may not accept the explanation, but the psychological motivation is there nevertheless. The child in responding to such questions is accepting some of his responsibility for his own learning. He is taking upon his own shoulders, of his own will, the obligation of pursuing learning. This is not pampering a child. This is not spoon-feeding him. His behavior requires an explanation. "Why have you not come up to read to me?"

is a valid and important question. "How can I teach you to read better when you do not come when you have the chance?" is another way to frame the same query.

The research we now have available indicates that children are not reluctant readers when they choose their own books and have an individual conference with their teacher. The shoe is on the other foot. Teachers are the ones who complain that children take too much time and insist upon too many conferences, and plague them mightily to listen to the stories they have chosen. The problem is the lack of time on the part of the teachers, rarely upon the recalcitrance of the children.

When the powers of self-choice are set in motion, the climate for learning is at its best. One-to-one conferences provide the most harmonious atmosphere for instruction that is possible. Evidently it is as important to a child to decide when he is ready for his conference as it is to choose what he is going to read.

Problems of the individual conference with children in the first grade or those just beginning to read have not, at this writing, been adequately explored. Surely the need for much small-group activity on sounds of letters and other word-analysis problems will use class time that, at a later stage, would be taken by individual conferences.

Some first-grade teachers kaleidoscope a series of conferences in rapid succession as a "keeping-track" operation on whatever seemed crucial at the moment. For example:

1. Carryover of sight vocabulary developed by experience charts to self-chosen books, or
2. Ability of child to use technique or substitution on unknown word, or
3. Specific word analysis problems

Word Analysis Belongs in Writing Activities

Gathering experience reveals many teachers' concern that *not enough* information of the pupils' ability to use word analysis techniques appears in the individual conference. More definitive research will probably demonstrate this clearly. Even so, such a deficiency in the individual conference only underlines the point of view of this text, that basic instruction in word analysis essentially belongs in spelling, or written composition.

A pupil can read by recognizing words by sight, whether or not he can identify and sound out a word. But he cannot *write* (i.e., spell) unless he is able to *hear* letter sounds, particularly vowels, and know what letters make those sounds.

Therefore, it is vital that phonics be carefully taught first in writing. After a child recognizes, by sight, about 75 words, he begins to *see* parts of words. Then is when he must be taught phonics—or letter sounds.

All should have been writing vital life experiences from preschool days (sending XX's and OO's to grandma as hugs and kisses is beginning writing). The letter-by-letter analysis of words fits best in such writing. Then the transfer of the skill to *reading* is made when word recognition fails and the child is stuck on a word.

Too much word-analysis emphasis in reading slows up the brain's acceptance of the symbols that it sees. The flow of the eye across the page must be maintained.

Individual Conference Aims at Meaning

Thus the individual conference *need* not be primarily devoted to word analysis techniques. The diagnosis of the child's ability is made through his writing, not his reading. This releases the teacher to concentrate on the development of comprehension, speech, and audience-holding ability. These are the true reading skills.

THINGS TO THINK ABOUT BEFORE STARTING

Once the class has settled down into independent work, as described in the preceding chapter, the teacher is freed to carry on his instructional activity with individuals and groups. As the next chapter is devoted to grouping, this one will deal with all aspects of the individual conference.

Who Should Be the First?

In a quiet working room the teacher meets with the child who is to have the first individual conference. But who should be the first? This is not simply a matter of teacher choice. It can be—but it is best to involve all of the psychological drives that have been set in motion since the beginning of the period. The pupils have several decisions to make. These are best made by the child himself. They can be made by the teacher, but to do so would interfere with the progression of motivation that began with the selection of books.

These are areas in which pupils must make decisions: They should ask themselves questions, as follows:

1. "Shall I present this book to my teacher in an individual conference?"
2. "Has my teacher worked alone with me in reading recently? Because if not, I may have to prepare something I have already read for this conference."
3. "I just had my conference yesterday. So shall I prepare this book for my next conference in two or three days? Or shall I just read it and record it in my notebook?"
4. "I am not going to take this book to my individual conference. Shall I do some kind of a project in connection with it?"
5. "This is a book I want to do something special with. What shall I do?"

As discussed in the preceding chapter, these decisions may need the teacher's help ahead of time. Not each day, perhaps, but the development and practice on anticipation of the ways in which children can learn to make such decisions independently. The work period cannot run quietly if children must interrupt the teacher for directions. Turn to pages 66–68 for details.

Question-Asking Principles

There are a number of areas that must be assessed, examined, evaluated in greater or lesser degree during each conference. This takes a skillful teacher, but the skill of any teacher can be developed with a bit of help. Our earlier suggestion still holds—namely, that a "first-timer" in an individual conference take only one child for the first day. Maybe that teacher will need to work only with that child for several days until he feels he is beginning to master the technique of inquiry that will bring out the necessary reactions that are needed in order to further learning. There is a genuine technique that must be developed. It varies with every individual teacher. Each must explore and experiment until he finds the types of questions that work best *for him.*

Thousands of dollars are being spent upon research devoted ONLY to the asking of questions. The open-ended systems of learning require open-ended questions. These are the kind that cannot be answered quickly, or briefly, nor with any knowledge that is a simple regurgitation of what someone else has found out. Teachers fall into the trap of expecting children to become parrots, repeating only what they have found out that someone else wrote. Questions must encourage *thought,* not memory.

An individual conference with next in line.

Here is an example of a fourth grader being questioned about *Tall Man in the Pivot*, a basketball story.[3]

Teacher: What is a pivot?
Boy: A circle on the floor.
Teacher: How do you know?
Boy: I guess I don't.
Teacher: Well, if the book is called *Tall Man in the Pivot*, do you think a pivot might be a part of the story?
Boy: Yes.
Teacher: What would you guess, then, that a pivot might be alive or not alive?
Boy: I'd guess that a pivot would have to be alive—it must be one of the boys in the story.
Teacher: Yes, I just didn't want you to tell me the story—but to think through something without really depending upon your memory.

Later the teacher helped this boy understand that the pivot was indeed a person on the basketball team and not a painted circle on the floor. The example shows that she questioned him in such a way that in this case he had to resort to reasoning, not memory.

[3] Matt Christopher, *Tall Man in the Pivot*, Boston: Little, Brown & Co., 1959.

Another example was found during the filming of practice sessions of "From the Bookshelf."[4] Several children had come up to talk about *Billy Goats Gruff*, as they had already read it.

Miss Carr: Which character would you like to be?
Boy No. 1: I want to be the BIG Billy Goat Gruff.
Miss Carr: Why?
Boy No. 1: Because he is the strongest.
Boy No. 2: I want to be the Big Billy Goat Gruff, too.
Miss Carr: Why?
Boy No. 2: Because he helps the others.
Miss Carr: What is the difference between being strong and helping others?

Thus a superb question pushed these children to compare—at age six—the difference between what could be described as a power complex and the Golden Rule.

Open-Ended Questions

Open-ended questions cannot be answered with a mere "yes" or "no." They require the element of thought, of reason, of guessing, of hypothesizing, of probing. They are a high form of the teaching art. Some questions stop all thought quite effectively. Others can be so provocative that they needle a mind throughout life. The skill of inquiry is the teaching technique that produces the inventive mind. Interrogation also produces the brainwashed mind, as American prisoners in Korea can attest. The third degree[5] in some police stations is composed of a series of questions—with one aim in mind, namely: "Tell us what we want to hear. Eliminate your own thoughts." In earlier times the Spanish Inquisition sought heresy by closed-end, limited-answer or fixed-answer questions. There was no alternative for he who was on the rack. Thinking or reasoning was not allowed as he answered his inquisitors. "Conform. Don't think for yourself. Believe."

Improving Inquiry

School teachers must improve their skills in question asking in the direction of Inquiry. It is the hope of democratic education.[6]

[4] Lyman C. Hunt, *"From the Bookshelf,"* kinescopes, National Defense Education Aid Fund, Penn State University Film Library.
[5] See William Sargant, *Battle for the Mind,* Garden City, N.Y.: Doubleday & Co., Inc., 1957, Chap. 9.
[6] Richard Suchman, "Inquiry Training," *Merrill-Palmer Quarterly,* Vol. 7, No. 3, July, 1961, p. 147 ff, and many other publications mentioned in this text.

Even though these preceding arguments may seem very grand and earth-shaking, they can be brought down to the simplest of levels for beginning readers. For example, compare these two questions that might be asked of a child about the same story:

1. Do you think the third little pig was kind to his brothers?
2. Why do you think the third little pig was kind to his brothers?

The first obviously calls for a "yes" or "no" answer and no other. The second question needs thought. To answer No. 2 the reader must recall some of the story, but he must do it in the context of making a judgment, of thinking over and deciding something that is *his to decide*. The first question could be a "loaded" one, i.e., the answer is tipped off by the teacher's smile or gesture, and the child must get the "signal." Guessing what is in the teacher's mind is not far removed in technique, even if it is removed in political importance, from the third degree. We have no research that indicates how crucial this is in our developing society. But the writer is concerned.

Questioning and Some Social Issues

We do know that the incidence of mental illness is on the upgrade, and that the ones who weaken under inquisitorial stress are the weak in psychological adjustment.[7] Dewey's essential precept was that a society must train its children in its image if its pattern is to be perpetuated. Are we really training for democracy? Are schools blameless in the rise of juvenile delinquency? Of brute force conservatism? It is hard to say. But the thought cannot be put aside. And questions asked in school by teachers during the reading period or other times cannot be ignored.

Some Pointers on Asking Questions

The following are some specific pointers in asking questions that may be useful to teachers:

1. Use questions that, while based upon the reading matter, help a child relate real life to what he has read.
2. Ask short provocative questions that produce long thoughtful answers.
3. Ask questions that help a pupil to widen his horizons from whatever limited base the reading matter might hold.

[7] Bruno Bettelheim, *The Informed Heart*, Glencoe, Ill.: The Free Press of Glencoe, Inc., 1961.

4. Frequently begin questions with the words, "Why, what, when."
5. Ask questions that stretch a child's ability to answer. Without making the situation unduly embarrassing, be hesitant to provide answers.
6. Encourage answers that are original with the child and, better yet, new to the teacher.
7. Present questions that show a pupil he has the right to his own opinions, even though he is asked to consider more than one point of view.
8. Ask questions that drive behind the actual facts presented in the material.
9. Ask questions that have worth in themselves, and are not designed to help a pupil guess the answer in the teacher's mind.
10. Give the pupil opportunity to think over an answer after the question has been given. Rapid-fire questioning may disorganize some pupils.

The teacher who uses open-end questions and follows the hints listed above will find that he will get much information with little or no prodding.

The open-end question provides more information per question than any other type. It permits a child to form his own judgments, opinions, values, etc. As a consequence, the open-end question lends itself to a better teaching-learning situation because the responses give the teacher more mileage per question. More can be revealed; more diagnoses can be made. In short, the teacher can pinpoint exactly what has to be taught to which child. He does not need to waste time teaching children something they already know—even if, as one experienced martinet said, "It won't hurt 'em to go over it again." It might not hurt—but it takes up time that could be spent in a dozen more valuable ways. One must always wonder about the teacher who "puts 'em through it again." Are they really teaching? Or merely taking up class time? Don't they know what else to do?

The Conference—A Guidance Function

Old reading hands will recognize, from the preceding description, that individualized reading provides for the transfer of clinical and remedial teaching into the normal living situation, the regular classroom. Teachers who are trained to conduct such individual conferences are, in a real sense, practical clinicians. Reading instruction is taking place where it should take place, in the classroom. The isolation, the segregation, the banishment of the pupils "down the hall" with a special teacher cannot be justified in terms of mental health, efficient learning, nor in research findings that are favorable.

Yet remedial reading classes "down the hall" can also mean escape from a poor classroom teacher—an escape route denied to the average and gifted. But whatever may be the case in a given situation, it

The conference: a guidance function.

cannot be denied that the BEST place to teach reading is in the classroom, because there it is possible (whether it happens or not!) for the teacher to know a child better, to be more concerned for his personal welfare, to know the details of his difficulties that a short-term teacher can never know.

In the classroom the teacher holding an individual conference, and learning all of the "tricks of the trade" of that conference, should do a better piece of work than any 30-minute reading period with a reading specialist "down the hall!" Such a conference can hold much chance to get acquainted on a far more intimate level than in any other situation. One teacher said, "I never really knew my children before!" Another said, "I was absent the other day, and when I came back my children asked, 'What was the matter?' I told them I was sick, but they still asked 'What was the *matter?*' They never cared about me like that before."

Thus the conference offers teachers much opportunity for guidance and counseling. It offers much in the establishment of rapport —so important to learning success. It continually offers additional chances for teachers to learn more about their children's limitations, needs, personal problems, loves, hates, and all of the things that people learn about when they are friends.

The Reading Specialist Helps Teachers

The reading specialist in a school system or school building, we recommend, should NOT work with children. Instead he should serve as an expert for teachers. He should make himself available to any teacher who is stumped by a reading problem in his class. The teacher would then come to the specialist and receive help in analyzing all pertinent behavior of the child with the reading problem. In so doing, the specialist can proceed to teach the teacher, so that the latter may become more and more able to deal with reading problems. The teacher learns more and more. The specialist has less and less to do, and perhaps later could be spread more thinly throughout the school system.

The Advantages of the Individual Conference

The individual conference provides the prime opportunity, however, for intensive instruction. It also provides the best setting in which a child may share not only his interests in life, his concerns, his goals, but also his anxieties, his fear of failure, and his shortcomings. The individual conference is a marvelous guidance situation. There is something objective to work upon, and yet it is non-segregative in character. It is a poor teacher indeed who cannot accomplish a great deal in such a spot.

Another advantage for the individual conference is the push it gives to the teacher to become a master of the reading skills. Chapters 8, 9, and 11 deal with those in detail, but suffice it to say for our present purposes that the better teacher knows how the panorama of skills *should* unroll or unfold. The actual pattern or sequence of reading skills must await far more definitive research than is now available. But a rough approximation of the breakdown can be cited as: whole words into parts, the progression from left to right coupled with the increase of visual acuity in seeing from large to small.

The point is that in a self-selection program the teacher does not follow a set of skills that are preplanned for him *before* he has met his class. Rather the teacher must first teach some reading, or hear a child read something, and THEN decide what is the next skill on the docket. The beauty of an individual conference is that it allows every child to have his skill-needs pinpointed without regard to those of any other pupil. This is done best by knowledgeable teachers. The interaction and pleasure accruing from a one-to-one situation provide a unique incentive for teachers to develop their knowledge of what sequence of skills can be expected. It is like the backdrop of a stage set. The backdrop is what the teacher knows. The teaching is the action in front of it.

What Happens After the Conference?

A similar advantage to the individual conference, and perhaps its greatest strength, is that it is the determiner of what is to come next. During such a session the teacher can decide what needs to be:

1. Taught right away in the conference.
2. Taught via group instruction as soon as possible.
3. Taught through assigned individual or self-directed materials of a self-help nature.

It cannot be overemphasized that the individual conference with self-selected material is the best way to meet individual differences. The writers contend that there is no other way to be so sure of what needs to be taught than the diagnosis that can occur during such a side-by-side meeting.

A New York City teacher sums up the functions and purposes of the individual conferences as follows: "The individual sessions are used to:

  ..bring the child and the teacher together for mutual understanding and benefit.

  ..capture the children's interests and to use these interests for developing reading.

  ..develop positive attitudes toward books and the whole process of reading thru happy experiencing.

..feel secure with books and to develop increasing power in reading books.

..develop specific needed skills along with continuous reading.

..diagnose and point up needs and to make necessary plans and assignments to help overcome liabilities.

..provide opportunity for developing good work–study habits.

..relax the children and leave them laughing and wanting more."[8]

GETTING READY FOR THE CONFERENCE

A third grader told his teacher, "You know, it is nice and quiet during our reading time now." Another said, "You don't have to move around the room so much." His friend said, "The kids used to talk, kick their chairs, and waste time." These are examples of child comments that show a classroom that reflects pupil acceptance of tasks. Things go well because the children not only know what they are going to do, they also participate in deciding what they are going to do. The class runs more smoothly.

To help teachers organize their operations better, the checklist on page 140 might prove useful. Check the ten points to answer the questions.

THE CONFERENCE ITSELF

Areas To Be Examined During the Conference

Although the activities or the procedures or the form of each conference may be the same, or similar, for each child in a given class, the variety will come in the questions, the discussion, the reading material, the learning for each child. There are several areas that must be examined frequently. Some might be omitted occasionally, but none of these patterns may be ignored. If a teacher skips an area for one day, he must watch to see that it is picked up on the next conference. His record-keeping should show what he should do. Nor is there any specific order that is sacred to these areas. Most teachers seem to prefer to get mechanics "out of the way" first, so that the fun of the oral reading and the story itself can be enjoyed to the hilt. For most, however, let us say that it is not the order so much as the *depth* to which each area is explored for the best reading growth. The areas are as follows.

[8] Lazer, Draper, and Schweitert, *op. cit.*, p. 34.

Question	Conference No.									
	1	2	3	4	5	6	7	8	9	10
Yes										
No										
Partly										

1. Is the class settled down and absorbed in independent work?

2. Has each child planned his independent work so that he will be continually absorbed until it is time to stop the reading period?

3. Is your notebook ready with a page and plenty of blank paper for each child?

4. Is your place for the individual conference suitable? I.e., is it out of earshot and line of sight of the rest of the class? Is the blackboard near? Is paper handy for on-the-spot teaching side by side? Can you still see everyone well enough to keep tabs on the whole class?

5. Have you thought through those few unique individual's problems that you know you will be facing that period?

6. Are you comfortable about your plans for the ensuing group sessions?

7. Will the classroom arrangement permit smooth sailing from activity to activity during the independent seatwork period?

8. Are children aware of and trained in classroom routines such as: changing their books, securing supplies; leaving the room, coming for a group, etc.

9. Are you clear in your own mind as to questions you must ask, or steps you must take, with each child even if you do not know the particular book the child brings to the conference?

10. Are you sure you know how to involve each child in his own learning so that he recognizes and begins to tackle that which he does not know?

Checksheet for teachers new at conferencing.

I. Comprehension skills as:
    A. Central thought
    B. Inferences and critical reading
    C. Value judgments
    D. Author purpose
    E. Necessary plot sequence

II. Personality adjustment and the selection
    A. Insight into personal interest in story, enjoyment, satisfaction, knowledge
    B. Awareness of peer group reaction to his interest
    C. Insight into possible personality behavior change

III. The mechanical skill
  A. Word definitions
  B. Study skills—indexing chapter headings, etc.
  C. Ability to analyze unknown words
  D. Reading for details
IV. Ability to hold audience attention
  A. Oral reading of selection
  B. Retelling long story briefly

New York City found that many specifics were "fused in the individual conferences—diagnosing, teaching, listening, sharing, evaluating, discussing, planning, extending . . . the child and the teacher might discuss the choice of the current or future books; explore the child's feelings toward a book; discuss and plan possible follow-ups."[9]

Developing understanding in the conference.

These areas hold many skills and abilities of a highly specific nature. The chapter that is devoted entirely to the development of the skills deemed important is Chapter 11. The reader is referred there for details on actual procedures. This present chapter does overlap, but it is more concerned with classroom management than

[9] Lazer, Draper, and Schweitert, *ibid.*, p. 28.

an emphasis on skill development. How, for example, does a teacher design a conference to begin to explore these above areas? Where does he begin? How does he close? What does he listen to, discuss, inquire about? These are the concerns of this present chapter.

Comprehension Skills

To read with comprehension is, of course, the crucial ability in gaining the main idea of a piece of material. Children who are reading for the sense of what they read cannot possibly make ridiculous mistakes of, say, reversing "was" and "saw." A child that is getting sense out of a story would reject "house" for "horse" or vice versa. It is not understandable why so many texts on reading instruction concentrate on a kind of mistake that is made when a reader gets no meaning from his material.

Gaining central thought cannot be accomplished by drill on words. It cannot be accomplished even by working on a supposed skill called "sequence of events." A story must have a sequence to pass the test of being a story. A weak story or one that is *forced upon a reader without his choice* must be studied for sequence. But the nature of the human animal is to seek and find absorbing tales. A child who is supposed to read a story he does not prefer must be persuaded to read it. Persuasion is conditioning, not unlike that carried out in dog-training, and, of course, in brainwashing. The child must be conditioned to read the unchosen story. The view of this text is that such teacher activity is to be stopped as it is ineffective from a learning point of view and undemocratic from a politicosocial point of view.

Questioning for Central Thought

The questions a teacher must ask to discover whether or not a pupil is gaining the central thought of his reading are therefore basically simple. There are many variations of the following, as these are intended only to be suggestive in nature.

What kind of a story is this?
What is it mainly about?
Does its setting make a difference?
Does its time (of year, in history) affect the story?
Does this book remind you of any other book?
Did you think it a happy (sad, frightening) story?
Could you describe this in a few words?

These above questions are cited in many excellent discussions of the reading skill called skimming, or scanning. The above questions are useful in discovering the degree of understanding when material has been skimmed.

Inferences and Critical Reading

Here the teacher should work to discover if the child has not only gained the central thought or main idea, but is aware of the "between the lines" meaning of the selection. The point of his personal approval or disapproval is not germane here. Does he see, does he realize what is being implied if not actually said? Does he catch subtitles? Has he been fooled in some way?

Here are some questions:

Do you think the story is really about . . . . . . ?
Is there something here that isn't actually said?
Is there a lesson to be learned in this book? What?
Was there anything in the story that was not the same as you've heard somewhere else?
Do you think you can believe what it says? Why? or Why not?
What is the problem of . . . . . . (a character) in the story?

Value Judgments

To believe everything that one reads should not be a goal for teachers in a democratic society. Healthy suspicion of the motives of all reading material promotes human welfare. The old saying "Don't believe anything you read and only half of what you see" is not far afield. Not that children should be raised to be anxious, neurotic, fretful human beings. But vigilance is the eternal price of freedom. The world has seen totalitarian regimes come and go and they invariably develop ways of controlling their mass media—i.e., radio, television, newspapers, and magazines. Even certain forces in this country are guilty of the same offense—thought-control. American teachers thus have an obligation to understand how that certain ability to make adequate value judgements about mass media, especially publications, is fostered. Judging reasons behind written material is an ability. It is not an automatic ability. It is learned behavior. The individual conference is a fertile place to promote this skill, even though there are other portions of the school curriculum and schedule that are similarly fruitful.

Questioning for Value Judgments

To help a reader—of any age—to analyze the motivation behind the printed word, certain questions can be useful. Some of these are suggested:

Do you agree or disagree with this story?

What is your own opinion about . . . . . . in the story?

Is this something everyone should read? Why?

If only a few people should read, whom would you choose?

Is the story making fun of us all?

If you could pass a law, or have your own wish, would this book influence you?

Do you trust what you read?

Is it right for someone (writer, publisher, organization, etc.) to print only part of a whole story (event, argument, etc.)?

Do you believe everything you read? Why?

Do all of your friends believe what they read? Should they? How can you change that if you would want to?

Can you trust what this author (publisher, newspaper, magazine) says? Why? Or why not?

If you cannot find out whether or not a story is true, what could you do that would help somewhat?

These are provocative beginnings. Many teachers will probably learn as much as the pupils. But we must make a better world than we now have. One way to begin is to be able to analyze the goals and objectives of all authors and publishers.

Author Purpose

The teacher pushes further here to help the pupil evaluate authors. Do they always write in the same way? What is to be remembered in particular? Here are some questions?

Who is this author?

What do you know about his family (home, etc.)?

What other books of his do you know about?

What do you feel he is trying to tell people in his stories?

If you could talk to him, what would you tell him?

Do you think he has children of his own?

Does he like animals (nature, etc.)?

What ideas are you sure about when you read him?

Necessary Plot Sequences

The ability of the reader to follow a plot, and understand why it unfolds the way it does, deepens comprehension. This is quite different from the "teaching of sequence" skill described in so many basal reading manuals. The latter is, intentionally or not, advice for 1) killing time of the reading period, and 2) making palatable the diet of reading material chosen by the teacher.

In a self-chosen story, on the contrary, no drill is needed on *what* series of events makes the plot, only probing of *why* the incidents came as they did and how the story was retarded or enhanced.

Some questions that will expose these thoughts are suggested:

Tell me (us) the story.

After . . . . . . (an incident) what happened next?

Tell me (us) what happened first, then

If such-and-such happened before so-and-so, does it make any difference in the story?

If you could, would you change the story around at all? Why?

What was the best part of the story to you? Was this best part in the beginning, middle, or end of the story? Would you have any idea why that part was where it was?

Personality Adjustment and Reading Selection

Psychiatrists tell us that insight is the first step toward changed behavior. Insight is the realization of one's own motives, or reasons for action. Much has been written about the phenomenon of bibliotherapy, i.e., the working out or, at least, the working at personal problems through choosing books that meet an emotional need. Teachers can move in these directions of insight and resolution of personal problems at quite simple levels.[10] Teachers are not therapists and should not be tempted to play such parts. But neither are teachers medical doctors; yet they are most useful in spotting cases of measles, mumps, impetigo, and the like and isolating the disease from the total group. It is this kind of initiative, or perhaps sensitivity, that we should help teachers develop.

A pet-lonely child will devour books on dogs, cats, and horses. A child who is overburdened in the home may become lost in *Half-a-Team*.[11] A cultured Negro girl yearning for recognition will love

[10] See also S. Weingarten, "Reading As a Source of the Ideal Self," in *Reading Teacher's Reader* (Causey, O. S., ed.), pp. 151–55.

[11] M. Drury, *Half-a-Team*, New York: David McKay Co., Inc., 1960.

Hold Fast To Your Dreams.[12] Forcing children to read in areas in which they are not interested will hardly "broaden" them. This may be a shock to some, but this text supports that point of view. As long as a child is reading at his independent level, reading avidly, eagerly, and with genuine inner motivation, what difference does it make WHAT he is reading?

To these points, as we noted at the beginning of this chapter, the individual conference lends itself notably. The nature of its privacy and intimacy assists the child, who needs to, to realize his own identity, his own interests.

Teachers frequently report the eagerness of poor students, or those with severe problems, to come to an individual conference. The reasons for such behavior of seeking the teacher's personal attention may well lie in a self-realization not possible under any other classroom circumstances. We need more research in this area.

The shy child who needs to "find himself" can be encouraged when his teacher really talks with him. The individual conference can well be, at times, a kind of personal confession, in which it is easy to talk over troublesome matters. Teachers can be the safest of human beings to some children. All teachers should work harder to become a confidante to all of their pupils—confidante, *not* therapist.

Insight into Personal Interest in Story

There are questions that facilitate the kind of useful, helpful interchange that we are describing. For example:

Was this a good story?

Why did you choose this book?

Did you ever have an experience like this?

Would you like to be just like the person in the story?

What about this story or material made you angry (sad, laugh, etc.)?

If you could become one of the characters in this story, which one would suit you just fine?

Which character are you sure you would not like to be?

If you could, would you wave a magic wand and live in this time (place, house, etc.)? Why?

Talk to me about your feelings when you read this story.

Do you know anyone like this character?

If you could change anything about this story, what would you change? Why?

[12] Catherine Blanton, *Hold Fast To Your Dreams*, New York: Julian Messner, Inc., 1955.

These are stimulating and provocative questions. If the teacher treats the pupil with dignity and respect, or at least his *responses* with dignity and respect, he is in a better position to improve the behavior and adjustment of the pupil. These are the elements that probably explain one major research finding in studies on individualized reading—the improvement of discipline. When children have a person to turn to and talk with, and an objective that is safe, such as a book, they can move in healthier directions. One teacher said, in fact, "We talk about the *book* together, then I don't have to bring up something that he did. This is the first time I have done this. I can tell you it was a shock to realize that I had never had such personal talks with my children!"

Awareness of Peer-Group Reaction

Because children are normally gregarious, and the lonely child is the unhappy, or even sick, child, some exploration into the reader's awareness of his place in his group is useful. Here are some questions that have that objective.

Who do you know that likes this type of book?
Would they like this one?
Are you going to tell them about it?
Do you like to have those friends tell you about books?
Do you ever read books with someone else? What books were they?

With this kind of question, groundwork is laid for pupil-with-pupil activity.

Insight into Possible Personality Behavior Change

Insight and awareness must precede change of behavior, for good or bad. The old saying of "having the game as well as the name" indicates an impending negative behavioral change. Positively stated, a person can see the why's of their actions and so work for self-improvement. Such insight is possible in a reading conference where the object of the discussion is *not* the reader's behavior, but a fictitious person, or at least a person who is not right there.

Here are some helpful questions on this point.

Did you have a problem like this person in the story? Did you get some help with your problem from reading it?
Does this story make you feel like doing something? What?
Did you see something about yourself after you finished this story that you didn't know before? Tell me about it.

Is there something here you didn't like and never would do yourself? What?

As can be seen, these are quite personal questions. Thus the need for some degree of privacy during the conference can be understood.

The Mechanical Skills

Keeping in mind the suggestions about open-ended questions, teachers need to practice their skills in ferreting out the reading difficulties of each child.

First, the teacher should capitalize on those deficiencies that the child *knows* he has.

Second, the teacher should find out those difficulties the child is unaware of and try to bring them to his conscious attention.

The child who knows his problems is apt to be more willing to work at them, unless, of course, he is overwhelmed by them. The major portion of the teacher's task is to diagnose problems in such a way that a pupil is not overwhelmed, but rather sees a problem as a challenge. Mistakes can become incentives for progress when encountered in bite-sized chunks.

The reduction of difficulties in the area of sheer mechanical skills has been reported. The use of contextual clues comes into full glory with material with which a reader is personally involved. It makes guessing permissible rather than sinful.

Research is needed on this point, but the writers would surmise that difficulties are much more numerous and of different character in a self-selection program than with a teacher-assigned piece of reading material, particularly in an ability-grouped situation. It would seem that with self-choice material the pupil struggles to gain meaning, *because that is why he chose that story.* He works from the whole to its parts. He unconsciously seeks to read by leaps and bounds, in ways so well described by those in the area of speed-reading. When he gets stuck, then he resorts to word analysis, and that is the time that he NEEDS specific and detailed help in breaking down a word. The motivation is not to analyze and then to read; to drill and then to read; to read parts before he reads wholes. Rather the reader uses his eyes to sweep along whole lines and pages to the best of his ability at the stage of development.[13]

[13] It is notable that Robinson, in *"Why Pupils Fail in Reading"* (Chicago: University of Chicago Press, 1947), a major contribution for its time, analyzes many reasons why pupils do fail in reading with one startling omission. No emphasis is noted as to the possibility that children fail to read because they cannot abide what they are being given to read. Obviously, Robinson was not discussing the reading difficulties in a self-choice program.

The work of the teacher during an individual conference is not so much to find out where the child has been in his reading, but to see how far he can be taken.

Word Definitions

Vocabulary development is a school and home responsibility. Family conversation is important. Class discussion is equally important and has been proved to improve reading achievement.

On a person-to-person basis a teacher can push horizons further by inquiring about certain words in a child's book. For example:

Here is an unusual word. Can you tell me what it means?

Here is another (and another, etc.).

Can you tell me another word that means the same thing? Or almost the same thing?

If I said _____ (naming an antonym or homonym), would you say this word was the same or opposite to it?

Did you find any words that meant something different when you read them somewhere else? What was the difference?

So the teacher expands verbal understandings.

The Study Skills

Although these are broad curricular skills, rather than reading per se, there are opportunities in instructional reading periods for their development. Later on these skills must be transferred into their proper spheres, the content areas—music, social studies, science, and the like. Here are some questions:

Show me the index (table of contents, chapter headings, etc.).

Find the page where such-and-such is described.

How do you find things in the index (table of contents)?

Did the pictures help you read this book? How?

Can you find the place where this story was laid on the map?

Can you find the general topic of this story in another book? In any of our reference books? Our texts in other subjects?

These questions on locational skills and other study skills can be woven profitably in an individual conference. Their transfer into other curriculum areas will be made easier when handled with such self-chosen material.

Ability To Analyze Unknown Words

As mentioned earlier, the time and place where detailed word analysis is best taught are with written composition, especially that concerning spelling. The nature of word analysis is letter-by-letter, phoneme-by-phoneme dissection of a word. The nature of reading is synthesis or overall perception—seeing wholes and seeing them rapidly in flashes. The seeing during the stops in eye-movement is reading. To stop reading too frequently in order to dissect words brings on word-calling. However, there are occasions, even with self-selected materials, when all perceptive skills fail and a word must be analyzed, from the inside out or the outside in. It is this ability that must be *used* in reading, even though *taught* during writing.

Here are some conference questions in this area:

Show me a word that you didn't know. How did you figure it out?

(After oral reading reveals an unknown word, pick any of the following questions that will help.)

What is in this word that you know? (small word-digraph-initial letter-initial blend-vowel sound, etc.)

Let me cover up part of it. Now what do you see? Say it. Now here's the whole word. Can you say it?

This word starts like _____ but rhymes with _____. Try it.

These are but a few questions that might be asked. Answers, particularly when specific words are mentioned, should be recorded in the teacher's notebook or by the child for later study, and probable group assignment. There are key signals of difficulties that the well-trained teacher can spot. But the above questions, and others like them, will serve to raise the problems to the surface.

Working with Unknown Words

The child in each case would point out, *if he knew*, those words that had been stumbling blocks to his reading of his story.

Often the teacher makes an on-the-spot decision as follows:

1. Shall I teach him these words now?
2. Shall I teach him how to figure out these *types* of words now or shall I put him in a group with other pupils with the same trouble?
3. Can this be fixed with self-help material?

The determining factor would be the drastic character of the difficulty. A minor fluke can be taken care of without further ado. A major problem—say, ignorance of short vowel sounds—would need depth instruction and should therefore be delayed for concentrated work during a group meeting.

Here are two examples from actual tapes of individual conferences that show procedures[14]:

EXAMPLE NO. 1.

Pupil: I don't know these words. (Pointing.) "Cobbler," "skinny," "football," "trouble," "thought."

Teacher: Well, they are several different kinds of words to figure out. How did you read your story?

Pupil: Mary told me when I got to them.

Teacher: We must work on these with some others who have the same problems. Let us go ahead now, and I will put you in a group later on.

EXAMPLE NO. 2.

Pupil: I know this word. "Armor."

Teacher: Look at the first part of it.

Pupil: Oh, it is "amber."

Teacher: Amber is a color, but in your book it's the name of a cat.

In the first example, the teacher decided that the difficulties were too numerous to deal with on the spot. She postponed her instruction for a later group session or sessions. In the second example, the teacher made the decision to work on the word right then and there and did so.[15]

Reading for Details

If nation-wide standardized tests are to be believed, our children have been taught to read for details better than any other reading skill. But is this good? Probably reading for details is the least important of all the skills as it is so seldom needed.

Reading for details means slow reading, thorough reading. It is the opposite of speed or rapid reading or skimming. By implication teachers have assumed that thorough reading, which must be slow in order to be thorough, is "good" reading. This text questions such philosophy.

---

[14] Courtesy Imogene McIntire, University of Cincinnati, unpublished material.

[15] See also, for more examples: Lazar, Draper, and Schweitert, *op. cit.*, pp. 29–33.

Noting Details a Function of Content

Certainly there are some kinds of material that must be read more carefully than others—recipes, legal documents, directions for complicated toys or electrical appliances are but a few examples. But the slow-up of the eye span to read such cannot be proved, or at least has not been proved, to be a function of *training*. One reads slowly because of the nature of the situation or of the material. In brief, reading for details should be a function of content, not a function of training. If a reader does not recognize that the material to be read calls for thoroughness, he is not reading for meaning. If reading has purpose that is accepted by the reader, there is no training necessary to make the reading careful.

Noting Details in Excess Causes Disability

More seriously, reading for details has too often come to be a punitive matter. Teachers punish children for reading rapidly, and require them to read and reread to get some minor point. Regressive eye movements are a reading disability. The rare times that such details are needed should not be a result of such poor teaching as to produce a disability. Yet this can happen. Much of what is needed to be found out will occur in the word-analysis area. When a child is blocked from absorbing his story because of unknown words, he MUST look at the details of that word. But then that is a proper thing to do. Details are a barrier to reading itself.

Questioning for Details

When does a teacher probe to assess the child's ability to read for details? First, the type of material will dictate whether or not such an activity is necessary.

Three third graders had found a set of directions to make an electromagnet. During the individual conference with the teacher one of them brought this to light. The teacher called them all together for a session as follows:

Teacher:	You all want to make an electromagnet?
All:	Yes.
Teacher:	What is the first thing that you do?
Boy No. 1:	We need to get one or two dry cells, and some wire.
Teacher:	How much wire? What kind?
Boy No. 2:	Two or three feet of insulated wire.
Teacher:	Yes. Are the cells and the wire all you need?

Boy No. 3: Oh no. We need some thumbtacks and a large nail.
Teacher: O.K. What, then, is the first thing to do?
Boy No. 1: Put it all together, and make it work?
Teacher: How do you know when it is working?
Boy No. 2: When the nail becomes a magnet?
Teacher: I would like you to experiment with these materials first to see if you can work it out *without* the directions. That is the most scientific way to do it. You will be better scientists in the long run if you depend on your hunches than if you depend upon written directions. But, nevertheless, there is a place for printed or written directions. Can you figure out what that place might be?
Boy No. 2: Sure—to see how our own experiment is like the directions.
Boy No. 3: We may find a short cut to making the electromagnet that we hadn't thought of.

This interchange during a regularly organized group conference shows how a teacher can help children to see that details are important under certain conditions. It is incidentally a fine example of why teachers need to have knowledge in all curriculum areas!

Another example of reading for details because the content demands it follows:

Teacher: We are going downtown to the radio station. What is the first thing we must do to get ready?
Child No. 1: Find out where it is.
Teacher: Where do we do that?
Child No. 2: Phone book?
Teacher: Yes. Go to the office and get it. While she is gone, what else can we do to get ready for the trip?
Child No. 3: I found a story about a radio station. It isn't a real station—but it is just like a real station. It's in those folders. (Pointing to sets of Informational Classroom Series).[16]
Teacher: Find it and let us see what to do and look for.

The folder was unearthed and lists were made on the chalk board of important parts of the radio station that must be observed. Eventually the address of the station was found in the phone book (and if THAT isn't reading for details, nothing is!) and methods of transportation were discussed. The school bus was to take them, but the best route—use of the map of the city—and regular bus routes also came in for discussion.

Above we see the melding of many skills, often placed in widely separated categories, into the purpose of the material to be read. In both of these examples, reading for details is clearly a function of the content, not of training. The purpose dictated WHY details were important. The next example has similar implications.

[16] Ray Fidler, *Informational Classroom Series,* Grand Rapids, Mich.,

Teacher:	Our June picnic menu calls for cookies. Many of you have brought recipes. Which one shall we use?
Girl No. 1:	The ones with the little chocolate things in them.
Teacher:	Fine. Chocolate Drop Cookies. I have dittoed enough recipes for all of you to have your own copy. Now, we will need partners to do the different parts of the recipe. What is the first thing to do?
Boy No. 1:	Mine says, "Preheat the oven." Does that mean turn it on?
Teacher:	Yes. But there is another part of that direction. What is it?
Boy No. 1:	Oh—"to 375 degrees F." What is "F?"
Teacher:	Look in the index of your science book under the "F's" and you will be able to figure it out. If not, ask me again. Now, you and John will turn on the oven. O.K.? What is the next thing to do?
Girl No. 1:	Mine says "Sift together 2¼ cups sifted flour."

So the teacher forces the group to read the minute details of the recipe—not to be punitive—but to underline the fact that the cookies would not come out right unless the directions were followed in detail. This *is* valid reading for details.

On a negative note, some questions might be cited that are a waste of time, as they stem from a teacher's suspicion and mistaken notion that children do not read well unless they read "thoroughly." These follow as horrible examples of questions not to ask. Be sure to read Chapter 11 on this matter.

Who saved Little Red Riding Hood?

Find the part of the story where it tells what Gepetto's work was.

What kind of a house did the third little pig build?

Recognizing pertinent details means exactly that. There must be a real purpose for the question other than testing the pupil to "make sure he has read what he was supposed to." To trip up a child, to make them guess the *one* right answer the teacher might have in mind, is not good teaching. When the questions lead to more and more discussion, to deeper examination of the topic involved, to the extending of "living area" beyond the limits of the story—then the teacher is truly an educator.

Ability To Hold Audience Attention

Reading orally is also mechanics of reading and serves as a fine diagnostic tool. It is a separate section in this list to emphasize its unique characteristics and the importance of its role.

Reading aloud is the climactic point of the individual conference. None should end until some portion of the book has been read to the teacher. Reading orally is indeed a skill that must be taught directly. It is a matter of training, and must be so considered. Again Chapter 11 deals with all manner of methods in accomplishing good oral reading.

For the purposes of this chapter, we see that oral reading is a good way to find out a child's reading difficulties of which he is unaware. It is true that skilled questioning serves this same end. But a sharp-eared teacher during a reading-aloud session can pick up difficulties that may or may not have arisen.

Oral reading is no trouble in an individual conference. In fact, it is some problem to hold off until all else has been assessed. Pupils are usually intensely flattered to have the sole attention of their teacher—and reading aloud is the frosting on the cake.

Here are questions that are good starters:

What part of your story did you choose to read to me?

Tell me what happened up to this point.

(After the reading.) Now tell me what happened next—as it is time for me to stop this conference.

Why did you choose this part of the story?

Are you sure you are ready to do your best reading for me?

If the pupil asks, "What shall I read?" the teacher should always tie his answer into purpose of reading as well as skill of reading, as follows:

Read the part that you liked best—maybe it is the most exciting, the funniest, or has something else that you particularly like. But be sure I hear your BEST reading. I will help you, as you know, but it isn't fair to others if you do your reading practicing with me when you could do it by yourself.

Another example shows a far more serious problem and the teacher elected to deal with it later in a group session.

When the teacher is sure of the pupil's ability to read aloud, he can proceed to other matters or move into the closing seconds of the conference. There is much else to be done in this area, and other times of the school day are as good as during the individual conference.

Outline of Individual Conference

Now let us present a more easily followed outline. The next few pages will list the major headings and subheadings of the areas to be examined in the individual conferences. The suggested questions will be listed, without the explanations made in the preceding pages.

Thus a teacher can follow, on a pick-and-choose basis, a list of questions, using those and only those suitable for the moment.

Lists of Suggested Questions

I. Comprehension Skills
  A. Central Thought
    1. What kind of a story is this?
    2. What is it mainly about?
    3. Does its setting make a difference?
    4. Does its time (of year, in history) affect the story?
    5. Does this book remind you of any other book?
    6. Did you think it is a happy (sad, frightening) story?
    7. Could you describe this in a couple of words?
  B. Inferences and Critical Reading
    1. Do you think the story is really about _____?
    2. Is there something here that isn't actually said?
    3. Is there a lesson to be learned in this book? What?
    4. Was there anything in the story that was not the same as you've heard somewhere else?
    5. Do you think you can believe what it says? Why? or Why not?
    6. What is the problem of _____ (a character) in the story?
  C. Value Judgments
    1. Do you agree or disagree with this story?
    2. What is your own opinion about _____ in the story?
    3. Is this something everyone should read? Why?
    4. If only a few people should read, who would you choose?
    5. Is the story making fun of us all?
    6. If you could pass a law, or have your own wish, would this book influence you?
    7. Do you trust what you read?
    8. Is it right for someone (writer, publisher, organization, etc.) to print only part of a whole story (event, argument, etc.)?
    9. Do you believe everything you read? Why?
    10. Do all of your friends believe what they read? Should they? How can you change that if you would want to?
    11. Can you trust what this author (publisher, newspaper, magazine) says? Why? Or why not?
    12. If you cannot find out whether or not a story is true, what could you do that would help somewhat?
  D. Author Purpose
    1. Who is the author?
    2. What do you know about his family (home, etc.)?

    3. What other books of his do you know about?

    4 What do you feel he is trying to tell people in his stories?

    5. If you could talk to him, what would you tell him?

    6. Do you think he has children of his own?

    7. Does he like animals (nature, etc.)?

    8. What ideas are you sure about when you read him?

E. Necessary Plot Sequence

    1. Tell me (us) the story.

    2. After _____ (an incident) what happened next?

    3. Tell me (us) what happened first, then _____.

    4. If such-and-such happened before so-and-so, does it make any difference in the story?

    5. If you could, would you change the story around at all? Why?

    6. What was the best part of the story to you? Was this best part in the beginning, middle, or end of the story? Would you have any idea why that part was where it was?

II. Personality Adjustment and Reading Selections

A. Insight into Personal Interest in Story

    1. Was this a good story?

    2. Why did you choose this book?

    3. Did you ever have an experience like this?

    4. Would you like to be just like the person in the story?

    5. What about this story or material made you angry (sad, laugh, etc.)?

    6. If you could become one of the characters in this story, which one would suit you just fine?

    7. Which character are you sure you would not like to be?

    8. If you could, would you wave a magic wand and live in this time (place, house, etc.)? Why?

    9. Talk to me about your feelings when you read this story?

    10. Do you know anyone like this character?

    11. If you could change anything about this story, what would you change? Why?

B. Awareness of Peer Group Reaction

    1. Who do you know that likes this type of book?

    2. Would they like this one?

    3. Are you going to tell them about it?

    4. Do you like to have those friends tell you about books?

    5. Do you ever read books with someone else? What books were they?

C. Insight into Possible Personality Behavior Change

    1. Did you have a problem like this person in the story? Did you get some help with your problem from reading it?

    2. Does this story make you feel like doing something? What?

    3. Did you see something about yourself after you finished this story that you didn't know before? Tell me about it.

        4. Is there something here you didn't like and never would do yourself? What?

III. The Mechanical Skills

    A. Word Definitions

        1. Here is an unusual word. Can you tell me what it means?

        2. Here is another (and another, etc.).

        3. Can you tell me another word that means the same thing? Or almost the same thing?

        4. If I said _____ (naming an antonym or homonym), would you say this word was the same or opposite to it?

        5. Did you find any words that meant something different when you read them somewhere else? What was the difference?

    B. Study Skills

        1. Show me the index (table of contents, chapter headings, etc.).

        2. Find the page where such-and-such is described?

        3. How do you find things in the index (table of contents)?

        4. Did the pictures help you read this book? How?

        5. Can you find the place on the map where the story was laid?

        6. Can you find the general topic of this story in another book? In any of our reference books? Our texts in other subjects?

    C. Ability To Analyze Unknown Words

        1. Show me a word that you didn't know. How did you figure it out?

        2. What is in this word that you know (small word-digraph-initial letter-initial blend-vowel sound, etc.)?

        3. Let me cover up part of it. Now what do you see? Say it. Now here's the whole word. Can you say it?

        4. The word starts like _____ but rhymes with _____. Try it.

    D. Reading for Details

IV. Ability To Hold Audience Attention

    A. Oral Reading of Selection

        1. What part of your story did you choose to read to me?

        2. Tell me what happened up to this point.

        3. (After the reading.) Now tell me what happened next—as it is time for me to stop this conference.

    B. Retelling of Long Story Briefly

Summary of the Areas To Be Examined

The preceding section has dealt with those areas that cover the total reading pattern of any individual. Imbedded within the suggested questions are all sorts of avenues of exploration. These four points are bridgeheads or stepping stones. Each teacher *in each conference* may vary the complete interview without departing from these four points. Under mechanics, for example, are a dozen skills that must be evaluated. Under the development of value judgment different material will sharply alter the pattern of talk between the teacher and pupil. Personal identification cannot possibly be the same, beyond the broadest of outlines, for any two people. This is good, as it moves teachers toward the ideal condition of being able to meet any contingency. As a good athlete may be ready to move from either foot in any direction, so, too, must the good teacher be ready to strike while the iron is hot. He must be able to take advantage of all events in an individual conference. The concept of the "teachable moment" is implicit in this philosophy.

Teachers using open-ended questions cannot anticipate many answers. The excitement, the variety, the "out-of-the-rut" feeling is desirable. As for the role of supervisors in such practice, it revolves around a true helping action, in the sense so well propounded by Kimball Wiles.[17] The supervisor that must be sure that all teachers "follow the manual" must resort to *policing* actions, not helping actions. It is essentially a law enforcement act to be sure that teachers are doing exactly the lesson, the book, the workbook, that is decreed by the sacred book of the manual (or administrator's guide.) Manuals insist on absolute sequence—to the tittle and jot. Not so, when the teacher must wait for the child to read, to answer, to react before a question can be proposed. Supervisors must be better supervisors in order to help rather than to police. They also must have different types of personalities to enjoy their work. If they can neither help nor police, they should lose their jobs, or find some good graduate training, or quit.

The preceding sections on suggested questions in four important areas that are an umbrella for all reading activity are presented as nudges to supervisors as well as suggestions to teachers.

Closure of an Individual Conference

With a weather eye on the clock, the teacher must begin to search for a good stopping point as the time begins to approach the five-minute mark. This need not be as formal a stopping point as is to be suggested for groups in the next chapter (see Chapter 7, page 335),

---

[17] Kimball Wiles, *Supervision for Better Schools,* New York: Prentice-Hall., Inc., 1950.

but it should nevertheless put a kind of period, an ending, on the action.

In each case the conference should end with some kind of a summary statement by the teacher. The statement should be a kind of winder-upper for their work together. There should also be assignments, if necessary, in self-directed activities with specific times for their checking scheduled or planned for. Some kind of positive comment, such as praise, should be included in the final seconds of a conference. There is always something that can be found—even if it seems only minor to the teacher. A change of attitude toward reading, a longer time spent in silent reading, better planning of the independent work *after* the silent reading are examples of praiseworthy actions.

The teacher in individual, group, and class sessions must cultivate the sense of when to close. Reaching a climax, and then stopping even if there is still time, is better than dragging out a session that has lost its punch.

To conclude, closure is best done when the teacher:

1. Indicates follow-up with:
   a. Self-directed activities
   b. Group sessions
   c. Individual assignments
2. Finds something to praise
3. Concludes upon a high point.

How To Close an Individual Conference

The following are samples of statements that illustrate each of the above points:

1. Indicates follow-up with:
   a. Self-directed activities

Teacher: We worked on finding the root words in these words that had many syllables. I would like you to take this work sheet that has some practice on that very thing. Finish it right now and leave it on my desk for checking.

   b. Group sessions

Teacher: There are several children that have the same problem of reading aloud as you do. I will set up a group tomorrow after the individual conferences and we will work at that skill.

   c. Individual assignments

Teacher: You read this story with real interest. I can tell that you liked it very much. But you missed the main point, as I showed you when we talked it over. I would like you to go back and read it over again and see why it is that William had trouble in his new school.

2. Finds something to praise:

Teacher: You certainly have come a long way in making your voice sound as if you were talking. I think you are nearly ready to read a story to the first grade.

or

Teacher: I am glad to see that you are looking at the beginning letters of words that you don't know. That is where you start to figure them out.

3. Concludes upon a high point:

Teacher: We have talked over the story and worked out some words that you needed help on. Now let me hear you read aloud. Pick the best part. I will like it if you like it.

or

Teacher: You certainly like horse stories, don't you? This was a dandy. Have you found the next book that you want to read? Good. Go to it.

or

Teacher: So this is the story you will read to the second graders? Let me hear you. I am sure I can help you read it better.

In all of these the deep personal interest of the teacher in the material selected by the children shows. The respect for ability, the concentration on the reading, rather than on discipline or behavior, is notable. Knowing how to close an individual conference well leaves the pupil eager and ready for the next one. A poor conference is one that is a chore. Each child must always have this high degree of stimulation, challenge, and excitement. The sense of closure helps in this goal.

Record-Keeping During the Conference

As noted elsewhere, the teacher is able to take notes during an individual conference, when he is too busy to take notes during a group session. Chapter 12 describes the details of notebooks and other means of keeping records. For the purpose of this chapter the discussion will dwell upon the management thereof.

A teacher must have ample paper or cards for each child. The effectiveness of a loose-leaf notebook has increased its popularity. Large cards tend to get dog-eared and lost. However, this is a personal matter that each teacher should solve for himself. The writers prefer a loose-leaf notebook after observing many teachers. It seems to work better.

When the teacher has some sort of duplicated form for each pupil such as this:

John S.		
Book—Date	Word Analysis	Notes & Assignments

it doesn't matter when any child comes up. The teacher simply turns to the page for that child.

Let us imagine an individual session. Child and teacher are sitting side by side with the child's story in hand. They talk. The interaction and the recorded comments could go like this:

> *Teacher:* Let me see, your book is *The Big Ball of String* by Marion Holland.[18] (She records as follows:)

John S.		
Book—Date	Word Analysis	Notes & Assignments
9/21 *Big Ball of String*		

> *Teacher:* What kind of a story is this?
> *Child:* It is about a boy who makes a big ball of string.
> *Teacher:* Why did he want a big ball of string?
> *Child:* I don't know, but maybe he just wanted to collect something. I collect pretty stones.
> *Teacher:* You do? Would you like to find a book about stones?
> *Child:* We don't have any.
> *Teacher:* O.K. I will ask the school librarian. (She records in the note book as follows:)

[18] Marion Holland, *The Big Ball of String*, Beginner Books, New York: Random House, 1960.

John S.		
Book—Date	Word Analysis	Notes & Assignments
9/21 Big Ball of String		Lib: Stones ?

Teacher: Did you have trouble with some words?
Child: Yes. But I guessed them or figured them out. But I might miss them again.
Teacher: What ones were they?
Child: (Turning pages rapidly.) This one, "Ker-flop"
Teacher: We could go faster if you would bring these words all written down for me to look at. (Teacher writes this down as follows:)

John S.		
Book—Date	Word Analysis	Notes & Assignments
9/21 Big Ball of String	Kerflip – OK	Lib: Stones ?

Teacher: What other words?
Child: There were lots and lots of words that rhymed. I had to figure out "dumped" from "bump," and over here I figured out "trike" from "bike," and "anything" from "string" and "thing." I had a hard time for a minute with "machine," but it just had to rhyme with "between," and so that was the only thing that fitted what was happening.
Teacher: Good for you. (She recorded the following:)

John S.		
Book—Date	Word Analysis	Notes & Assignments
9/21 Big Ball of String	Kerflip – OK	Lib: Stones ?
	dumped (bump) trike (bike)	
	anything (string - thing) machine (between)	

Teacher: Now pick the part that you wanted to read aloud to me.
Child: (Turning to page 43.) I liked this part because my mother has a hard time to keep me in bed when I am sick.
Teacher: Tell me about the story up to this point.
Child: Well, there was a boy who got an idea that if he had a BIG string ball he could do lots of things. But he has a bad time finding string. His Dad got mad at him. His Mother chased him away. He went to the dump though and got all he wanted. He had a balloon and he kept getting into trouble. Finally he got sick and had to stay in bed. He couldn't get out. He shot all his darts. Then he got the best idea yet for what to do with his string. That's where I want to read.
Teacher: O.K. Go ahead. (Child reads several pages woodenly, and without expression, although he seemed to enjoy it. He miscalls "rig" for "fix.")
Teacher: You have a problem, John. We need to work on your oral reading. I will make a group tomorrow and see if that helps. (She records as follows:)
Teacher: Look at this word. (Shows piece of paper on which she has written "rig.") You missed it but you still made sense. What is the first letter?
Child: "R"—it is rig.

John S.		
Book–Date	Word Analysis	Notes & Assignments
9/21 *Big Ball of String*	*Kerflop* – OK	*Lib: Stones ?*
	dumped (bumps) *trickle (trike)*	*Knew story*
	anything (string-thing) *machine (between)*	*Oral Rdg Expression (Group)*
	rig / fix	

These kinds of notes, in whatever kind of personal shorthand a teacher might use, are invaluable in planning for the next day's reading period. A quick glance over the notebook will reveal what needs to be done. Perhaps notes on a separate piece of paper would look something like those on page 165.

SUMMARY

This chapter has been devoted entirely to a discussion of the individual conference. Its basic philosophy is that individual differences cannot be met unless the teacher frequently works with each child separately. The criteria for managing a large class are hinged to the child's presentation of a representative sample of his reading, and to

```
10/23

Groups
    Oral reading for expression        Beginning consonant substitution
        John                               Susan
        Mary                               Ethel
        Joe                                Shirley
        Phillip                            Yvonne
                                           Bill

Individuals
    John — see librarian re books on stones
    Sam — check comprehension on yesterday's story
    Manny — check "My Own Word List" in spelling for structural analysis skills

Self-Directed Assignments (in Group?):
    Maria, Chuck, June, Ardelle, Walter, Vada, Murray, Scott

Overdue Individual Conferences. Why:
    Bob, Rennie, Maude
```

the ability of the teacher to conduct an effective conference in a brief period. The scheduling, time allotment for each child, questions and procedures, and decisions that must be made by both pupil and teacher are all discussed in detail.

The areas that must be examined include the mechanics of silent and oral reading, development of value judgement, and pupil insight into his personal identification with material chosen. Suggestions for closure of the conference as well as for keeping records were made. In brief, the structure of a good individual conference was described with an eye toward the classroom teacher who wishes to move in these directions.

7

GROUPING

What are the principles of grouping that allow the most effective teaching to take place? What must a teacher watch every time he puts two or more children together? The following guidelines may be helpful as basic to open-ended learning in groups:

1. Groups are to be organized for single, specific purposes.
2. A group exists for the duration of its purpose and no longer.
3. The activity of a group and the amount of teacher help are determined by the reason for which the group was organized.
4. The reason or purpose of the group must be clearly understood by each member.
5. The reason for the group must provide a purpose and personal challenge for each member.
6. Each member must be aware of the group purpose prior to its organization and activity.

These principles provide the framework for any teacher in any curriculum area to proceed in a most fruitful fashion. They indicate reason as well as method in good classroom practice. These principles are just as applicable in social studies, arithmetic, or the language arts other than reading. However, they are specifically designed for reading and find greatest usefulness there.

The orginality of these principles must be emphasized, inasmuch as other texts de-emphasize these concepts, or offer an opposite point of view. Rather than using the widely accepted practice of assigning children to various groups on the basis of generalized ability, a teacher would do better to meet with children individually, assess their specific needs, group, and then proceed accordingly. Such analysis of individual needs become the "lesson plan" for the teacher. When two or more children have the same need, purpose, or interest, a group is indicated.

GROUPING AS A FUNCTION OF WHAT CHILDREN NEED TO KNOW

Grouping in these terms is thus a function of curriculum, of what children learn. Grouping is not a function of what children ARE. They can be dull, brilliant, blue-eyed, or pig-tailed. It does not matter. What does matter is what they need to be taught. Therefore, grouping of children cannot be decided before the teacher sees the pupils. Children cannot be grouped until some kind of exploratory teaching takes place that helps identify these specifics that need to be taught. Decisions must be made for each child as to who should work on which item—and with others facing the same problem.

GROUPING NOT A METHOD

That grouping is not a method would appear to be obvious. But the years of nonspecific, assigned groups of slow, medium, and bright children have clouded the issue. Whatever measure or manner in which the Bushytails, Robins, or Tigers have been segregated

or separated has nothing to do with what or how they are taught, once grouped.

There are literally thousands of ways in which one class of 35 children can be grouped over a semester's time. But these thousands can be put into categories. Some of these are:

1. Ability groups based on:
   a. Tests
   b. Texts
   c. General achievement or reward
2. Skills groups
   a. Letter sounds or phonemes
   b. Word recognition
   c. Oral use of language
   d. A stage of development
3. Social groups
   a. Friendship
   b. Interest
   c. Project
   d. General cooperation

These preceding categories or types of grouping have differing philosophies. A method of teaching has nothing to do with the way children are put in groups. "Method" is not the way people are clumped together. "Method" is what a teacher does with a group. We are concerned with classroom management at the moment, and grouping is just that.

GROUP-TEACHING NECESSARY

Learning to read is a highly individual and personal process. Yet, when many pupils need to be taught in the same classroom at the same time, many approaches need to be used. Certainly the best evidence of a good reading program is the presence of a variety of patterns within the same class. Because an approach to reading is based upon an individual conference is no reason to assume that grouping never occurs. Quite the contrary. Groups have specific, valuable uses and as long as class size remains where it now is, groups save teacher and pupil time. In short, they provide for more efficient use of classroom time. In a usual reading period of 60 to 90 minutes, groups for the teaching of reading should take approximately half of such a period.

The problem is to help teachers learn how to set up individual conferences and to recognize those purposes, needs, and interests that are revealed in such an intimate situation. Teachers need to become sensitive to procedures in a group session. In short, teachers need to know:

1. The kinds of groups to organize
2. How to teach what children need to learn when they need to learn it

The point of the matter is that it is mainly in the individual conference that the teacher gets the clues and evidence of what learning *must come next*. It is the analysis of evidence from any portion of the day's work that is the basis for succeeding days' programs. It is these notes that show the teacher which children have common needs. Let it be stated that grouping during the reading period can be derived from spelling disabilities as well as reading disabilities. The following discussion, while emphasizing the teacher-pupil conference in reading, does not exclude evidence from other areas of the curriculum. It is these notes, then, that show the teacher what GROUPS are needed. The records of each conference are a gold mine for lesson-planning.

Much group teaching is necessary. Much group living is necessary. The teacher who fails to see this denies pupils learning opportunities, and, just as seriously, socializing or working-together opportunities. Our society is one that likes to live in groups as much as it cherishes individuality. Groups are essential in the classroom, not only for healthy citizenship, but to provide teachers with the most efficient and businesslike method of teaching the most material to the most children in the shortest period of time possible. Children are thus grouped when a SINGLE PURPOSE is to be served. This purpose may be learning a certain reading skill. It may be enjoying the same story *together*. It may be pooling efforts to charm the rest of the class with choric reading or panel discussion or dramatization. It may be a hundred things.

Grouping is a process that enables children to learn. But the process relates to classroom management. What children need to know is either content or skills. Managing the class works best when the content is fitted to children—not children to content. Such fitting with a class of 30 to 40 pupils requires that the teacher know the content in such great detail as to see what can work for certain pupils. The analysis of content must allow it to be applied to any pupil, in any quantity, in any sequence, in any step in any sequence, at any time.

The scope and range of what is to be learned, and its progression, *must* be at the command of the teacher. Materials and skills are the servant of the teacher. No manual can be followed page by page because no manual is omniscient enough to know what a particular group needs from one day to the next. But a manual *could* list range and progression in such a way as to be of help to the teacher no matter what the individuals in any class needed. Then the inanimate material truly serves the human being, the teacher.

TYPES OF GROUPS

A discussion of the progression in group activity must deal with the several types or categories of activity that do occur in a classroom. Whether or not the groups meet simultaneously or consecutively, there are rather typical ways in which children divide themselves, or are divided by the teacher. Wide differences within each group are of no account as long as the purpose is clear to its members.

1. Special Needs or Task Grouping
2. Friendship Groups

3. Interest Groups

4. Special Project Groups

Special Needs or Task Grouping

This is a term that is to be found in the professional literature, but is usually mentioned as one way of dividing up children who have been put together on the traditional ability basis. We feel there is no measure of generalized ability that is suitable for effective grouping. Thus, to save time in the classroom, children can be grouped when their PURPOSES are the same. When each member of a group has an identical specific need, whatever that might be, this term is properly applied. More details will be described later.

Friendship Groups

The second category of grouping comes at those times when a child may work with his friends. The whole field of group dynamics has explored the potentials for learning, as well as good human relations, that accrue when friends work together. That the accent be not on the friendship, but on the learning, is our concern here. It is fine to work with someone you like, but the purpose must be other than pure friendship. They must DO something constructive. Otherwise, justification for spending time in school with one's friends is slim indeed. There is no question that given an excellent and rich purpose, friends will carry it out with more dispatch. But it is also possible that nonfriends be put together if great accomplishment is desired. The question is: What must be done? This is the key to the whole matter. Surely friendships help, but alone are not sufficient for group organization.

Interest Groups

The third category, Interest Groups, organize themselves around a mutual concern. Joe, Mary, Jim, and Bob want to test cans of peas in their study of nutrition for the amount of water in comparison to the amount of solids. This is an absorbing interest of these four. They pursue it until finished, then go their own ways for other tasks.

"Interest" applies to those groups that are characterized by a central interest of the membership. Such grouping occurs frequently in the setting up of committees or groups for a social studies or science unit. Each committee has an interest that it chooses to pursue. In this case, the teacher will need to do relatively little direct teaching. He will act in the role of facilitator, or one who gets action started or sees that appropriate materials are available.

For example, a sixth-grade class is studying the history of our nation. The Bill of Rights is under scrutiny. Eight children decide they want to concentrate on Article III: "No soldier shall in time of peace be quartered in any house without the consent of the owner, nor in time of war, but in a manner prescribed by law." They find all of the books bearing on the subject. They divide up the responsibility in order to explore why this article was included in the Bill of Rights. Once the teacher has made sure that they have enough work to do, he goes on to other matters.

In short, the difference between "Interest Groups" and the other types is the element of pupil choice in the activity, be it work-type or recreational. "Interest Groups" should be set up and operate with relative independence of the teacher, who can conduct his class in a roving fashion moving from one group of children to another. The element of independence, either in the actual choice of activity or in the sessions themselves is a key factor. The cohesiveness of the membership depends upon the responsibility undertaken.

Special Project Grouping

Perhaps this is an arbitrary term, but it is intended to convey a characteristic in these groups activities that might be called "the good and welfare" of the class. For example, special projects might be cleaning out the terrarium, planning for a special event such as a parents' tea, or getting the classroom library in order. There should be an element of doing a "chore" together in this kind of activity, even though the "togetherness" is the "sweetening" for the work. There is a job to be done and so several children volunteer to put their shoulders to the wheel to do it.

Summary of Types of Groups

As can be seen, the "Special Needs" is the type of group that teachers will use mostly for direct instruction, although there can be a high degree of independence once the group attacks the purpose for which it was organized. All skill-teaching takes place in this type of situation. Such groups require the teacher's presence and are not very fruitful without much teacher attention. In fact, continuing attention is usually a requirement for these activities.

The types of groups other than "special needs" have a larger element of independence than direct teacher intervention or instruction. In each case, the job is set and the membership "gets on with it."

Although these definitions and terms are admittedly arbitrary in character, they do indicate the infinite possibilities of arrangement and rearrangement of pupils. This, it would seem, is true flexible grouping. In rare cases does the organization become long term. One to five days would be more apt to be the average, and usually one day will suffice.

Using a class as a sample, let us set up a schedule that shows how a teacher might plan to meet his class, first in individual conferences, and then in groups upon the needs or interests that might be revealed. The chart below could describe procedures for any grade that has some measure of independent reading ability. (See Chapters 8, 9 & 11, for beginning procedures relating to children who have little or no independent reading ability.)

This schedule will show the bridge between individual conferences and groups in a situation where the class has long since set up its routines and is familiar with the management pattern. Teachers who wish a description of the changeover from traditional, three-group, basal reader systems should turn back to Chapter 4 for assistance.

CLASSROOM ORGANIZATION FOR GROUPING

Setting Up Groups

How teachers observe, note, and diagnose the needs of the pupils in an individual conference is described in detail in Chapter 6. A teacher can take notes during an individual session, but while teach-

Name**	Conference No.*									
	1	2	3	4	5	6	7	8	9	10
1. Allison, Claude	11/13									
2. Barbour, Isabelle	11/9	11/12								
3. Bentley, Saide	11/6	11/12								
4. Faulk, Clayton	11/13									
5. Gray, Hilda	11/14									
6. Hall, Alfred	11/9	11/13								
7. Holt, Gerald	11/10	11/13								
8. Hultz, Yvonne	11/13									
9. King, Marshall	11/6	11/10	11/14							
10. Manners, Sue	11/6	11/11								
11. Milton, Olga	11/7	11/12								
12. Oltman, Ross	11/7									
13. Peters, Margaret	11/7	11/11								
14. Prince, Becky	11/8	11/12								
15. Radman, Joel	11/14									
16. Reese, Mabel	11/14									
17. Richman, Warren	11/14									
18. Saltzer, Marietta	11/13									
19. Solomon, Kathryn	11/7									
20. Sotolski, Alex	11/7									
21. Thomas, Wilma	11/11	11/14								
22. Thulman, Jane	11/8	11/12								
23. Upton, Hope	11/14									
24. Wassel, Della	11/7	11/14								
25. Weston, Eunice	11/6									
26. Wishinski, Gwen	11/7	11/11	11/14							
27. Wooster, Roger	11/14									
28. Wurton, Barney	11/11	11/14								
29. Young, Lynn	11/6	11/13								
30. Zigetti, Joe	11/13									

*Dates of individual conferences. These are listed in such a way as to represent the way the conference sheet in a teacher's notebook might look. See also Chapter 11.

**All names are fictitious and any similarity to living people is purely coincidental.

A sample class roll.

ing a group he is too busy to do much writing. The quality and values of the one-to-one relationship are not destroyed by whatever note-taking during an individual conference the teacher feels necessary. Of course, too much is too much. But the teacher's own good sense should tell him when the climate of the conference is being destroyed.

Therefore, a rich supply of information about each child's performance is recorded each time he sits alone with his teacher. A record of each pupil's strengths and weaknesses is noted in the teacher's note-book or record cards. These notes are a great help to a teacher, when planning the next day. He sits down and on a separate piece of paper lists the various deficiencies, skills, interests, projects, or other myriad items that have been revealed during the conferences. This paper is the reference for future teaching. Children's names may be listed on the board or simply announced when their time comes for group-teaching. The groups meet, are taught, or discuss whatever the item might be, come to a closure point, and then disband.

Let us take one class as an example and show how it might be organized into groups without resorting to the traditional generalized ability classifications. Needless to say, there are several ways in which this might come about. Every teacher puts his own stamp upon his own methods of procedure.

Schedule of Individual Conferences and Follow-Up Grouping
FIRST DAY (say November 12th)

Reading period (9:00–10:30 A.M.)

9:00   Planning for independent work period
Book selection time

9:15   Silent reading begins and each child moves into his own independent work when ready—usually from 30 to 60 minutes later

9:20   (approximately) Individual conferences begin

These children have indicated their readiness and preparation for same. They come, in turn, as they had signed up for the conference:

Jane T.	Kathryn S.	Becky P.
Sadie B.	Isabelle B.	Gerald H.
Ross O.	Eunice W.	Lynn Y.

However, the teacher was not able to get to the last two signees, Gerald and Lynn. So these two are to be first during the next conference time. In addition, Marietta S., Joe Z., Claude A., Clayton F. and Yvonne H., in that order, have indicated they are ready.

10:00   Group sessions begin as planned previously by teacher. The content to be taught is noted by the heading. These topics arose in the preceding day's conferences, or, at least, in a very recent conference.

Skills Groups

Voice Inflection Problems

Questions	Quotation Marks	Sentence Structure
Alfred H.	Joel R.	Wilma T.
Gwen W.	Alex S.	Hilda G.
Roger W.	Mabel R.	Warren R.
Barney W.		Marietta S.

The teacher calls all of the above children together at the same time, as voice inflection problems can so be handled. A record is kept of date, content and suggestions, if any, for future meetings.

10:15   Consonant Substitution Problems
Della W.   Olga M.
Claude A.   Hope U.
Margaret P.

10:20   Interest Groups (Alligators)
Marshall K.   Roger W.
Gerald H.   Alex S.

10:25   Choric Reading Group (choosing a poem)
Jane T.   Eunice W.
Isabelle B.   Kathryn S.
Hilda G.   Becky P.

SECOND DAY (November 13th)

9:00   Planning, etc.
Book selection

9:15   Silent reading begins—Individual conferences begin
Gerald H.*   Lynn Y.*   Marietta S.
Joe Z.   Claude A.   Clayton F.
Yvonne H.

NOTE: Independent Work Period proceeds as planned at 9:00
On deck for coming individual conferences:
Hilda G.   Mabel R.   Hope U.

See Chapter 6 for procedures for children slow in signing up for individual conferences as:
Alfred H.   Olga M.

10:00   Group Sessions Begin
Skills Groups
Smooth Oral Reading
Jane T.   Warren R.
Wilma T.   Isabelle B.
Joel R.

Digraph Group of Words with CH and TH
Ross O.   Eunice W.
Hope U.   Gilda G.

Consonant Substitution Difficulty
Marshall K.   Isabelle B.
Kathryn S.

* Did not have time for conferences the preceding day.

Interests and Projects
Choric Speaking Practice

Jane T.	Eunice W.
Isabelle B.	Kathryn S.
Hilda G.	Becky P.

Diorama Partners

Log Cabins	Woodland
Warren R.	Eunice W.
Marshall K.	Hilda G.

THIRD DAY (November 14th)

9:00 Planning and Book selection

9:15 Beginning of silent reading and individual conferences

Hilda G.	Barney W.	Warren R.
Mabel R.	Roger W.	Wilma T.
Hope U.	Della W.	Joel R.

10:00 Group Sessions Begin
Need Individual Conference
Alfred H.
Marshall K.
Sue M.

10:10 Skill Group Sessions

10:20 Interest and Project Groups

FOURTH DAY (November 15th)

Repeat previous patterns

Progression to Grouping

As the scheduling chart provides, the teacher must learn to analyze each child's needs through diagnosis of notes made during *the individual conference* and from word-analysis disabilities revealed in his daily writing, not to mention observation of his daily performance. On the basis of these observations it will be necessary to plan daily for each child—as an individual or as a member of a group. The teacher will listen to each child frequently and alone so that his reading techniques, habits, strengths, weaknesses, his attitude toward reading in general, and all his reactions to reading can be studied and analyzed. No step shall be so large that he will stumble; none so small that he will waste time.

Grouping as an Extension of the Individual Conference

It might be said that while the adult society, the Board of Education and Administration, sets the broad outlines of what is to be learned, it is the child that becomes aware—and accepts—those specifics of what HE needs to learn. Much careful teacher-planning, teacher-pupil planning, and pupil-pupil planning are of the essence of open-ended systems of learning. They are the dynamic forces— the energy—behind all instruction. Planning begins long before the actual time the children come and sit together for the purposes that have been decided upon. The roots go deep. Experiencing, living, learning mean more rather than less planning. The better the teacher, the more organized is the operation—organized and structured for those skills and needs that are to be learned as tools that lead on to greater and greater heights of human knowledge and accomplishment. Once a child knows HOW—he is freed to proceed on his own.

Grouping Saves Classroom Time

Of course, he can learn some skills in an individual conference, and does. The major point of grouping children is that it saves classroom time. It saves wear and tear on the teacher energy. It teaches much to many in a short space of time. These have always been the advantages of grouping. But grouping upon specific needs or tasks is a major breakthrough in concept, as it allows the teacher to work only with what is needed by those who need it at the time they need it. Grouping, in this sense, is truly an extension of the individual conference. That is the best way. That is the way it should be.

A sort of partnership must exist in classrooms where teacher and pupils plan the kind of future our democracy needs. For children fortunate enough to be living in such a classroom, instruction becomes more than learning one of the facets of the curriculum—it becomes a way of life.

When To Group

The knowledge of when to organize a group usually comes, as can be seen, from the individual conference. Reading progress in a group is determined frequently by the way children work together. These groups, as can be noted, are temporary, on a day-to-day basis. Children move in and out of them as skills and other needs require. The way children work together provides clues for grouping. Note on the preceding scheduling chart that several children met in more than one group on a given day, as Alex S. on the first day; Hilda G., Jane T., Warren R., Marshall K., and others on the second day. This is the wisest way to use the time allotted to the reading period, because it pinpoints the exact needs of the pupils. It also makes a short cut for the teacher—i.e., more can be taught faster.

Gregarious human instincts require that children work together. For this, as well as reasons of efficient and economical teaching-learning situations, teachers must perfect their skills in developing ever-changing well-organized groups. It is a matter of classroom management and derives from knowing how to analyze the individual conference data and organize procedures from what is indicated.

Preplanning Is Essential

In getting ready for the next school day, the teacher lays out the notes made on cards or in a notebook from the day's individual conferences. On a *separate* piece of paper he should make a listing of everything indicated that needs personal *instruction*. One of the most disastrous of practices, if a child is to be educated, is for the teacher to assign workbook pages instead of personally teaching the indicated skill. Workbooks might be used as a final check. But there is no substitute for an instructor in the flesh, whatever inanimate audiovisual instrument might be used.

When the notes have been analyzed, a matter of a minute or two on each record, the teacher thinks through his lesson plan on each item. He decides which needs can be grouped (see the Voice Inflection Problems at 10:00 A.M. on the first day of the scheduling chart) and taught together. He decides which needs cannot be grouped at all. Beside each list, then, on this piece of paper he notes his lesson plan for the coming day.

Once the analysis and listing are made, some teachers like to put the names of the children on the board so that the latter will know what to expect. More important, they will know why they are being placed in a particular group. There will be no guesswork for the child. He will know he needs help on such topics as: reading questions, substituting consonants, or recognizing the sound of long vowels. He will know that that is what he needs and will not be ashamed. He is being grouped on what he needs to know, and not on what he is—which is a far different matter.

Announcing Group Membership

If the teacher does not have board space, or does not wish to make a public list, he can make an announcement during the first planning period saying something like this:

After the individual conferences there are several groups that need my special help. Jane, Warren, Wilma, Isabelle, and Joel: I need to help you read aloud better. Ross, Eunice, Hope and Hilda: You will remember that each of you had trouble with words that had the diagraphs "ch" and "th" in them. I will work with you four on that this morning. Now, Marshall, Isabelle, and Kathryn, you are having trouble with the sound of consonants. We will work on that together this morning. Also, the choric speaking group that chose their poem yesterday will need my help in getting ready to practice. You will need to decide how you are going to divide up to say the different parts of the poem.

And so it goes. Each child knows what to expect. Because learning is a highly stimulating and exciting activity when the learner is personally involved, these children will have a favorable mind set when their group is called. It will not be a chore, but a task that is accepted as worthwhile and valuable—for itself alone. This task will not need any kind of grading or checking. It will be done face to face. While there might be a follow-up exercise, if the teacher feels it would nail down the learning, the accent is upon doing something for its own sake—and not because the teacher decides, for unfathomable reasons, that something must be done.

The Need for Systematic Routines

Another aspect of planning is that of setting up routines so that children will be sure of what they are to do at the proper time. Routines can be deadly—witness the usual weekly spelling lesson—but they must be there. There must be some kind of habitual way of going about the classroom business that allows enough freedom and still does not stifle individual initiative. For example, the teacher that has monitors hand out every piece of paper is promoting rigid conformity, not to mention dependence upon others for basic personal needs. But the teacher who places the paper in an accessible place, encourages children to take whatever they need when they need it, and holds them accountable for wastage has set up routines that promote personal independence. There is a clear difference.

In reading, too, the placement of books dictates the manner in which children may choose them. When may a child go to the book center? Always or just sometimes? How long may he stay there? As long as he wishes—or long enough to get one book—or two minutes by the clock? How does a teacher know when to let some children engage in independent work, read or work on their own projects, while others browse through the book corner? Still others may be looking with a speculative eye on the art supplies to produce a piece of work for the sharing time. Each teacher will do all of these things differently. Some will be overplanned, some will be underplanned, others will have just the right amount of planning.

The right amount of planning allows children to:

1. Carry on their work with little need for self-interruption (such as keeping busy for 30 minutes at a stretch).
2. Change materials or activities at a time when it is necessry, rather than when it is convenient.
3. Meet emergency needs (of a learning nature or otherwise) without upsetting the whole class.

Variety in Group Activity

The well-ordered classroom can keep its serenity even though every group (or for that matter every child) is undertaking a different activity. Whether groups meet with or without the teacher, simultaneously or consecutively, all manner of activity is possible. A dozen different kinds of group operations going on at the same time need not cause an uproar. The teacher helps the class organize those who are noisy and insists that they not meet while quiet working groups need to work.

For example, one group is working with the teacher on some skill in word recognition. Another is sitting in a quiet spot memorizing a poem for its turn with the teacher to practice choric reading. Another is researching some books in the book corner for a specific topic. The rest of the class is working individually on a variety of personal assignments, both teacher- and self-imposed.

But the group that is getting ready for the puppet show *may not* practice during the quiet working time. They must wait until there is no direct teaching going on. Also the group that is reading *Homer Price*[1] aloud in turn must wait until later. Similarly, the group dictating the day's diary must wait, but the children transcribing, in their *best* handwriting—yesterday's news—can proceed because there is no noise involved in copying those sentences.

Yet, with all of the need to be quiet at the appropriate times, there should be an immense amount of variety of activity as described in Chapter 5. Routines have their place—but not when routines and repetitiveness deaden learning. Teachers should stretch themselves to make each hour different, each day different, each month different, each year different. A mark of professional growth is the realization that you "did it better this time." Things are apt to be better when done differently.

The Place of Uniform Assignments

Uniform assignments do have a place in good grouping practice. There are times when the teacher does insist that every child do the

[1] Robert McCloskey, *Homer Price*, New York: Viking Press, Inc., 1943.

same thing in the same way at the same time. But what characterizes *acceptable* uniform assignments, for surely they are undesirable under many conditions? The difference is what knowledge the members of the group have as to the exact and specific reason for which they were organized. For example, the group that knows its oral reading is word by word, accepts the fact and goes to work as rapidly as possible to correct that deficiency. The teacher has isolated exactly what needs to be done. In that respect, and in that respect only, is that group homogeneous. Thus, it can read the same material, or carry on the same activity at the same time. Because the teacher knew how to ascertain the needs of individual members, he can proceed to teach the necessary skill in a uniform way. In short, when a common need has been found in two or more children, the teacher may use the same material to teach that skill. This is what is meant by uniform assignment.

CHANGING GROUPS

Obviously children will work in many groups. Thus, they will need to change from one to the other. Changing seats or places in the room can become chaotic or it can be orderly and business-like. This depends upon the kind of directions each teacher gives. Children need to practice changing their "place of business," so to speak. They should arrive where they belong with a minimum of fuss and noise. No stopping on the way. No visiting with friends who are not moving. No teacher waiting an unnecessarily long time for a given group to arrive and get settled (And no "Thank you" upon arrival. Coming to a group is an expected act, not a courtesy to the teacher).

A major problem of such shifting around is that of moving chairs. If it is at all possible, teachers should request an extra set of chairs for group meetings. It saves class time to move the children themselves *without* their seats, rather than have them bring their own chairs. It is also good for short term five- or ten-minute sessions to use what the Girl Scouts call "sit-upons." They are made of folded strips of newspaper woven in and out, that last a surprisingly long time and can be made in two minutes upon demand. Children themselves can make them.

Changing children without their chairs should rarely take longer than the time it takes them to stand up, walk to where they should be, and sit down. The author has timed this often, and 60 seconds is ample for an entire class to change places. Good classroom management requires that the teacher help children know exactly what to do. A "walk-through" is a way of perfecting skills of changing seats!

If it is not possible to use "sit-upons" because the group session will need 20 minutes or more, and if there are no extra stools or chairs available, then the teacher must grit his teeth and really plan how to move the children around. Moving chairs greatly complicates the task of changing groups. In the first place, simply picking up chairs and carrying them, going back and getting any necessary materials, or arranging the chairs so that everyone is in an advantageous spot takes time that should be "learning" time—that is, learning-how-to-read time. There is always learning, of course, in any situation. But school time is better spent primarily on reading skills, rather than on how-to-bring-one's-seat-to-the-reading-group skills.

Direct teaching in a group.

When the problem of the chairs is resolved one way or the other, the teacher must make a decision on where the meeting place for groups should be in the room. The spot chosen should be out of the way of general traffic for leaving the room, or getting new books, or securing supplies from the closet. The normal and unavoidable foot traffic in a classroom should never be allowed to interrupt or interfere with individual or group sessions. Yet the teacher must be sure that he has clear view of all the pupils. See Chapter 2 in the session "Helping Teachers Change Over to New Patterns,"[2] for ideas about preliminary planning, map drawing of room arrangements, that will help in deciding the places to be occupied by the seats, the groups, the books, and the other necessities of classroom living.

GROUP SESSIONS WITH OR WITHOUT THE TEACHER

When do groups of children work alone, and when do they work with the teacher? How are such decisions made? The third principle at the beginning of the chapter gives the clue:

3. *The activity of a group and the amount of teacher help is determined by the reason for which it was organized.*

This leads us to a discussion of groups meeting one after another, or all at the same time.

SIMULTANEOUS AND CONSECUTIVE GROUPING

Simultaneous grouping could be a term applied to a class that had several groups working away at the same time with the teacher roving from one to the other to make sure all was going well. The teacher need not be with each group continuously; nevertheless, in a sense, he has worked himself out of a job, and acts in a sort of supervisory, facilitating kind of way, once the activity has been organized.

"Consecutive" might be a term applied in a class whose teacher worked in succession with different groups that for some reason could not carry on their purpose without the teacher's being in charge.

In this latter case, the group finds the teacher's presence necessary for its survival, ie., for the carrying out of its purpose. This does not mean the teacher is needed to keep order. No group is well organized if its purpose is not good enough to *provoke effort on its own*. Groups are for collective action and, when an adult is needed to keep order, that purpose is very weak indeed.

Probably consecutive groups deal more with activities that do not require the teacher's experience. Simultaneous groups proceed to absorb content and knowledge that are directly dependent upon teacher-training and knowledge.

A teacher decides when groups are to meet simultaneously, with only roving teacher attention, and when they are to meet with him

2 Pages 24–25.

in succession. For example, several children have been noted to need special attention to improve their oral reading—i.e., "reading like you talk." This cannot be done without the attention of the teacher. That group session cannot be interrupted without weakening the learning situation.

On the other hand, a group of children have found several copies of the same book with the story of "Rumpelstiltskin" in it. They decide that they want to read it to each other in turn. The teacher's attention is not needed in this group, beyond making sure that they have a spot to retreat and that they have enough books.

Similarly, a group of children have found the directions for doing an experiment with chlorophyll. The teacher again is needed not continuously but only long enough to make sure of their organization, supplies, and plans. Then they can be on their own.

But one group of children have chosen Vachel Lindsay's "The Potatoes Dance" for choric speaking. They need the complete attention and assistance of their teacher until they arrive at the point where each knows what line he is going to say. This takes teacher time before the group can be independent.

These are examples of group activities in which the purpose clearly dictates whether or not the teacher's presence is essential. There is no blanket rule. It depends on what has to be accomplished.

Variations in Simultaneous Grouping

Another way a teacher might group children is to place together those children most able to work independently with very little teacher help. A second group could be made up of children who are less able to work for a length of time without teacher help and a third group could be those children who need a great deal of assistance at frequent intervals.

Thus the familiar pattern of three classroom groups is obtained, but the division of children cuts straight across intelligence, reading ability, or any other talent. In these situations children who are very bright sometimes develop a project that is so complex that they need frequent assistance to bring it to its ultimate end. Similarly, a very slow child in reading or other areas of the curriculum might be quite capable of keeping himself occupied for relatively long periods of time. Thus this kind of grouping is not derogatory in nature nor psychologically destructive to the children themselves. Yet, it gives the teacher the needed freedom to concentrate on those children needing help regardless of ability.

Teachers wishing to shift from the traditional three-group patterns can follow the above suggestions by simply shifting the children in the groups and not disturbing the basic pattern of his classroom organization.[3]

SPONTANEOUS GROUPS

But with all of the need for preplanning, planning, and setting up workable routines, the need for spontaneous action is undeniable. Often such activity is the richest source of learning of all. The class weekly newspaper comes and ten children want to read it immediately. Why not?

There are many kinds of opportunities for children to get together in spontaneous fashion. A group of first graders (of varying achievement levels) wanted to read "Jack And the Beanstalk" in one of their supplementary readers. The teacher was delighted. Over to the corner they went, made their circle, decided who was to read which part, and "Fee-Fi-Fo-Fummed" at a great rate for about half an hour.

One third-grade boy, finding a dandy description of how to make an electromagnet, asked two of his friends to help him make it. Teacher permission was granted and they started to work. It took them two work periods of two days, but they soon had the magnet working and demonstrated its capabilities with great pride.

Why do American teachers so often deny children the simple pleasure of helping one's neighbor? Questions such as: "What is this word?" "Do you know how to do this?" "Do you think I am ready to read this to the whole class?" Such help makes for nicer human beings —and allows learning, to boot.

These are all examples of spontaneous grouping that require only the teacher's awareness or permission. There is certainly much valuable educational opportunity in such getting together. But their purpose is not necessarily *directly instructional*. Children, or anyone, learn a great deal from their peer group in such a way. But the learning is incidental, and indirect.

CLOSURE FOR GROUP SESSIONS

For good operations in group-teaching, the recognition of the proper time to close the group and send them back to their seats or to some other activity is essential. It is a teacher skill and must be

[3] The author is indebted to Mr. Edward Wright of the Public Schools of Warren, Mich., for this unique way of organizing classrooms.

learned in a conscious way. The appropriate closing of group sessions can save hours of class time.

Groups rarely need to meet more than five or ten minutes at a time, and some can be closed within a couple of minutes. In Chapter 6, in the section "The Individual Conference," the decision as to closing the conference was a matter of teacher ability and skill. It is a learned ability and skill. So, too, does closure of group sessions require similar awareness or recognition of a good stopping place.

GENERAL RULES FOR CLOSURE

Short-Time Groups

In general those groups whose needs are highly specific, with a single item of definite, tangible nature, can be instructed in a very few minutes. Such groups would have such purposes as the following:

1. A certain letter sound or phonemic element in a word.
2. A single word recognition skill, such as final "e" in a word like "name."
3. Some specific choice requiring teacher help in organization, such as:
   a. Choosing a poem.
   b. Choosing characters in a story to be read aloud.
   c. Deciding on certain materials for a project.
   d. Assigning jobs in a chosen project, etc.
4. Check-up on previously assigned follow-up exercise.

Long-Time Groups

Although short-time groups might frequently extend their sessions, there are nevertheless certain types of activity that by their nature take a longer time than those types listed above. The key difference would be the necessity of direct teacher involvement. That could not be speeded up. Such types of groups might be:

1. Skill practice that requires the teacher's direct attention, such as:
   a. Learning to read aloud meaningfully.
   b. Running through a dramatization.
   c. Dictation of a chart story, or daily newspaper.
   d. Working on certain word recognition skills of more complex nature, such as use of prefixes, suffixes, syllables, and small words within larger words.
2. Groups requiring audience participation:
   a. Sharing of a follow-up project for a story.

b. Demonstration of some kind.
c. Presentation of some kind.
3. Emergency situations that cannot be closed until the teacher is satisfied that a stopping point has been reached.

These are a few examples of those kinds of acceptable group sessions that build on the sound principle of teaching children "what they need to know when they need to know it." The reader could probably supply a hundred other examples.

The members of all groups will vary widely in all characteristics *except* the one for which the group was organized. That will be the same.

Closure Is Reached

The teacher must recognize when the peak of learning for a given group is passed. How does a teacher know when to stop and not drag on, wasting class time?

First, the children's attitude in the group is important. When the wiggling starts, that group has finished. Better that the teacher should cultivate the ability to move smoothly and rapidly through a brief series of steps and dismiss the group too soon, than drag out a session. Children will show when they "catch on." Their faces will show it. The emotional need for achievement shows teachers when children are delighted when they "learn" something. They will ask for the next step. They will want to go on to new worlds. They will seek to leave the group—not because they are bored, but because they are eager to proceed, to progress. A wise teacher will build on this eagerness. He might have a good follow-up exercise. He might say:

"How can you prove to me that you now know this long "a" (or whatever) no matter where you meet it again?"

Children can respond:

"Go on! Give me something. I will show you. I KNOW I know it now."

or

"I can hear it when I can't see it. I think that I will be able to use that long "a" when I am writing a story. Watch my next story."

or

"I think I will take my word list in my speller or in the back of a reader. I will find all of the words that have a long "a" in them. You check my list. O.K.?"

or

"I am going to write a story with all of those long "a" words in it— and more, too, if I can think of them. That will help me practice."

or

"I am going to find all the words I can with "a" in the middle. Then I will see if I know which ones have a long "a.""

These types of wind-up activities might well bring in the use of workbooks and other published materials. Should the teacher have a dozen different workbooks on his desk, from which he might pick and choose an appropriate exercise for a given child or children, he would have material that is often pinpointed to bring out specific learnings. The mistake that most publishers make, however, is their insistence that these materials[4] teach without the help of the teacher. This is simply not so. But they can be most useful adjuncts to the teacher who knows what he wants for which child.

The simplest way of closing a group session, of course, is just to have the children quit when they are finished with their job. There is nothing more to do. A new project, or interest, or assignment is needed.

But usually, closure depends upon the sensitivity of the teacher to a point at which action can be suspended, and the children have had enough to do for that day. Perhaps the phrase "working oneself out of a job" is the most descriptive. A teacher works always to increase learning power so that it may be applied independently in other situations.

Closure Comes When Next Step Is Seen

Closure is the most recognizable when the next step in the learning is sharp and clear to teacher and children alike. When all know where they must go next, or what they must do next, then is the time to stop.

Finally, the teacher needs to develop a "stopwatch mind"—so that all teaching efforts in an individual conference or in a group session are used to fullest advantage. The key to the whole matter, of course, lies in the concept of grouping that does not consume time for time's sake, and so becomes a kind of "busy work" for children (albeit peace for the teacher). But it is designed for a single, identified group purpose. No group, then, is really finished with its meetings, even if they take more than one day, until that purpose has been fully realized.

[4] See Agatha Townsend, "Workbooks—The Research Story," *The Reading Teacher*, Vol. 17, No. 5, February, 1964, pp. 397 ff.

SUMMARY OF GROUPING MECHANICS

The preceding section discussed matters of progression and operation in grouping. Realizing that the subject is by no means exhausted, we nevertheless move on to a more philosophical and analytical discussion. What is to follow has its practical aspects, also, but it examines some of the basic assumptions under which an approved approach to grouping must operate.

ANALYSIS AND PHILOSOPHY OF GROUPING

In order to straighten out the confusion long prevalent about this classroom practice one must turn to the philosophy that governs the appropriate separation of children in a learning situation.

Assignment of Pupils

First is the matter of teacher assignment of pupils into groups. When is it all right for a teacher to place children in a given group? When does it violate profound principles of mental health, of learning theory, and of wise use of classroom time?

Pupils may be assigned into groups when they are aware of, or when they have a part in setting up the group. The question arises:

Do you, or do you not, in best school instruction, group children when they do not know the specific reason for which they were put together?

The point of view of this text is that if children do not know the effect will get in the way of learning, and will produce serious psychological repercussions. Yet this kind of classification of human beings is described in practically every piece of writing that discusses grouping. More seriously, the discussion is conducted with seemingly little awareness of the errors of such a practice. It is not that teacher classification is never to take place, but it is that it takes place in the full light of what needs to be discovered, or worked upon, or carried out. Teachers always have assigned and always will assign pupils in some way or other. What is objectionable is when such an assignment is generalized and therefore inadequate for the learning of particular items.

HETEROGENEOUS AND HOMOGENEOUS GROUPING

The practice of "ability-grouping" goes on and on in the face of most experts who admit there is no such thing as an homogeneous group. Why such an unsound practice continues is a result of a shocking situation. Ability-grouping is an admission that teachers and/or administrators cannot, will not, or do not know how to deal with individual differences. Ability-grouping then, is a symptom, a sign of poor teaching.

The term refers to that practice that puts children together on the basis of general similarities. In such cases, children are considered "close enough" for all practical teaching purposes. However, such segregation is a waste of classroom time, pupil time, and teacher time. But teachers have rarely been trained for any other kind of grouping. Worse yet, the practice lends itself to less effective teaching because teachers frequently make less and less pretense of meeting individual needs under such an organization.

The only true homogeneity is to be found when some kind of activity or learning takes place that allows each learner to arrive at *his* learning place in accordance with *his* own ability, endurance, and energy. Thus, such a learning activity must have a long broad continuum that has literally hundreds of progression points, each one dependent upon the next, and allowing a pause if such is necessary. Programmed learning, of course, is based upon these principles. And there is much that is mechanical in character that lends itself well to programming. But, for the purposes of this section, let us assume that the successive progression points are part of the knowledge of the teacher, and need his direct, human attention.

Hammond, in a short, but excellent leaflet "Homogeneous Grouping and Educational Results"[5] sums up the evidence as follows:

[5] Sarah Lou Hammond, *Homogeneous Grouping and Educational Results,* Curriculum Letter #40, Middletown, Connecticut: Department of School Services and Publications, Wesleyan University, no date given. Dr. Hammonds' bibliography is well selected:

Hopkins, Thomas. *Thirty-Fifth Yearbook of the National Society for the Study of Education,* University of Chicago, 1936.

Keliher, Alice V. *A Critical Study of Homogeneous Grouping,* Contributions to Education No. 452, New York: Teachers College, Columbia University, 1931, p. 76.

Burr, Marvin Y. *A Study of Homogeneous Grouping,* Contributions to Education No. 457; New York: Teachers College, Columbia University, 1931, p. 41.

Courtis, S. A. "Contributions of Measurement," *The Second Yearbook.* Bulletin of The Department of Elementary School Principals, 1923, p. 161

Cornell, Ethel L. "Effects of Ability Grouping Determinable from Published Studies," *The Grouping of Pupils, Thirty-Fifth Yearbook of the National So-*

That homogeneous grouping is only one of many devices that have been developed to attempt to provide for the individual in the process of mass instruction;

That verbal intelligence tests are not reliable as a single measure upon which to group children;

That homogeneous grouping has not reduced the range of variation with a grade;

That homogeneous grouping has not made superior provision for individual differences;

That homogeneous grouping has not brought superior learning results.

Analogy with Swimming Instruction

Perhaps an example from a field other than reading might make things clearer. Take swimming instruction for example. At one end of the continuum is the nonswimmer. At the other is the accomplished water expert. The learning points in between can be diagrammed as on page 193.

The Continuum in Reading Instruction

Now let us take the continuum concept and apply it to the field of reading. In Chapter 8, in the section "Child's view of reading," we list the following major reading for a progression. They are:

Getting to know people

Creative expression and talking

Seeing, writing, and hearing our own words

Moving into sentence recognition

Reading our own sentences

Early level word perception

Moving into word analysis

Word analysis

Word analysis again becomes word perception

---

ciety for the Study of Education. Part I, Bloomington, Ill.: Public School Publishing Co., 1936, p. 290.

Wyndham, Harold S. *Ability Grouping.* Educational Research Series, No. 31, Melbourne: Melbourne University, 1934, p. 156.

Miller, W. S., and Otto, H. J. "Analysis of Experimental Studies in Homogeneous Grouping," *Journal of Educational Research,* XXI: 95–102, February, 1930.

Alberty, H. B., and Brim, O. G. "The Relation of the Newer Educational Practices to Grouping," *The Grouping of Pupils, Thirty-Fifth Yearbook of the National Society for the Study of Education.* Part I, Bloomington, Ill.: Public School Publishing Co., p. 129.

	Nonswimmer
	Can hold head under water 5 seconds
	Can hold head under water 10 seconds
	Can sit on bottom
	Can pick up object from bottom
	Can do "jelly-fish" float
	Can float face down
	Can kick while floating
	Can kick and use hands
	Can do dogpaddle
	Can float on back
	Can kick while floating on back
	Can do flutter kick
	Can do crawl stroke
	Can do breast stroke
	Can do back stroke
	Can master life-saving techniques
	Can teach others swimming and life-saving
	Expert swimmer

The continuum of swimming proficiency.

Van Allen, in *Learning to Read Through Experience,*[6] has a similar list of progressions that also provide a continuum for the guidance of a teacher. These are:

"1. What a child thinks about he can talk about.

2. What he can talk about can be expressed in painting, writing or some other form.

3. Anything he writes can be read.

4. He can read what he writes and what other people write.

[6] D. M. Lee and R. Van Allen, *Learning to Read Through Experience* (rev. ed.), New York: Appleton-Century-Crofts, Inc., 1963, pp. 5–8.

5. As he represents his speech sounds with symbols, he uses the same symbols (letters) over and over.
6. Each letter in the alphabet stands for one or more sounds that he makes when he talks.
7. Every word begins with a sound that he can write down.
8. Most words have an ending sound.
9. Many words have something in between.
10. Some words are used over and over in our language and some words are not used very often.
11. What he has to say and write is as important to him as what other people have written for him to read.
12. Most of the words he uses are the same ones which are used by other people who write for him to read."

As in swimming, at one end of the continuum of reading there is the blank inability to read. At the other end is the ability to read the most provocative, the most challenging fiction, or fact, materials available. Between these two extremes lie, as in the swimming analogy, thousands of possible learning points or plateaus—each one a bit more progressive than its predecessor depending, however, upon the need of the individual that is progressing. Each level would lead away from the nonreading extreme to the rapid reading stage.

In these progressions the emphasis lies in the way the learner moves. The teacher, patiently, yet eagerly, must encourage and yet *wait for*, the evidence that shows him that the child is moving along to ever higher stages of achievement. In these above steps, it is the child that moves, through his own efforts and help from the teacher, through self-selected reading. He is not pushed through a predigested, preplanned, predetermined set of inanimate materials foisted upon him by his teacher. He takes himself through. Yet he is not alone. He has help as he shows he needs it. *What* he reads—outside of very broad outlines of range of difficult—is of little concern. He must like what he reads. He must choose what he reads. He must be able to handle what he chooses.

The learning situation is beautifully wide open. Identical assignments are a follow-up of a revealed need. They do not *begin* a reading lesson. In such a situation, when two or more children reveal, in an individual conference, or in some other kind of open-ended learning situation, identical needs, interests, purposes, then and then only may they be grouped.

This denies the practice of teachers that say "I'll teach them all the series of skills systematically. Then they will know it when they need it." More likely they will have forgotten it when it is needed. But more seriously, it is a monumental waste of time to so teach children who are not ready for the skill, or who already knew it. Certainly one of the great weaknesses of education is the inability of many teachers to see that they do waste time when they teach children what they already know.

Heterogeneity or Homogeneity Is Not the Point

Currently, these terms indicate that homogeneous groups are usually organized on four bases. They follow with a critique of each.

1. On the basis of an achievement test, *before any actual teaching has taken place* in the new situation. Such measures are too broad, and too soon outmoded in terms of skill needs of children, to be very helpful. There is no question that many school systems waste thousands of dollars on such instruments that could well be spent on tradebooks and other needed materials.

2. On the basis of I.Q. tests, which are questionable except when given individually and are nonverbal. Of what use is an I.Q. test to help a teacher find out the exact skill a pupil needs to know? Even bright children learn some things at a slower pace than the less able, so what difference does it make what a child's I.Q. is? Again, most of such testing is a waste of money that might be spent more usefully on school supplies and books.

3. Teacher judgment that certain children will "do well" in certain groups, or worse yet, are "lazy" and are held at lower rank than necessary as a punitive measure. This certainly is not a learning measure.

4. Assigning children to books rather than the other way around. A teacher says, "Will the White House group come up," because the entire membership is reading in that text. Because teachers fell compelled to "cover" certain texts simply because the school system has purchased them, they lose sight of the fact that they are letting the inanimate, the mechanical, the machine, if you will, control what happens to the human being. In this practice the chances of meeting individual differences by such group organization are small.

If it is best that children be grouped on the basis of what they need to be taught rather than upon the several arbitrary measures cited above, then it follows that the matter of homogeneity or heterogeneity simply has nothing to do with the grouping. In every one of the four instances above, the groups are widely heterogeneous.[7] As was

[7] J. W. Wrightstone, *Classroom Organization*, No. 13, pp. 8, 9. "What Research Says to the Classroom Teacher Series" Washington, D.C.: Department of Classroom Teachers, American Educational Research Association, National Education Association, 1961.

stated in the beginning of this chapter, the term homogeneous is intended to segregate children on the basis of *what they are*. The only proper grouping is that which separates children on the basis of *what they need to know*. What children are and what they need to know are two opposed and irreconcilable points of view for group organization. A teacher may, perhaps, group children homogeneously for some portions of the curriculum and heterogeneously for other portions of the school day. But homogeneously on what? Test results or diphthongs? As the saying goes, he must fish or cut bait—if he cares about the efficient use of class time and the learning attitudes of children.

Homogeneity Non-Existent

There is, in truth, no such thing as a homogeneous group. It is impossible to find more than one child exactly like another on ANY general measure. The practice of having slow, middle, and bright groups on the thought that such children are *close enough* for teaching purposes is a fiction. Suffice it to say here that irreparable harm has been done children, the least of which is a rather universal dislike of reading.

As far as heterogeneous groupings are concerned, they, too, miss the point, as they, too, are organized on the basis of what children ARE, not what they need to know. What children need to know makes the difference in grouping practice. Yet, if children are grouped on the basis of specific need, such groups are heterogeneous in the extreme. There will be children of widely varying abilities in a thousand (literally) ways. But the point is that they will be identical on one single teachable item. And even that similarity will pass within a few days or hours. To repeat, children may be blue-eyed, pig-tailed, dull, or brilliant. It does not matter. What does matter is that special learning that is needed. In this sense, such a special needs or task group is homogeneous. But such is a far cry from the slow, middle, and bright groups of Bushytails, Robins, and Tigers so prevalent on the current educational scene. Task-grouping must form a central core of instructional practice.

DIRECT AND INDIRECT TEACHING

The matter of teaching groups on the basis of what they need to know cannot be complete without an examination of direct teaching— i.e., teaching that requires the continuing action of the teacher for the duration of the lesson. It is true that Prescott[8] has come to question

---

[8] D. A. Prescott, *The Child in the Educative Process*, New York: McGraw-Hill Book Co., Inc., 1957, p. ix.

whether or not there is such a thing in the traditional sense: "These experiences [i.e., with child study groups of teachers on the inservice level] . . . have forced me to accept the fact that children learn and cannot be "taught" in the usually accepted sense. . . ." He may be right, but that thesis cannot be accepted without discussion. There are too many instances of children and adults learning with eagerness, drinking up knowledge in numerous "direct teaching" situations. Could it be that Prescott worked mostly with teachers who were unskilled in setting up groups on the learning purposes of the child?

"What is Teaching?" and "What is Learning?" are age-old questions that still tie the theorists up in knots. A teacher surely can be said to be teaching when he sets up a situation *within which* pupils learn. There may be directness in the instruction and there may not be. But there are very specific times when direct teaching, in the sense of *showing how*, must take place.

When are we sure of a reasonable chance of the pupil learning? Does this depend upon direct or indirect teaching? No one can learn *for* a child—which fact has saved many a human being in his early years—saved, that is, from some then current idiocy of an educational practice. A child WILL learn what he choses to learn WHEN he chooses to learn it—no matter how much teeth-gnashing takes place on the part of his elders. The whole Progressive Education movement has suffered from the lack of comprehension of this matter of direct teaching, indirect teaching, and the sureness of a child's learning. When, indeed, can teachers be sure what to teach their charges?

Learning takes place most surely when a child knows what he doesn't know because the teacher has isolated a specific. When that is clear, the teacher can go ahead without fear with the most direct kind of teaching. If the teacher does not teach well that which a child wants to know, a great opportunity is lost.

Direct and indirect teaching are connected to the purposes with which children are grouped in a classroom. The situation of a cluster of children coming together spontaneously lends itself mostly to indirect teaching and learning. (Within such an event, however, the teacher may see an opportunity—but that does not change the original statement.) A spontaneous group is usually not the kind of a situation in which children say "Show us" to the teacher, although it can be.

The Role of Self-Choice

The element of pupil self-choice is imperative. Personal commitment does not contradict the need for compulsory attendance in school, nor need it product laissez-faire practice. When a child chooses to learn something, it is not a result of a whim. No one can force a child to learn. A school system has the right to set the patterns of what shall be learned. Within those patterns, which of necessity must be broadly stated, children can be helped to recognize their own needs. Totalitarian societies do this by means of brain-washing. And too few teachers in democratic societies understand how to avoid such persuasion tactics in their classrooms. Grouping that shows children their specific disability is a practice that is basically democratic. The child has a goal. He knows what he needs to do to get there. More importantly, research in self-selection in reading clearly identifies the incentive factor. Children prefer to choose their own books in no uncertain terms.[9]

TEACHABILITY FACTORS

Some groups are easy to teach. Others are difficult. Aside from the personality of the children themselves, their background, their degree of acceptance of the "unchangeables," there are several characteristics over which teachers DO have some control. These characteristics are what are being called "teachability factors," for example:

GROUP MANAGEMENT IS ONE SUCH FACTOR. A group needs a place to sit where it can see the board or the paper that the teacher is using to demonstrate a particular piece of learning. Little children see the board in a distorted way—it is out kilter, so to speak—if they are too low and the writing on the board is high. The sheer arrangement of the physical bodies of the children in relation to communicative factors determine teachability. A group that is so large that it cannot see that which is necessary to see to learn the particulars involved is not a well-managed group.

THE RANGE AND EXTENT OF KNOWLEDGE IS ANOTHER FACTOR. The narrowness of the range of what is to be learned greatly increases the teachability of a group. When a teacher has singled out one item that needs attention by a given group of pupils, it takes very little time to teach it (usually—although there are some items that would require a length of time). In brief, ONE item is easier to teach than several. When the reason for the group is clear cut and specific, it is easier to finish its business. But when the purposes for the group are multiple or amorphous, that group is difficult to teach. The very *amount* to be "covered" is so large as to make it hard to decide how to proceed.

[9] Esther Schatz, *Exploring Elementary Reading in the Elementary School*, Columbus: The Ohio State University, 1960, p. 7; Russell Stauffer, *Individualized and Group-Type Directed Reading Instruction*, Winston Consultant Bulletin C2. New York: Holt, Rinehart & Winston Co., 1961.

Another example might be the necessity to teach a certain six children how to recognize the short vowel sounds "ĭ" and "ĕ" in such words as "let," "lit," "pen," "pin," "tilt," "bend," and the like. The pupils of this group—whatever else they needed to know, whatever might be their achievement scores, whatever might be their I.Q., whatever might be their personal interest in reading—would come together for work on this single item, the short sounds of "ĭ" and "e," and that is all *for that session.*

Another type of group might be several children who wished to read *The Last Horse* by Steiner[10] aloud to each other, and look at Beatien Yazz' illustrations. Another might need the teacher's help in choosing a poem for choric speaking, and then help in deciding who would say the various lines of the poem.

These are ways in which a teacher might separate his class into groups, consecutive or simultaneous. In each case the decision rests on the purpose of the group. The children reading *The Last Horse* do not need the teacher's presence. But the other groups do. They could not be successful *without* the teacher.

In concluding this point, there is no necessity of teaching anything else in a group needing the teacher's direct presence. The specificity, the setting apart of a certain topic, is the heart of teachability. There are no high-ways and by-ways to pursue. The teacher and children say "What are we here for? Let us get on with it!"

GROUPING FOR A PURPOSE

A beginning first-grade teacher noted, during the morning sharing time, that seven of her children showed clear ability to apply the alphabetic principle to the letter "b" in the following experiential material that was dictated by the pupils:

> Our room has a new ball.
> It is a bouncy ball.
> Jim's brother plays baseball.
> Bill has a bat.

That teacher knew that the 25 other children sat without awareness of the letter "b" (although they were aware of other things). But seven clearly did in response to her questions. So those seven were grouped later on. They needed to solidify their knowledge of "b"—its sound in a word, its feel in their mouths as they say it, its looks in many words, its looks anywhere, words that could be *said* that began with "b" or had a "b" in the middle somewhere.

[10] Stan Steiner, *The Last Horse,* New York: Macmillan, 1961.

As the purpose of this group was single, its range was narrow. Both were determined by a single item. No other characteristic did that teacher need to consider. No other characteristic of those seven children *mattered.* And the group was eminently teachable.

Groups Depend On What Is To Be Learned

To repeat, then, the purpose and range of what is to be taught determines how children are to be grouped. *Grouping is a function of curriculum, of what children learn, not what children are.*

As the daily panorama of classroom living unfolds, the teacher will note that usually those groups with the narrowest range tend to be those groups to which he teaches skills. And those groups that have the widest range and scope are those related to the personal interests and purposes of children. In both cases, let it be emphasized, the originating reason for the group is singular, not multiple.

Thus, we are saying that, if what is to be taught is narrow, then that element in each member of the group is narrow. If what is to be taught is wide-ranging, then the members of the group, as far as that element is concerned, can be wide-ranging. In either case, the group purpose matches that which is to be learned on the part of every group member. The trick is to match up child and item to be taught.

The Myth of Flexible Grouping

For decades, even centuries, educators have worked upon "fluid" and "flexible" grouping without coming to grips with the central problem. Fluid or flexible grouping has meant that a teacher must not maintain groups with any kind of permanency. But just telling teachers to change children around a lot has not worked, as Groff has shown.[11] When a group is organized for multiple reasons, its beginning and its ending are fuzzy. Groups that are organized on specific, identifiable items, the starting and stopping points are sharp and definite. Thus the years of trying to help teachers be fluid and flexible as to group membership has simply missed the point. The whole matter lies in the cause of the group organization. This is, WHY group? And better still, why THIS group? What specific learning should these children have that no other children need TODAY? What has the teacher

11 See Patrick Groff, "A Survey of Basal Reading Grouping," *The Reading Teacher,* Vol. 15, No. 4, January, 1962, pp. 232–35, with special reference to Theodore Clymer's evaluation on p. 235.

found in her teaching on one day that needs special attention with certain children on the next? There are thousands of reasons as the months roll on for separation of children into clusters. The most teachable ones are those that are organized with the most highly specific need. The least teachable ones are those whose lesson plan deals with indistinct, broad, generalized subject matter.

Therefore, when are groups BEST organized? How can teachers know these things *for themselves* and not be the servants of someone else's manual?

THE MENTAL HYGIENE OF GROUPING

Why are these principles good? Why are they better than current practice in ability grouping?

In the first place these principles bring into action, within each child, the finest kind, the healthiest and most productive kind, of good feelings about one's self. The needs of the psyche have various names but for the nonpsychological reader let us cite the ones, in our own terms, with which we are concerned:

1. The emotional need for achievement.
2. The emotional need for self-dignity and worth.

When these and other demands of the self are poorly met, children, and adults, too, react in several negative ways:

1. They become sick.
2. They become isolates and have no friends.
3. They become silent and withdrawn.
4. They become angry, hostile, and aggressive.

Without repeating previous points of argument, let it be said that grouping, based on OTHER reasons than ability (in its generalized sense), yields quite *positive* values because there is no degradation of self producing one or more of the above *negative* reactions.

The emotional need for achievement shows that learning in itself is something everyone must do. Not to learn is frustrating. Therefore, it is all right when a person does not know something. What is destructive is when a person is not clear about what it is he does not know. It is destructive to personality when an individual *realizes a job is hopelessly beyond his capabilities*. Thus, let us specifically examine our first principles of grouping from a mental health angle.

The Acceptable Principles of Grouping and Mental Health

These principles allow each to grow at his own pace, and this, in itself, gives the person a sense that his own pace is something of value. Take each principle in turn:

1. GROUPS ARE TO BE ORGANIZED FOR SINGLE HIGHLY SPECIFIC REASONS. The reason for such grouping is definite. There is no confusion. Confusion is destructive. There is only one thing to be accomplished. Doing only one thing is nonconfusing. "Do it and be done with it" is the motto. Such definiteness lends organization to one's world. A well-organized person is, all things being equal, a more healthy, happy, productive person than a poorly organized one. He gets things done. He is useful to society and, people being what they are, he is *praised* for getting things done. People like praise. It makes them feel worthy, of value. In addition, such a principle requires a single element to be common to all group members. Man is by nature gregarious. He does not thus feel isolated in this situation.

2. GROUPS EXIST FOR THE DURATION OF THE GROUP PURPOSE AND NO LONGER. The reasons for organization and disbanding are the same. The sense of achievement is aroused when there is no other reason for being with one's peers than the accomplishment of a certain purpose. No other factor is involved in such grouping. There is, as in the above, no confusion.

3. THE ACTIVITY OF A GROUP AND AMOUNT OF TEACHER HELP IS DETERMINED BY THE REASON FOR WHICH IT WAS SET UP. This is, in effect, the third guarantee that group activity will conform to the original purpose for which it was organized. Thus it is triply important in terms of helping the pupil feel nonconfused, well organized, and purposeful. Nothing else will be "rung in" by the teacher—strengthening the whole activity. There is one thing and one thing only to be done.

4. THE REASON FOR THE GROUP MUST BE CLEARLY UNDERSTOOD BY EACH MEMBER. The pupil, knowing what he does not know, and knowing that it is within his grasp, will reach for it. It is satisfying to learn. It enhances the emotional need for achievement. Man is born with this need. It is his nature to want to know, to want to learn. To prevent learning is to produce boredom or revolt. To have attainable knowledge within reach is a stimulating situation to the human animal. He is born with curiosity. He is tantalized by something he does not know, and particularly so when the unknowable is attainable. Nothing succeeds like success.

5. THE REASON THE GROUP MUST CONSTITUTE A PURPOSE AND A PERSONAL CHALLENGE FOR EACH MEMBER. Again, the need for achievement is enhanced. Not to know is tantalizing, but there are so many hundreds of thousands of things to be learned, how does one choose? With the guidance of the teacher, choices can be made. Of the dozens of groups that should be organized certain ones are a must for each child, depending on his stage of knowledge and development. There could be many that would constitute a challenge. But the one chosen must constitute the challenge, or the needed learning will not occur as fast as possible, or as easily as possible. Challenge is another word for interest. It is the basic motivation for all learning. Without it nothing happens.

6. THE EXACT REASON FOR THE GROUP MUST BE KNOWN TO EACH MEMBER PRIOR TO ITS ORGANIZATION. The need for achievement is enhanced here. It, as has been said, is tantalizing not to know something that is there at hand. Then it follows that a pupil will be highly motivated to learn what he needs to know if he is aware of the exact nature of what he needs to know. The basic question in this principle challenges much current school practice: Do you, or do you not, group children when they do not know the specific reason for which they were put together? This principle insists that children *must* know why they are put together. If they do not, then whole motivational drives are lost, not to mention the decisiveness, the order and nonconfusion so evident in preceding discussion of principles. All is lost without the active cooperation and basic concern of the pupil for what he needs to find out.

SUMMARY

Learning to read is a highly individual and personal process. Yet, when many pupils need to be taught in the same room at the same time, many methods need to be *used* simultaneously. One of the best evidences of a good reading program is the presence of a variety of methods within the same classroom. Although the author of this book believe that individual differences cannot be met without highly personal, private, individual conferences, this is not to say that groups are to be eliminated. Quite the contrary, grouping has a specific use and is enormously valuable. Perhaps, in the total amount of time spent during the formal reading period, half of the period should be used for group activity and the other half in individual conferences.

The best functional teaching of skills occurs when the learner recognizes his need for knowing particular "things." The best source for discovering these needs is in observing the behavior of each child when he is reading, reacting, or performing at something. He, the child, will show the teacher what he needs, if the teacher will but look.

Ever since McGuffey brought forth his first set of graded readers, plans have been suggested and carried out to make education of children function through some form of administrative organization for classifying pupils. But the personal, face-to-face relationship between the teacher and each child will always be the keystone of any teaching-learning situation. And no administrative device can guarantee human friendship. But distance and proximity hinder or help. We count ourselves on the side of proximity.

III

PROGRESSION

AND

DEVELOPMENT

8

THE CHILD VIEWS HIS
PROGRESSION IN LEARNING
TO READ

One way to analyze the way reading comes about is to try to get inside the child and see what happens, as much as is possible, from his point of view. In order to do this, we have set up a series of major bridgeheads somewhat overlapping to be sure, but, in general, running along developmental lines.

The developmental pattern clearly starts with the child's talking with others. It finally arrives at that state of Utopia where he has resolved all manner of technical, operational reading problems, and is reading his way rapidly, voraciously, and happily.

THE TEACHER'S ROLE

With the accent on the stream of consciousness of the child, the teacher enters into the picture as one who encourages, and yet waits for, growth. These stages of development or progressions have great importance to the teacher. When she knows—even if in generalities—the next step that a child might logically be expected to make, then that teacher can help that child reach that step more easily and with less fumbling.

For example, the following statement to a child shows him exactly where he is in his pattern of growth, and what he and his teacher can expect to take place next.

"Now, Jim, when you can find your own words, on the chart stories over there, you can begin to look for them in other places."

If Jim continues to be unable to find his own words on the class chart stories, no harm is done. He still can keep on looking for them while the teacher keeps working to have him give her dictation so that there are more of his words to be found. The day will come when he does spot his own words. Then he can look for them elsewhere—or do any number of other things with them.

These bridgeheads flow from the first hand—to the vicarious—to the abstract. While even very young children are capable of vicarious experience, the more a teacher can proceed from the known to the unknown, or at least the untouchable, the more sure is the progress of the child. Some children may hop, skip, and jump throughout these progressions without seeming to need any instruction whatsoever. Others jump ahead one and then back two, in contradiction to a peer who does just the reverse. Research is very limited about what details are to be expected. But the general patterns are clear.

A child may vocalize vowels before he does consonants. But when he is getting meaning from spoken words, whether they are made up of such letters or not makes no difference. They must have power and meaning for HIM, personally, and no one else. Hence, each child must learn to read the words that are his own. They must have a personal connection to his life. They must express something that produces profound reactions in him. If not, he will take forever to learn to read. And he will hate it.

Teachers Need To Know the Progressions

In effect the knowledge of these general developmental patterns emancipates the teacher from commercial materials produced by writers who are not acquainted with a specific group of children. The teacher who is following the personal needs of his pupils can fit the manuals and workbooks to the ones in his charge. Knowing what to expect from children, even if generalized around a major heading, frees the teacher to search through many manuals and workbooks for what he wants at the time it is needed.

To pick and choose from a variety of materials is much more of a guarantee of meeting the exact and specific needs of pupils than when one piece is followed page by page. Teachers, of course, need to be trained to know what to look for in these kinds of materials, and to fit them to the expressed level of the child as it comes around as discussed earlier. This would be the prime role of the reading specialist, it would seem—to work on the diagnostic skills of teachers rather than the never ending assembly line of children.

Teaching reading, then, is done with the knowledge of a general progression through levels of skills and accomplishments. Children will proceed at their own pace anyway because of or in spite of what a teacher might do. No one can learn for a child. Yet the teacher must know what is reasonable to expect within limits, and do all that is possible to entice children through these stages as rapidly as his health, ability, and adjustment will allow.

We wish the teacher to "get inside" the child's mind as much as possible. We have used the "stream-of-consciousness" technique in hopes that it will make it easier for the reader to think as a child thinks as he learns to read. For this approach it does not matter too much if the teacher is working with single children, those in groups, or the total class. Classroom management is not of immediate concern here, although it can never be entirely discounted.

These progressions are not absolute. There is a gradual process of increasing ability within children. But sometimes the skills needed come according to the following detailed description. Sometimes children will leap over some progressions. Sometimes children will mix all these up together. In general, however, the headings of these progressions provide a reasonably safe road map for the teacher to follow.

Progression Titles

Getting To Know People

Creative Expression and Talking

Seeing, Writing, and Hearing Our Own Words

Moving Into Sentence Recognition

Reading Our Own Sentences

Early Level Word Perception

Moving Into Word Analysis

Word Analysis

Word Analysis Again Becomes Word Perception

Remember that there is no guarantee that every child will proceed along the outlined path. But there is a good chance that he will. These are intended to improve the teacher's hunches as to what will happen next—to each child—regardless of what any other child does, in that class or on the other side of the nation.

GETTING TO KNOW PEOPLE

The child thinks:

1. I hear what people say, and I usually know what they mean.
2. I try to say what I want.
3. I play with my friends.

4. I can look at books.
5. I like to look at pictures in books.
6. I like to make up stories of my own when looking at books.
7. My friends and I can talk together.
8. My teacher (Daddy, Mother) can talk about what I want to talk about.

Getting to know his world.

This series of statements illustrates that this child is in an elementary stage of development as far as verbal communication is concerned. The teacher must take the child and work to loosen the ability to communicate—even one-way communication is a starting point. Taking each statement separately, let us see what is meant.

1. "I HEAR WHAT PEOPLE SAY, AND I USUALLY KNOW WHAT THEY MEAN." This statement expresses an awareness of environment and

what could be called "listening ability." Hearing people and understanding them is part of learning. Children need help in this direction, and teachers will find it helps ease other learning procedures. Understanding others precedes making others understand us.

2. "I TRY TO SAY WHAT I WANT." This child is on the verge of being able to ask for whatever he wants. Undoubtedly he has been doing this at home for some time. But the child in school is not necessarily the same, as concerns asking, as the child at home.

The teacher watches for the chance to get a child started.

"Go ahead, Ethel tell what you want for the party tomorrow."

or

"Tell me, Sue, do you want to play in the doll corner or look at books?"

3. "I PLAY WITH MY FRIENDS." Playing, believe it or not, is directly related to reading in that it is the climate within which a child learns early to communicate with his peers. He has long been talking with his family, but, now in school, he must work to interact with his own classmates. The teacher can help bring about better playing with less fighting, rejection, and more inclusiveness as opposed to exclusion, but she cannot play FOR children.

4. "I CAN LOOK AT BOOKS."

5. "I LIKE TO LOOK AT PICTURES IN BOOKS." How children react to books is the subject of many fine discussions, notably by Larrick,[1] Monroe,[2] and Gesell and Ilg.[3] The squirming delight of children hearing *Make Way for Ducklings* by Robert McCloskey[4] or Margaret Wise Brown's *Goodnight Moon*[5]—nursery rhymes of Mother Goose—making noises of their own as well as the ones in books—all contribute to what has been called "book behavior."

These two statements indicate children need to be near books, to be surrounded by them, all kinds, all shapes, all colors. There must be ample time—and that means an hour or two a day—for free and spontaneous exploration of books in the classroom. The child who pours over books—and, for that matter, colorful magazines, too—is saying, consciously or not, "I am starved for books and their pictures. I need them. I am interested in them." There is no need for artificial

[1] Nancy Larrick, *Parents Guide to Children's Reading*, Garden City, N.Y.: Pocket Books, 1958.

[2] Marion Monroe, *Growing Into Reading*, Chicago: Scott Foresman & Co., 1951.

[3] Arnold Gesell and F. L. Ilg, *Infant and Child In the Culture Today*, New York: Harper Bros., 1949.

[4] Robert McCloskey, *Make Way for Ducklings*, New York: Viking Press, 1941.

[5] Margaret Wise Brown, *Goodnight Moon*, New York: Harper & Row.

and commercial readiness activities here. Just piles of attractive books, and a teacher who encourages their examination and who often reads aloud from many of them, help to begin reading.

6. "I LIKE TO MAKE UP STORIES OF MY OWN WHEN LOOKING AT BOOKS. I TELL STORIES BY SCRIBBLING." This statement shows a child who is on the verge of knowing that books and his own words have some relationship. Books SAY something—and he can approximate whatever it is by grandly mumbling along to himself—telling a story. He may even be "reading" to a friend with great aplomb—neither knowing nor caring that the exact words he is "reading" are not on the pages he is turning.

A teacher noting this kind of behavior can well say something like this:

> You are certainly good at telling stories from that book. Next you will be telling me your own stories. Then I will write them down for you, and then I can teach you to read.

Making up stories of one's own is the necessary step to learning to read by reading. Number 6 above is a step before that magical stage. It is a signal to the teacher that says "Watch this child. Get him talking during the next sharing time. Be sure you write down some of his words and see if he can recognize them."

From babyhood children are exposed to books. They sit side by side with daddys on the davenport. "Read to me, Daddy," over and over again is a refrain in most American homes. In this process of sitting beside Daddy, or Mother, or Grandma, children have a growing awareness that the pages have a kind of magic that Daddy can translate. Another kind of magic occurs, too. A man in the book becomes "Daddy." A truck in the book becomes a real truck that comes down the street. The window in the house is recognizable as a window in the child's house. And the whoops, snorts, and gurgles in *The Noisy Book*[6] by Margaret Wise Brown are noises that the child knows. This transference from book pages to real life is the beginning of awareness that there is symbolic meaning to print, a meaning that can be decoded, that can be READ. Perhaps the child only realizes this vaguely at that time. But it is the stuff upon which the teacher can build when she begins to connect actual speech to print.

A classroom without books is an outright denial of opportunity to children. Many will leap over this book-examining stage right into higher levels of ability. But no matter—the ability to compose from someone else's writings and pictures is latent, nevertheless. To dis-

[6] Margaret Wise Brown, *The Noisy Book*, New York: Harper & Row.

cover that books have ideas—whether or not children "read" the ideas verbatim or not—is crucial to a good start in reading. This whole process requires freedom of exploration and an ample supply of books. There must be many books of many different titles— small, large, thin, fat, and few titles of the same book. Teachers must go on a treasure hunt for books, hound librarians and anyone else who promise such riches. The teacher who says, "No, we will only have basals in this room" is violating not only advice from the basal manual, but also the developmental plan of children in learning to read.

7. "MY FRIENDS AND I CAN TALK TOGETHER."

8. "MY TEACHER [DADDY, MOTHER] CAN TALK ABOUT WHAT I WANT TO TALK ABOUT." These two statements exemplify the way in which human beings important to young children communicate verbally. They *talk together*. Research has shown us repeatedly that the "talking" home produces children who have less trouble with reading than those that come from homes where there is little discussion between older and younger members of the family.[7]

First graders who talk easily with their friends and also with adults on subjects of their own are showing their readiness for the crucial step of dictation. Ideas come from within, and the teacher must work in such a way that there are "legal" talking times, as described in Chapter 9. It is in this sense that the eerily silent classroom damages—*seriously* damages—beginning steps in reading. For that matter, the room that continually rocks with racket and noise is not much help either. There is a happy medium, and teachers can check their own practice by questioning themselves: "Can I hear someone talking to me?" "Is this room tranquil enough so that children want to talk to each other and to me?" "Why do children tell me things? Because they know I want them to talk?—Or because they truly have something to say."

TALKING AND CREATIVE EXPRESSION

The child thinks:

1. We sit together for talking times now.
2. My teacher and I sit alone each day and talk.

[7] The reader is referred to Esther Milner, "A Study of the Relationships Between Reading Readiness in Grade One School Children and Patterns of Parent-child Interaction," *Child Development*, XXLL:95–112, 1951; and Dolores Durkin, "Children Who Read Before Grade One," *The Reading Teacher*, Vol. 61:163, January, 1961, for, detailed discussion on this point.

3. It is not so hard to talk now. I can say a lot.
4. She talks and we talk. She wants us to tell her about ourselves.
5. I draw with my crayons.
6. I paint on the easel.
7. I make things with clay.
8. We all make things and tell our teacher about them.
9. Our teacher writes what we tell about what we have made.

Here we see the child as a part of a class. Sometimes he is alone, sometimes in a group, and sometimes together with everyone. The teacher is getting ready or is anticipating the children's readiness to give dictation. The magic of writing and reading is coming closer to the child's awareness that such symbols are a consciously controlled action.

1. WE SIT TOGETHER FOR TALKING TIMES NOW. To organize such an activity, some kind of ground rules need to be set up. A teacher might say:

"You all have so much to say, and that is fine. But you can't all say it at the same time. Why?"

The children should respond to the effect that no one hears "exactly," as one first grader said, what others say. Then:

"How can we fix it so you can hear exactly what each of you says?"

And so the socializing influence of communication affects the group. They take turns. Whatever fears existed are lessened. Maybe the teacher worked consciously toward this end as:

"Good, John. We all liked it when you told us you had a cat. Next time I expect you will be telling us a big long story about the adventures you had with your cat. O.K.?"

Or maybe the teacher said:

"John, I heard somewhere that _____. Is that right?"

John replies it was.

"Well, tell us about it."

Developing expression is a matter of encouragement and good planning for sufficient talking time. The actual teaching skill involved is not as direct as might be found in other skills. A warm and friendly personality is as important as knowing what to say.

2. MY TEACHER AND I SIT TOGETHER EACH DAY AND TALK. When the class is busy with their drawing, painting, and clay and block

My teacher and I talk.

play, the teacher works with each child, one by one. She calls each to her and engages them in conversation. They must know that this is THEIR time to tell matters of the heart or mind that concern them. The teacher must consciously say to herself:

I must get this child to talk with less and less push from me. That means I must be interested in what he says, even if I am not. It means that I must help him say things so that other children will want to listen to him later. I must help him say things so that he will know that someone cares what he has on his mind.

3. IT IS NOT SO HARD TO TALK NOW. I CAN SAY A LOT. In the personal conversation or in the group assembled, the children should

begin to feel the power of their ability to speak and be heard. Particularly as school can be a too formal and too quiet place, each child must learn the power of his own words, and at the same time acquire the self-discipline to listen to others. But his own language comes first. He must know it is welcomed. He must know that his ideas are acceptable, and that they can lead to the activity we call writing.

Teachers must keep an eye on the audience as children speak. When a class knows that the teacher wants them to talk, sometimes they will merrily go on when not a single person is listening. Part of the skills, then, of speaking is learning to charm the audience. How is this done? A dozen, a hundred, ways. For example:

"Did you notice we all were fascinated by David's story. How can you tell when we are all fascinated?"

So the teacher helps the class analyze the actual facial expressions —"everyone was looking right at him"—"I could see everyone's eyes" —"No one was punching anyone," etc. The quiet of a listening group could be noted, and other evidences mentioned that serve to bring to the speaker's (and others') conscious level of when he is a "spellbinder." Once raised to this level, a child will know, rather instinctively perhaps, how to talk to bring the same situation again. As all good speakers know, this is an enormously satisfying experience. With some people it borders upon addiction! But the development of an awareness of how to hold an audience is very much a skill of communication, and therefore a part of the reading program.

4. SHE TALKS AND WE TALK. SHE WANTS US TO TELL HER SOMETHING. This statement shows another side of the child's awareness of the power of communication. The individual turns outward, so to speak, to involve other persons. Next to the family, a child's teacher is most important. Approval of conversation under these kinds of conditions lays the groundwork for the coming approach to specific reading skills. The flow of language is the necessary beginning of formal reading. In a sense, it is the start of formal reading instruction.

Teachers are leading up, from an informal spontaneous interaction sharing time, to a more formal and structured dictation time. When teachers record dictation, normal speech patterns can interfere. Children must be aware of normal speech before they can give dictation. The slowdown of speech, in order to write what children say, needs to be speeded up to natural levels when read back. The halting, jerky, oral rereading of children can be prevented from this very early starting point.

The necessity of a free give-and-take under a nevertheless structured situation is geared to the need for children to recognize that base of all reading instructions—oral language.

5–9. I DRAW WITH MY CRAYONS. I PAINT ON THE EASEL. I MAKE THINGS AND TELL OUR TEACHER ABOUT THEM. OUR TEACHER WRITES WHAT WE TELL ABOUT WHAT WE HAVE MADE. For years children have probably been "drawing" and "writing" (scribbling) in the sense that they are recording something either in color or with pencil. However, the indeterminate scribbling stages (see Viktor Lowenfeld[8] on the developmental stages of drawing) are only preliminary to the need for representational drawings and eventual writing that we need for the reading program. As words are symbols for experiences, so drawing, painting and clay objects symbolize something for the child. He makes his house, his cat, his Mother, the airplane he saw, the cowboy he saw on T.V. These represent specific things to him—no matter how confusing it might look to anyone else. Whatever the whole gamut of creative experience might be, those with which we are concerned here are the ones that can be *labeled,* or captioned. Labeling leads to reading.

The teacher writes down words upon a real picture, or as a caption of a vivid mental picture. What must happen is the awareness that language has meaning—and writing is language.

Many activities are possible when children have pictures with labels—sentences, phrases, or single words—*that they know.* In fact, the formal reading program can begin right then and there. No fuss. No bother.

"What did you draw?" asks the teacher. "What word do you want today?"
The child tells her.
"Then what do you want me to write on your picture?"
The child tells her.
"That is what that says. Now go ahead and READ it."

Such an interchange will continue into the next progression and necessarily so. The teacher is the good teacher who senses the "teachable moment." To strike while the iron is hot can occur at different times. Should it be when the child watches his teacher write HIS words? Or when he brings up several pictures to a group after they are a day or two old? It doesn't matter. When the teacher says, "Go ahead—read what you just said," is the important thing. Perhaps the sooner after the taking down of the dictation the more certain the learning.

[8] Viktor Lowenfeld, *Creative and Mental Growth* (rev. ed.), New York: Macmillan Co., 1952.

But there is much that can be done before children even try to dictate messages and read them back. That is the story of the next progression.

SEEING, WRITING, HEARING OUR OWN WORDS

The child thinks:

1. Our teacher writes our stories for us.
2. We use our stories to learn words.
3. We use our own words to make stories.
4. We learn about the alphabet.
5. We use the alphabet and our words and make new words.

This is the progression that illustrates how children can be taught to use their own words to learn the sounds of letters of the alphabet. This is the stage at which the child must have a vastly expanded program of *hearing*. He must hear similarities of beginnings of words whether or not he can say the letter that they begin with. He must hear words that rhyme or end with the same letter. He must hear all sorts of sounds so that his ears become a useful tool in teaching him to discriminate between various pitches, or tones, or noises in general. But most particularly must the child begin to recognize that the alphabet is useful when he is trying to hear various letters that are like those in his own words.

This stage is the beginning of phonics. It starts with auditory discrimination and is based SOLELY on the children's own spoken language.

Phonics

No word lists are needed from any other source. When a teacher has developed enough communication skills, or ability to talk, if you will, then there are abundant words—sentences, phrases—to teach ANYTHING required at this level.

No separate drill from phonic charts are needed now—or later. Only the child's spoken language, and the teacher's keen ear for what will help her teach sounds of letters in words.

Beginning phonics must be rooted solidly in the child's own words. They are free. They number into the thousands. They come with every child, bar none. They walk through the door in each body, mind, and mouth.

The stress upon children's own words is not accidental. The reason for it lies in the principle of self-selection. People, by nature, are interested in their own experiences, therefore in the sound of their own voice telling about their own experiences. Thus, there is present an intrinsic, or built-in motivating factor. Children like to deal with their own talk. No need to say: "Here are some words. I want you to say them. Now sit quiet and listen, etc." Children will sit quiet when the teacher is working with their own words. She can show children how a simple matter of talking can develop into a reading skill.

An Example of Using Children's Own Words To Teach Sounds

What follows is an account of how a teacher could go about teaching from an experience story. It begins with a conversation. Comments are inserted in parentheses to instruct the reader as to why the teacher did what she did.

Boy No. 1:	My Daddy works downtown.
Boy No. 2:	So does my Daddy. He drives downtown every day. (Murmur of children chiming in with similar statements about their father's work and where it is located, etc.)
Teacher:	You have been talking about your Daddys' work. I want to show you something. Say these words after me (children repeat):

"Daddy"
"Downtown"
"Day"

Does anyone know anything about Daddy, downtown, day? Do you notice anything? (Comment: The teacher has had all children say these words that begin with a "d." She is not sure which child recognizes that the letter is common to each word. So she asks one quick question as a probe. It takes little time and provides evidence for more advanced stages of teaching.)

No response from children . . .

Teacher:	Never mind. I'll see if I can help you find something. Everyone look at my mouth. (Everyone does and she carefully and distinctly says:) "Daddy!" Now all of you say it.
Children:	Daddy.
Teacher:	Now *start* to say "daddy." Don't say it. START to say it. Let me see how your mouth looks. (Looks over class). Now say another word that feels just the same way.
Several children in succession:	Dog
	Doll
	Diddle—oh hey, diddle.

(Comment: This teacher was successful in helping children say words that begin with a "d." This does not happen always. Let us see what would happen if there was no successful response.)

Teacher:	"Get ready to say "Daddy"—etc."
	(Silence.)
Teacher:	Keep your mouth set to say "daddy." Let me help you find a word you know. I am thinking of a word that begins just like "daddy," but it is what girls play with.
Girl No. 1:	"Doll."
Teacher:	Everyone say "Daddy."
Children:	"Daddy."
Teacher:	Say "doll."
Children:	"Doll."
Teacher:	Get ready to say "doll." Look at my mouth. Is your mouth the same? Try to find another word that is just like it. (Comment: The teacher will keep working until some one or two children respond with a word *of their own* that begins with a "d." She must be sure not to overrun the children's span of attention. Let us see how a teacher might work if a child responds with a completely wrong, i.e., unwanted response.
Teacher:	. . . get ready to say "Daddy."
Child:	"Boy."
Teacher:	No, you don't understand, watch. Say "Daddy." (Child does.) Now, say "boy." (Child does.) Are they the same? Feel your mouth. Can you tell?
Child:	No.
Teacher:	(Using the child's own word) Say "boy" again. (Child does.) Now get your mouth ready to say "boy." Don't say it. Get ready to say it. See my mouth when it is ready to say "boy." Now your mouth is right. See how your lips go? (Demonstrates.) (Comment: Now this teacher could go on to have the child find a word in his own vocabulary that begins with a "b"; or she can go back to the original difficulty of that child with the letter "d." Her own judgment should dictate the decision. Either is acceptable. There may be reason, at times, when the situation is too embarrassing for a child, that it might be wise to change the subject entirely. But some day the teacher will have to help that child cross this bridge of using his own spoken vocabulary to identify similar elements in words).

These examples show teachers working to help children use the alphabet to hear beginning letters. However, there are some children who hear and use *rhyming* words before they use the initial letter. There is no great problem about this. Remember there is no research that clearly shows us whether children hear or see the LEFT side (i.e., the front part, of the word) or the LARGE part (i.e., the rhyming part) of the word first. In any event, it is not crucial which part of the word a child sees.

The important thing is that teachers must work almost entirely with children's own words. They must use sparingly those words that come from some adult's list. The transfer from thought to sym-

bol—from idea to letters—from talk to words written down—comes
about more rapidly with the child's use of his own words.

Our Trip to the Library

Miss Williams showed us around the library. She read two stories to us. Miss Williams let us look at many story books.

Our trip - The Post Office
We saw a big safe where stamps are kept.
We saw a tying machine.
We saw lots of mail and packages

My teacher writes what we say.

MOVING INTO SENTENCE RECOGNITION

The child thinks:

1. My teacher sometimes writes those words we say so we can see the parts that are alike.
2. I can say all of the alphabet looking at it or not.
3. I can write my own name, and copy other words for my pictures.
4. My teacher writes what we say.

5. Sometimes she writes one word, and other times she writes a lot.
6. I know my own words when she writes them.
7. I know what I said so I know what she writes.
8. I am looking at books that have nice pictures in them.
9. My teacher says soon I will be reading some books.

This progression shows how sight builds upon hearing. First a child speaks and is taught to listen to certain things about his speech. Now the speech is turning into something that must be seen. From hearing and speaking to seeing and hearing, as drawn in the formula, is this stage of development.

Teacher taking of pupil dictation is beginning to come into full flower. This stage is crucial if the bridge between talking and reading is to be made. Therefore it is important that the most exciting, the most thrilling of children's experiences be the ones recorded—nothing trivial, and nothing that is unrelated to a child's life. The incentive to learn is even more strongly bound up in the pupil's recital of events important to him. To drill on a list of words from someone's sight vocabulary is to retard children's drive to read. Children learn to read from reading, and their own words are first.

1. MY TEACHER SOMETIMES WRITES THOSE WORDS WE SAY SO WE CAN SEE THE PARTS THAT ARE ALIKE. This statement connects directly to the preceding discussion of letter sounds and rhyming words. To listening is added vision, or seeing, whatever element is to be noted. For example:

The talking has been about the work of "Daddies" and their place of business. The teacher has been able to get children to find words that start alike. We take up from that point. (See pages 219–20.)

> *Several children in succession:*
> "Dog"
> "Doll"
> "Diddle"—oh, hey, diddle, diddle.
> *Teacher:* Yes, those words all begin with a "d." Let me write them down
> for you to look at. (Writes on easel or chalkboard.
> dog
> doll
> diddle
> all in a row so that the "d"s are all under each other.) See these
> words. Can you show me the part that is alike?
> (Comment: It may well be that no child can focus on such a small
> element as one letter in a word, even if they are all written in a
> line to make it easier. But there *might* be one child who can find
> the letter "d" in each word and show it to all. This signals the
> teacher that this child is further ahead in his development than
> those who cannot isolate a letter within a word. Therefore, that

teacher must be sure that that child proceeds at his own rate and is not held back by his less mature peers. He must be grouped with others who reveal the same signal, if any, or he must be worked with alone during an independent work period when the rest of the class is busy. The teacher proceeds with the probing in such a way that the "ready" children show up.)

Changing from sight recognition to beginning letters to rhyming words, let us continue.

Girl No. 1:   Ball-fall. I fell down yesterday.
Girl No. 2:   Ball-tall.
Teacher: Fine for you. Those words do rhyme. Let me write them on the board. (Writes down in a row—saying each word as she puts it down.)

> ball
> fall
> tall

Now can anyone show me something about these words that is alike? (Comment: Again it may be that there would be no one in the class that recognizes the similarities of these endings. The teacher accepts this. She knows, then, that she must continue to work at hearing until she gets the beginning signals from those children who can SEE the similarities and show where they are. As before with single letters, such children must not be held back but grouped with others, if any, for more practice in identifying similarities in other words from their own dictation. Nevertheless, the teacher leads children on, whether or not one child is revealed as advanced. The teacher need not be repetitive with the rhyme of "all" in order to give practice at this developmental level—as there are numerous other rhymes available. In short, a class need for practice at a certain level (in this case, rhyming) should not require boredom with the drill on the same *words*—but can be vital and interesting doing the same *activity*, with different words. The teacher simply records another experience.)

2. I CAN SAY ALL OF THE ALPHABET LOOKING AT IT OR NOT. This statement illustrates that the teacher is about to tie the sight of the letters in the alphabet to their sounds in words. Children who are able to hear that "dog," "doll," and "diddle" all sound alike when they start to say them must move next to recognizing that that similar sound is a part of their alphabet.

Knowledge of the alphabet is necessary. They must be able to say it—even a sing-song style is useful for instructional purposes. This is not to say that each letter must be recognized at this time on a one-to-one basis. But the transfer of the *feel* of certain letters to the mouth and their sound on the ear to their sight in words begins here.

Thus all children must be taught to say the alphabet early. It is a helpful, useful thing to know. Educators, the writer included, have not always seen how valuable such an activity might be. But it is valuable simply because names of letters and sounds of letters are enough alike to serve the beginning reader (and writer).

3. I CAN WRITE MY OWN NAME, AND COPY OTHER WORDS FOR MY PICTURES.

4. MY TEACHER WRITES WHAT WE SAY.

5. SOMETIMES SHE WRITES ONE WORD AND OTHER TIMES SHE WRITES A LOT.

6. I KNOW MY OWN WORDS WHEN SHE WRITES THEM.

7. I KNOW WHAT I SAID SO I KNOW WHAT SHE WRITES. Writing is the other side of the coin of reading. It is a necessity for reading. When children know what words they have said because they watched the teacher write them, they need little drill on those words. Sylvia Ashton-Warner calls them "one-look" words and summarily throws away those words children do not remember instantly. We can be grateful for the guidance she has given in her book *Teacher*.[9] In short, she works with children to have them tell her those words that have power to the child. She found words that relate to "Sex" and "Fear" most powerful, hence useful.

As children come to her, one by one in the beginning of their work period, she involves them in conversation. Soon she asks what word they want for that day. They reply with some word power-packed for them—"Jet," "Snake," etc. She then *writes that word on a large cardboard*. The child repeats it as she writes, and then takes that precious piece of cardboard to do with as he wishes, although first he must say the word and trace the letters with his finger, in a practice reminiscent of Montessori. Then he uses it in creative writing or in games, or whatever he wishes. But later on each child brings his word card to his teacher to see if he still remembers it. If the word is loaded enough with emotion and life force, he knows it from that time on. Or if it is a pallid word, he forgets it and it is thrown away.

Whether a teacher follows the highly exciting and satisfying regime of Ashton-Warner, or has one of her own that merits her loyalty, children will need to write what they have said and read back if they are to learn to read easily and with little drudgery.

Children must write their own words frequently for their own reasons. Connecting what they want to say and what they actually put down is a vital bridge to the world of books. We have already mentioned the "scribble story" of the preschooler who cannot even write his name. This is a rudimentary and important step in learning to

9 Sylvia Ashton-Warner, *Teacher*, New York: Simon & Schuster, Inc., 1963.

read and write. There is magic to one's own name, as many psychologists have pointed out. There is magic in one's own words as we stated earlier. It helps a child straighten out the "big, buzzing, booming confusion" that is his world. When he names himself or an object, it takes its place in the realm of reality for him. He can control his world when he can name it.

Copying words on pictures is clearly portrayed in the motion picture "Skippy and the Three R's"[10] when Skippy is helped to write "bicycle" on his picture of the bike that he saw. The more dramatic the material, as this picture well shows, the faster, the more certain the learning. Often, when educators insist that children follow their own basic interests in their life, lay people feel that this pampers the child, and so prepares him badly for adulthood. But the old saying "You can bring a horse to water, but you can't make him drink" illustrates why educators use pupil interests. They simply serve to guarantee more and better learning. That is all there is to it.

To continue, the copying of sentences, phrases, or words on a picture sets in motion beginning skills in word recognition, particularly the acquisition of a sight vocabulary. Children must come to appreciate what other people have written, too. The best way to foster such appreciation is a realization of the function that one's own words serve.

8. I AM LOOKING AT BOOKS THAT HAVE NICE PICTURES IN THEM.

9. MY TEACHER SAYS SOON I WILL BE READING IN BOOKS. Reading in the sense of looking at books has been going on since babyhood. Children's delight in books has pulled them toward them long before they entered school. These statements indicate an on-going awareness of the place of books in the child's scheme of things. He likes them. He looks at them much of the time.

Most children come to school having been read to at home. Most parents teach their youngsters nursery ryhmes. Most parents, if not actually book lovers themselves, nevertheless, rarely are book *haters*. In these blessed days of the supermarket book rack of inexpensive books—sold into the millions—we find parents arguing their children OUT of candy in favor of books.

Work should be vital, dynamic and satisfying. When work is ugly and harsh in school it defeats the purpose of school—i.e., to learn. The library corner must be wide open to all comers and be part of the on-going "work" and therefore part of the on-going learning. Teachers must always "permit" children to read books.

[10] "Skippy and the Three R's" (film), National Education Association, Washington, D.C.

These statements reflect the child's awareness that he can probably find something if he looks. He is ready or he soon will be ready to read in books, which, of course, is reading in the child's, perhaps the true, sense of the word.

READING OUR OWN SENTENCES

The child thinks:

1. I can find my own words in our stories.
2. I can read the lines.
3. I can read them when I can remember what we were talking about when my teacher wrote the story.
4. If I forget what we were talking about, sometimes I can find words that I know that help me remember.
5. I can write the words that I can read in letters, in my own stories, in captions for my pictures.
6. I can find my words in books.
7. I want to write my own stories.

This progression presents an over all picture of the child's development from hearing or listening skills to the identification of ideas of his own that have been written. Although he is still largely in the stage of seeing whole lines, the Gestalt is breaking down and he is beginning to find words as signposts to meaning of those lines. The child's own choice of words makes his own road map, so to speak, to guide him through the new land of written language.

While his vision is sharpening and he can spot greater detail than ever before, the dominant feature of his reading ability at this level is his security in knowing that a single line—or sentence or phonological unit—is a single unit of thought. A whole story may be more definite than a peculiarly shaped blob of hieroglyphics, but he is beginning to seek out lines—words as a matter of challenge and self-achievement.

In addition, this stage illustrates the skill of writing becomes the companion skill of reading. While a child develops his reading through his own language, he must begin to move into the world of books in the sense of finding IDEAS in the world of books. We see here the onset of vicarious learning. No one will get very far in learning to read if he is always bound to his own thinking. The first move away from that which signifies absorption with self is not only to seek and enjoy books but also to begin to write down one's own ideas as a major step in the appreciation of ideas of others. First-hand learning is fine as far as it goes. First-hand learning always will have unique uses at all levels of learning. But if we never move into the vicarious, the world will be narrow indeed.

Breakthrough in Writing

Somewhere, sometime in these stages will come the evidence that all teachers should work for. The child has been watching his teacher write what he says. He has been copying from his own dictation, from others' dictation, from stories his teacher has written about the happenings of importance. Eventually will come the well-known request. "I want to do it myself."

When the teacher hears that hoped-for phrase, she should react with delight and approval, bustle about making sure the child's efforts will not peter out after a word or two, and pridefully send him to his seat to write—at last—on his own, really his own.

Finally, this stage represents the increasing complexity of the recorded experiences. If sentences are coming into their own as whole thoughts, then stories, written as charts or as typed personal sheets, can be longer and can begin to assume the more usual paragraph form. Lines will not always have to begin at the extreme left-hand side of the page regardless of where the previous sentence ended. Some can begin where the previous one left off. The return eye-sweep for a two-line sentence can be expected to be started, particularly with the teacher's guiding, moving hand, and perhaps even be mastered.

EARLY LEVEL WORD PERCEPTION

1. I can read my own stories, letters, labels (etc.).
2. I know lots of words.
3. I can read when my words are the same as some other children's words.
4. I can read my words when they are in other children's stories (etc.).
5. I know some words no matter where I see them—in books, on the street, on television, in stores, lots of places.
6. I can write any word I see.
7. I can read a lot of words that I can write if I know what they are when I write them.
8. I know some words because they are bigger or smaller than other words.

This progression finds the child in the full flower of word recognition. He has no trouble in spotting words in a sentence. He takes delight in finding words wherever he may. The commercials in television have not, as yet, been adequately assessed as to their role in developing sight words, but it seems safe to say that they have a powerful effect, if parents and other observers of young viewers are to be believed. The connection of such specific written parts of language to the environment is proceeding rapidly. "That says 'Harbor Lane.'" said a six year old, firmly pointing to the street sign of his own street. "Yes" said his aunt, "and if you keep looking you will be able to read the street signs of all the streets that you know. When you find one you don't know, you will ask—and then you will know these, too."

Writing is proceeding strongly along the lines noted in the preceding progression. Not only does the children's authorship of books come with more pages, but each page has a longer message. More importantly, the increased resourcefulness of children to find words they need to know has sharpened their powers of observation and all that that means for reading skills.

What is happening on this more advanced level of word recognition?

Visual discrimination is now taking precedence—for the first time—over auditory and speech or articulation discrimination. This tendency will never regress unless trauma of some kind occurs. Vision becomes the means by which a reader improves his reading. He will seek help from sounding, yes, but it is becoming automatic and it is no longer dominant. Listening to one's own speech has served its purpose.

Building of the stock of sight words is also approaching its peak. Just as one forgets faces and names when introduced to too many people, so do children forget the words they know when they must rely on memory alone. When the stock of sight words nears the figure of 75—and that is approximate—the Gestalt of seeing whole words begins to break down into seeing parts, i.e., letters. Just as whole lines of experience stories broke down into separate words, so this process continues to even smaller units. The child is fast approaching his final breakdown stage of seeing details.

MOVING INTO WORD ANALYSIS

The child thinks:

1. There are so many words I know that I can't remember them all.
2. I can see that some words begin like other words. I can see and name the beginning letters.

3. I can see that some words have different beginnings even though they have the same endings.

4. I can think of words that begin with the same letters.

5. I can see some little words in bigger words and parts of words sometimes.

6. I know that words I write have letters in them. I know the different letters.

7. I watch my teacher make stories with words, and she does it with writing letters, one after another.

8. I know what those letters sound like in words. I can skip around the alphabet.

9. I am reading books now with longer stories in them.

This progression embodies the first clear breakup of a word into its parts, syllables, and letters. The ability to read independently has passed the point where it can be done solely by sight vocabulary. We have come to the peak level of the "whole-word method." The child needs instruction at this point to help him learn how to apply, independently, the principles of sounding that he should have been aware of since the very first days of dictating stories. If he is not helped at this stage, he will develop his own methods of word analysis. Whether or not his methods are effective, and to what degree they are effective, depends, of course, upon sheer accident. A child may stumble on a homemade system that works for him in reading, but could leave him greatly handicapped in spelling later on.

The Progession of Word Analysis in Capsule Form

Taking the statements that follow one by one will show a systematic and sequential progression for the individual. First, an outline of what these steps are:

1. The stock of sight words is so abundant that he can no longer remember them all and is found to have forgotten words he once knew.

2. He begins to identify the left side of the word—the initial letter— and can begin to set up a one-to-one relationship when looking at and saying the alphabet.

3. He can identify words in families, or words that rhyme, and syllables.

4. He can now master the art of "substitution."

5. Parts of words in the form of small sight words and syllables become apparent.

6. He recognizes that words are made up of letters that he can find in the alphabet.
7. He observes the writing of his teacher and sees, in a precise way, that writing is done letter by letter.
8. He is able to proceed to sound out those first initial letters without help. Auditory discrimination training begins to pay off. Hearing and seeing each letter becomes possible.
9. More and more books can now be read. He moves into more numerous and more difficult books, and is ready to begin individual conferences.

This above outline sketches the message of this section.

The stage provides one of the most important signals that children can give their teacher.

Right-handed children see more naturally from left to right. Left-handed children go more naturally in the opposite direction and need to be taught more directly that western society does most things from left to right. This kind of retraining is not difficult, as most left handers will attest. But, above all, the teacher must be sure that the line of direction of left-to-rightness is automatic or nearly so. When this does become automatic and the number of sight words climbs to near 75, the first part of the word a child will see is its left side—the initial letter, whatever it may be. The eyes, prior to this development, tend to see only large masses because they look straight ahead and converge in the distance. The ability to focus on small, near objects was thus limited.

The Technique of Spontaneous Response Protects Child

We spoke earlier about "conditioned aversions" in terms of hearing and seeing. No child will violate his own development unless highly motivated to do so. No child needs to violate his own development if the teacher knows how to maintain progress by means of the technique of spontaneous response. This is a term that can be applied when children have the right to respond to the teacher's question *in their own terms*. Of course, those who are most ready, or the most verbal, or the most mature will respond first. Those not yet ready will simply sit—maybe interested spectators—but not yet seeing what it is all about. A teacher must learn to run his classroom so that this kind of choice is all right. To volunteer or to sit during the talking time is a pupil's decision. But the method of spontaneous response comes from "open-ended" questions. Here is an example of spontaneous response in action.

The children are discussing the hurricane. The teacher has used the words to teach sounding, to build sight vocabulary and the like. She has worked rather specifically in probing to teach the sound of the letter "H" in "hurricane, hard and had." It was the letter "H" that was her concern. Now is the time to throw out a provocative open-ended question. She knows it could have a *different* answer from each child. She says something like this: To produce spontaneity in the reaction, still keeping control of the talking, she says:

"Now I would like to see what you can see without my showing you. Look at that story. Tell me anything about the words in it that you notice."

The children look. Maybe nothing happens at first, but under probing questions that are *still* open-ended such as: "Are there any words alike?" "Do you see two words that have something alike?" etc., some child will recognize some initial letter. He may say: "Hey, that word starts like my name!" or "Look, 'wind' and 'went' start just alike," or some similar response.

Using Resources for Teaching Letter Sounds

Once a teacher has discovered that the particular item that the class or group or child needs to know, he may use any material available to teach that item. For example, a teacher finds that a group needs to work on the letter "S" while rereading a dictated story. After using the *original* words that began with the letter "S" the teacher may turn to any list, or workbook, or exercise that reinforces that item, the letter "S." This principle works whenever a teacher finds he must teach something to a class. At later stages he might uncover the need for teaching plurals of words. So he proceeds by using first the situation in which the need appeared, and then anything else that will further the learning of plurals no matter where it may be found. As in a detective story, the teacher gets his clue. It comes from some spontaneous language situation and is expanded to resolve the total problem.

All of the letters of the alphabet must be taught in words whose origin is in the dictated material that the teacher records. Probably all letters—at least as they appear as first letters in a word—can be taught within a very few weeks of the opening of the first grade.[11] By midyear most of the children should be moving into more complex developmental stages.

As a craftsman has a built-in interest in others performing his same craft, so does the child, in his dawning consciousness of the role that letters perform to make words, become fascinated to watch his teacher—hopefully the best craftsman of the schoolroom. In this level we can see the pay-off to the stress on the oral memory of the alphabet. Whereas formerly the saying of letter sounds was done by

[11] Z and X might be difficult and if *needed* (how often are "z" and "x" needed?) can be discovered by use of non-experiential material—movies, photographs of zoos— zebras, xylophones, x-rays, and the like.

the oral repetition of words containing similar letter sounds, now a one-to-one sight relationship between the sound of a letter and what it looks like in the alphabet becomes apparent. The child comes to a precise awareness of the fact that letters make words.

9. I AM READING BOOKS NOW WITH LONGER STORIES IN THEM. The transition of sight vocabulary is proceeding rapidly. He finds that the teacher told him correctly that words he knew from experience stories are also to be found in any number of books. He senses the triumph of independence and is glorying in his ability to read in more and more difficult books, even though he—to others—has hardly progressed out of the primer level (whatever that is).

This statement is the child's awareness of his own reading progress and his ability to read independently. This is when the teacher must arrange the schedule to set up individual conferences for such children.

We move to the final stage, now, of word analysis. We are, in short, on the home stretch.

WORD ANALYSIS

The child thinks:

1. I can read better from anything anywhere, books, television, etc.
2. There are still some words that I don't know, of course, but not so many, etc.
3. I can figure out those words I don't know by first looking at their beginnings.
4. I can figure out a word I don't know by looking to see what it rhymes with.
5. Sometimes I just need to work out the first part of the word and I can guess the rest of it.
6. Pictures and other things help me recognize words.
7. You don't need to know every word in a good story.
8. If I still can't figure out the word, I look at the middle of it.
9. I figure out what the vowel (vowels) sound like.
10. Then I put the front of the word on the vowel sound, and, if I need to, the end of the word. Then I know what it is.
11. Small words and syllables are easier to find now when I am stuck on a word that has them in it.

Here we see the child in the most analytical stage he will ever know. He is being forced to break down—to disintegrate words—in order to put them together in meaningful form. Never again in his life will he need to be so piecemeal about his reading. The method by which he breaks things down and puts them back together is what we have called word analysis. But he needs only clues to get him started. A single clue may unlock a large word for him. He need do nothing further but go on with his reading once he has put that word, just discovered, back into a meaningful context.

There is the sequence of word analysis here—and a possible series of steps can be seen. But whether or not each child must go through each step is not known. The logic of the progression indicates that something of the sort must take place.

The pupil is getting ready, then, to move into the adult stage of reading, not unlike the sight vocabulary stage in that the eye sweeps magnificently along a line. But there is one major difference. In the sight-word stage the child has no way of pulling himself through material that stumps him, when the contextual or other clues failed. Now the child is almost truly independent, and has resources at his command. He has a way to unlock words. If he gets stuck, all is not lost. He is ready for increasingly difficult material on ever widening circles.

One first grader told her teacher how she worked out words she did not know, as follows: "Look to see how it begins. Look all-l-l-l across it to see what other word it looks like. Then read the sentence, and if what you *think* it *is* fits in, that's *what* it is!" A better definition of analyzing a word without forgetting contextual clues can hardly be found.

1. I CAN READ BETTER FROM ANYTHING ANYWHERE—BOOKS, TELE-VISION, ETC.

2. THERE ARE STILL SOME WORDS THAT I DO NOT KNOW, OF COURSE, BUT NOT SO MANY. These two statements show that the child is moving into a higher level of reading. The heady sense of power stems from his increasing ability. He has begun to fall in love with reading—and could even be considered a compulsive reader. That is, it is now so satisfying for him to recognize words wherever he meets them, that he seeks out words—on billboards, on labels on trucks, on appliances in his home, in comic books, on television commercials, if not actually in programs themselves. He is revealing his fascination with learning. The hen tracks, the hieroglyphics, those marks, now carry meaning.

He is quite accepting, however, that he is not "over the hump." He still needs help and is willing to find it. But he sees the end—i.e., he sees the day when he can be completely independent of anyone's help. He is moving toward being his own master, at least as far as reading is concerned.

Because he is aware that he still has some rough edges to be honed down before that state of bliss arrives, he searches more and more for clues that will aid his growing power. The mere fact that he has come so far, in itself, is an incentive. He will clutch at suggestions and helps if they hold the future promise of putting him on his own. Psychologically, he has tasted the sweet wine of achievement and it is good. There may be pitfalls ahead. But his push toward independence, self-reliance, is now indomitable. He is in a marvelously teachable frame of mind. The logistics of word analysis are no bugbear. He is ready to become an expert in this business of reading, and the cumbersome details that may block the way will be mastered—just as other blocks have already been surmounted.

Statement Nos. 3 to 11 follow a pattern that can be presented in an overall form that may simplify the teaching of word analysis as far as reading (not writing) is concerned—if the reader will realize that there are patterns of word analysis that hitch to the concept of Gestalt seeing wholes. In short, when children look at words they probably see them in smaller and smaller parts—*starting from the outside in.* That is, the child will see as follows (see also page 387):

1. Beginnings of words
   a. Beginning letters (consonants or vowels).
   b. Beginning blends or digraphs.
2. The rest or remaining portion of the word (i.e., the ENDS of them)
   a. Rhyming words.
   b. Families of words.
   c. Everything except the beginning in No. 1 above.
3. The middle of words
   a. All vowels short and long, diphthongs, "r" rules, etc.
   b. All syllables or helpful small words.
   c. Prefixes and suffixes and other helpful signposts.

With this general pattern in mind the teacher can simplify his teaching to a large degree. For example, it does not matter how a child proceeds *within* each of the above three stages. A child will usually proceed from the front OR the back of the word he needs to work out. The last and most complicated step is the analysis of the middles of our English words. Keeping three major bridgeheads is simpler than worrying children through a long series of a dozen or more steps, particularly when those steps fall so easily into an overall pattern.

Word Analysis Becomes Word Perception

1. Now I am reading faster than ever.
2. There are many books that I can read.
3. I am finding out about many things from books.
4. I am learning more about myself from my reading.
5. I like to read more than ever.

This stage, as can be seen, includes the increasing ability to enjoy and benefit from reading. It is the rapid reading stage. It is the stage where children devour books with great enthusiasm. In this stage the insurance for a lifetime habit of liking to read is finally paid up. The learning-to-read difficulties are largely past. Interpretation of material, rather than the mechanics of reading it, bothers the most. The pupil that has come this far with few diversions, as the saying goes, has it made. He not only can read—he does read.

SUMMARY

The purpose of this chapter is to help teachers see inside a child's mind as he learns to read. By using the "stream of consciousness" technique, even though the progressions listed are not intended to be arbitrary, it is hoped that teachers will gain more insight into the workings of a child's mind.

As important as the unusual point of view presented is the suggestion that a child, marooned on a given level or stage, need not be doomed to repetition of assigned material as is so often the case in basal programs. Rather such a child can have an infinite variety of material used, all at the same level, until he finds his way toward more advanced levels.

9

BEGINNING READING

GETTING READING STARTED

Children learn to read by reading. Not by drilling on words in hopes they will be recognized later. Not by playing games that supposedly develop some kind of skill. Nor by doing exercises that are supposed to transfer into some kind of reading skill at a later date. No. Children learn to read by reading. They learn to read their own language that they bring to school.

The major task of the teacher of beginning reading is to help children realize that the language they speak is the language that can be written, and then read back. It is language that changes a child from a human animal into a social being. He learns to be human through talking.

Reading has intrinsic value in itself. It does not need any other kind of motivation beyond the satisfaction that comes from gaining meaning from printed symbols—the "hen-tracks"—the hieroglyphics that we call sentences, phrases, words. Reading does not need artificial gloss to make it attractive. It is good enough by itself to attract. To put any other reward upon it is to deny the basic concept of reading.

Reading is also, of course, the *seeing* of sentences and words in order to gain their meaning. But merely looking at words does not guarantee that they have been understood. The connection between speech and writing is crucial to reading growth. The fastest, most efficient way, and, in the opinion of this text, by far the BEST way to teach beginning reading is to show how talking can be turned into writing and then read back. All the necessary reading skills can be taught through this process. In fact, the teaching of skills can be greatly simplified when reading is taught by these means. Some call the approach the "language-experience" approach. We are not so concerned with labels as we are what happens to children.

The reader who is looking for ways to use commercial readiness programs and other articial and extrinsic modes of teaching beginning reading will not find it here. Their value is questionable at best. The most important reason why these commercial programs fail is that they deny the most fundamental linguistic law of all—the priority of spoken language. Children speak and talk before they read or write. Therefore the shortcut to reading is through their own speaking and listening. Why use materials based upon the language of a mythical set of children? Although it is true that some words in the reading readiness books and pre-primers are the same words as some of the children commonly use, they are supplied in situations that are different from the life experiences of the particular class. As they are about *fictitious* children, a real child will tend to block out when he tries to identify his own spoken language in that written form. As one first grader said, "I don't catch."

Using Oral Language in Reading Instruction

The language that children bring to school is of more than a little importance. *It is the best material that the teacher has to use.* It contains every important pattern of structure that is found in adult language. It is never the same, but has flexibility and variety. It carries its own high level of interest with it because it expresses the most dramatic, organic element of every person—his own life. It is an emotional reservoir that can be made the most powerful instrument for learning a teacher could find.

The progressions in the process of learning to read hold infinite possibilities for classroom activity. Problems that arise, as they will, can arise at any level, and any *level* can be taught at any age. Adult illiterates should be taught in similar fashion to the approach that we will describe for children. There is an unrolling panorama of skill development that moves and shifts in peaks, valleys, and plateaus. There is only general progress. There is much "backing up to go ahead." None of the development can easily be pinpointed *as to age level* even in the best of adjusted children. There is a system of development that does follow a sequence, but only in the broadest and most generalized terms. Teachers can predict *what* might happen next to a given pupil—but there is no guarantee that it *will* happen nor *when* it will happen.

Progression of Communication

Talking, as we have tried to indicate, is a learned skill. The level of expression is truly a mark of the excellence of the training in talk-

Trips.

ing, in spite of the variations in children. But the following scale from Monroe[1] allows for the talented talkers to proceed at a more rapid rate, and to higher levels of communication. Children are never consistently at one level, but vary according to their mood, the friendliness of the adults with them, their state of well-being and other similar factors. Variations are to be expected. For teachers, though, to have some indication of *what to expect* is to help them listen to their pupil's talking with better understanding of the child himself. We quote:

> Level 1. *The child does not respond until encouraged.* Adult encouragement to talk is met with embarrassed squirms and

[1] Marion Monroe, *Growing Into Reading,* Chicago: Scott, Foresman, and Co., 1951, p. 77.

People.

will respond only when urged, and then with a single remark.

Level 2. *The child responds with one or more spontaneous remarks
but cannot continue.* This child may blurt out a comment,
relevant or not, without being especially invited to talk, but
cannot continue in spite of further encouragement.

Level 3. *The child responds with one or more spontaneous remarks
and continues with another remark or two when requested.*
This child is not a compulsive talker demanding the adult's
attention nor can he be considered a withdrawn or quiet individual. Probably he talks when HE wants to, rather than
waiting to be invited.

Level 4. *The child responds freely, continues when requested, and is highly productive.* This is the child who enjoys communicating with his adult world. He has learned the satisfaction of expressing ideas, and delights in exploring them. He loves to talk and enjoys anyone who will listen.

Level 5. *The child's responses are at Level 3 or 4, but he includes the teacher in a conversational manner.* This is a child who loves interchange. He is so accustomed to it that he feels natural in involving adults in a conversation. In fact, it is hard for an adult to avoid the conversation. The give and take is easy and unforced.

Fostering Progress in the Beginning

The teacher who sees reading instruction as a sequential development that must—at one and the same time—be encouraged and yet waited for is the teacher who can learn to meet individual differences in pupils. Reading progress must be waited for, it is true. But our lack of knowledge as to the exact stage of development, or more accurately, the exact details of the development often finds teachers waiting for something that has already happened! There is much that can be done to *encourage* development. A teacher only wastes time if he tries to go further than the human organism is ready to go. He cannot build what is not yet there. But he can help bring to a conscious level existing abilities.

The use of mechanical and artificial means of development is wasted energy. Our purpose here is to present patterns of classroom activity that will set in motion the most exciting of all learning—gaining meaning from the printed word.

We present these patterns in a rough sequence. Quite obviously, the first item on the agenda of a teacher of beginning reading is to explore the speech—the linguistic experience and proficiency—of pupils. In brief, teachers must begin to teach reading by encouraging pupil-talking.

Group Size and the Flow of Conversation

Size of a class in its relation to communication cannot be ignored. Sometimes the whole class sits together to begin its day and talk over problems, make plans, and share the overnight happenings that are of interest.

On the other hand, there are times when the whole class together intimidates the shy, or, in any event, dampens their urge to enter into the discussion. Also, as the whole class involves many children, the sheer number of contributions can prevent getting around to all who wish to say something, or to react to that which has been said. In these types of situations the teacher would be well advised to meet the class in groups—on whatever basis might be appropriate. With smaller numbers more can enter into the conversation.

Finally, if conversation is to be important, the teacher will need to meet daily with as many individuals as possible. As Sylvia Ashton-Warner points out, "It's the conversation that has to be got."[2] She describes an activity during which her pupils are working with each other with their word cards while she calls one after the other to her individually to push their horizons in word recognition—or, as she calls it, the Key Vocabulary.

There can be single, group, or total class interaction. But let us begin with whole class activity.

READING BEGINS WITH TALKING TIMES

This activity is variously known as "Sharing Times," or "Show and Tell" and other titles. What it is called is not as important as what happens in the activity itself. We are referring here to an instructional pattern. The informal conversation of children and teacher during the school day is not, at the moment, our concern. This is a discussion of a regularized, scheduled, organized time to talk involving the whole class, and occasionally a smaller group.

Exploring Ideas Together

The overall content of the talking must have real impact and interest to the total group. Usually this means that the topics come from the children themselves, but does not mean that the teacher must be a blank-minded observer. The role of the teacher is to pick up on the topics the children begin and further their knowledge. Topics are literally endless and only limited by the experiences of the children themselves. As we noted in the individual conference, the teacher should see how far, or how widely, he can take the discussion.

From any one of the topics suggested, the use of free association can push a class down many avenues of exploration. Just following a single word, or a single idea, is useful. See what happens when we take the word "paper," for example: See where "paper" can take you!

"Paper"   pencil-writing-pen-typewriter-ink-ball point-letters-post office-U.S.A.-Washington, D. C.-the President-etc.

[2] *Teacher,* Simon & Schuster, Inc., 1963, p. 35.

"Paper" news-newspaper-reporter-television-announcer-radio-broadcast-Telstar-
         space-space men-rockets-moon-etc.
"Paper" papyrus-Egypt-Nile-bull rushes-Moses-Biblical times-history-etc.

These three examples do not even begin to exhaust the possibilities
of the one word "paper."

With this kind of free-swinging open-endedness, it is quite normal
for some children to talk too much and some to be withdrawn. Managing these differences is not difficult, when the teacher keeps a
weather-eye out to shush the frequent talkers and encourages the
shy. The teacher cannot abdicate as chairman. He must act.

"The World Is So Full. . . ."

Teachers can move children ahead in communication to the limit
of their potential. The teacher encourages interaction, but also other

The world is so full of interesting things.

things. They walk around the block. They go down to the engineer's room. They take a trip—a walking trip to the fire station. They learn how to use their own classroom to advantage. Magnifying glasses, the terrarium,[3] the rabbit hutch, the fish bowl; magnets on a special table with all sorts of metal; the primer-size typewriter, the easels, the blocks, and the like expand children's worlds. These provide an incentive to explore, to think, to observe, to experiment. Exploration, thought, observation, experimentation can be *seedbeds of language expression*. Children learn to use the magnifying glasses on the fish bowl, the floor, chalkdust, sand, snowflakes. They learn what magnets will pick up and what they won't pick up. They learn, in short, as Stevenson said, That "the world is so full of a number of things . . ."

They find out that their seemingly confusing and frightening world is loaded, every hour, every minute, every day, every mile, block, and inch, with wonderfully exciting, interesting, absorbing, and unusual things.

What Ideas To Talk About

Where do the ideas come from? Mostly from life experiences, the ideas, the thoughts that interest the group, these provide the content, the topics of talking times.

Some kind of system is needed to see that children take turns, do not interrupt, contribute as frequently as possible, and enjoy the conversation that develops. If some children are shy and reticent, the teacher must work to unlock their reluctant minds and so loosen their tongues—and probably later struggle to figure out ways to control the "unreluctant" tongues.

As a starter, however, the following are areas that a teacher can inquire about. She[4] can begin with some kind of an invitation as:

"Tell me what you like to do at home."

or

"Do you have any pets? Tell us about them."

or

"What scares you?" (if teacher and pupils feel comfortable together)

[3] See activities for Independent Work Period, pp. 114–16.

[4] The use of the pronoun "she" in this chapter is a bow to the fact that most beginning teachers are females. Let us hope that another decade will bring a significant influx of men into these early grade levels. Until then, it feels more realistic to refer to teachers in the feminine.

Something to talk about later.

Teachers can also open these sharing or talking times by showing something:

"I have several pictures here that I brought from the museum. I thought you would be interested in them."

or

"Here is a new book that the librarian let me take for this morning. I would like to read it to you" (or "I'd like to tell you about it").

or

"Here is a collection of stones. Look at _____."

Another gambit to get the school day started is to discuss the plans for the day (see also Chapter 4).

"We need to plan what you will do after your work period today."

"Now John's group must finish———etc."

The following are general headings that might prove provocative to help teachers have rich and engrossing sharing.

Ideas come from all kinds of pictures:
   Children's own, magazine, book pictures, newspaper pictures, film strips, motion pictures, colored slides, picture collections from museums, art galleries, etc.

Ideas come from feelings:
   Talking about an argument somewhere
   Talking about a dream
   Talking about a great embarrassment
   Talking about an event that was funny
   Talking about an event that was frightening
   Talking about something that meant happiness
   Talking about something make-believe

Ideas come from events:
   Accidents in the street, home
   Happenings in the home, neighborhood, going to and from school
   Happenings in the school
   Events in the news, on television, radio, etc.

Ideas come from trips:
   Walking trips nearby to gas stations, children's homes
   Trips within the school building
   Trips by bus and car

Ideas come from people:
   Visitors to the class or school
   Friends and neighbors with interesting occupations or hobbies
   Owners of businesses and other adults
   Children in other classes in the school

Ideas come from class activities:
   Making plans for the day, week, term
   Making and discussing collections, experiments, construction projects
   Cooking, baking, eating
   Caring for living creatures at home and at school
   Telling stories, riddles, jokes

Here are two examples of ideas that Mary Beth asked her teacher to print at the bottom of two pictures she had drawn:

                                                    Mary Beth

This is me and my friend's cat.
I am looking at myself in a mirror.
These are flowers. ————————

                                                        Mary Beth
I am wearing pink.
I am riding a bicycle.
I am trying to kill this monster.

These sources cover a lot of territory, but perhaps children will
bring up discussion about ideas not mentioned. The point, of course,
is that the ideas come from the children and that the teacher handle
the discussion wisely. Talk must be promoted, controlled, but not
hindered. While the content might possibly wander into bizarre,
wierd, and ugly fields, the teacher can use his judgment and shift
the emphasis. Nevertheless, the use of powerful and emotionally
tinged ideas can and must be used to advantage in reading instruction. No one has written more eloquently on this, and described it
more forcefully and movingly than Syliva Ashton-Warner in *Teacher*.[5]
Without exploiting her young pupils, she showed them how to *use*
their feelings in constructive ways. She never criticized the content
of what the child said or wrote—that, she said, was not her concern.
She worked to help them say what THEY wanted to say easily, and
in good English.

Listening Ability

We cannot discuss talking without mentioning listening. Whether
it is a skill or an ability is perhaps a semantic difference and a bit
irrelevant here.

Listening involves the ability to FOCUS on something that is heard.
It might be called "hearing perception." A child perfects this ability
to focus on sounds when he is not overwhelmed by a confusion of
sounds, and when he is concerned about what he is hearing. How
does a teacher help a child to become selective in listening?

Needless to say, a classroom must vary in its noise levels. A
teacher must avoid absolute silence and excessive noise. A teacher's
"overtalking" is a common problem. One teacher said, after listening to herself on a tape recorder of an hour's teaching, "I nearly
died after the first fifteen minutes. I never dreamed I talked so much
and said so many things over and over."

Then, too, a teacher must avoid the trap of considering "listening" as another form of disciplining children. Listening does not
mean "Be quiet"—but rather, "Pick out from what you hear that
which you are interested in."

[5] *Op. cit.*, pp. 263–64.

A teacher must help a child to focus on that which he has interest in. For example, "John, you were talking about model planes. Did you hear anything in Mary's telling us about her butterfly collection that applied to airplanes?" (i.e., referring to similar principles relating to wingspread in model airplanes and wingspread in butterflies). A teacher serves as a guide to a child to extract from a confusion of sounds that which serves his interests and purposes.

Finally, the teacher helps children to understand what they do hear. What do they want to know more about? Is there something that *must* not be answered by the teacher, but left tantalizing and dangling for the child to pursue on his own? Understanding often is a matter of personal attention.

"When may I tell you about my new baby brother?" asks one child. Talking times, or individual conference times, help a great deal.

Hannah Trimble said, "Always children are busting to talk with you. Always they are being shushed."[6] The teacher must be encouraging, gentle, yet insistent. These beginning days of expression can be checked by the too brusque and "business-like" teacher. She waits. She smiles as she brightens and nods encouragement and makes supporting murmurs or says things that invite the child to break through the speech barrier. She shushes others in order to give the hard-to-talk a better chance. Only when it is clear that the situation is wrong *for that day* does she change the subject. Then she might say, "Will you tell me later when we are all alone?" or she might say, "If I said the doll corner, would I be right? Shake your head yes or no," or she might say, "Can you tell us tomorrow?" and so close that part of the talking session.

Play Is Communication

Playing may not be directly related to reading, but it is communication, as is reading. Beware of the child that has no friends. He is in need of help. (Incidentally, isn't it interesting that we do not have remedial classes in making friends as part of the school curriculum?) Nevertheless, children need to play with friends and teachers need to help them understand the joys and pains of such. And pain does arise!

"He swiped my ball."

"He hit me."

"He kicked me in the leg."

[6] *"Out of the Mouths of The Third Grade," New York Times,* Magazine Sec., Sunday, June 2, 1947, p. 28.

"He called me a————."
"They won't let me play."
This is not to say that teachers must TEACH children how to play together. It doesn't work that way. But teachers can help children resolve—or understand—the stresses and strains that always arise when several children are together. For example, during a talking time, a teacher may start a discussion like this—and then only participate to MANAGE it, not to issue moral judgments.

Teacher:	John was saying that Mabel came to the table and took the saw out of John's hands. I have my own ideas about who was right and wrong. But I am grown up. I should know about such things. I want you to think about this situation and then, when you think you are right about what you are thinking, tell us about it.
Boy No. 1:	Mabel could have waited.
Girl No. 1:	Yes, but John ALWAYS has the saw.
Boy No. 2:	We need two saws and then everything would be O.K.
Girl No. 2:	(to the teacher) Can we have two saws?
Teacher:	I will see. I don't know. But would it help if we had a saw for everyone?

The discussion went on in this vein until one child suggested something about taking turns, which brought forth the idea of a time limit for use of such tools for one child.

This teacher was helping these children "play with their friends" by means of helping them smooth out the rough spots of sharing. The teacher did this by oral language. She could well have continued and used the whole incident as a basis for a chart entitled "Rules for Tools." Thus "playing with friends" can serve as a part of the reading program, at the least, as far as simple communication is concerned, and, at the most, as a lead into pupil dictation.

One teacher set up a "Complaint Box." Without identifying[7] who complained about whom, the teacher 1) refused to help with spelling—"If you can't spell it, don't complain"; 2) regularly opened the box and led a general discussion of problems mentioned.

Class and Caste Language Differences

One final note in passing, however, needs mention. It centers around the common opinion that lower class children have nothing

---

[7] (Observers report a Communist school practice that trains children for tattletaling by designating the actual child who does something undesirable.) Hence our wariness on this "finger-pointing." Problems need airing, surely, but carefully.

to talk about. They most certainly do. The problem is that their environment is so different from other children that they honestly consider themselves to come from another world and so SEEM to have nothing to say. The teacher's problem is to be sensitive to these dramatic social differences and to be sure that contributions are made. Church[8] suggests that the great disparity in language between Puerto Rican and Negro children and their white peer group living in large cities may not be so much the poverty or the limited book and verbal culture of the former, but rather the drastically differing *living* conditions.

Dialects No Barrier

This same idea applies to different dialects. A child from Boston area may be quite aware that "park" has the letter "r" in it, even though there is no "r" sound when he says the word. In the same way children in the eastern United States may say "sore" for "saw," but THEY know they mean "saw"—so they mentally see "saw" and not "sore" as would their mid-western cousins. Dialects are no barrier to the teaching of letter sounds. But the teacher must be aware of differences of letter sounds when helping a pupil with a dialect. The pupil can be easily confused if his normal speech patterns are criticized, and if there is an effort to force change on him. His ears will bring change in due time.

If a teacher is aware that some of the class have a speech difficulty, or a unique dialect, and she proceeds to *accept that way the given children say* the word under study, progress can be made. This is not to say that the teacher cannot work to clear up a difficulty. But the matter of dialect is touchy and needs to be handled with all due respect to the individual pupil concerned. It is, after all, quite proper for people to reflect speech patterns they have known all their life. What is wrong with it? Being made to feel ashamed of how one talks is not far removed from being made to feel ashamed of one's skin color, or religion, or one's parents. In these days of desegregation, many teachers realize that Negro children and white children might just as well have been brought up on opposite sides of the earth, as their customs, their mores, and their speech are sharply different and reflect that we have had, and will continue to have for a long time, two different cultures in the

[8] Joseph Church, *Language and the Discovery of Reality*, New York: Random House, Inc., 1961, p. 139.

same cities and towns. We must accept speech differences as legal, even though we proceed to make them more intelligible to everyone.

MECHANICS OF TALKING TIMES

There are matters of classroom management, or mechanics of organization of such class discussions that can be mentioned to aid the uninitiated. Total class talking will be made easier when problems of time-scheduling, floor space, squelching those who dominate, and other things are resolved. Let us begin with scheduling.

The Scheduling of Talking Times

Although the authors prefer that such an activity take place at the very beginning of the school day, many teachers have other quite acceptable ideas. Good education should bring the outside world into the classroom, and the first thing in the morning is a good time to do that. Just the sheer effect upon tardiness is something to be considered. The teacher who has learned how to begin the day with an absorbing, provocative period is the one whose pupils rush in to the school building. They are afraid they will miss something. Those teachers who start with excruciatingly dull opening exercises are the ones who have pupils dawdling about coming into the building. They couldn't care less if they miss something.

A caution about the activity called "Show and Tell" is in order. Its emphasis upon a single child "showing and telling" is too often a denial of any interaction or conversation. *The whole point of scheduling talking times is to develop language facility.* A series of children showing something without response, or with an artificial this-is-what-the-teacher-wants response, hardly fills the bill. More seriously, the accent upon material wealth in the very name "show and tell" is a discouragement to the "have-nots" of our classrooms. The spectacle of a child with a new and expensive toy before a class in which some children have never had such a thing is not desirable or fruitful.

Talking sessions can be held at all times of the day when the "state of the union" requires it. Sitting down together to solve unexpected problems not only promotes a fine classroom climate, but also encourages language facility about things that children care about. "The gold fish is dead (or dying). What shall we do about it?" "The kindergarteners are scared to play where our room plays. What can we do?" are samples of things that happen that call for group discussion.

Seating During Talking Time

Everyone should be as close together as possible without crowding. The distance between the last child in the back to the teacher, who usually acts as chairman, should be as short a distance as possible. Yet children must have room to sit comfortably without pushing a neighbor.

Seating during talking times.

If the floor of the schoolroom is particularly dirty, then "sit-upons" can easily be made. When the children are all settled on their sit-upons or what have you, and the teacher is settled upon her chair (not a child's unless she is unusually small, nor a large adult chair. The best is an in-between size. It often can be found in a fifth- or sixth-grade classroom.)

The Place for Talking

Most teachers like to have these sessions in the part of the room that has the most floor space. Usually this is in the front. Certainly it should be in a place that does not let the children face the light and is free from cold drafts and noise. There should also be a chalk board (or easel with large paper and a black crayon) ready for the teacher to write upon if necessary.

If teachers feel that they have no floor space large enough for such a gathering, they might look at the wasted floor space of the room. For example, for some unfathomable reason, some teachers are devoted to a seating pattern of single rows of seats. They do not seem to realize that it is just as easy to have double rows of seats—making not a whit of difference in classroom control. Doubling of the rows saves many square feet and so provides the floor space for talking sessions (or other activities). Squares of desks or tables of children often are not well situated in terms of efficient use of floor space and also permit some children to face the light all day long. If teacher would draw a map of her room, and see how changes could be made, much more floor space would be available. This is usable not only for talking times, but also for building projects in connection with social studies units and many other worthwhile activities.

A diagram of a typical classroom in which the talking times take place in a group around the teacher appears on page 23 in Chapter 2.

Meeting Individual Differences in Talking

The teacher, knowing that the ones who say little must be helped, must plan to work with them separately at some time. She observes and takes notes or makes records as has been described. Sitting close, cross-legged, on the floor, makes the teacher's observation chores easier.

What do we do *after* talking time to help facilitate language expression?

The teacher closes the talking session and sets the class busy with various centers of activity that should be a part of every first-grade classroom. Some draw pictures with crayons at their desk. Some paint on the easel. Some play with the blocks—or in the doll corner, the house-keeping center, the book corner—or cut pictures from colorful magazines. When all is calm and relatively quiet (i.e., a conversation can be held), the teacher says something like this: "I would like to talk to some of you in small groups. Will you come when I call your name?"

Using the records and notes that she has made during or after the talking period or even relying on her memory, she decides to call certain children who have *revealed similar abilities in talking.* The teacher must listen long enough to note the degree of language facility. Children who are highly verbal might be called on first. Then a group of those who talk less easily would be next and so on, until the teacher has worked through a succession of groups. The teacher's purposes are:

1. To facilitate oral expression.
2. To record language on a chart paper.
3. To take dictation for inscribing upon a picture, etc.

in all ways clearly showing children the connection between their oral and written language.

In this way the teacher meets individual differences by a kind of grouping that depends upon a single characteristic. After a day or so, the teacher will see that new arrangements, i.e., new groups of children are necessary. Light dawns upon a previously quiet child and he bursts forth with speech. These groups should change from day to day. They are organized only to allow for all children to have *equal* talking opportunities. Shy children whose communicative spirits are dampened by the loud and boisterous must be grouped together and helped to talk. They, literally, need practice in talking.

On the other hand, a teacher could invite those children who are playing in the block center to come to her for a talking time. If some children just happen to be together at a time when the teacher is ready for them, they can be called for a group. Groups must be ever changing, and it is easy to keep them that way when the teacher is seeking to develop the children's verbal expression.

Evaluation of Talking

The ability to talk, naturally, varies from child to child. The amount of conversation, the degree of unique ideas, the free flow of interaction between child and adult, as well as between child and child, are all related to intelligence, personality development, and other similar factors. Certain types of mental illness bring complete silence to its victims. Verbal intelligence test scores can be upped startlingly by an increase in vocabulary. But, for the classroom, teachers must know and ACCEPT that the fluent talker is the one who will have an easier time learning to read, to write, to spell, and to do almost anything in the field of language.

In order that teachers may have some way of measuring or evaluating the conversation that goes on during the school day, the following progressions may be helpful. They deal with both quality and quantity of the contribution.

Monroe[9] suggests that a teacher might want to measure pupils with this scale by putting each child in an identical situation (such as reacting to a certain picture, or finishing up an opening gambit of a story). However, this can become artificial, and may not be helpful to those teachers who are working to improve communication. The teacher's notebook could be set up for taking notes on children and recording growth over a period of months. These records then are sufficient and artificial situations are avoided.

For example, a form like the following might serve on occasion[10]:

Name	9/10-14					9/17-21					9/24-27			
	M	T	W	T	F	M	T	W	T	F	M	T	W	T
Philip	6		6	6		4	5		6	5		6		
Donald	2	2	2	4		4	2	3	6			4		
David		2		2	5	3	4	5			4			
Mabel	0	1		0	4		3		3	0	2	2		
Esther	4			2	6		2	4	4		6	6		

Symbols to use:
0 – Out of contact with conversation.
1 – Listens and shows reaction by face or body movement.
2 – Nods, raises hands, joins in requested response.
3 – Timidly, or hesitatingly, indicates desire to speak.
4 – Insists upon speaking from place in group.
5 – Stands before group to speak.
6 – Speaks before group and interacts with them on topic.

Chart of quality of contribution.

To use the foregoing chart effectively the teacher should indicate the highest level for the day for as many individuals as can possibly be evaluated. Let us assume that the teacher has helped the group to understand and to practice the mechanics of the discussion. During this period the teacher will probably have less time to note the quality of individual children's contribution. Nevertheless each child should be rated as frequently as possible, perhaps twice a

---

[9] From *Growing Into Reading* by Marion Monroe; Copyright 1951 by Scott, Foresman, & Co., Chicago.
[10] NOTE: Not every child needs to be evaluated every day.

week. Once children are easy in their organization of the period, the teacher can make the proper notations and still listen and promote the conversation.

Name	9/10-14					9/17-21					9/24-28			
	M	T	W	T	F	M	T	W	T	F	M	T	W	T
Philip	✓	✓	✓	✓	✓		✓	✓	✓		✓		✓	
Donald				✓	✓	✓	✓			✓				
David	✓		✓		✓	✓	✓	✓	✓	✓	✓			
Mabel									✓			✓		
Esther	✓	✓			✓	✓			✓	✓				

Chart of frequency of contribution over a period of time.

The teacher will make a check for each child on each day that he makes one or more contributions that hold the attention of the class, however briefly.

Names	9/10-14					9/17-21					9/24-		
	M	T	W	T	F	M	T	W	T	F	M	T	W
Philip		/			/		//		/	//	//	/	/
Donald	///	//	₶			///	/	////	₶	/	//		///
David	//	//	//	/			/	/		//		/	//

*Could be checked by a child, or observer.
 1 — One time volunteered to talk.
 2 — Two times volunteered to talk.
 3 — Three times volunteered to talk.
 4 — Four or more times volunteered to talk.

Chart of frequency of daily participation. (Could be checked by a child or an observer.)

If the teacher did not want to bother making these judgments every day, he would have quite adequate records even if an evaluation were made on certain days. This, however, would not give a pattern of how frequently different children talked. Quality could be indicated with the use of numerals rather than checks on certain days and the chart would look something like the following. It is similar to Chart IV but shows degrees of quality rather than frequency of participation.

Names	9/10-14					9/17-21					9/24	
	M	T	W	T	F	M	T	W	T	F	M	T
Philip					2		5		3		3	3
Donald	1	4	4			4		2	2		3	
David	4	2	1		1	3			4			

*Not every child everyday.
1 — Nods, raises hand, or otherwise signals.
2 — Offers monosyllabic responses.
3 — Occasionally offers brief thought.
4 — Offers to speak regularly.
5 — Always would react verbally.

Chart of quality of expression.

"But I can't keep 'em quiet!" wailed one desperate second-grade teacher. "They always have something that they think is important to say." But teachers *must* cut off discussion when the group has lost interest. The teacher could say something like:

"John, I'm eager to hear what you have to say. Will you be first tomorrow? (or this afternoon?) or tell me about it when everyone else is busy?"

or

"There are many of you who have not talked yet, and we want to hear you. We'll hear from Scott today. Suzie, will you be first tomorrow? Then we'll hear from Andy and Eugene. You are getting tired so we must stop. Scott, will you be the last one?"

or

"We don't need to tell everything here in talking time. We can do other things besides talk. What else can we do to tell others our ideas?"
Children: We can draw our ideas. We can write a story about our ideas. We can make our ideas in clay (blocks, etc.).

Closing sharing or talking times does not depend upon every last child expressing every last idea. The old-fashioned movie serials held over an excited audience for a week at a time.

CLOSURE FOR TALKING TIMES. Children are frequently so talkative that it is difficult to know when the time comes to shift to another activity, or for that matter to another child! Such a decision to close a group session is sometimes not easy, but the attitude of the children will give the teacher the signals, if he will but look.

Teacher's taking dictation must always be a fast-paced, stimulating experience. Once the pupils begin to show signs of boredom or fatigue—that is the time to find a good stopping point. Children will sit far beyond their normal attention span for a teacher that they like and admire and who listens. But even so, highly motivated learning cannot occur, in the best behaved of classes, when yawns, wiggles, and poking one's neighbors become common. The teacher might as well give up. The "teachable moment" is lost. Drain learning of its dynamic, organic, emotional characteristic, and it disappears.

"Leave 'em wanting more." is an old stage adage. Teachers should run a "cliff-hanger" of a discussion and then—at a propitious moment —say:

"Many of you have some wonderful ideas. Quick now, go back to your seat and find a way to tell us about them. Talking time is over, but there are other ways to talk—with crayons, with paints, with lots of things."

or

"This was one of the best sharing times we have ever had. But we have other things to do. We must stop now, and go back. Now, who is going to. . . . ?" (and she quickly plans the next period of activity).

Even in upper grade levels and as adults, there is a mistaken notion that discussion is the *end* as an activity. Quite the contrary—it is a *beginning*. Talking begins all learning. And because it is only a beginning, teachers do not need to drag every last dreg of knowledge out of every comment made by participants. "Keep them guessing as to what is next." Leave them in a state of anticipation for the next session. There is no educational sin much worse than teaching that is boring. Thus the activity, be it talking or otherwise, that is producing bored and dulled children must be changed for another.

SUMMARY OF TALKING TIMES

To move on to the next area in the use of oral language in reading instruction, we might summarize our discussion of talking times by indicating that they are scheduled and organized in such a way as to allow children to feel free to bring up ideas that interest them in a setting that encourages cooperative efforts to speak and to listen. Some teachers might be helped to note the levels at which some pupils might be able to participate, and provide for daily opportunities to meet individual differences. Records are useful and provide information for later activities.

TAKING DICTATION

As the children talk—at whatever level—the teacher listens and begins to prepare in her mind which words she will write down to use for beginning reading instruction. She encourages pupil participation with as little use of her own voice as possible. She will lift her eyebrows and nod to a child bursting to say something. She will wiggle her finger invitingly at the one who should have a chance to talk while making a gesture to "be quiet" to the one who has been talking too much.

There are helps to teachers in preparing to take pupil dictation. They follow a progression that is geared to development—rather than to age or grade level. Illiterate adults would be taught in the same way as six year olds—the only difference lying in the experiences dictated.

How To Make a Chart from Dictation

The teacher should know how to write down the words and sentences that are dictated for the thousands of ideas that arise. This is a simple matter of mechanics. A ream of news print is better than 50 sheets of expensive construction paper or tag board. As was stated earlier, quantity is necessary where pupil dictation is concerned. The more charts the better. They are to be cherished, loved, hung up, duplicated, cut up, and clamped together in bunches (on the same dates, or on the same topic, or for whatever reason). When wall space gives out, the teacher should have them reprinted in booklet form to be used over and over again—to read to Mother at home or to search through for a spelling word that is needed. Again may we repeat that the better the ideas, the more exciting the trips, the more vital the experiences, the more easily will children recognize and learn to read the charts. And that, of course, is the whole idea in the first place.

Chart Construction

Materials
> Large paper 2 feet x 3 feet (by the ream) much that is cheap and some that is of good quality, (newsprint, construction and tagboard).

Writing implements: ball point pens for Indian ink, felt pens, large black crayons (bowling-alley type is OK), Magic Markers. (N.B. anything that makes a broad dark mark is suitable.)

Chart holder: homemade clamps or spring-type clothes pins or thumb tacks on a 2-foot piece of wood, hung from a nail by a string from each end, holds 10 to 20 charts. Commercial types with clamps that hang up. Easels of any type.

Use of Print or Manuscript Writing

Use of manuscript writing or print writing large enough to be seen easily from all parts of the classroom, i.e., approximately 2 inches high. Words and lines clearly separate. 1 inch between words, 3 inches between lines (approximately).

Illustrations

Should be used sparingly and only on charts with topics that cannot be described without a picture of diagram. Should be placed at top, bottom, or on right and not interfere with left to right, or top to bottom progression.

Arrangement of Material

Balance necessary—do not crowd right hand side of page. Title, about three inches from top, well centered, and three inches above the first line, with capitals used for clarity. One-line sentences if possible, especially for beginners, all starting evenly on the left.

Two-line sentences are to be treated as paragraphs, unless return eye sweep is puzzling as to meaning; then second line begins in the middle. As soon as possible treat material as full paragraph (see examples below).

One-Line Sentences:

Our Trip to the Market

We went to the market.

We walked over there.

We saw lots of good things to eat.

We saw grapes, oranges, and carrots.

We all bought an apple.

Two-Line Sentences:

Making Cookies

We are going to make cookies
for our party.

We will make chocolate chip
and oatmeal cookies.

Making Cookies

We are going to make cookies
for our party.

We will make chocolate chip
and oatmeal cookies.

Paragraph Style:

Making Cookies

We are going to make cookies
for our party.   We will make
chocolate chip and oatmeal cookies.

General Guidelines

Every situation is different, but there are some general guide lines that will help, whether a teacher is working with a group or whole class. First, a teacher knows she is on the right track if the pupils are alert and interested. Once the wiggling begins, the teacher must change the topic, the activity, or both.

Once the teacher hears the pupils expressing themselves in all of the ways that have been suggested, decisions must be made as to what to record. How much of the flow of language must be recorded? What portion of all of that talk should the teacher write down? How can a teacher know that she is proceeding wisely? Putting down one-word captions is a good way to start.

ONE-WORD READING. The teacher must listen intently for the *general idea* of what is being said. What are they talking about—boats? Dogs? Going to town? Wagons? What?

Children talk about their homes, their pets, their fights, their families, all the things that go into a youngster's life. The more dynamic, or "organic" as Sylvia Ashton-Warner says, the better.

As children talk, the teacher listens for the general trend of the conversation. What are they talking about? Is it something that happened the day before? What was it? The teacher may even move to keep the talk on the subject, if it can be done without damaging the spontaneity of what is being said.

As the teacher hears a single topic, she can reach for the chalk, or marker, and write a single word that entitles that subject under discussion. For example, one might see:

Birthday

as a one-word summary of John's birthday party the afternoon before. Or one might see:

Rocket

as a one-word recapitulation of a successful launching of a rocket from one of the nation's bases. In like manner:

Puppies

is the best word to bring back the whole experience of a basket of puppies that were brought to school by Mary. So it goes. One word is a caption, a title for a whole lengthy experience, and gives the teacher a beginning on such skills as word recognition, and reading for comprehension and central thought.

With those words on the easel, the teacher takes advantage of a break in the flow of conversation before another child speaks up, and *reinforces the fact that she has written those words as a caption* of one child's contribution. The teacher may say: "John likes his dog. Here is "dog" or "Mary went downtown with her mother. Here is "downtown." The teacher may also point to a word on the easel, and ask who knows it. Rapidly, casually, she goes from word to word and notes who knows what word.

CAPTIONS LEADING TO STORIES. The next step is for the teacher to go back and ask a question like: "We have talked about several things today. I want you to help me write a story that we can use for reading. What story would you like to write about?" The children indicate whether the boat, or dog, or Mary's shopping expedition is their choice.

Once the general topic is decided upon—and these steps should all be in rapid-fire order lest interest wane—the teacher then begins to question in such a way as to recapitulate the idea in its proper sequence. Then she records the children's language as faithfully as possible with an eye to needs for future skill development.

STORIES FROM CAPTIONS THAT HAVE BEEN ERASED.

Writing No. 1—The Captions

Wagon
Boat
Downtown
Dogs

Writing No. 2—What follows after captions are eraed

The Wagon

A wagon went by schod.
An old man was in it.
It was a junk wagon

Writing No. 3—Another story from a caption

Dogs

Dick has a dog named Blackie.
Jane has a dog, too.
It is a great big dog.
She calls her dog "Heidi".

Use of Dynamic Ideas

From a recent novel, certainly one of the most eloquent descriptions of teaching that has ever been written[11] we read how a teacher stumbles upon the effect that emotion has upon children's sight vocabulary, although the author never uses such a technical word. We quote:

He is reading my Maori book about Ihaka . . . he comes to the line "Kiss Mummie Good Bye, Ihaka."
"What's this word" he asks.
"Kiss."
A strange kind of excitement comes over him. He smirks, then laughs outright, says it again, then tugs Patchy nearby and shows him. "That's 'kiss.'" he says emotionally. "K-I-S-S."
Patchy lights up too in an extraordinary way. They both spell it. The reading is held up while others are called and told and I feel something has happened although I don't know what.

[11] Sylvia Ashton-Warner, *The Spinster*, New York: Simon & Schuster, Inc., 1959, pp. 160–61. Reprinted with the kind permission of the publishers.

The next morning Patchy runs in, his freckles all agog. "I can till pell kitt!" he cries. "K-i-et-et! Tame simply gallops in. He brushes past me, snatches the Ihaka book from the table, opens to the page and points out the word to others nearby. "Look, he says profoundly, "here's 'kiss!' "

Why this sudden impetus in reading, I wonder. . . . What's this power in a word like "kiss"?

Later I say (to the inspector) "This word 'kiss.' Look at what it does to them. . . . It's got some relation to a big feeling. I can't put my finger on it."

"Do you mean i is a caption?"

Caption! Captin! Caption . . . the whole question is flood light. This word is the caption of a very big inner picture . . . It's the caption of a huge emotional picture.

Sylvia Ashton-Warner searches for more and more words that entitle "the big inner picture," and, so, too, must American teachers. Rarely do we find a novel describing classroom management so beautifully.[12] But she is right, and we must do likewise.

The term "caption" is an appropriate one. It is the grease that smooths the child's expression. Once out, the teacher selects the overall idea—the caption—of the talk. The use of such captions is the beginning of the reading skill "gaining central thought."

Different Types of Chart Content

Once a teacher knows the mechanics of chart-making, the myriad ideas of children can be recorded.[13] There are so many types or categories of such records that a word or two about them might be in order.

EXPERIENCE CHARTS. These are recordings of pupil dictation about actual experiences. Some interesting, dynamic event or observation, at home, at school, or elsewhere is set down in black and white. Experience charts are only about experiences, and the term should only be used in that sense.

HOW-TO-DO CHARTS. These are statements about how to accomplish something that needs to be done, such as some schoolroom chore (feeding the goldfish), some experiment to be carried out (how to make an electromagnet), or something in which a sequence needs to be followed.

OBSERVATION CHARTS. These are a series of notes that have been recorded about something observed, such as the weather, science experiment with growing things, animal behavior, and the like.

---

[12] Another book describing her work with children, *Teacher, op. cit.,* is also available.

[13] The reader is also referred to V. E. Herrick and M. Nerbovig, *Using Experience Charts With Children,* Columbus, Ohio: Charles E. Merrill Books, Inc., 1964.

Air Experiment

1. We had two pumpkins.

2 We cleaned the pumpkins and made a Jack-O-Lantern of one of them.

3. We put a lighted candle in each pumpkin.

4. The candle in the pumpkin went out because it got no air.

5. The candle in the Jack-O-Lantern did not go out because it had air.

A how-to-do chart.

KAPER CHARTS. Borrowing a phrase from our camping friends, these charts list necessary chores that can be checked off as completed. Cleaning desks, washing the aquarium, feeding the white rats are all items that need to be accomplished. A chart with a check-off system that provides for pupils taking turns fills the bill.

A LIST OF————CHART. A list of similar things lends itself to recording in this fashion. Books brought from home, father's jobs, and birthdays are the type of time that can be so listed.

There will always be, of course, charts that fall into no category at all. No teacher should feel that she MUST have a chart of every

The subject of an observation chart.

variety. Undoubtedly, the teacher who runs the best talking time will have the most charts about life experiences. As long as children's feelings and ideas are being expressed and recorded with sympathy by the teacher, learning will be served.

What To Do with What Is Said

The role of the teacher can be expressed in the following self-question: "What can I do with what these children have said?" It is not so much where the children have been but where can the teacher take them. "How can I make just a walk down the street mean more?" is another question the teacher must ask himself. The secret, of course, is the development of eternal curiosity about what has been seen.

We have said that seeing and hearing perception is a result of experience. The child who is never encouraged to "Look at that!" or "Can you hear what I hear?" has a harder time relating to his environment *intelligently* than the child who is consumed with curiosity and drives his elders wild with his questions. Hearing and seeing, in the sense of exploration, are necessary, and, if they are not

The subject of an observation chart.

part of the child's behavior when he comes to school, the teacher must develop such.

Building upon that, the teacher then must take whatever was seen, heard, or thought about and turn it into written words, sentences, and phrases. This is not to say that the teacher is stumped if she finds that children come to school frightened and unable to say much. There are all kinds of things that can be brought up at the level of their talking ability. The teacher ACCEPTS what a child offers, even if it is a brief sentence or even a single word.

"What kind of a pet do you have, John?"

"Dog."

"What is his name?"

"Rover."

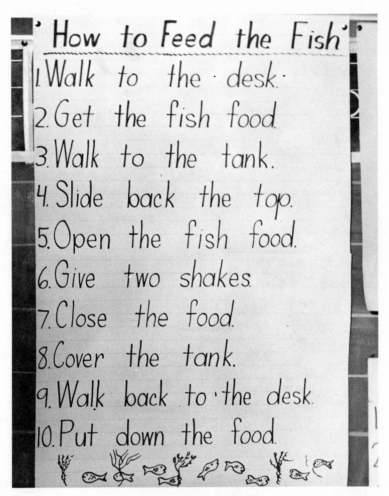

A "kaper" chart.

With that the teacher could simply write on the easel one of the following:

ROVER

or

JOHN'S DOG IS ROVER.

She would have then made the transfer—even at that admittedly limited level—*for John*, between what he said and the written language on the easel or board.

The development of the transfer between spoken language and written language is the major effort of the teacher in having a talking time and in writing down some of it for all to see. The teacher is thus developing sight vocabulary—but the words are the words of the children.

The Teacher Must Edit

For the total class, however, we have presented ideas as to: 1) the frequency with which charts should be made, 2) the role of the teacher, 3) the way to construct a chart, 4) the guidelines for what to include, 5) and the impact of a child's emotional life on his recognition of words. We are ready to proceed in much greater detail into the matter of the actual editing done by the teacher.

As speech is the representation of real-life experience, it cannot possibly include everything. No matter how much a person tells about some experience, no matter how long he talks or how many sentences he uses, the words can serve only as a symbol for the whole experience. For example, everyone can remember trying to tell another about an incident that was hilariously funny, and then wind up saying, lamely, "It was so much funnier than I can tell you." Of course it was, because all of the elements of the experience cannot possibly be put into words. The words are, in a very real sense, the caption, the heading, the title, the subtitle, the outline of an incident. How does this apply to beginning reading?

Recording the Language Most Helpful in Instruction

The application of these facts about language means that the teacher cannot possibly write down everything a child says when she is taking dictation. Therefore, she must take down that portion of the child's language that *will help him learn to read best.* How does the teacher recognize that portion? These are the choices:

1. The most dynamic, emotional, and organic part of the pupil dictation.
2. The part that can be transcribed in the most natural language of the pupil.
3. The part that allows the teacher to develop any one of a number of reading skills.

Examples of Class Dictation

The following are several examples of teachers in action. Note how they listen to the child's language and reproduce its meaning while still preserving its ownership.

A partial recording of the news.

The first example that follows shows how a teacher selected the organic, dynamic, and most emotional part of the children's discussion.

> *Teacher:* We had quite a storm last night.
> *Boy:* My Daddy said we got the tail of the hurricane.
> *Girl:* One of our windows got busted.
> Several Children (excitedly):
> "Our cellar was full of water."
> "That's nothing. Our whole street looked like the ocean."
> "Water—lots of it."
> "You know that big tree in our front yard? It blew down."
> *Teacher:* Let us make up our own story about the storm. Tell me some of those things again and I will write them down. O.K.? First what shall we call the story?
> *Child:* Our Big Hurricane.
> *Teacher:* Wonderful. Here are those words. (And she writes "Our Big Hurricane" on the board.) What shall we say next?
> *Child:* We got the tail of the hurricane. (Teacher writes that sentence on the board.)
> *Child:* Our big tree blew down.
> *Teacher:* Was that the only tree that blew down?

Chorus: No—lots of them did.
Teacher: If I wrote "It blew down trees," would that be all right? Would
it be what you said? (All agreed and the teacher wrote it down.)

Through this kind of questioning and encouragement the teacher
had the following story[14] ready in a few minutes. She later copied it
and did it over in manuscript for display on the wall as shown on
page 431.

Our Big Hurricane

We got the tail of the hurricane.

It blew down trees.

There were floods.

It blew windows out.

The wind blew very fast.

It did a lot of damage.

The next examples show how a teacher can rework children's
language into a natural sounding repeat of certain words that will
help in developing a sight vocabulary, as well as provide a set of
words that may trigger off a child's recognition of similar initial letters, similar endings or rhyming words, similar "middles" of words,
or vowels.

EXAMPLE 1. The child said: "I saw a wagon go by the school. It
had a horse and an old man driving it, and all kinds of junk, tin cans,
mattresses, old pails and lots of other things."
But the teacher wrote:

> "A wagon went by school with an old man driving it.
> It had all kinds of junk, tin cans, papers, and mattresses."

This teacher in listening recognized that she could get some natu-
ralistic repetition of words that began with "w." She saw the possibility of teaching the sound of that letter in the words, "wagon,"
"went," "with."

14 An actual story from a class in Glastonbury, Connecticut, Public Schools.

EXAMPLE 2. Another example might be similarities of endings of words.

The child said: "Can we go to the playground and play ball? Everyone wants to use the new ball. You can come and get us when the time is up."

The teacher wrote with this comment: "May I write what you said this way?" She wrote this version:

Playing Ball on the Playground

Do you all want to play ball?

We have a new ball and

it belongs to all of us.

So go ahead and play.

I will call you to come in.

The teacher is reaching for good ways to show that certain words rhyme. The "all" family seemed a natural in this case. So she re-worked the words—but not the idea—to make it easier for her to teach the rhyming words, "ball," "all," "call."

EXAMPLE 3. The teacher might be working to see if children could hear and see differences in the middles of words, usually vowels.

The child said: "I sure like to swim in Lake Michigan. It has waves and sand. I can make things in the sand, and I can dive through the waves, too. It was sunny and warm. I liked to be there."

The teacher wrote, again requesting approval for the slight re-drafting:

We like to swim in Lake Michigan.

Jim swam there on Sunday.

It was warm in the sun.

Lake Michigan has waves and sand.

It is fun to dive in the waves, too.

For the teacher looking for words that will help teach vowel differences, this story, even if a bit stilted, has much to offer. The teacher can take her choice between "like" and "lake" or "dive" and "waves" or "sand" and "sun" or, for that matter, "swam" and "fun." This chart is particularly good to teach many word attack skills.

Sentence Structure of Charts

Before moving to the next part, a comment must be made about sentence structure of experience charts. Those samples can be seen to have the simple common form of subject-verb-object.

Recent research[15] shows that such short and simple 1-2-4 patterns (i.e., subject, predicate, objects) are more common to basal readers than to children's spontaneous speech. It could be that such sentences by teachers are a carryover from the memory of those readers. Research is needed that explores the effect of sentence structure upon the ease of reading. Research. is also needed as to HOW FAR a teacher can depart from the dictation of pupils.

We have suggested that as natural a reproduction of the children's informal speech as possible always be made. But some editing is necessary because of sheer quantity of words to be recorded. It may well be that future investigations will show that the more closely reading matter imitates children's normal speech, the better will be the reading. Nowhere is it easier to imitate the children's speech than in taking dictation. It is probably true that when children have the privilege of selecting their own reading material, they will tend to choose those books that "sound like me." It is also probably true that when children *are put into books* a basic objection or conditioned aversion to reading could be set up, simply because the writing is so different from the given child's normal talk. This could explain the notable improvement in attitudes of reading in research studies where the practice of self-selection is under examination, particularly now when so many tradebooks are available. Certainly, these current studies would suggest caution to teachers making experience charts so that they avoid the language of the basal readers, as these are clearly unlike children's normal language. Caution is in order even about so simple a matter as a teacher repeating the words she is writing on the board, She can find herself in imitation of the jerky oral reading pattern so prevalent. Teachers *must* go back line

15 Ruth G. Strickland, *The Language of Elementary School Children: Its Relationship to the Language of Reading Textbooks and the Quality of Reading of Selected Children.* Bloomington: Bulletin of the School of Education, University of Indiana, Vol. 38, No. 4.

by line after taking dictation and orally reread such sentences in normally inflected tones. Loban says in his classic study "Competence in the spoken language appears to be basic for competence in reading and writing." [16]

The Place of Vocabulary Drill

The practice that provides for the repetition of words in order to read a pre-primer later on cannot stand the test of efficient learning. Drilling upon words that come from a list that have no connection to the life experience of the child is waste of classroom time.

We know that interest is the prime motivator of learning. How can a child be interested in words, phrases, concepts, sentences that are totally divorced from his own life? Therefore, to "motivate" a child to "be interested" in those sentences and words is to erase his mind of any other interest. Teachers are too frequently evaluated upon how well they can instill motives other than the child's into their pupils. This practice is a waste of time because it takes longer, it takes more argument, it takes more discipline, it takes more EFFORT on the part of the teacher. Worst of all, it is not necessary.

There is no place for vocabulary drill upon words unrelated to the child. If they are truly related, no drill is necessary. Word drill can be advocated when it comes from a child's need to complete gaps in a sentence between his "power" words or when such drill provides the necessary words to read a book of his own choice or some other material. Word drill will come automatically when the child has something he must read to himself because it absorbs his mind, when he must write in order to make something important happen, or when he must read aloud to develop his own sense of pride and accomplishment.

In summary, the teacher must edit with a judicious eye as to the children's own unique language patterns. If these are destroyed, there is no sense in even bothering to take dictation. One might just as well use the phrases in readers. However, there is no reason, even if it were possible, for the teacher to record the *exact* wordage of the children's speech. Keeping the recording as close to natural speech patterns as possible, the teacher can still do enough editing to speed up the operation of reading instruction. The mild editing that we are suggesting will still have enough richness to be useful for teaching a great many skills.

[16] Walter S. Loban, *The Language of Elementary School Children*, National Council Teachers of English, Champaign Research Study No. 11, 1963, p. 93 (back cover).

Primer-Size Typewriters

The emphasis of the preceding description has been upon total class activities with the teacher using a chalk board or easel to record writing in a large enough size for all to see. Groups and single individuals can also come into their own as they give dictation to their teacher. Teachers may take down in longhand (or shorthand, too, sometimes) as the child sits or stands beside her. The side-by-side position is of real importance. Psychologically, it promotes the sense of teamwork—a we-are-doing-this-together kind of feeling. It is hard to feel antagonistic to a child who is beside one. More often the teacher succumbs to the feeling of wanting to hug the small body on her right or left. The light in a child's eyes as he looks up at his teacher who is his alone, for that short time, is bright indeed.

Whether or not the teacher writes with pencil or pecks away at a primer-size typewriter is not of great moment—beyond the fact that *typed* material, on its own, holds much glamour for children. Probably, the same motivation that drives authors and writers the world around is at work here. In any event, typewriters—primer-size or not —enhance the language arts activities in any classroom. Recent studies underline many advantages of these machines.[17]

Taking dictation directly onto the typewriter with the child at the teacher's side is to be done in the same way as taking dictation in any setting. However, because of the advantage of the one-to-one situation, much more word mileage per minute is possible. Editing does not need to be so stringent. Some children can dictate pages and pages without seeming to run out of breath. Others run out of juice when they come to the end of the incident or episode that they are describing. Teachers can use this material, typed or written, for endless activities in reading instruction. And like the rest of children's language, it is free, it is always available, and it is easily stored for future use.

Frequency of Taking Dictation

Charts of pupil dictation should be done in quantity. Two a day is not too many, and perhaps more than that for some groups of individuals within a class. After a degree of independent reading is

---

[17] *The Manual Portable Typewriter as an Instructional Tool in the Elementary Classroom*, Boston University School of Education; University of Illinois College of Education; Teachers College, Columbia University, 1960.

achieved so that much reading in books is occurring, then the charts can be reduced to one for every talking or sharing time. Their form may change to diaries, or "The Second-Grade News," but experiential material is vital at all grade levels.

Application of Guidelines to Other Media

Let us apply these guidelines to various ideas, materials, thoughts that might arise in the classroom, and follow a sequence of events.

EXAMPLE NO. 1: CHILDREN'S PICTURES AND LANGUAGE.[18]

1. Children draw pictures that represent some aspect of their lives.
2. Children talk, in turns, about their pictures.
3. Children allow or request the teacher to put down the main idea, i.e., captions, of their pictures. (See the film "Skippy and the Three R's[19] as an example.)
4. Teacher takes dictation during independent work period.
5. Children develop their own skills throughout the days and weeks, and move toward the breakthrough of putting their own words on their own pictures.
6. Children talk about their pictures and, as independent writing ability increases, write longer and longer captions, phrases, and eventually sentences for their pictures.
7. Teachers take advantage of this written language and help children write without pictures, at a higher level, or compile many stories with pictures that have now become illustrations into their own booklets.

EXAMPLE NO. 2: MAGAZINE PICTURES.

1. Child or teacher selects and shows a magazine picture for personal and horizon-expanding reasons.
2. Discussion follows upon each picture shown.
3. Teacher writes single-word or phrase captions on the board or easel.
4. Volunteers take the picture to write more.
5. Volunteers seek other pictures to write about

or

Teacher takes dictation as needed.

---

[18] See also D. M. Lee and R. VanAllen, *Learning to Read Through Experience* (rev. ed.) New York: Appleton-Century-Crofts, Inc., 1963, for other descriptions of ways to proceed.
[19] Film available from the National Education Association.

FILMS, MOVIE STRIP FILMS, OR COLORED SLIDES.

1. Teacher shows movie.

or

Child brings series of kodachrome slides.

2. Discussion of film ensues.
3. Teacher writes as many captions as feasible for situation.
4. Volunteers undertake to write their version of the films, as in preceding cases

or

Teacher takes dictation as needed.

EXAMPLE NO. 3: SOMETHING BROUGHT TO SCHOOL.

1. Children bring living creatures, or inanimate objects, for talking time.
2. Children show to the whole class, and explain the background.
3. Teacher makes sure all understand and that truth has been served.
4. A caption goes up for all to see.
5. It is erased or discarded.
6. The teacher invites all to contribute to a story about the object.
7. The teacher records the story line by line.

Let's Rerun These Guidelines Again

1. The teacher listens and records important words, as a kind of caption for the topic being discussed. Children are not interrupted for this recording.
2. The words are pointed out by the teacher and connected to:
   a. The topic that had been discussed.
   b. The child who initiated the topic.
3. The teacher writes down on the board or large paper a sentence that captures the child's idea. She states what she is going to write down and asks if it is right.
4. She continues until the piece of material has a wholeness of content.

Now we are ready to go into greater detail about the use that teachers make of the outpourings of children. We discussed the problems of encouraging speech, of taking it down in writing. Now we must move to how we use what has been taken down.

READING INSTRUCTION WITH CHARTS

The previous section showed some specific examples of how and why teachers took down the particular dictation that they did. Now what do teachers do with recorded speech? The skills that the teacher is mainly concerned with at this stage of development are:

1. That there is a connection between what the child said and what the teacher wrote.
2. That writing is composed of ideas transcribed in meaning units, i.e., sentences (or phonological units),[20] phrases, words, and letters.
3. That the meaning of these segments is discoverable.

in brief, that reading is the simultaneous bringing of life and thought to a page in order to extract its meaning. A child must *find his own speech patterns* on a page in order to read it. So what does the teacher do next?

Work with the Dictated Materials

1. The teacher works extensively and intensively with the given pieces of material, using the innate interest of pupils in their own work for motivation.
   a. Important words are identified.
   b. Important words become the clues to the ideas, the total meaning of whole lines.
   c. Reading back from the charts (paper) occurs
      1. By individual children in a one-to-one situation.
      2. By a group of children who are concerned with the idea.
      3. By the class who participated in the chart preparation.

Reading from Charts

Within the major goals cited above there are many small details. Now, however, the teacher must work with these charts to teach:

1. The identification of words by sight and shape until enough of a word bank or sight-vocabulary accumulates or
2. Until children mature enough to see that words have parts, i.e., letters, phonemes, syllables, etc.
3. The sounds of letters in words.
4. The carryover of normal speech into oral reading.

Thus the child moves into the stage of word analysis and stays in it until he recaptures the ability to read by whole words again—of course, at a much higher ability level. All along this developmental line, the teacher helps pupils make the transition from their own

[20] See Ruth G. Strickland, *op. cit.,* p. 16.

An alphabet card to teach a short "U."

words on charts to books, and other printed material. The teacher, in short, labors to build a bridge between the child's spoken language and any book that he chooses to read anywhere.

Once the experiential material is ready, the teacher begins something like this:

"What are your favorite words here?"
"This one tells about what Martha brought. So what is it about?"

The following example is illustrative. An overaged, retarded, rebellious child in second grade was asked about the trip they had taken to a farm on the previous day.

Teacher:	What did you like best at the farm?
Boy:	I liked the cow.
Teacher:	Let me write that on the paper. (She does and shows it to him.) Want to read it back?
Boy:	I can't read.
Teacher:	But what did you just tell me?
Boy (diffidently):	That I liked the cow.

Teacher:	That is what that says. Go ahead read it back. (She put her hand under the words.)
Boy:	I liked the cow.
Teacher:	Anything else about that cow?
Boy:	It was black and white.
Teacher:	Let me write that down. (Does and shows it to him.) Go ahead read it back.
Boy:	Does that say what I said?
Teacher:	Exactly. You can read when you know what you said. Go ahead.

This boy slowly, laboriously, with increasing industry, picked up the wrecked threads of his reading life and eventually was able to learn the skills of word analysis and become quite independent before the next two grades were finished.

Teaching Connection Between Sights and Sounds of Letters

Saying "A" as the teacher points to "A," on the posted alphabetical cards, and "B" when the teacher points to "B," connects sight and sound. It connects it fastest and most certainly when the teacher switches from the cards to the beginning letter of a power-laden, spoken word. For example, a group of children have discovered that "peach," "pumpkin," and "Pop-eye" all begin with the same letter. They do not know what letter it is—yet. The teacher says, moving over under the alphabet and points to "A."

> *Teacher:* Do "peach," "pumpkin," "Pop-eye" begin with "A"?
> *Children:* No.
> *Teacher:* With "B?"
> *Sue:* Yes. (Comment: The teacher's judgment should make the decision of whether or not to ignore the one child who was not getting the idea. However, in this case, perhaps because both "P" and "B" are labials and so feel similar on the lips, the teacher should take an additional few seconds to say "Sue, you aren't right. Let me see if I can help you feel—with your mouth—why you are wrong. OK? Say 'peach' (Sue repeats 'peach') Get your mouth ready to say 'peach' but don't say it. (Sue does) now say "B." Now say "boy." Can you tell that they are different?"
> Sue might not "catch on" at that moment—but groundwork is laid for later individual work. The teacher should be sure to make a note of this on Sue's page in her notebook.)
> *Teacher:* Everyone say "peach" again. (All do). Now look at this next letter in the alphabet. It is a "C." Does "peach" begin with that letter?
> *Children:* No.

The teacher proceeds until the letter "P" is reached. Most children should feel the similarity between the name of the letter and its sound in "peach," "pumpkin," and "Pop-eye." If not all, she makes a note of who has trouble for later lesson-planning and goes on to other things. Of course this procedure is not necessary very often. It is intended only to help children get the idea.

These statements do not show that the child is yet aware of the difference between words, sentences, phrases, or anything else. A whole chart story may be one big blob to him. It is difficult to tell. We have evidence that children have remarkable ability to see details in books from which their parents read. Woe be to the parent who skips a page—or a word, for that matter! The ability of children to discriminate by vision alone between various objects in their environment has puzzled more than one family. Ability to recognize certain phonograph records, distinguish between other similar objects occurs at preschool ages. Whether this same ability applies to verbal symbols in schoolbooks and other school materials is not nearly so well known at this time.

Identification of spoken words can be safely assumed to be made on the basis of whole meaning of the lines in which they appear. When the Gestalt of these wholes breaks down, children do not keep it a secret. They give out signals with enthusiasm! Teachers must learn to recognize them for what they are.

Gaining Central Thought

What reading skill is being developed when key words or captions are used? Don't such words help children to gain *central thought?* Maybe one word won't serve. If not, then more than one, a phrase, is needed. But this kind of "headline" focuses children's ideas upon the overall idea of the talking. Even the immature child who still is unaware of the connection of talking and writing will get the glimmer that "Daddy" is the main subject in the class that was talking about where their Daddys work, or that "Ball" was the topic of the discussion about the ball game. The element of assisting children to *focus* on meaning eases the later more complex skill of finding central thought. In fact, it is a foundation for it.

Gaining Sight Vocabulary

Another reading skill that is developed is the acquisition of sight vocabulary. We define sight vocabulary as those words that are learned by their shape only. They are long, or short, or tall in the middle, or what have you. Let us follow an example of a teacher in action to depict procedures of giving children a good start in accumulating a sight vocabulary.

Teacher: You wanted to tell me about some of the things you did this summer.

Lyle: We went to the Big Pond and rode on all the rides. I liked the ferris wheel.

Susan: My daddy took us, too, and I rode ponies, and threw balls at the monkeys. We went on the ferris wheel. I was scared. (Conversation continues with other children telling of similar experiences)

Teacher (slipping the comment in between two contributions): Let me put the words BIG POND on the board so you can see what they look like as you are talking. (Writes Big Pond on board or easel.) (Comment: This is the first week in the first grade. The teacher quickly catches the topic of discussion as being about an amusement park. This is clearly of vital interest to the group. Therefore, this is the key word to be shown. A simple statement that that is what she is doing makes her act educative, rather than just a random motion of standing, sitting, or scratching her eyebrow. Her action is keyed to what the children are saying. She connects writing to it.)

Teacher (as topic runs its course): You have been talking about Big Pond. I want to write a story about it. What happened first?

Child: We went to the Big Pond.

Teacher: When?

Child: This summer.

Teacher: I will write what she said. So you all can see what it looks like. (As she writes she speaks each word as it goes down. But she is careful to read it back, when finished, in normal, spontaneous speaking fashion.)

Teacher: What shall we say next in our story?

Girl No. 2: You can ride lots of things at Big Pond. May I say it this way— "Big Pond has lots of rides?"·

Teacher: Yes—let me write that. (She does in same fashion—speaking each word as she writes, then rereading in normal talking style.) (Activity continues until the following story is on the board.)

(Comment: The teacher retained most of the child's expressions, but did not hesitate to do minor editing when it would serve the purposes of developing the use of the alphabetic principle or rhyming, or acquiring sight vocabulary.)

The Big Pond

We went to Big Pond this summer.

Big Pond is a big park.

Big Pond has lots of rides and things.

Lyle, Bob, and Susan rode the Ferris Wheel.

Susan was scared on the Ferris Wheel.

Her Daddy held her tight up high.

We went swimming at Big Pond.

We rode the little train.

We loved it !

What skills can this teacher teach with this record of a group's experience? There are so many that can be taught that an easier question to answer would be what skills *cannot be taught*.

Skills that can be taught—i.e., taught directly and not incidentally with this story—are a matter of judgment certainly, but it also depends upon the maturity of the pupils and what they need to know. There are some helps, though, that can steer the teacher through the maze. For example:

1. THE DEVELOPMENT OF SIGHT VOCABULARY.
    Teacher: Look at this story. Find where it says the name of the park. Come and show all of us by putting your hand under the name of the park every place you see it.
        or
    What line has the names of three of you?
        or
    Find some words that are the same.
    (Comment: At this level the sense of achievement is enhanced by recognition of simple words. This is a good time to develop recognition of the nondramatic words, such as "went" (two times), "we" (five times), "rode" (three times), "Big" (four times). Even a game of "what is this word" is valid at such an early stage—when later on such a game can insult the intelligence of pupils.)

2. MAKING LEFT-TO-RIGHT, TOP-TO-BOTTOM DIRECTION AUTOMATIC.
    Teacher: Come and show that you know which word is the first word in the line—any line.
        or
    When you start to read a story where do you start? Show me.
        or
    Why do I always make my hand go along under the lines this way?"
    (Demonstrates.)
        or
    Notice this big letter. We call it a capital. It is a signal to you. What does it tell you?

3. AUDITORY DISCRIMINATION.
    Teacher: I see a lot of words that start the same way. Can you find them?
    (Comment: The children should be able to hear, even if they cannot *see:*

pond	went	held
park	was	high
ponies	we	etc.

and proceed to repeat the other words from their own vocabulary beginning with the same letters.

With such a variety possible, the teacher could go on far beyond the attention span of the children. Thus after three or even four of such "striking-while-the-iron-is-hot" situations, the teacher should watch for the give-away wigglings and signs of fatigue. There will be another day, and there should be a hundred more experience records. The other skills can be taught later.)

There are literally thousands of ways that teachers may help children to read back the material that they have dictated. In the very beginning, the teacher may work only with the single words that have been written as the "captions" of the topic that has been discussed.

Here is such an example of a class BEFORE the children could recognize any word.

> *Teacher:* We have talked about Mary's puppy and Joe's house getting painted. I want you to say "pup."
> *Children:* Pup.
> *Teacher:* Paint.
> *Children:* Paint.
> *Teacher:* Now get ready to say "pup"—don't say it but get your mouth ready. What word can you think of that goes the same way?
> *Child:* Pop.
> *Teacher:* Soda pop?
> *Child:* No, Popeye.

And another instance of the same skill with the child looking at the words:

The child shows the teacher the word "bottle."

> *Teacher:* It begins like "bat." Let me see your mouth get ready to say "bat." Now say something that soda pop comes in without changing your mouth.

Reading Back to One's Self

Pride and achievement are well served when children find dictated material—of their own or others'—and choose to read it or attempt to read it independently. One teacher, frustrated and annoyed by a continual lilting murmur somewhere in the classroom during the quiet time, found one little girl happily chanting out experience chart after experience chart that were hanging from a clamp on the wall. As she triumphantly finished reading each, she threw it back over her head and went on to the next one. The teacher found her half hidden with a dozen charts over her head, and another dozen to go!

Reading back a chart.

Reading Back As a Group

Sometimes groups need to check their assignment or work at specific tasks that need mastery.[21] Groups are set up for hundreds of reasons. Children work at skills, or follow interests, or finish projects. Reading back from dictated material can serve in any of these aspects. One group has made butter during the activity period. With

---

[21] The discussion of grouping in Chapter 7 stresses the activity that develops pupil responsibility for mastering some aspect of their reading.

the help of the teacher they have dictated the whole process and are ready to report to the class. They must read it back in order to make a good presentation.

Some groups have not yet mastered some skill in word analysis. They need to recognize certain sounds of letters when heard in words. The teacher takes an appropriate chart and teaches them this skill.

Another example of a group in action in reading back material might be the baking of cookies for the Christmas party from the same recipe that was so popular for the Halloween party. Following the directions written out by the Cookie Committee for the Halloween party, this group could proceed with their task.

The Whole Class Reads Back

There are numerous opportunities in every school day for the whole class to read some previously dictated material. This is one of the most important reasons that charts should be hung up all over the walls in full view of the children. Teachers must insist that they be allowed to put up these charts, and those in charge of building new buildings should be urged to make sure that teachers have the KIND of walls that makes it easy to put up material for display—and therefore learning.

Oral Reading in Normal Speech Patterns

The skill of oral reading must be stressed in connection with the reading back of pupil-dictated material. ALL oral reading must reconstitute the natural speech patterns of children. A child cannot read material that does not represent his living experience. Research is desperately needed in this area, but there is reason to believe that the teacher's editing of the children's dictation should be similar to what was said, rather than resemble the sentence structure of basal reader materials.

Under no conditions, even from the very first read-back of the very first chart, should teachers allow word-by-word oral patterns to develop. A warning to teachers is necessary on one point. As children dictate something to be written, the teacher writes the words down one by one. It is advantageous for the teacher to SAY THE WORD as she writes it, if only to connect speech and writing. But if this is done, the teacher must read what she has written aloud *after* it is completely written in normal talking tones. The memory of the halting word-by-word repetition of the words as it was being written must be erased by a proper reading of them at the end.

Child Sets Child Upon the Path of Reading

A fine independent activity that can be carried out, when a quiet working classroom is absolutely necessary, is that of child reading to child. Before enough sight vocabulary has developed to pull children into searching through books for words that they might know, the many charts that had been dictated, transcribed, and displayed can be used by friends to read to each other—for the sheer joy of accomplishment expressed in the wonderful story about the boy riding the bicycle—"Look, Ma. No hands!" While the boy came a cropper with his bike, the child reading to his friend has someone to turn to. If they BOTH are stuck on a word, they still can seek help from another friend, another chart, or, in a case of last resort, the teacher.

Independence in Reading Back

Teachers must train their children to have initiative, inventiveness, in working out their own reading problems. The teacher, then, is the last person to whom a child turns, and then only when other resources have been exhausted. The teacher should inquire as to what other steps a given child has made before asking for help.

For example:

Boy: What is this word? (Pointing to "from.")
Teacher: Where else have you looked for that word?
Boy: No where.
Teacher: Who else have you asked for help?
Boy: I asked Joe. But he didn't know it.
Teacher: What could help you that we can both see from here?
Boy: Our stories on the wall?
Teacher: Yes—look over by those near the window. I can see your word from here. Maybe you will know it in that story. If not, come back.

Teachers can also train children to ask for words without saying anything. Just pointing to an unknown word is sufficient to indicate that it is unknown.

The opportunities for reading back pupil-dictated material are almost limitless. Whatever limits there are would be set by the lack of charts! There must be, we repeat again, a minimum of two a day for the whole class and perhaps another one or two for individuals or groups. ALL of these must be considered as reading material. Their vocabulary *does not need to conform* to any designated list. The words that children use in their speech come from all grade levels. To refuse to write certain words that first graders say, simply because those words are not on the first grade list, is the height of educational folly.

NEWS

I use to be sick with Grmin mesles. I had a big bump on the back of my neck.

Hilary C.

NEWS

The girl mouse will have babies soon. They will be squirrly
I like mice. They are nice.
They nibble on paper towels.

Barbara

NEWS

Andy R.   May 21, 1964

We had some visters.
They came from India.
The lady a 6 yard of silk. it was 25 yard whyed.
The man had a Gandhi-Cap.

NEWS

Cindy Wood   May 28, 1964

In morris town.
They had a crash up.
The man were dead.

Cynthia

The little snow man
by Debbie Prewitt

Once there was a little snow man. He was lonesme. He want
to play. Oh dear I can not walk. He get smaller and smaller
and one day a girl came. Oh dear said the girl. What a snow
man. He is small. I will helpe you said the girl. I will put on
snow. you are geting bigr mr snow man.

The End

A first-grade story written independently, using some words, as needed, from
an experience story developed during talking time.

Children's Vocabulary

Teachers may feel safe in using any word that she feels helpful
for her purposes, as long as it has the quality to stir feelings within
a child. These dynamic words will hold together other words—such
as "from," "were," etc.—that have little importance on their own, but
that serve as building blocks in our language structure. Simply because various investigators have discovered these words that children (of given ages) use ninety-eight per cent of the time is not to

say that those words are applicable in a given school situation. The test for the use of the word in dictated material is its importance to the child who says it and the others who hear it said.

"Hurricane" is not a word on any first-grade vocabulary list, nor are several others from preceding charts, but a teacher who would refuse to use such words on that chart is denying learning opportunities to the class. The fitting of words to children, rather than using what a class says, is why basal readers are so drab. There is no guarantee that the few chosen from word lists by the basal authors will meet a given class's interests. Rather the expression of the children works in the opposite direction, and rightly so. Children are the masters of the words they speak, and whatever any other group of children speak is of little importance in reading instruction—particularly in the beginning stages.

WRITING AND READING

From the very first day of school, children can begin to write.[22] Indeed they MUST begin to write if the teacher is to take advantage of her total instructional opportunities. Writing is entwined in all reading activities from the beginning.

Children begin, as has been noted in the many excellent texts on curriculum and language arts, by writing their name. Children show early in life their interest in, not only their own name, but the names of everything about them—animate and inanimate. Knowing what a cart is, what a cat is, what a fireplace is gives the child a sense of personal power.[23] If he can identify, he can use—because he can extend himself into the seemingly magic area of communication. In the classroom, children's names go on everything that belongs to them. Everything about the room is labeled—the door, the table, the crayon drawer, the chairs, ad infinitum.

From this simple labeling children's concepts are spread to other children's names. One first-grade teacher took roll by means of an alphabetized box of her pupils' first names with the initials of their last names. The day started with each child going through the box for his own name. Paul soon learned that his name was in the middle of the box. William never hesitated in looking behind the "W" section. Cornelia knew hers was in the front of the box. And so it went. All those present brought their cards to the talking time. The teacher

---

[22] See Alvina Burrows, *They All Want to Write* (third ed.), New York: Holt, Rinehart & Winston, Inc., 1964; D. M. Lee and R. VanAllen, op. cit., for excellent discussions of this area.

[23] This concept underlies the whole "Operation Headstart" program.

used these cards in many ways. Names with the same first letter were then compared. Initial consonants were taught by ear through "getting ready to say 'Paul.' " The absentees were pulled out and listed on the board. Soon someone could copy off those names, too, for the teacher's records (takes longer—but look at what it could teach!). The absentees' names were used for purposes of hearing letter sounds and recognizing similar shapes and configurations. The copying leads to writing.

Because it is important that a child write a book of his own as soon as he can do so, we must examine the interdependence of writing and reading.

Breakthrough for Children's Authorship

Teachers experimenting in San Diego, California, in taking dictation report that after so long, one by one, a child will want to write his story himself. This is a tremendously important development, a real breakthrough. As we have said, the child reaches the point where he says "I WANT TO DO IT MYSELF!" When this demand occurs, the teacher must see to it that the child does write *what he can*. A few moments must be taken to help him see where the words are that he might need—how to get help when he can't find the words he wants to use—and in all ways, to proceed down the path of independent writing and self-expression.

The Child As an Author

Appreciation of the effort and understanding of what is involved in making is essential to learning to read. Without such realization, learning to read can become a meaningless exercise without reason, without need, without cause. The child who struggles to write his own book is the one who rapidly gains the feeling of what it means to write a book. Even if he DICTATES it in its entirety to his teacher, he still gains this sense of appreciation of authorship. This appreciation cannot be overemphasized as the incentive for good reading. It provides the driving energy that surmounts all those difficulties in the way of he who would become a reader.

Children who do read tend to be the ones who cannot resist reading. Like eating food when hungry and going to sleep when sleepy, reading is a way of life. Writing one's own book is full of that kind of incentive.[24]

[24] See also J. A. Cutforth, *English in the Primary School*, Oxford: Basil Blackwell & Mott, 1959. Vicars Bell, *On Learning the English Tongue*, London: Faber & Faber, Ltd., 1953.

What is a book to a six year old? Probably a series of pages suffices to represent a book in the mind of a young learner. Then what is on a page? A single idea written, or drawn, or both.

In the beginning a teacher may call up those children ready for this activity into a group. For that matter, children not ready to write can also come. Why not?

As writing upon charts appears, and needs to write letters, stories, and other items occur, children can copy words, letter by letter, without any damage to their progression in learning to read. The time for the formal instruction in spelling—i.e., instruction in learning words letter by letter—should not come until the child's maturity as to vision and his store of sight words have served to move him to the stage where he can see the middles of words. In fact, the child who gives some kind of a signal that he hears and sees the middle of a word is ready for formal spelling. Before that day, teachers will run the risk of upsetting the steady progression of seeing from left to right, and the breaking down of wholes into parts, if formal spelling instruction is begun too soon.

Once words are there for all to see—up on the wall—on their pictures—all over the place—children not only can, but should begin to copy them for various purposes. Independent writing of some kind should occur every day—just as there should be two experience charts done each day. Teachers must help children write the words they need to use. Instruction on letter shapes and forms must begin —left to right—top to bottom—and large letters on the board are fine starting points for six-year-old muscle coordination. Writing is not innate. It is learned. It must be taught.

In the same way that teachers show children that the words they SAY can be written down by the teachers, so must they show children that those same words can be written by themselves. Copying a word letter by letter is not spelling instruction unless drill takes place. Teachers, then, assist and promote all kinds of writing *as a part of the reading instruction program*, and must provide constant opportunity in this direction.

Progression for Child Authors

There is a progression that can be followed for young authors. While individual variations are always desirable, the following steps may serve as guides to the teacher.

1. The child draws a picture.
2. The teacher says: "When you have several pictures, bring them to me and I will show you how to make a book of your pictures."

3. The first "authorship" may be a book of pictures.

4. Eventually the teacher will suggest to the child, "Why don't you write a story about your pictures? I will help you with the words."

5. Pictures begin to carry captions, phrases, and then perhaps sentences—either on the picture itself or upon lined paper attached or lines provided underneath the picture space.

6. The teacher moves in the direction of making a book with such labeled pictures.

7. Eventually the teacher says, "I have these blank notebooks[25] (or "Go to the dime store tonight and buy a notebook.") and when you are ready to make your own book I will help you work."

8. The teacher works with the child (or children in a group) on ideas for their books as follows:
"What will your book be about? Your pets? Your family? Your playing? Who would like me to take your picture with my camera and then you can make your book about you?"

9. The children proceed, during their independent work time, along the lines planned with the teacher. The teacher works for greater and greater independence on the part of the "authors."

10. Eventually, these pages can actually be bound into a book. It is a high incentive for children's reading and writing.

Here are some examples and suggestions of ways in which writing can become part of the daily reading program.

Copying Words

Teacher: Here is our story. What are your favorite words? Choose those you like and go back to your seat and write them.

or

Look at all of our stories around the room. Choose some words that you know and write them down. I would like to see them.

Writing to Others

Teachers' notes to pupils:
Teachers write individual notes to pupils upon matters that concern only them, as:

1 "Would you bring your hamster to school for us all to see?"

2. "Your new pencil is ready for you. Come and ask me for it."

---

[25] Many school systems provide inexpensive tagboard-covered notebooks. If these are not available, the pupil can purchase some at the dime store. This act of purchasing is, in itself, a true motivator toward making a book.

3. "I like your new short hair cut."
4. "It was fun to meet your mother."

Children's notes to teacher:

1. "May I have a new pencil?"
2. "Will you come to my house for lunch on Tuesday?"
3. "May I bring my sister to school?"
4. "You did not see my new shoes. I like them."
5. "You are the best teacher in all the world. I love you."

Pupils write to family, friends, or anyone, who must be contacted, as:

1. "Dear Mother and Daddy: Will you come to the PTA meeting?"
2. "Dear Uncle Joe: Will you come to school and tell us about working on a train?"
3. "Dear Mr Voigt: May our First Grade come to see your paint factory?"

Skills Involved in Authorship

WORD COPYING. Copying words for such material usually means copying words *that are known.* The child needs to know how to spell "This is my house." He knows what these words look like as they are part of his sight vocabulary. He searches with the help of the teacher, if necessary. He searches by reading and rereading previously done experience charts, books, and anything else that will be helpful. As he is on the verge of seeing words themselves in reading whole sentences, he is pushed to move in that direction.

Sentences, as we have said, govern the meaning of the words in them. Sentences, particularly in the beginning, should be read back *as they were spoken.* Thus children in muttering to themselves, groping for the words they want for their books, follow normal oral speech patterns. They want the word "puppies" in a sentence like:

"My dog had _____."

They read the sentence as they have it so far, come to the missing word—that is, the blank space—and the search is on. The teacher has said:

Look over all of our charts. See if you can remember where the one is that you *know* has your word on it. Look in any book that you know will help you. Can you put down the first letter of the word? If you can, do it, and go on to write the rest of your story. Later I or someone else will help you. Maybe your neighbor knows how to spell your word. Don't bother him too much, but once in a while is all right.

USING SIGHT VOCABULARY. Here is another example of how to transfer sight vocabulary that has been accumulating into a reading situation.

From some experience story a teacher might say to each child: "What are your favorite words in this story?" And each child will go and show a word or two. Then the teacher might say, "Would you put your favorite word in your alphabet book?" And so a child records his own pet words. In fact, this could well be a beginning step, leading into "writing" their first "book." To write a letter is to write words. Reading and rereading are a vital necessity when writing. In all truth one cannot write without reading. They are two sides of the same coin.

The skills that are begun by writing at this level are the beginning skills of word analysis, which occupies us vitally at the next two levels. Words are composed of letters. Copying "D-E-A-R M-O-T-H-E-R" starts the first awareness that these whole words have parts. We might note in passing that the reason formal spelling cannot be taught until the child shows he sees—easily sees—letters in words is that formal drill upon letter by letter will interfere with normal breakdown of the Gestalt of seeing wholes.

Finally, books can become true works of art. The child, instead of starting with a picture, may start with a story and then illustrate it. The carryover into social studies is particularly useful in the upper grade levels.

One sixth grade was studying the problem "How Man Has Kept Records Through the Ages." Groups in the class variously worked on paper-making projects, i.e., real paper made from real rags, ink-making, book-binding, block-printing, type-setting, and printing by machine. The respect for craftsmanship that grew among these pupils was notable. For our purposes here, however, the expanded knowledge of record-making developed tremendous appreciation of book-making. Those who love books appreciate the art of construction and also the art of writing.

A BOOK OF THEIR OWN

With writing experience of this nature a matter of daily diet, children pile up a further store of sight words that they know—either by total shape or by some part of them. As soon as possible, and here individual differences come strongly into play, the teacher urges them to write a "book of their own." The teacher can, and perhaps should have each child make a "book of his own," a necessary task before he may read a book written by someone else. This is a common practice in England and has much merit.

Children can write their own books on a hundred subjects. But the egocentrism of the early grade levels would probably lead them to write something about themselves—their homes, their pets, their families, their trips, and the like. One teacher gets her first graders off to such a start by taking photographs of each of her pupils, and then using the snapshots as an incentive to write "books" about themselves. Her success is notable. The children write pages and pages.

Those who remember the film classic "Passion For Life" (*L'Ecole Buissoniere*)[26] recall the effect on Albert when he had a camera. The entire class in that film wrote about things that mattered to them, a kind of experience story at older grade levels.

The suggestion of an "own book" as a prerequisite to reading other books is not meant to be arbitrary—and for that matter, such an activity can go right along with any kind of a reading program. Whether writing his own book comes first, last, or concurrently is not nearly so important as whether or not it happens. The child as an author is more likely to become the child as a reader, more easily, more rapidly, and with greater appreciation than if writing is not so used.

Writing one's own book involves skills of writing, of course, but just as importantly, it involves skills of reading, and therefore becomes a necessary part of the reading instruction program.

TRANSITION INTO PUBLISHED BOOKS

The approach to reading through experiences will provide anything that is needed to read books. The rich vocabulary of children's speech is available to any teacher who knows how to use it. More importantly, that same richness of vocabulary is the bridge the teacher can use to promote the reading of "real" books.

The School and Classroom Library

In school a child voluntarily goes to where books are—the library corner—the school library—and selects those he likes. Nice pictures attract him.

[26] Brandon Films, New York, N. Y.

What is the teacher's role in this? There are several. One is making sure that books surround the children. There must be many. No classroom is complete without three to five books per child of different titles. For that matter, no school is complete without a school library and librarian. That means, as of this writing, that the vast majority of American schools are incomplete.[27]

The teacher must search for books everywhere and, if he fails to find them, organize his colleagues and his community to pressure the powers that be for money to purchase them.

Making sure of an adequate supply of books does not guarantee that they be properly used. Children, if permitted, will find them irresistible. But do teachers so permit? Or do they too often treat books as mothers treat spinach and ice cream? "Eat your spinach. Then you can have ice cream," Mothers say. "No, you cannot have your dessert until you eat your dinner" they say, as if dessert was not part of dinner.

Teachers say similar things. "No, you cannot go to the library corner until you finish your work." The room library corner becomes something that is not part of the work of the room. It is extra. It is a reward. The library corner must assume every bit as much importance as the child's own desk. The class "work" in reading must be *centrally* based upon such trade books. In the same way the school library is *central* to class work.

Finding One's Own Words in Published Books

As soon as each child can recognize ANY word and remember it for himself, he can begin his search through the library corner, or the school library, for *that* word in a book. This is precisely the incentive that teachers can use so well. A child learns a word for whatever reason that arises. Probably the child learns a dozen words, then two dozen, then a hundred. It does not matter. But when he knows a word his feet must be set on the path to finding that word elsewhere. Although we are using the term "word," the child may just as well learn to identify a phrase, a sentence, or a phonological unit. Whatever it may be, the shape and configuration of that word are in his head. He *knows* it. The teacher then says to the one child or the many children who are at that stage:

[27] In passing we cannot refrain from commenting that the same amount of money that sends one spacecraft in orbit would pay for most of this lack of books. A society that blows up its material wealth in one way and yet neglects the development of the intelligence of its children through the written word needs to examine its expenditures!

See these words that you have told me and that I put down on our charts? Some of you know those words no matter where you find them. I want you to look everywhere you can think of to see how many *of these same words* you can find.

Into a book.

So the children are urged to seek words of their own choosing. A teacher needs but the first child who, with triumph, shows a word (phrase, etc.) in a book that is the same as that on the chart. Praise is indeed in order, and can hardly be overdone. This is, perhaps, the most important step of all in the process of using oral language to teach reading in books. The teacher should not view this accomplishment of pupils calmly. Enthusiasm, delight, and clear-cut approval must be the order of that day. A milestone has been reached. It is not a class milestone, or a group milestone, but an individual personal milestone. It is the key to all future reading progress. Sight vocabulary is being accumulated on the daily experience charts, and other reading skills pile up through the days and weeks.

In addition, the teacher's role is to read aloud from books. Once a day in the beginning—until children have heard many of them read by their teacher, who should be the best oral reader in the room.

The teacher is the best reader, or should be (!)—oral and otherwise—in the room. The literature period should be a daily delight, and children set on the path that leads to that library corner to read *The Story of Ping*[28] and *Millions of Cats*[29] for themselves.

"See all of those words you told me to write on these charts?" says the teacher pointing to what should be a large collection hung on the walls.

"Look at all those words of your own in those stories. You have heard me read *If I Ran the Circus*[30] to you. You heard me read *Peter Rabbit*[31] and oh, so many of those books in our library corner. *Did you know the same words are in books that are on your chart stories? You didn't? You don't believe me? Go and see!* Who can be first to find a word? Just one word, mind you. Or maybe two. Who will it be?"

Moving into the Individual Conference

As children find themselves able to read a book, in whole or part, they must have an individual conference with their teacher on that book. The teacher should always have a notebook and record the progress of pupils in the direction of developing independence. Even if a teacher's records are not complete, it takes a blind teacher, indeed, to miss the child's excitement when he finds himself able to read SOMETHING for himself. Usually children announce the event to the heavens. They are thrilled and they should be. When a child exhibits such enthusiasm, the teacher must make arrangements to work individually with that child.

Each day there must be some kind of an independent work period. Often this period is a noisy, banging, building kind of activity. When the teacher sees that one or more children need a conference, then the rest of the class must be occupied with independent work that is quiet (see Chapter 5). The time has come for teachers to differentiate for her class two kinds of work periods: 1) a quiet one that allows the teacher to work with individuals or groups, and 2) a more noisy one that allows for building and construction and allows the

---

28 Marjorie Flack, *The Story of Ping*, New York: Viking Press, 1935.
29 Wanda Gag, *Millions of Cats*, New York: Coward-McCann, Inc.
30 Dr. Seuss, *If I Ran the Circus*, New York: Random House, Inc.
31 Beatrix Patter, *The Tale of Peter Rabbit*, New York: Frederick Warne & Co., Inc.

teacher to move from group to group or child to child holding a paper here, suggesting next steps there, and so on. In the latter period, the teacher is not *formally* teaching anything. She is moving around the room assisting children in work projects of various types.

When a classroom is quietly absorbed in some activity, then the teacher is released to work with single children. But teachers must insist that there be few interruptions, and only those of emergency nature. Children must be trained to be resourceful without bothering teachers unnecessarily. Independent work means just that. Individual or group conferences have priority at such a time.

The Role of Books in Reading Instruction

Tradebooks are the best materials for teaching reading that are available. They are most like children's normal speech patterns. Basal readers saddle teachers and children with artificially controlled vocabulary in ways that have never been justified by research. The assumption that a few words are learned *before* reading takes place is considered insupportable by the writer of this text. Rather than learning words to read, one reads (i.e., recognizes what he has said) in order to learn words. The entire progression of reading instruction presented herein is predicated upon a quite opposite philosophy. While needing more exploration research-wise, it is based upon facts that children speak and think and work out their own lives. Their thinking and speaking are the most important parts of their living, because the speaking communicates thought and ideas to others. Man cannot exist *as man* in isolation. He must communicate with others. Books are one way in which others can communicate with him. It is that simple.

Those readers who may feel that the presented method of reading instruction in this text is intended to supplement or support basal reading have not read with much comprehension. Language teaching must be approached through experience. As the skills develop, then the horizon is limitless. Any book, anywhere, is proper fare for the reader as he chooses. Tradebooks are the richest source of man's knowledge. They are written by far better writers than textbooks, the present author not excepted. They usually provide depth, variety, and scope not often included in books that are supposed to be read by all in the same way. Perhaps books of simple vocabulary can be used, as some children grow in confidence when they are able to read such. It is not the *books* of basal readers that are so objectionable. It is the insistence of authors and publishers that all use them in the same way.

Children's Literature

A teacher must read aloud frequently from books of literary merit. Before children are able to read for themselves, a literature period— i.e., a reading aloud from the best literature available is vital. Once independent reading comes into its own, the teacher can space such literature periods to less frequent periods, although in our opinion, never less than once a week at any level. Children must get to know those stories that have stood the test of time, and sometimes, perhaps, are so difficult that years must pass before they are able to read them for themselves. *Dr. Doolittle, Robinson Crusoe, Swiss Family Robinson*, the *Jungle Books* are but a few. But modern classics are not to be ignored. *Misty of Chincoteague* will outdo *Black Beauty*. It is this kind of material that expands children's horizons. It is this kind of literature of which children's dreams are made. When teachers neglect literature for workbook exercises, or the repetition of the directed reading lesson, they are doing so at dreadful sacrifice to learning. It is not too much to ask how much conformity, or lack of inventiveness and ingenuity, has resulted in our nation from such neglect.

Saying that tradebooks are the best instructional material also says that they may not be used *en masse*. They are best used on a self-choice basis. Each child may have the privilege of choosing his own. The province of this chapter on beginning reading is to describe how we get children to that point. We continue with a description that takes children up to and through the stage where they are past the word analysis stage. Once the rapid reading stage is reached other kinds of activities must be planned.

SUMMARY

The discussion of beginning reading concludes at the point where children's reading abilities move into the rapid-reading phase, and they are well on the way toward adult patterns of reading. The chapter might be recapitulated by stating some of its major points in slightly different form and order. We have said in several ways, for example:

1. Reading instruction must take advantage of and promote all psychological developments of the child.
2. Reading instruction must follow a pattern, a system, a structure of broad enough stages to allow elasticity of application.

3. Reading instruction cannot be preplanned in a closed fashion for an unknown group of pupils.

4. Reading instruction must begin with and proceed from the language and experience of the pupils.

We have also said that the organization of a beginning reading program must involve the following principles:

A. Operational
   1. The setting of classroom routines as:
      a. Provision for organized talking times.
      b. Provision for individual conference.
      c. Provision for grouping on specific needs.
      d. Provision for use of the child's total environment.
B. Philosophical
   1. The use of the children's own spoken language for:
      a. The development of the concept of reading.
      b. The development of certain abilities.
   2. The use of self-selection in reading:
      a. To reduce the problem of readiness.
      b. To develop incentive, initiative, interest, and attention.
      c. To provide for all differences between individuals.
      d. To transfer recognition of own words to others' words.

In sum, the chapter has presented practice and method designed to start children on the road to reading in the most efficient way possible. It is, indeed, a royal road.

10

READING AT THE MORE ADVANCED LEVELS

PHILOSOPHY AND BACKGROUND OF READING AND THE CONTENT AREAS

A reading period, as such, cannot be justified at the more advanced levels of achievement. It is a waste of classroom time to set aside time for only reading instruction. All the skills related to the upper levels of reading can be taught, and, indeed, should be taught, as part of the content areas that form the basis of the curriculum at older age levels. There is much agreement in the research literature that generalized reading ability is not enough to help pupils attack the problems of content learning. The excellent discussion by Spache[1] and Smith[2] underline the lack of relationship between general reading ability and specific reading in social studies, mathematics and the other subject areas.

Coulter[3] writes, ". . . the teaching of reading skills and the teaching of subject matter are inseparably related. The studies show that merely the fact that a child reads well from a general reading text is no guarantee that he will successfully master the unique reading skills required of arithmetic, science, and the social studies . . . this is not an automatic coupling."

Once pupils have come through the word analysis stage, and their need to take words apart in order to recognize—thus *read*—them has passed, they will move into the rapid reading stage, as we have described. When word analysis becomes word perception, the ability to read is over its major hurdle. From that point on, reading as a process changes in degree perhaps, but not particularly in form.

[1] George Spache, *Towards Better Reading.* Champaign, Ill.: Garrard Publishing Co., 1963, p. 49.
[2] Nila B. Smith, *Reading Instruction For Today's Children*, Englewood Cliffs, N. J.: Prentice-Hall, 1963, pp. 308–9.
[3] M. L. Coulter, *Changing Concepts of Reading Instruction,* Int'l Reading Assoc. Conference Proceedings, 1961, Vol. 6.

A reader will always use reading to discover what he wants to know from the printed page. But at the advanced levels he *knows* how to read. Therefore the amount of time formerly spent on attaining mastery of the printed page is no longer necessary. He is freed from the task of learning how to read and can give attention, as never before, to the task of learning what books say.

The American publisher has presented his public with the finest collection of tradebooks the world has ever seen. In 1963, twenty-one hundred tradebooks *for children* came off the presses. These are, in large part, good books, written and illustrated by professionals. Some of them are truly great literature. Some are inadequate or unusable. With these riches a teacher in the elementary school, not to mention those at the high-school level, can use tradebooks alone for content learning.

Geography must be taught. Why not use the many books on rivers of the world, for example, as one area of the learning? History is important. *Pioneers Of The Press*[4] is another example of a fascinating discussion of the experiences of early printers and newspaper editors. The West must be opened all over again, every year, for hundreds of thousands of children. What better source material than in the legions of books, many of which would give television programs of the "old days" a run for their money.

The Negro question has never received adequate attention in either formal texts or informal instruction. The generations of children who absorbed the stereotype of the Negro female from *Little Black Sambo*[5] are many. Only recently the social conscience of the nation has pushed the publication of books presenting more authoritative pictures of Negro life, such as *Southtown*,[6] *William*,[7] *A Snowy Day*,[8] *Hold Fast To Your Dreams*,[9] and others. The Civil War—its armies, its generals, its horses, its spies, and, above all, Lincoln, is to be found in hundreds and hundreds of books. The possibility of learning facts, of understanding social problems, from tradebooks makes the use of single texts in the area of social studies a mark of incredibly poor instruction.

To put matters more bluntly, the teaching of reading in the content areas cannot be carried out satisfactorily unless teachers are emancipated from single texts and are allowed to teach from multiple sources. The trouble is, however, that teachers so frequently do

[4] *Pioneers of the Press*, New York: Crown Publishing Co.

[5] Helen Bannerman, *Little Black Sambo*.

[6] Lorenz Graham, *Southtown*, Chicago: Follett Publishing Co., 1958.

[7] Anne W. Guy, *William*, New York: Dial Press, Inc., 1961.

[8] E. J. Keats, *A Snowy Day*, New York: The Viking Press, Inc., 1962.

[9] Catherine Blanton, *Hold Fast To Your Dreams*, New York: Julian Messner, Inc., 1955.

not know how to use multiple sources. That is the task of this chapter. In order to do this we need to refer to the various parts of the book where we have described such teaching.

Is Reading a Subject or a Process?

A "subject" is an area of knowledge that has been selected from a larger area by someone, supposedly informed enough to make a wise selection. Therefore a "subject" must be a selection from a body of knowledge *that is known.* A "subject" cannot be original, or creative, or be related to the future. A "subject" in a curriculum cannot even be an invention, because an invention is not known. Therefore, the very nature of a "subject" roots it in the past. It must be static.

A skill is something by which we can study a subject. It is a tool of examination, a tool of learning. It is the means by which a given body of knowledge is learned. By its nature, it can and does change from day to day, from teacher to teacher, and from pupil to pupil. It has or can have a quality of immediacy, of invention, of dynamism. It should change and grow. Therefore, a skill is a process. Processes are ever changing, and are more oriented toward the future than toward the past.

Reading Is a Process

Reading, on this basis, is a process. We employ a skill in furthering reading. We use reading in all curriculum areas. It cannot be a subject in that it does not exist as a body of content. It is something that happens to bodies of content. The act of reading is not an end in itself, but is a means to another end. Reading therefore is essentially a process.

Traditional patterns of three ability–grouped, basal book–centered instruction treat reading as a subject, therefore static. It has required certain types of material that have been supposedly correctly graded as to difficulty, from simple to the more difficult. Present research calls into question the control of vocabulary as a measure of difficulty. Vocabulary control was the crux upon which the planned sequential nature of these graded materials swings. Within this framework of alleged control, reading skills were theoretically cemented into the interlocking sets of publications, the reader-manual-workbook triumvirate. The teaching of skills was intended to be implemented from one to the other to the third. Unfortunately, there is little if any, existing research at this time that substantiates this claim. More to the point, perhaps, is that this theoretically interdependent trio of publications caused reading to lose its characteristic as a process and, instead, helped it become a body of content.

To the extent that the body of content outlined in the reader-manual-workbook combine was used verbatim, to that extent was the process of reading frozen and rigidified into a body of content. Questions need to be raised. Townsend[10] notes that "current research furnishes very little evidence supporting workbooks except perhaps in the upper high school. . . ."

If reading should be a means to an end, then drastic change is called for from the traditional patterns developing reading as a body of content to those patterns developing reading as a process, and a thought process, at that.

The Dilemma of Teaching in the Content Areas

Teachers in the middle and upper grades are skewered on the dilemma of the single text book, usually with an accompanying workbook, in the social studies, science, and arithmetic. Although the onset of modern mathematics has brought some relief in that area, there are still teachers who, as do the vast majority of their peers in social studies instruction, "follow the book" page by inexorable page. More seriously, a kind of guilt feeling has been developed among teachers that they are somehow "sacrificing" their children if they skip a page or fail to grind through the ineffective and uneducational workbook exercises that go with these types of texts. The truth of the matter might be in that few teachers *know what else to do* to take up the class time during that portion of the school day. To keep children occupied is a worthwhile teacher goal. But the broad streak of Puritanical thought too prevalent among teachers confuses many into believing that such business must be painful. It must be hard work. Hard work is good for the soul, they say.

As we reject the value of single texts in reading at any grade level, so we reject the single text in any content area of the curriculum. There simply are no books that are so good that every child must read every page. The following comment on American history texts is typical of many authorities:

. . . The conditions surrounding textbook manufacturing practically guarantee that the textbook content will be conceptually empty at the same time that the students, particularly the bright ones, will be led to believe that they are learning great and significant truths. . . .[11]

[10] Agatha Townsend, Reading Consultant, Stroud Union School District, Pa., "What Research Says to the Reading Teacher," March, 1964, p. 6.

[11] Lawrence E. Metcalf, "Research on Teaching Social Studies," *Handbook of Research on Learning* (N. L. Gage, ed.), American Educational Research Association, Chicago: Rand McNally Co., 1963, p. 953.

The problem, of course, can be traced to the quite understandable publisher desire for as wide a market as possible. No segment of the population can be offended and so facts are watered down to this end. The publishers' laudable intention of meeting the needs and interests of all children from coast to coast without offending anyone while still including a proper account of accurate information is an impossibility. The sooner administrators realize that history, geography, economics, and science cannot be limited to one text, the sooner will the teachers under their jurisdiction be freed from an intolerable and impossible task of "covering the material." The answer is that single texts, preferably in the teachers' hands, might be used in conjunction with a variety of tradebooks and other materials. Such texts might be available in small sets of five or six, but to have every child have a copy of his own seems a patent waste of precious taxpayer money. Let the teachers have several texts, and spend the money saved on a grand diversification of materials now flooding the market. The publishers will, of necessity, need to shift their operations from single texts to more widely varied books of other types.

Reading problems that have arisen and have caused teachers and administrators to expand their emphasis on reading *for its own sake* have, at least in part, and we believe in major part, come from the incessant and mandatory use of single texts. Social studies is not the only area that is taught from a single book to the whole class at the same time. Science is being taught the same way, as are English, health, music, and other areas.

The dilemma of the teacher is to resolve the reading problem with such texts—as they are aimed at the median achievement levels of the grade—thus by definition, half the children find them too hard and the other half are left unchallenged. Teachers trying to fit the variety of human beings to nonvaried material are doomed from the start. Diversification of material is a crucial first step toward reading independence at these advanced levels.

Curriculum Reform Will Bring Reading Improvement

What must happen is a fresh look at the curriculum practices of the teaching of social studies and the rest.

The many sources[12] to be found on the teaching of the content areas are based on the assumption that content areas must be taught

---

[12] To mention a few: Spache, *Towards Better Reading, op. cit.*, Chap. 16; Smith, *Reading Instruction for Today's Children, op. cit.*, Chap. 10; Paul McKee, *The Teaching of Reading in the Elementary School*, Boston: Houghton Mifflin Co., 1948, Chaps. 12–16.

from a common text. These and other references like them present many panaceas so that teachers will receive help in working with these content area texts. These references are replete with reading exercises, informal tests, and practice sessions of various types. They give one the feeling that if one reads to master the "study skills," whatever they are, one will eventually find his pupils mastering the texts. There is little hope in this. Quite uniformly, the overemphasis upon the reading of the text has prevented real education in the given area from taking place. As most of the specialists in reading are not trained in curriculum practice and too often have little classroom experience, it is no wonder that their remedies for poor reading in the content areas are largely ineffective.

The fresh look at the curriculum involves an acceptance of, or a return to, the problem-centered curriculum. Hopkins' book *Interaction*,[13] the British film, *Near Home*,[14] Noar's *Freedom to Live and Learn*,[15] and the writings of Frederick G. Bonser[16] in the practical arts are helpful in this area.

The problem-centered curriculum includes reading, not for its own sake, but for the sake of teaching children to work and learn about their own society. Reading, then, assumes its proper role of a tool, a process. It can never be anything else but a means to the end of education. Teachers obscure the meaning and role of reading if they pluck it out of the curriculum and treat it as an area of content.

If we believe that we should teach as well as we know how, we find it hard to accept a program composed of isolated subjects, or a program in which drills or fact or subject-matter mastery are the chief concerns. If schools are to make each child the type of adult that a society needs, then his day-to-day learning and in-school living must have much of the qualities expected in later life.

The problem is not really one of "isolating" subjects, as there are many times in a school schedule that the whole class will do nothing but handwriting or geography or arithmetic, because that is what is necessary to proceed along the path of social development. The problem is to refrain from disintegrating the learning situations that the child faces. These may or may not fall into the neatly compart-

[13] L. T. Hopkins, *Interaction: The Democratic Process*, Boston: D. C. Heath & Co., 1941.

[14] *Near Home*, Ministry of Education (part of Visual Unit "Local Studies") London, England. Rentals from film libraries of The Pennsylvania State University, New York University, University of Illinois, and others.

[15] Gertrude Noar, *Freedom to Live and Learn*, Philadelphia: Franklin Publishing Co., 1948.

[16] Bonser, F. G. *Industrial Arts for Elementary Schools*, New York, Macmillan Co., 1923. Bonser, F. G., *Elementary School Curriculum*, New York: Macmillan Co., 1921.

mentalized subdivisions of the all-encompassing areas of human knowledge—but it is the learning situation, and not the logical sequence of subject matter that gives the cue to teachers as to what needs to come next.

Children learn to read, not by means of isolated drills and exercises, but by means of all the reading activities that have significance to them because of self-selected materials and projects from a variety of possibilities. We learn to speak and write as we need to use speech and writing to communicate. We learn to use arithmetic as the concepts bear directly—the more directly the better—upon our daily needs and in the solution of daily problems. The content of the social studies is examined as it bears upon the understanding of our present problems or as it sates our appetites about man's past. We study the world of science for its own sake, as we seek a solution to our problems as gardeners, cooks, hobbyists, simply because it interests us.

COVERING THE SUBJECT MATTER

The question arises in some minds "How are we going to cover the subject matter?" The answer is not satisfactory, but it is simple. No one ever "covers the subject matter" no matter how bright he is or how able his students are. Even the most committed of single textbook teachers move on, bemoaning all the time (and blaming the poor reading habits of the children) without insuring "mastery" on the part of even a minimum of the students. There is simply too much to learn. In any event, someone must make a decision, arbitrary or by guess, of selecting that small fraction of material to be taught from the vast reservoir at our disposal.

The final reward is not whether or not children have "covered" a prescribed—and largely unproved as to value—block of skills, subject matter, facts, etc., but whether or not they have been started on a path of insatiable and eager curiosity that will never fail them.

Learning To Be Curious

The proof of the pudding lies in viewing the child's increased ability to see a problem, to research for pertinent data, to see unexpected ramifications, to make effective application of what he finds out. As a profession, teachers should seek to trigger, to stimulate, to energize an ever-increasing and indefatigable sense of inquiry for appropriate knowledge of the world. Given this, the matter of reading, of figuring, of experimenting, falls into its proper sphere. The studies that show pupils asking decreasing numbers of questions as they proceed through their schooling is a damning piece of evidence of poor instruction. Hopefully this text will be a nudge in the direction of increasing the curiosity of children.

Teaching Skills Directly or Indirectly

We come again to the problem of when and how to teach skills. A direct attack, as we have said elsewhere, should come when the teacher has discovered that a pupil, or several pupils, does not know a specific item. Then that teacher rolls up his sleeves and teaches directly, specifically to that need and no other—with, perhaps, a follow-up exercise of some kind.

The problem of reading skills in the higher achievement levels is not a *reading* problem. It is a problem of using a tool to explore the unknown, to investigate, to analyze, to experiment, to learn, to categorize, to outline problem solutions. In short, to read in the middle and upper grades is to fit reading into the pattern of all the curriculum.

Repetitive Drill Signals Poor Teaching

This is the pedagogical problem for teachers at those levels. In open-ended learning, provisions for skills mastery is made directly and indirectly, formally and informally. In every situation, however, the skills are learned—not as ends in themselves but as a means to well-planned, well-defined ends—even though they be labeled exploratory or inventive. Spelling, mathematics, writing, etc. drills occupy a very small proportion of the school day. To drill, in truth, means that what is drilled upon was never really taught. Reinforcement is the product of reward, not repetition. To repeat is really to defeat reinforcement. Drill is needed only when the teaching has been poor. Drill is needed when the learning has had little relation to the pupil's own self. Drill is something that is piled on top of a child but is not OF him.[17]

Most of the schoolday's schedule is given over to an ever-widening series of individual and group meetings to work out operations that will solve the daily problems of living together—classroom rules, letter-writing to learn about new things, letter-writing in general, discussing news events, dramatizing to reinforce knowledge discovered in various places, planning for next steps in the unit, and so on.

The sequence that can be categorized as "Word Analysis" or "Word Breakup" will be needed in reading. The child at the higher

[17] See Ashton-Warner's discussion of "one-look" words on this point, *Teacher*, New York: Simon & Schuster, Inc., 1963, p. 49.

levels of achievement who needs to analyze a word, IN ITS PARTS, is not at this stage as long as that need is his problem. He is at an earlier stage.

The teacher must return to a teaching technique of those earlier levels. In short, he must return to the proper place in the curriculum to learn word analysis—i.e., in spelling or written language. Learning to spell *in order* to write is the best way to teach these analytical skills as we have urged from the very beginning.

Fallacies of Skill Teaching at Advanced Levels

Obviously, there are other skills, *unique to reading*, that belong in the higher achievement levels, and in no other. The teacher must make a decision, usually an on-the-spot decision, whether or not the child's problem is one of word analysis or of word perception. If the need lies in the word breakup category, the teacher tells the word immediately in order to help the child get on with his task, and records, or has the child record, a reference for use during instructional time in written language, especially spelling.

On the other hand, if the problem lies in the area OTHER than the need to break up a word, the teacher must plan to teach what that child needs in the most efficient manner. Which of these needs, for example, are purely READING needs? Very few indeed. Which of these skills is taught *by reading itself* without need to refer to any content area of the middle- and upper-grade curriculum? For example:

Location Skills	Are Best Learned:
Title of book	At pre-primer level
Table of contents	During book selection in recreational reading, or problem-solving in science, geography, etc.
or	
Index	During request time in music class using music book
Footnotes	During social studies unit problem-solving
Copyright, Preface, Glossary, Appendix	During unit problem-solving
Library Skills	
Use of card file	For recreational reading, or solution of unit problem, as soon as needed in first grade.
Understanding guide cards in card file	During problem-solving during unit or news discussion.
Special reference materials: atlas, encyclopedia, etc.	During problem-solving in social studies, discussion, science, etc.

Paragraph Development	Written composition, especially letter writing, newspapers and periodicals, and news analysis
Outlining	To organize steps in unit development or to organize content of a personal letter, or planning creative dramatics
Adapting Rate of Reading	
Skimming	In selecting material to solve problems or other purposes to find a specific point
Rapid reading	Recreational reading or to assess a book in terms of a problem to be solved, to rearrange books on shelves
Rereading for details	To substantiate an arrived-at point of view
Oral reading	To charm and/or inform an audience at all age levels

This is an incomplete list, but it serves to point up how skills should be taught, not as reading skills per se, but in other curriculum areas. To teach outlining by means of a workbook exercise is inefficient. What research even suggests any value to such a practice? Yet the teacher who allows or helps his class to develop a working unit based on a genuine problem that needs solving will probably teach more outlining without a workbook even though a reference would be helpful. The workbook thus *assists*. It does not dominate.

Pacing Devices

Similarly, we know that the speed of reading is not the speed with which the eyes go over a series of sentences, but the speed with which the brain absorbs what the eyes see. This is common knowledge. Although some value of increased speed is to be found with gadgets to speed up the EYE movements—to pace eyes more and more rapidly across the page, their current sales are out of all proportion. One goes slow or fast in reading not by the conscious knowledge that one *should* go slow or fast, but by the need to absorb what the simple or the difficult material has to say.

Thus to say that:

"Reading for central thought"
"Reading for details"
"Varying the rate of reading"
"Critical reading"
"Etc."

are the reasons for reading is to get in the way of the real reason for reading. If we are taught to read for central thought, will we always read for central thought and ignore details? Will we read for details and ignore central thought because we are taught to read for details? When will we skim? When will we read for details? How will we decide when to do either? Will it be the direct teaching of these so-called skills? Or will the *reasons* for reading dictate these variations in the reading act?

Skills at the Rapid Reading Stage

What is different once children arrive and pass into the rapid reading stage? What is different about the way they read? What is different about the way they work with subject matter? We would say that the main difference is that everything happens faster and more easily. Word analysis techniques, from the beginning, are in the spelling-writing area. Gobbling up great quantities of reading cannot be done when the pupil needs to stop and work out each unknown word. Word analysis is needed in reading, but its technique has been learned in writing as we have shown. The transfer of skill is made only when the child cannot guess ("use of context") or otherwise find a shortcut to the meaning of the page.

WORD ANALYSIS REGRESSIONS

Word analysis must become word perception—then sentence perception—and with the onset of true speed reading—whole unit perception. Thus one major difference between the struggling era of learning to read and the arrival at rapid reading rates lies in the change between letter-by-letter and phoneme-by-phoneme analysis to flash-gun type of recognition where the shape of the word comes into its own and becomes an instantaneous act that eats up meaning from the page without awareness of how the meaning got from the page to the mind. Word analysis becomes instantaneous meaning recognition. This is the major characteristic of this stage.

To sum up, skills of word analysis are not to be taught at these levels. They should have already been learned. But if there comes a breakdown, and that breakdown is major—a true regression—then the teacher develops the skill in spelling and in the independent writing time. But if the child does get stuck in reading, he need stop only long enough to figure out the word (using previously learned techniques) and get his train on the track and go rolling along.

Skills Not a Thing Apart

Skills are not a thing apart. They are, regardless of the curriculum area, a phase of the learning of that area. To practice on words in a vocabulary list *before* one reads a story is to deny the role of meaning in reading. To read, and reread, the same story five times in order to "master" it is a violation of the psychology of success and failure. To expand vocabulary by studying lists of words is a misconception of the meaning of transfer of training, as well as an ineffective instructional practice. To assume that the so-called "work-study" skills can be taught as a "reading" exercise that will magically operate in any other situation is erroneous.

All learning stems—without exception—from the deep personal reactions of the learner to his environment. Life simply cannot be divorced from learning, nor learning from life, for that matter. The place of skills in reading is squarely on top of living experience, which sets all of education in motion.

When purpose for reading is part of the act of learning, the necessity for working on isolated skills in reading is enormously reduced. When there is no personal purpose for reading—usually because the child has no choice in what he is to read—the need for "teaching" a multiplicity of skills is the only hope for the teacher. Purpose is the dominant driving force in learning to read. How many and what skills are needed are simply phases of that purpose.

It is reasonable to suspect that a careful study of the *way* reading is taught at advanced levels would have a bearing upon achievement. One clue, we believe, lies in the studies of Fay,[18] Shores,[19] and Robinson and Hall.[20] They, and there are other studies supporting these findings, underline the need to supplement *general* reading skills with *specific* reading skills geared to content areas. They underline this need by consistently pointing out that these are two different, although related, aspects of reading.

If there are two different aspects of reading and one only relates to the content areas, then that aspect only should be the one included in the curriculum where the content areas are of prime concern. In short, the teaching of reading for reading's sake cannot be justified. Reading must be integrated into the total teaching pattern at these older age levels.

[18] Leo Fay, "Responsibility for and Methods of Promoting Growth in Reading in the Content Areas," *Better Readers for Our Times,* International Reading Association Conference Proceedings, 1956, Vol. 1, p. 92.

[19] Harlan J. Shores, "Skills Related to the Ability to Read History and Science," *Journal of Educational Research,* 36:584–93, April, 1943.

[20] F. P. Robinson and P. E. Hall, "Studies of Higher Level Reading Abilities," *Journal of Educational Psychology,* 32:241–52, April, 1941.

WHAT KIND OF READING PROGRAM?

What kind of reading program is needed? We urge that it not be a reading program at all, but instead, a wide-angled language arts program, with diversified materials, using all areas of the curriculum to teach whatever skills of reading become necessary.

How would such a program be set up? How does reading become integrated into all phases of the curriculum? Briefly, these are activities of such an approach:

1. *Reading* from a wide variety of materials in every phase of the curriculum.
2. *Oral language,* i.e., talking, discussing, dramatizing, sharing, reading aloud.
3. *Written language,* practical, personal, imaginative, discursive, non-discursive, always independent and original.
4. *Demonstrations,* experimentations, and exhibitions.
5. *Listening* for literary values, for speaking, and other values.

What materials and equipment are needed to further such activities? A variety of materials in each area of the curriculum are needed.

What Materials Are To Be Used?

1. *Trade Books,* three to five titles per child, that run the spectrum of needs in:
   social studies, such as peoples of the world, geographical features (rivers, mountains, plains, etc.), machines at work, man's livelihood, transportation, communication, etc.
2. *Texts,* few copies of each of several, in social studies, mathematics, science, language, health, etc.
3. *Workbooks,* reference copy, for teacher use and resource, of various drill texts, exercise books, and the like.
4. *Science Equipment,* supply of, for experimental, demonstration, and exhibition purposes.
5. *Manipulative material* for learnings in mathematical areas.

This is a program that is not reading for itself alone. It is an integrated program designed for a teacher to meet individual differences.

Reading in the Social Studies

Once the hurdle of diversifying materials is overcome, a teacher can teach social studies as it should properly be done—i.e., as a PROCESS, rather than rigidly set content that squeezed certain concepts and ideas into the specific age levels or grade levels. There is currently, and long overdue, a challenge to the traditional social studies sequence of home and family in the first-grade community and its aspects in the second grade, on up through the world and all of its connotations in the sixth grade.[21] Experts in the field find it hard to agree upon what must be "covered" at the various levels. Nevertheless, it is not true that children need to be allowed to wander willy-nilly through an unplanned and whimsical social studies program.

The development of social studies learnings cannot be properly mapped as to sequence and content, and rightly so, but they can be clearly organized, systematized, and patterned around the process of learning about "the human drama," to use Edwin Reeder's phrase. To get off the hook of what needs to be taught to what class of children at what grade, the teacher needs to know how to conduct children through the process of inquiry and curiosity so that each child, to the extent of his ability and power, will never become a complacent, accepting "tell-me-what-to-do-next-teacher" kind of pupil. Such an approach drives a child, energizes his ever-present talent for exploration, and helps him to pursue knowledge, as it should be pursued—*for its own sake.*

In short, the teacher sets up a problem-centered curriculum. Specific content cannot be required, but *process* can be. The teacher learns how to help children investigate, in an organized fashion, problems that arise from the many sided experiences of life—in or out of a classroom.[22]

What Are Problems in a Problem-Centered Program?

Problems that children can get their teeth into need to be stated in their terms. For example, a fourth-grade study of United Nations might well have the problem statement:

[21] The writings of J. D. McAulay are notable in this respect.

[22] For more detailed discussion of such social studies program, the reader is referred to R. S. Fleming, *Curriculum For Today's Boys and Girls,* Columbus, Ohio: Charles E. Merrill Books, Inc., 1963, pp. 207–24, 245–313.

"How Do Children in Other Countries Dress?"
or
"What Do Children in Other Countries Eat?"

How do children in other countries dress?

On the other hand, a similar study at the sixth-grade level might be entitled:

"What Are Civil Rights in the Middle Eastern Countries?"
or
"How Did Man Clothe Himself in the Middle Ages?"
or
"How Has Man Kept Records of His Nation?"

So problems arise, are identified, and their solutions are plotted and outlined. Books are secured. The school librarian, as always, is a helpful resource.

How Reading Meets the Problem-Centered Curriculum

Once the problem has been stated and the class has divided itself into committees or groups on the parts of the problems, the reading material must be found and used. For example, let us take the first problem above: "How Do Children in Other Countries Dress?"

Subproblems stemming from this might be:

1. What does man wear from the neck up?
   a. Hats
   b. Hair styles
   c. Facial decoration
2. What clothes do women wear in Latin America?
3. What clothes do men wear in Latin America?
4. What effect does climate have upon the way people dress?
   a. Warm climate clothing
   b. Cold climate clothing
5. What kinds of material do people use in their clothing that is easy to get and does not cost much?
6. How do different people make their clothing beautiful?

The problem for teachers is to learn how to fit reading instruction into this kind of classroom management. It has excitement and adventure and makes for highly dedicated teachers. But teacher training has not been notable for helping new and inexperienced teachers to know what to do when.

Children learn in a myriad of ways. They are always looking at that which is new to them. They ask questions. They poke around. They may politely accept imposed knowledge, but they take fire and get excited when teachers come close to what intrigues their interest. Maybe one reason why teachers, as well as children, welcome school parties on birthdays and holidays is that so rarely does the school day hold anything quite so dear to a child's heart as a party. The dynamic classroom really does not need parties—and a teacher might well check his own performance by noting the degree of enthusiasm for a party. Evidence of wild delight should give the thoughtful teacher pause.

Not all learning comes from books or direct teaching. Experiences that children have in their normal daily out-of-school life can be valuable sources for learning when used in school. Yet in school they can reconstruct these ideas, and, in so doing, gain control over them. This serves to clarify their thinking and makes them owners of these non-school concepts.

Children build, draw, and copy, developing thoughts and ideas creatively with simple, readily available raw materials. They reconstruct ideas they have learned in some tangible way. This serves to clarify their thinking and thus aids closure in making these ideas their permanent possessions.

Concrete Experiences

Understanding of maps, for example, grows out of a natural, logical sequence of experience with copying or reproducing scale tabletop models. A trip to the airport or seeing the operation of an airport on film often results in setting up an airport on the classroom floor or project table with blocks, boxes, and model planes and people. The children or group or class reproduce a large space in a small one, keeping the general configurations and patterns. The next step in constructing maps is the making of picture maps. The last step in the sequence is the abstract symbolic representation that has real meaning to children because they have lived through the early steps of going from the concrete to the abstract.

Role-Playing and Dramatizing

Role-playing is a learning experience that is especially useful in the intermediate grades. Playing the role of the doctor or nurse reduces fear in some children. Dramatizing the work of the bus driver, policeman, the governments of the village, state, or Federal government teaches each child the importance of relationships in any of our highly complex organizations. The therapy of social and mental hygiene in dramatic play is important enough to justify the class time devoted to it. Superimposed upon these values lie the intellectual implications. As the role-playing becomes more complex, more knowledge is needed. The children must return to books for additional information, more observations must be made, to add to, to refine, and to clarify the facts, so that the play can be more realistic.

Classroom Experimentation

Another aid to learning that children of all ages can use is experimentation. Trying out old ideas in new ways, testing them, and evaluating the products stimulate scientific thinking as well as the development of skills that make up the process known as the scientific method.

Field trips do the same thing. They can promote investigation attitudes. They furnish the materials for discussion, reproduction, and dramatic play in the classroom. They may furnish motivation to initiate study, provide material for an on-going class project, serve as a culminating activity, or justify the inspiration and interest of the trip itself. Audiovisual materials of all types, books, resource people who are interviewed or invited to visit the classroom—all are valuable sources for learning.

Problems and Difficulties of Reading in the Content Fields

Teachers of intermediate-grade children are aware of the large range of differences in reading abilities present in their classes. There will be children who need continued instruction in the skills of primary reading. There will be those who are ready for the high-level skills associated with reading at the secondary level; and then there will be those children who have reached rapid reading levels. These are the children who will need help in bridging the gap between the stages of initial reading experiences to the literary-type materials of the primary grades to the more difficult and varied reading in the content areas of the intermediate and the upper grades.

Materials in the Content Areas

In order to provide for the wide ranges in the teaching-learning situation in the content areas, adequate materials of varying levels of difficulty are essential for intermediate-grade classrooms. Encyclopedias, reference books, dictionaries, an abundance of library books varying in level of difficulty and interest, social studies and science books of many types are basic. Children's magazines, newspapers, pamphlets, and informational bulletins of all types are needed. Adequate chalkboard and bulletin board space is a must. Chart paper and black crayon are desirable for making charts to record group experiences, findings, conclusions, listing steps in certain procedures, such as note-taking, dictionary usage, word lists, etc. In short, the materials needed for teaching-learning in the content areas will be part and parcel of the library needed to teach the skills of reading.

Grouping in the Content Areas

Grouping comes into its own in advanced grade levels. As it should result from needs of content learning, interest in a group should be high. Grouping in teaching the content areas, just as grouping for reading instruction, must come after particulars are isolated in a preliminary, initiative kind of teaching action. Grouping upon identified tasks is tangible. The tasks are recognizable and immediately attainable. Let us go into a description of the actual procedures within the classroom.

Social and Science Experience Units

How does grouping apply to the area of social studies and science? Content areas have a peculiar role to play in achieving the personal and social objectives so paramount in a democratic society, since their content and materials deal with people—their interrelations and interactions as they deal with their physical and sociocultural environments in their quest to satisfy the basic needs associated with self-preservation. Basic to these programs is the need to learn problem-solving in living in large and small groups; the effect of environmental influences on man's living; the effect of inventions and technology on ways of doing things; and how our cultural heritage is dynamic and ongoing instead of a body of information about the dead past.

Children learn best the relationships they feel and live. This means developing an understanding of themselves and their dealings with others; with members of their family, class, school, neighborhood, and town or village. These must be the concerns of social studies and science. These relationships are learned most effectively when children face real problems on their level of maturity that have important meanings for themselves and others.

In short, science and social studies are the study of life—not a subject to be taught solely from a book. The difficulty in adjusting the reading level of such a text is not a social studies or science problem. But to those who conceive of these two fields as problem-centered areas within broad curriculum confines, suitable to age and grade, the matter of grouping is beautifully simple. The development of grouping for problem-solving would proceed as follows:

1. A mutually fascinating problem is discovered by pupils and teacher together.

2. The problem is examined to ascertain various parts that could lend themselves to group action.

3. Temporary groups are organized on the basis of individual pupil interest (*Not friendship—interest*)

4. Initiative first-hand, go and look, go and see, go and talk to—explorations, experiences, and observations.

5. Development of permanent groups on interest dictating self-assignment to task.

6. Preliminary investigation and early assembling of information, materials.

7. Planning for construction or other audiovisual presentation or exhibit.

8. Working at categorizing, organizing, and perfecting the progression of ideas and materials to be presented.

9. Final presentation.

Other Language Areas Push Reading at Advanced Levels

If reading texts are not to be used, at least as their publishers intended, then what must be done in these advanced age levels to promote reading? Surely the growth cannot be left to chance or incidental teaching. There must be a form, a structure for teachers of whom too many are prone to plow their classes through pages of workbook and teacher-made exercise material. In at least one state[23] the legislative mandate to teach reading in the junior high school years has produced LOWER reading achievement for the first graduating classes whose test results have been recorded. Quite obviously, this was not due to the fact that extra emphasis upon reading was NOT made, as it was. What happened was that the type of reading instruction[24] that took place was unbelievably poor, consisting of material-centered, packaged, filling-out-of-the-plans type of mechanical drill. The teachers commandeered to teach reading knew no better, so cannot be blamed. These results illustrate that whatever happens at these older age levels, reading is better taught in some other way.

Another way to put the matter would be to compare learning to read with learning to sing on key. We know that if children arrive at the fifth grade unable to carry a tune, that is a sign that those children have had ineffective music instruction. Children should be able to carry a tune after the third grade. There may be literally one

[23] Pennsylvania: 1963 high school graduates had lower reading achievement scores than 1953 graduates on the same test.

[24] For details see Arthur W. Heilman, "The Mandated Jr. High Program," *Reading and Child Development*, Proceedings for thirteenth Reading Conference, Lehigh University, Vol. 4, 1964.

of one hundred thousand who cannot—an infinitesimal percentage. Thus, in the area of reading, if teachers in the fifth grade NEED to have special drill-type reading classes, this, too, is to be noted as a mark of ineffective teaching in the preceding grades. However, we suspect that those middle- and upper-grade teachers who feel the necessity of having regular work-type (whatever that is!) reading lessons simply don't know what else to do. Anything other than basal readers and workbooks for certain hours of the day is not considered "reading." What we are proposing is a curriculum at these older age levels that will promote reading without teaching it per se.

To talk about reading, we must talk about *talking*—or oral language itself, for one thing—as well as independent writing. Reading instruction at these advanced levels must contain, as we have shown its presence in the earlier levels, a direct relationship to the other language arts. It gives the teacher a built-in set of reference points upon which all necessary skills can be built—often without the conscious effort or "now-I-am-teaching-skills" feeling on the part of the teacher. As we have shown, all through the developing years, spoken language provides the material for learning the sounds of letters, the recognition of how to read well aloud, and most important of all, the heartland from which all word analysis skill-learning arises.

At the advanced age levels also, spoken language has its unique role. That role is crucial if critical reading is to be developed to its fullest possible extent. Basically we are going to discuss the teaching of free speech and of creativity. Free speech demands responsibility; it also demands an intelligent citizenry. All of the words that have been used to urge "meaningful" reading, or reading for a purpose, will now come home to roost. The purpose and meaning involved in the following descriptions are the child's own. They do not read because it is reading time. They read in order to develop a point of view that they can defend before their peers or set down on paper with spontaneity and enthusiasm.

We are proposing that the planned sequential materials be ignored. We suspect that most children at these older levels learn to read in spite of such materials and not because of them. We insist that variety of language arts activities and the removal of straitjacketing will help children arrive at the Nirvana of their best reading better than any other means.

CRITICAL READING

Critical reading is probably not best taught as "critical reading." It must be a part of a curriculum in which the child reads in order to examine problems that worry him, to defend what he believes among his peers, to develop points of view. It is an ability that is developed as part of a larger goal. It is truly a thinking skill, although semantically we question that phrase.

William Eller[25] cites four blocks to critical reading:

"1. The single text methodology cheats the learner in several ways, one of which is its failure to provide for critical reading. . . .

"2. Related somewhat to the single-text evil is another school-fostered obstacle to critical reading: the halo attached to the printed words . . . they (should occasionally) read something that could be disproved on the basis of their own experience. . . .

"3. A third failure of the schools in the development of critical reading facility rests on the avoidance of controversial subjects. . . .

"4. Another enemy of the critical reading habit which would seem to be a product of both the educational system and the general society is the emphasis upon conformity."

An examination of the research that bears on the development of critical reading[26] reveals little that is conclusive. In the *Handbook of Research on Teaching*,[27] a presentation of related studies is made under the headings of "Critical Reading," "Creative Reading," and "The Teacher Encourages Interpretation." Yet the burden of the reporting is that little is known and little is done in the elementary school to develop this skill. Many basal manuals include suggestions in this direction, but a clear cut body of experimental data does not exist. Nor are there reading tests recognized as testing this particular ability. Particularly is there no suggestion within these reports that oral discussion could develop reading.

We are proposing, in effect, that one of the best ways to teach reading is to use other language arts—independent writing, speaking, and listening—to reinforce what is read. We believe that one way to develop the interpretive skills in reading, so necessary to the area of social studies, can be done through open-ended discussion in which the structure has certain elements to guarantee its freedom.

[25] In D. H. Russell and H. R. Fea, "Research on Reading," *Handbook Of Research On Teaching*, American Educational Research Association (Neil Gage, ed.), Chicago: Rand McNally & Co., pp. 901 ff.

[26] O. S. Causey, *The Reading Teacher's Reader*, The Ronald Press Co., p. 31 ff. contains many of the best articles on reading to be found. This book is one to be recommended highly for its wide scope and depth.

[27] D. H. Russell and H. R. Fea, "Research on Teaching Reading," *Handbook on Research in Learning, op. cit.*, pp. 865 ff.

Discussion, Writing, and Dramatics Aid Reading

A study completed by the author reveals some important learnings in this matter.[28] Classes of children, while not considered retarded in their building assignments were, nevertheless, two to three years below the national norms on the Stanford Achievement Tests. They came from the then segregated Negro schools in a large eastern city. Sixteen classes were paired upon age levels, teacher ability, and length of time with each class, academic achievement, and other social measurements. One teacher of each pair was selected as the experimental partner and was trained to conduct, as a minimum, open-ended discussion (one hour for three days a week), creative writing (one hour for one day a week), and creative dramatics (one hour for one day a week). The experimentation continued over a semester's time—Spring, 1952. Both experimental and comparison classes continued under the usual supervision following the school system syllabus or the entire curriculum. The hours devoted to these creative activities were subtracted from the language arts program, principally oral language, written composition, and reading, in part. All sixteen classes used the basal readers with the workbooks and extensive teacher-made, chalkboard-written exercises.

The results of school system-wide testing program, given the following September after the summer vacation, were used. There were no significant changes as to social behavior by the instruments administered by the investigator in June, 1952. These were not part of the city testing program. Either the sociograms, Ohio Social Acceptance Scale, were not sensitive enough to reveal any significant change or there were no such changes in friendship patterns. However, all experimental teachers observed and remarked upon the improvement of classroom climate. Children needed less formalistic discipline. They were absent less from school (for that matter, so were the teachers). They got along better with each other and exhibited concern for others in a way that the teachers had never noticed before. The teachers themselves reported their delight in finding, without help, ways to avoid the chore of correction of workbook exercises, or teacher-made exercises copied by pupils from the blackboard. The investigator did not discourage this development.

The formal test results, however, were dramatic but in only one area, that of reading scores. The comparison of reading achieve-

[28] Jeannette Veatch, *An Experimental Study of the Relation of a Program of Specific Creative Activities to Group Acceptance, Emotional Needs and Academic Achievement.* Unpublished Ph.D. dissertation, New York University, 1953.

Dramatics help reading.

ment over the five-month period of the comparison classes to the experimental classes was found to be .58 to .95 of an academic year and statistically significant at better than the one per cent level of confidence. The differences of the means before and means after showed that seven of the eight experimental groups outgained their comparison groups. When these differences were treated for significance, all eight experimental groups recorded gains. This is to say, three comparison groups failed to gain significantly over the year's time,[29] even though the factor of maturation was involved.

The Significance of the Study

While one swallow does not make a summer, there are implications in this single study that must be accepted by those who wish to face all developments in the field of reading. First, ALL groups used basal readers with continual reference to the manual for the teacher. The only variable between the groups was the substitution

[29] While the experimentation occurred only in the spring semester, the test results were used from the preceding fall and the succeding fall, from the regular city testing results.

of a creative activity in the field of language, using written and oral verbalizations for a portion of the formal language program. There was no attempt to change any portion of the reading program. In fact, the hypothesis of the investigator was more central to the improvement of human relations within these groups. There was no reading taught experimentally.

Yet skills in the language arts were certainly fostered through the inservice training programs of the experimental teachers. These three activities involved reading, writing, talking, and listening. It is unfortunate that other parts of the city-wide test (Stanford Achievement, Intermediate Battery) were not given to have provided findings on spelling and language usage.[30]

Lack of Research Attention of the Implication of Other Language Arts for Reading

The lack of interest of the reading field in other language arts is notable. There is much general agreement that there is a strong bond between reading and the language arts. But the curious "tunnel" vision of reading specialists when it comes to thinking of reading instruction in other terms than that of teaching reading from readers and other panoply of traditional practice is undeniable. The research that would support or refute the findings of that just described is either missing or listed in such an obscure way as to be lost to the major reporting in the field.

In short, it could be said that while most specialists will agree that reading is not reading alone, yet, when the chips are down, they have nothing to show that this is true. Research, as always, is needed in new and original directions. This text is in effect one long pleading that the field of reading needs a fresh look divorced from those patterns that at present comprise the bulk of reading instruction in America.

Reading cannot be reading alone. It cannot be reading at all unless it pulls into its tender center all the speaking, writing, and listening activities of creative independent nature. The need for research on the relationship between reading, writing, discussing or argument, and dramatization is obvious. Replication of the quoted study is called for, as well as original design in related areas.

[30] It should be pointed out that no significant changes were recorded in arithmetic. All groups made less gains than should be expected according to the national norm.

Presenting Activities That Aid Reading

To promote reading on these advanced age levels, there follows a presentation of 1) discussion, 2) dramatics, and 3) writing that are designed in this direction. Reading is inherent in each of these. Yet it is not the sole end-all, be-all of the approach.

These activities are inherently creative. Yet they were developed around a structure that, paradoxically to some, guarantee freedom of the activity. There must be structure, as Bruner so ably points out, but it must be a structure that allows each pupil to grow and contribute at the level of which he is best capable.

CRITICAL READING THROUGH OPEN-ENDED DISCUSSIONS

Much space was devoted in Chapter 9 to the development of talking time, or sharing time, as a means to help children become easier in presenting their ideas to their classmates. The following diagram will be recalled as a beginning step in starting what should be a long process of developing free, yet responsible, speech in the elementary school.

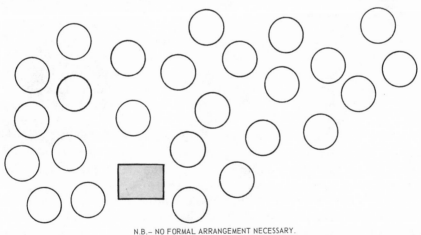

N.B.– NO FORMAL ARRANGEMENT NECESSARY.

Seating for talking.

The teacher is the skilled technician that coaches and abets the talking in such a way that children can truly exchange ideas. Although the ability to sustain a train of thought[31] is a product of mat-

[31] Jean Piaget, *The Language and Thought of the Child,* London: Kegan Paul, 1947.

urational forces, nevertheless, the readiness available within the child can be brought to the surface by some incentive inherent in the discussion situation. The incentive in this activity is the natural, instinctive reaction to other human beings. Man is a social creature, even in school, in spite of the child-isolating tendencies of some schoolroom practices. It is these natural social tendencies that are activated in discussion.

Yet some teachers can make such a fetish of creativity that they throw the baby out with the bath. They fall into the trap of stereotyping creative practices into a wild kind of laissez faire, and so set the cement of something quite different from that desired.

There must be flexibility of practice and of process. The directions and descriptions that follow are designed primarily as springboards. Yet they are not inviolable. The fact that they can be carried out at regularly spaced periods of the school week does not deny their inherent creativity. It might weaken them a bit, but set periods do not need to eliminate the creative element. These activities are not to be permitted according to the "good" or "bad" behavior of the children. They should exist, as do hunger and sleep, because that is the way things are. Talking and sharing ideas are a necessity.

Panel-Type Discussion

An initial gambit into this activity with an inexperienced teacher of the midde grades is usually best made with a panel type of discussion. The individual panel member does not know exactly what he is going to say, but he does know what he intends to talk about. His presentation of his topic is a secret from everyone, including the teacher. He is unrehearsed, so to speak. He talks without reference or notes of any kind. "If it isn't worth remembering, it isn't worth talking about" is one way to help children understand this point. In fact, it is unimportant whether or not the child *knows* much about the topic he wishes to bring up. All he must know is that it will, in his opinion, be something that the class will be interested in discussing. He must take a chance on that. But what better way to develop critical faculties than by silently making a decision as to whether or not his peers will LIKE his topic? This is critical thinking in anyone's terms.

Spontaneous Group Reaction to Topics

The spontaneous reaction, or lack of it, is the major factor that promotes better or more fruitful discussion. When a child speaks about the subject that strikes a vital chord with his friends in the class, he finds great satisfaction, if their response is immediate and intense. If he strikes a topic that finds little or no response, the speaker is disheartened and disappointed. The teaching of current events with activities that does not bring out exciting front-page, controversial discussion is not good teaching. We are suggesting a proved way of working. The child chooses a topic. No one else knows about it. HE broaches it to the group from his spot in the panel. He sinks or swims on the spontaneous response.

Beginning with Brief Reading Session

In terms of general structure of this discussion activity, the teacher initiates the period by setting a brief reading session in which various current periodicals, information bulletins, newspaper (adult and children), and the like are scanned. The teacher helps children in their search for topics of their choice. He suggests, but does not insist. He doesn't need to. The excitement of a good bull session is much better motivation than anything a teacher might attempt. Children are urged either at home or school to watch news broadcasts on television and listen to radio to gain ideas. They are encouraged to ask their parents for suggestions at home.

One parent asked "What are you doing at school? You should hear the arguments that are going on at our dinner table. My husband is having all he can do to defend his point of view!" Such is an example of the way children should expand their in-school lives toward their out-of-school lives. The purpose is to help the children find a topic of their choice, rather than have them well-prapared in that subject.

Discussions Not an End of Thinking

The basic assumption here is that TALKING STARTS LEARNING. It never finishes it. There is no such thing as a *completed* discussion. A group may agree to quit, but will pursue the topic in its own way, on its own time, forever after. The common practice of posting news clippings on a class bulletin board is quite ridiculous. Who reads them, really? (Unless it is an administrator who thinks such postings are truly an evidence of learning activity around current events.) The main idea is that such spontaneous, yet structured, discussion is a springboard to ever widening circles of expanding knowledge. It is a starter.

Empty Panel Chairs an Incentive

As far as the mechanics of the operation are concerned, the teacher sees that six or seven empty chairs are placed in front of the class. These are literally open invitations for occupancy. It has been found that children do not get into systematic discussion so easily or so spontaneously without this half circle of empty chairs.

As a child signals that he has something to talk about, the teacher has him come and sit in one of the chairs. When they are all full (except one on the end for the chairman, usually the teacher until another pupil-chairman can be trained), the panel is ready to begin. As the class' experience increases and the demand for more and more participation in a panel is too heavy, the whole class can turn their seats inward, in a large circle, to face each other and carry on in the same way as in the panel.

Chairman Role Is Crucial

The success of the discussion lies in the hands of the chairman. He is not to contribute to the *content* of the topics brought up, but only to facilitate their exploration. In the beginning the teacher must coach a child chairman (often by sitting close behind him and giving him whispered instructions). He should be helped to be independent as soon as possible. Successive chairmen learn from their predecessors. Their duties begin with some simple question as "Who wants to begin?" Any brief silence at this point, or any point for that matter, is not to be considered disastrous. On the contrary, such a silence can serve to build up a desirable tension that will make the subsequent talk more vital and exciting.

The chairman talks as little as possible, developing techniques of signaling to decrease interruption to the flow of talk. Individuals are encouraged to talk without a chairman's signal when no one else is talking. There is little in teaching that is more satisfying to a teacher when this happens. Children can and do learn to space their contributions when there is an open space in the discussion.

The Phenomenon of the "Blowup"

As children learn that they may insert their comments without waiting for signals of permission, and as they select increasingly important and exciting topics, there usually occurs a phenomenon, which, for want of a better term, can be called the "blowup." This comes when two or more children all attempt to talk at once, not to be discourteous or to behave badly, but because they are so excited about what they want to say. This "blowup," if mastered by the teacher successfully, will short-cut the development of discussion toward the desired goal of a truly adult-type of interchange. If it is not mastered immediately, the drive to talk, to share, to argue, to exchange opinions, is slowed—simply because the blockage to that talk is slowed by overly zealous chairmen—who must, of course, maintain order at all costs.

The manner of gaining control of the "blowup" can endanger the spontaneity of the talking, and a delicate balance must be maintained so that children do not become discouraged and then refuse to participate. There are several ways to establish this control, which paradoxically again, guarantees freedom.

USING THE GAVEL. One way is to have the chairman use a gavel. This can really be an incentive to wanting to be chairman! Once the group is in confusion about who is to talk, the chairman bangs the gavel (ed. note: Protect the furniture with a magazine!) and brings order. Then he chooses whomever he thinks should be the next speaker. He may choose arbitrarily. That is all right. But he must choose rapidly, with little hesitation. He cannot play favorites among his own peers—or all is lost. In extremes, the teacher must retrieve the chairmanship for himself.

EVALUATING THE "BLOWUP" AS AN EVENT. Another way to handle this crucial event is for the teacher to step in as soon as he is sure that a "blowup" exists and will not straighten out by itself. He can start an immediate evaluation something like this:

1. "What did you like about these last few minutes?"
2. "What did you NOT like about these last few minutes?"

The pupils will usually respond favorably to the right to say what they wish, and unfavorably to the fact that, as so many have said, "No one listened to me!" It is perhaps best that the teacher then close the discussion for the day, and change the activity (preferably to something opposite in nature, such as a skill exercise in handwriting). Skip a day and then try again, with the teacher quickly reviewing what went wrong previously. It has been found that once the "blowup" is resolved successfully, the class is really on its way to exciting, provocative, satisfying discussion—the dream of most teachers who care about freedom of speech.

Outline of Open-Ended Discussion

As a summary of the previous description, the following series of steps is presented.[32] They are not to be taken as absolutes, but merely as guides that a teacher may change and adapt to a specific situation. A bibliography is added here rather than at the end of the chapter for easier reference for a busy teacher.

Open-Ended Discussion—Panel Type—Upper Grades

1. Begin with a 10- to 15-minute browsing, silent reading, thinking period to develop ideas for discussion. Pupils peruse all sorts of publications, i.e., newspapers, periodicals, etc.

2. Place 5 to 7 chairs at a table in front of class in semicircle, panel fashion.

3. Encourage children to signal the teacher when they have an idea for discussion.

4. Teacher urges children to find a subject they want to talk about, either from the current literature mentioned in No. 1, or from listening to radio or television, or perhaps from their own thinking.

5. The idea is to be kept secret—even from the teacher. Pupils are helped to understand that ideas 1) should be controversial, 2) can be relatively new and unexplored by group or originator.

6. As children indicate they have a subject they want to talk about, they come up and occupy a place in the panel, but tell no one what their idea is.

7. When the panel is full of these volunteers, the teacher chooses a chairman rapidly, casually, and then withdraws as a major figure in the classroom unless he is chairman of the day. If not, he moves to side or rear of room and participates only if necessary or if requested.

8. All reading stops (all materials and notes are to be left behind by panel members). The phrase "It's not worth talking about, if it's not worth remembering" is useful to inculcate this idea. The chairman opens with a brief question, such as, "Who wants to begin?" and waits for someone to talk, without regard to length of waiting period.

9. A world map is displayed in full view, a pupil appointed to indicate places mentioned as discussion proceeds with a pointer or yard stick.

[32] Adapted from R. S. Fleming (ed.), *Curriculum for Today's Boys and Girls,* Columbus, Ohio: Charles E. Merrill Books, Inc., 1964. Printed with the permission of the Publisher.

Rules

1. No notes or references to materials such as clippings allowed except in extreme cases to settle an argument. The class becomes an audience.
2. Discourage the phrase "I read in the . . . " or "I heard over the . . . " as the emphasis should be upon main ideas gleaned from digestion of many sources.
3. Chairman talks only to keep the discussion going, to assist in a change of subject, to prevent any person monopolizing the floor, to bring in the audience, and to keep order.
4. If, after several discussions, topics are 1) boring or 2) questionably gory or horrifying, the teacher should interrupt the discussion and help children evaluate.
5. Order is kept by chairman, gavel is permissible if used properly. Pupils should be, however, encouraged to wait to speak until no one else is speaking, and to signal chairman only if needing help to get into the discussion.
6. Pupils are to be encouraged to keep the discussion smooth, not to interrupt, or to flag the chairman annoyingly for attention. Interruptions of the flow of thought are to be discouraged.
6. As interest in a given topic wanes, chairmen should learn to sense this, close topic and invite a new contribution.
7. The teacher should quietly coach pupils to be chairman as the days pass. They need to be trained.
8. Usually such discussion every day lacks vigor. It is suggested such open-ended talk to be held every other day.

References

Corbett, J. F. *et al. Current Affairs and Modern Education. New York Times,* 1950.

Fleming, R. S. (ed.), *Curriculum for Today's Boys and Girls.* Columbus, Ohio: Charles E. Merrill, Inc., 1963, Chap. 7, pp. 185–90, pp. 236–7.

Klein, Alan F. *Role Playing.* New York: Associated Press, 1956.

Ohio Farm Bureau. *Cooperative Discussion Circles,* Columbus, Ohio: 1939.

Pronovost, Wilbert. *The Teaching of Speaking and Listening in the Elementary School.* New York: Longmans, Green & Co., 1959.

Sattler, W. M., and Miller, N. E. *Discussion and Conference.* New York: Prentice-Hall, Inc., 1954.

Veatch, J. *A Study of the Effects of Specific Creative Activities upon Emotional Needs, Social Acceptance and Academic Achievement.* Unpublished Ph.D. thesis, New York University, 1953. Microfilm, University of Michigan, Ann Arbor, Mich.

In conclusion, when a teacher develops organized discussion on important things that matter to pupils (whether or not the teacher is the focal point), there comes a time when the children must be trained to argue and discuss in an orderly and courteous fashion without dampening the ardor of the ideas being discussed. Techniques of such management of discussion vary widely. Yet there are certain crucial factors that must be present. These are:

1. The teacher must become progressively dispensable, with less and less need to referee heated discussions.
2. The topics that are discussed cannot be subject to absolute censorship, although suggestions for improvement are very much in order.
3. Somehow children must arrive at that state where they realize—internally—that communication is a matter of getting the other fellow to listen.
4. Some kind of system must be developed, such as a chairman, or a panel, or system of signals, that will set up a respected and reasonable method of taking turns.
5. Whatever talking goes on must be extemporaneous and sink or swim on its holding power with an audience (the class).

As the status position of the teacher is untouched, he must be careful about teaching "good English" during such a time. Whatever corrections of speech that occur might best take place at another time or place. Reference to the speech patterns of children must remain, during this activity, incidental and casual. If such reference is truly necessary, an evaluation should be made about the mistake rather than who made it, as in all ways, such practices lift the whole level of the educative activity of the class.

Helps for Listening

To those who would like more specific help in working with children who need to listen to participate in a good discussion, the following list developed by Posz[33] is recommended as a useful set of principles.

PERSON-TO-PERSON LISTENING

Listening to Others

1. *Stop talking*—You can't listen while you are talking.
2. *Empathize with other person*—try to put yourself in his place so that you can see what he is trying to get at.
3. *Ask questions*—when you don't understand, when you need further clarification, when you want him to like you, when you want to

[33] A. Conrad Posz.

show you are listening. But don't ask questions that will embarrass him or show him up.

4. *Don't give up too soon*—don't interrupt other person; give him time to say what he has to say.

5. *Concentrate on what he is saying*—actively focus your attention on his words, his ideas, and his feelings related to the subject.

6. *Look at the other person*—his face, his mouth, his eyes, his hands, will all help him to communicate with you. Helps you concentrate, too. Makes him feel you are listening.

7. *Smile and grunt appropriately*—but don't overdo it.

8. *Leave your emotions behind* (if you can)—try to push your worries, your fears, your problems outside the meeting room. They may prevent you from listening well.

9. *Control your anger*—try not to get angry at what he is saying; your anger may prevent you from understanding his words or meaning.

10. *Get rid of distractions*—put down any papers, pencils, etc., you have in your hands; they may distract your attention.

11. *Get the main points*—concentrate on the main ideas and note the illustrative material; examples, stories, statistics, etc., are important, but usually are not the main points. Examine them only to see if they prove, support, define the main ideas.

12. *Share responsibility for communication*—only part of the responsibility rests with the speaker; you as the listener have an important part. Try to understand, and if you don't, ask for clarification.

13. *React to ideas, not to person*—don't allow your reactions to the person to influence your interpretation of what he says. His ideas may be good even if you don't like him as a person, or the way he looks.

14. *Don't argue mentally*—when you are trying to understand the other person, it is a handicap to argue with him mentally as he is speaking. This sets up a barrier between you and the speaker.

15. *Use the Difference in rate*—you can listen faster than he can talk, so use this rate difference to your advantage by: trying to stay on right track, anticipate what he is going to say, think back over what he has said, evaluate his development, etc. Rate difference: speech rate is about 100 to 150 words per minute; thinking: 250 to 500.

16. *Listen for what is not said*—sometimes you can learn just as much by determining what the other person leaves out or avoids in his talking as you can by listening to what he says.

17. *Listen to how something is said*—we frequently concentrate so hard on what is said that we miss the importance of the emotional reactions and attitudes related to what is said. His attitudes and emotional reactions may be more important than what is said in so many words.

18. *Don't antagonize speaker*—you may cause the other person to conceal his ideas, emotions, attitudes by antagonizing him in any of a number of ways: arguing, criticizing, taking notes, not taking notes, asking questions, not asking questions, etc. Try to judge and be aware of the effect you are having on the other person. Adapt to him.

19. *Listen for his personality*—one of the best ways of finding out information about a person is to listen to him talk; as he talks you can begin to find out what he likes and dislikes, what his motivations are, what his value system is, what he thinks about everything and anything, what makes him tick.

20. *Avoid jumping to assumptions*—they can get you into trouble in trying to understand other persons. Don't assume that he uses words the same way you do; that he didn't say what he meant, but you understand what he meant; that he is avoiding looking you in the eye because he is telling a lie; that he is trying to embarrass you by looking you in the eye; that he is distorting the truth because what he says doesn't agree with what you think; that he is lying because he has interpreted the facts differently from you; that he is unethical because he is trying to win you over to his point of view; that he is angry because he is enthusiastic in presenting his views. Assumptions like these may turn out to be true, but more often they just get in the road of your understanding and reaching agreement or compromise.

21. *Avoid classifying the speaker*—it has some value, but beware! Too frequently we classify a person as one type of person and then try to fit everything he says into what makes sense coming from that type of person. He is a Republican. Therefore, our perceptions of what he says or means are all shaded by whether we like or dislike Republicans. At times, it helps us to understand people to know their politics, their religious beliefs, their jobs, etc., but people have the trait of being unpredictable and not fitting into their classifications.

22. *Avoid hasty judgment*—wait until all the facts are in before making any judgments.

23. *Recognize your own prejudice*—try to be aware of your own feeling toward the speaker, the subject, the occasion, etc., and allow for these prejudgments.

24. *Identify type of reasoning*—frequently it is difficult to sort out good and faulty reasoning when you are listening. Nevertheless, it is so important a job that a listener should bend every effort to learn to spot faulty reasoning when he hears it.

25. *Evaluate facts and evidence*—as you listen, try to identify not only the significance of the facts and evidence, but also their relatedness to the argument.

CRITICAL READING THROUGH WRITING ACTIVITIES

Practical Writing

There are two aspects of written composition that must be considered in the context of this book. Even if space would warrant, there could hardly be an improvement upon the suggestions found in the writing of Burrows, Applegate, Mearns, Cole, and others.[34] They all specify, or at least suggest, that all writing should be independent and individual in character. But it is Burrow's major contribution to describe such independent writing as either 1) personal, therefore usually creative, imaginative, coming from internal pressures, subjective in nature, and property of the author; 2) practical, therefore factual, external in origin, objective, and intended for others.

There is no area of the curriculum, perhaps, that has more and better texts to help teachers than the area of written composition. Sadly, however, actual instruction in the nation's classrooms gives little evidence that these excellent references have been used to train teachers, either before they teach or later on the job. Yet reform and improvement must come. The National Council of Teachers of English has already fired salvos at the inadequacies of English instruction.

Burrows has kaleidoscoped a great deal into the following article that relates to "practical writing." While Chapter 11 *"Teaching Skills for Reading,"* discusses writing in terms of "word analysis," in this chapter writing is presented as word analysis plus all of the language-usage skills, oral reading, proofreading, and rereading one's own products for fun.

We submit that this type of writing contributes to reading instruction in all ways. Word analysis leads to word synthesis. Mechanics of usage leads to rereading. It puts FUNCTION on the act of reading in

[34] Mauree Applegate, *Helping Children Write*, Evanston, Ill.: Row, Peterson & Co., 1954; *Easy in English*, Row, Peterson & Co., 1960. *Winged Writing*, Row, Peterson & Co., 1961. *Freeing Children to Write*, Harper & Row, Inc., 1963. Board of Education of the City of New York, *Developing Children's Power of Self-Expression Through Writing*, Curriculum Bulletin, 1952–53 Series, No. 2. Alvina T. Burrows, *Teaching Composition*, pamphlet, American Education Research Association, Department of Classroom Teachers, N.E.D. #18 Series "What Research Says to the Teacher, 1952; *They All Want To Write* (2d ed.), New York: Prentice-Hall, Inc., 1952. A. T. Burrows, D. Jackson, and D. Saunders. *They All Want To Write* (3d ed.), Holt, Rinehart, & Winston, 1964. Natalie Cole, *The Arts in the Classroom*, John Day Co., Inc., New York: 1940, Chap. V. J. Ferebee, *et. al.*, *They All Want to Write*, Indianapolis: Bobbs-Merrill Co., Inc., 1939. Hughes Mearns, *Creative Youth*, New York: Doubleday Doran, 1928; *Creative Power*, New York: Doubleday Doran, 1928.

every bit as powerful a way as does self-selection of a beloved tradebook. It could perhaps be argued that it puts *more* purpose in the act of reading. Writing, in any way, is a drive wheel for reading.

Mechanics in Written English[35]

To teach children to write with originality and power while properly observing regulations of spelling, punctuation, and sentence form is no easy task. The elementary teacher takes this goal seriously and works toward it year after year.

Practice exercises, drill books, and other devices, pile up on our shelves, but we are now quite certain that filling blanks in these so-called "objective exercises" does not help our pupils very much to write meaningfully and correctly. We have seen children write "I have seen" many times over, only to shout, seconds later, on the playground, the unaccepted but accustomed substitute. Our youngsters can place the terminal periods in one dittoed exercise after another, yet the same children will write a letter or report, omitting these very items of punctuation we thought we had taught them.

Just how do children learn to express their ideas with clarity, vigor, and in correct form? Learn they must if our national interest is to be well served! For we are coming to see that learning to express ourselves well in speech and writing is as important as learning to read.

Writing in the Beginning

Children's compositions from the beginning can and should be in acceptable form. Usually a beginner's writing is a group-dictated message, perhaps a memo to bring a smock for painting or a rug for resting, a story, a message, or a brief note about his picture. The teacher writes for him, and the pupil "reads" his brief composition. If he forgets the precise wording, the teacher credits his rendition of the idea and reads it correctly for him. But *the act of composition* is the pupil's. In later weeks he copies his written message, or as much of it as he can without excessive fatigue. The teacher may need to finish it for him. The beginner's own illustration further individualizes it.

In all such dictated composition, children experience correct written mechanics and see the connection between thinking and writing. Clarity is an aim, as well as originality. Often the teacher begins teaching the mechanics by reading aloud and emphasizing the endings of sentences. He might next ask the pupils to listen and raise their hands each time the end of a sentence is heard. He shows them how paying attention to the period after each sentence makes the sentences sound finished. Children may discover that a capital letter begins each new sentence. As children's independence grows, they of course do more of their writings independently. But the expression of ideas, facts, feelings, and wonderings is still a hard task. Just as writing done by adults for important purposes must be corrected and rewritten, so too much much of children's writing.

Teacher-Pupil Conference on Written Material

But when the teacher merely hands back papers corrected and graded in efficient red pencil, she, not the children, has had the practice. It is the teacher-pupil conference about the child's written paper that brings learnings to a

[35] Alvina Treut Burrows, *The Instructor Magazine* (Supplement), March, 1962. Reprinted with the permission of the publisher, F. A. Owen Publishing Co.

crucial point. The pupil can be helped to see just where he needs to clarify, to add punctuation, to correct spelling, or to smooth out phraseology—when ability warrants. "How would you say it?" is a good teacher question, or "Read it to me aloud." Reading aloud what one has written to an interested listener helps one to see it in a new light.

Writing the rough draft, correcting, making a good copy, proofreading—this is a long process indeed for the learner. When children finish "a big job" of report or letter writing, special commendation is in order. The climax of accomplishment brings complete satisfaction to the author only if he hears from his public!

Other Methods of Helping with Mechanics

If classes are so large as to make an individual conference difficult, there are alternatives: (1) arrange for competent pupils to take turns at being editors to help four or five children, one at a time; or (2) correct papers outside of class and ask the children to check their corrected papers carefully before starting the good copy. The teacher confers with a few at each writing session, at first with those most seriously in need of encouragement or help.

Once a pupil knows his unique problem, a great service can be performed by specific English exercises. These former mainstays of teaching come into their own when matched to pupil needs. When pupils see the relation between an exercise and satisfying communication, exercises can be productive.

A fifth-grader who has seen some of his corrected sentences take their rightful place in a book he proudly gives to beloved grandparents is ready for a class exercise in completing sentence fragments. Children read aloud to hear their voice patterns end a sentence and then to note that punctuation agrees with what they hear. They can see that the following sentence fragment leaves an event hanging in midair:

When we left the camp where Jack and I had been waiting for the other kids for hours and hours. . . .

Nothing happened *when* the long wait occurred. The children see and hear this omission when the teacher reads orally. They may add—

. . . we wondered if they would find our message.
. . . we worried and worried about them.
. . . it was already dark and raining.
. . . we didn't know which way to get to town.

Thus, children in upper grades also notice varied patterns of expression as well as the remarkable flexibility of our language. They can be alerted to word groups beginning with *if, who, where, because, while*—dependent clauses easily mistaken by the hurried writer for a complete sentence.

Fluency and Imagination

Will a child still want to write after working so hard? He will, for two reasons. The first is pride in using one's product in true communications. The second lies in the fact that stories and verse, or other personal writing, are not subjected to this painstaking correction. Indeed, the writing of stories is focused on the art of entertaining one's peers. It is an activity carried out for sheer enjoyment, for the fun of doing it. Criticism is out of order, as it is out of order when any other personal gift is shared. After being read aloud, stories are not displayed; they are filed for private satisfactions. Only when "published" in an occasional classbook or magazine need they be corrected and copied. Rather than learning carelessness or error in the freedom of personal writing, children learn fluency and the value of their own imagination. These qualities will carry over to their writing of more objective material.

Research shows that the study of parts of speech and grammatical analysis of sentences makes no identifiable contribution to speech and writing in the elementary school. The real job is to establish clarity, fluency, eagerness to write, and reasonable correctness in form.

Similarities of Reading and Writing Instruction

In Dr. Burrows' article all of the main characteristics that have been urged in this text are present in her ideas about written language and the teaching of the mechanics thereof. Children write (self-selection) that which is of importance to them. They choose a portion of their writing to present to the teacher in an individual conference, while keeping other writings in their own folder in the file. The teacher talks over all of the crucial areas that are noticed in the writing. The teacher takes notes in his own notebook.

After several conferences on writing, the teacher sees that some of the pupils have the same needs, and so groups are formed to meet these needs. Perhaps the whole class could benefit from a mass attack upon an identified problem. In these ways the love of writing is learned, and the power of writing is developed.

In passing it should be mentioned that writing is most valuable in other areas of the curriculum. Arithmetic, for example, is greatly enhanced when children write their own problems. The concept is brought home, so to speak, when its origin is from the pupil's own experience, or even imagination.

Summary of Practical Writing

In brief, practical writing is noteworthy in that it is intended for others to see. Not at the desire of the author so much, but because of the nature of the communication. Newspapers are not written for one's own self. Letters are meant to be sent. Reports on social studies projects are for general consumption. (If they aren't, something is wrong with the project!) Outlines promote something to be finished in the future, and plans are made to be carried out.

Because of these *intents*, such writing must be in good form. Thus it is subject to correction, to proofreading. If it be shown in unreadable form, the author can expect to be criticized—preferably by his peers. Sylvia Ashton-Warner[36] says:

[36] *Teacher*, New York: Simon & Schuster, Inc., 1963, p. 82.

Since I take this original writing as a basis for reading, a strict watch is kept on grammar and punctuation. And as for the writing itself, the hand writing, I mean, it has to be at least the best that they can do, to save their own faces, when changing books. Which brings one more subject into the vent of creativity: Handwriting.

In the middle and upper grades, then, children will follow a plan that begins with the writing of an initial rough draft. This must be checked by the teacher in whatever time its intended audience needs it. If feasible, the teacher can set up a system of student editors—keeping a watchful eye on the lordly one who loves to reduce his fellow classmates to small bits. Eventually good copies are made and the writing moves to its destination—wherever, whomever that might be. It is published. It is presented. Its writer should feel a sense of accomplishment and be all the more eager for the next writing. Children should really like to write as well as they like to draw. If the art teaching in a given school is inadequate, then the children should like to write more than' they like to draw. This is a handy yardstick for a teacher: "How well do my children LIKE to write?"

CREATIVE WRITING

The jewel of the language arts, however, especially of the written language arts, is creative writing. Writing for one's self. Intended for no one else unless desired. A safe self-made explosion. A warm comforter against the cold. A steel blade against the world. An in-gathering of all that is wanted. Creative writing triggers the senses.

But the mind cannot be separated from the senses—at least, it is dangerous to do so. Creativity is the engine that runs the mind, runs the soul, runs the body. It is the power, the drive wheel, the energy, the electricity that will discipline a man's mind or a child's mind as will nothing else. The reading program that skips this kind of writing is the poor one indeed. The teacher who never heard of it is a disadvantaged teacher. The class that never wrote creatively is a deprived class. The curriculum that omits it is not worthy of the name. The school that forbids it does not understand the role of education in a democratic society. Such an activity gets at the vitals of learning. It is so important, we will deal with it in detail.

How Creative Writing Begins

The main concern of the teacher must be to help each child find, within himself, a major idea, story, adventure, or desire that he considers worthwhile enough to put on paper. Although it is preferable that he do the writing, the teacher may take his dictation if the child so wishes. In this way, and in all other ways, the teacher must aid this setting down of ideas on paper. Childhood, and adulthood too, for that matter, is replete with stories, adventures, wishes, and ideas that could be lost for lack of an adequate means of expression. In this instance, the teacher must use all means at his command to help a child bring one of these ideas to verbal—written—expression.

To promote this end, the teacher goes to unusual lengths to have the situation, for the time being at least, free from strain and tension. A mood is set that gives promise of excitement, satisfaction, and release. A pile of fresh paper and new, beautiful (the dimestore type is beautiful!), sharply pointed pencils are ready for the birth of ideas. The teacher in setting the mood keeps his voice low, serene, and yet warm and anticipatory of exciting things to come.

He offers whatever guarantees are necessary to the children to allay fears and anxiety about what he—the teacher—will do or not do about the child's writing. He develops what might be called the "civil rights" of the classroom. Each child may write what he wants. He does not write if he doesn't want to.[37] The choice of writing or not writing is solely up to the child. The lack of mechanical ability is taken care of through drawing or dictation. The privilege of privacy is the prerogative of the author. Critical comments of even a remotely destructive nature are prevented. And lack of ideas is not considered catastrophic.

Setting the Mood

The teacher then proceeds to help the group find whatever lies in the storehouse of the mind that might be considered worth recording. Perhaps he begins by reading the efforts of other children that have resulted from this same kind of situation. He may give suggestive ideas that are general enough in scope to trigger off the minds of individuals or set in motion a train of thought in the direction of some story or idea that has lain fallow for so long. He urges them to wait for a *really* good idea, as their satisfaction will be so much greater when the idea is good. The teacher will help, he will counsel, he will take dictation, but he will never coerce or require or assign. Each product must be uniquely personal to the writer.

---

[37] The reader may be interested to know that over a period of years of teaching undergraduate classes in language arts, upward of 3,000 students were taught to do a creative writing experience, unsupervised, in various grades of local public schools. The incidence of nonwriters does not average even one to a class. Such refusals by children in a free writing situation amount to less than .0003 per cent even with totally inexperienced teachers.

As the Writing Begins

As the bulk of the pupils become absorbed in their efforts, the teacher recedes to the background, literally and figuratively. Since the children have been urged to seek any help necessary, that help must never be denied. As the writing progresses, the teacher moves only at the request of a child. Music might motivate more and better writing. Fine, then. Let the teacher run the record player. If the spelling needs swamp the teacher so that he cannot provide words fast enough for the demand, there are ways to speed such help up.

The teacher can refer—before the activity really begins—to the alphabetic principle[38] and show the pupils how to put down a word beginning with the initial letter and going from left to right as long as they can hear the letter sounds. Then the pupils can draw a line for the rest of the unknown word and proceed with their writing with as little interruption as possible. The teacher comes around to each as fast as possible (note: going *to* the pupils, not having the pupils come to him), filling in the blank spots or leaving slips of paper with the needed word written upon it. The teacher does all in his power to make the children more and more independent.

The Dangers of Teaching Mechanics

The encouragement of independence should not lead to the use of those creative writing periods to teach grammar, and usage and spelling. True, the teacher can glean clues of what is needed from such spontaneous outpourings. But these writings are sacrosanct. They are not *intended* for purposes of teaching the mechanics of writing. They are intended to teach the LOVE of writing and they cannot be prostituted for a lesser goal. Teachers take some notes. But the correction of such problems takes place in an entirely separate situation. To be critical of these efforts is to criticize a child's BEING. These efforts should be so much a part of an individual.

Whatever mechanics of writing, spelling, or phonics are to be taught to the group as a whole, must be relegated to another time of the day or week and with another type of material. If mechanics are included on a group basis during creative writing periods, the drive to write, the urge to put ideas down on paper, can be endangered, It is only when the danger of damaging that desire to write is well past, and for some children it is never past, that the teacher can make suggestions of a mechanical nature. Drill in any form is to be disassociated from creative writing.

[38] See details in Chapter 11, p. 387 ff.

Toward the end of a given writing period a suggestion may be made, by the teacher or the children, that some members of the grup might want to share their products with their neighbors, their teacher, or everyone. If this proves desirable, emphasis of the prerogative of choice in sharing should be made, lest no one feel that he is forced to read his paper. A shy child might receive encouragement and there are ways to help the shy ones. The teacher might say:

"Would you like me to read your paper?"
"Yes."
"Fine. Then you come and stand in our sharing line and I will read it when the time comes. You hold your own paper for me."

Even with other children, who are not the slightest bit modest about reading their own creations, there will be occasional pauses while a word is being figured out. However, accenting the oral reading to hold an audience helps eliminate much of this. Thus, children who are hesitant will feel even less conspicuous by the time their turn comes. The teacher—in the assistant's role—moves along behind the line of budding authors. He reads over the shoulder of each child who so wishes. In the case of the shy child, the teacher will find a place to get stuck on a work without much trouble. If there is no such place, the teacher should make such a place! He stops. He points to where he is and asks the child what it should be. The child—usually—knows exactly what he means to say no matter what is on the paper. A few more stops like this, and the teacher can frequently say something like:

"Oh, go ahead and read it yourself. You do better than I do." This is not exactly a foolproof idea, but it works in an astonishing number of instances.

So the creative writing period draws to a close. Even with young children the fascination, the sense of accomplishment, the thrill of recording something that matters, will keep a class busy, productively busy, without disciplinary requests, for more than an hour. The final sharing line is the cherry on the sundae. Stories are read. Other-day favorites may be reread. Some may become so popular that a book may be published.

Some Creative Writing

William Hauer of New Paltz Teachers College has spent countless hours in the last few years compiling a magazine of children's creative writing. It appears twice a year and contains poems, stories, with the young authors and their schools listed.[39]

[39] For those interested, this nonprofit publication is called *The Creative Writer* and is available from Mr. W. M. Hauer, New Paltz State College, New Paltz, N.Y.

The following about the death of President Kennedy is especially poignant.

Lament

Bright skies
Billowing banners
Cheering crowds
Happy people
Shattering bullet
Fallen hero
Terrified screams
Stunned Nation
   "The President is dead!"

Starlit night
Winging plane
Silent cities
Somber people
Lonely hearse
Weeping heavens
   "The President is dead!"

November sunlight
Tolling bells
Marching men
Riderless horse
Muffled drums
Clopping hoofbeats
Horse-drawn caisson
Flag-draped coffin
Respectful people
   "The President is dead!"

Crowded rotunda
Endless lines
Motionless guards
Silent prayers
   "The President is dead!"

Visiting dignitaries
Filled church
Courageous lady
Quiet Arlington
Salute of guns
Mournful taps
Eternal flame for
   "The President who's dead."

Sixth Grade Class, Howe School, Schenectady, N.Y
Miss Ella Cohan, Principal
Miss Catherine Grattan, teacher
The Creative Writer, Spring, 1964, p. 32

Here are some other efforts by children from the writer's files that insist upon being included and in the text of the teaching of reading! Think of it!

My Alarm Clock

My alarm clock isn't round and isn't square. It doesn't have numbers from one to twelve. It doesn't have a bell to wake up every morning. You can't shut it off when it rings. You can't change its time, because my alarm clock is my dad.

Colleen
Nittany Ave. School
State College, Pa.

Halloween came shortly after the first Sputnick was launched. A whole class collaborated on this production.

This is the Night

Everybody is busy. Tonight is Halloween. All the children are getting ready. They will stop being boys and girls. Instead, they will become witches, goblins, ghosts and bats. Even some mothers and fathers change. They become fancy ladies and brave knights.

But what happens to poor pumpkins? Most of them just sit and burn themselves out. But *not* Poopnick. He decided to run away. He waited until everyone was out trick and treating. Then he rolled down the walk on his big fat belly.

Some of the children who saw him tried to catch him. But Poopnick just rolled faster and faster. When the cats and dogs saw him they got so frightened they ran backwards. It took their shadow ten days to catch up with them.

Soon Poopnick got tired. He stopped to rest. He did not see a witch hiding in the trees. How scared he was when he heard the witch ask, "Who are you? Where are you going?"

Poopnick answered. "I am Poopnick the Pumpkin. I am running away from people. Can you help me find a safe place?"

"Hop on my broomstick. I will take you to a haunted garden. There a poor headless horseman stands. He has been wishing for a head for a long time. He will be glad to have you rest on his shoulders."

So Poopnick hopped on the witch's broom and off they flew. They did not mind the shrieks and shouts of the children when they saw Poopnick riding on a witch's broom.

At last they came to the haunted garden. There the poor horseman stood without a head. When the witch told him about Poopnick he was very happy. "You may stay on my shoulders as long as you wish," he told Poopnick.

And to this very day, you may still find him if you look in the haunted garden. To show his appreciation to the helpful witch, Poopnick lights up every Halloween Night so that the helpful witch can see where she is flying.

Mrs. Friedlander's Second Grade
October, 1957
Levittown, N. Y.

Here are more writings from children:

The World Begins

I rose slowly out of the pool that had been my home. What a strange place out here, and it was so bright. Suddenly I wondered why I wanted to leave my dark slimy pool of mud and come out in this—place. I turned back, but something held me. Fascinated, I watched the palm trees sway. I clambered, slowly, hesitantly, but faster and faster, I ran from one thing to another. How cool it was here and how small. I was huge. A small butterfly settled on my back. I lifted my scales and crushed it. What were these miniature little things. They looked like tea flies, but they were black, and only the size of my littlest claw. Then I realized these were flies and I wasn't in my tarpool any longer. I was the first creature to come out of the seas, to dry land.

> Unsigned—Pupil in 4th Grade
> State College Public Schools, Pa.

From a child who said she had "nothing to write about":

Moving Day

I moved in November
but I cannot remember.
Maybe I moved here in September
but I cannot remember.
Whatever I remember in
November or September.
I still remember
What I remembered.

From a slum child in a large city.

I Wish a Wish

I wished a wish the other night
As hard as hard could be
That just a fairy would come in and talk to me.
I counted pictures on the wall
And patterns just the same
To give the time away until the fairy came.
I heard a step upon the floor
As small as any mouse
I watched the door so carefully
I didn't want to miss
But it was only Mother who
Came in to have a kiss.

Teachers, old and young, will write, too, if they are sure it is safe. Here are samples from our files. Hilarious or heart-rending, these provide what each soul needed at that moment.

A Dirty Deed

It all started when we decided we needed a telephone book. I say we, but I really mean my husband. Perhaps I should explain about "him whom is" my husband. Once he decides something, it is better to try to move Plymouth Rock than to try and change his mind.

We had just come into this area for a short business trip and he needed a phone book for various and sundry reasons. You say, "Why didn't he use the one in the public phone booth?" Good question, in fact, one which I'd asked him myself. Needless to say, his answer cannot be printed verbatim, but went something like this—"Because, *dear*, I wish to have access to this for a long period of time during which we will not be permanently located in this area."

In other words, he wanted to "lift" one from the local Greyhound Bus Depot.

He outlined his crafty plan to me and proceeded into the station to "do his dirty deed."

I remained outside in front of the place in our car. Needless to say, I had all sorts of visions in my head. I could just see a cop going into the lobby and spotting my husband stealing a phone book. By this time, I had worked myself up into quite a frenzied state. Then, remembering some of the excellent movies from my youth, I decided I had better start the car so we could make a fast get-away. At this point a policeman did happen along the street and he went into the bus depot, probably for his lunch. This was too much for me. I could almost hear the gun shots so I turned the key in the ignition and stepped down on the starter. In my haste I neglected to do two things. The first was to take the car out of second, and the next, was to move over to the driver's seat. There followed an ominous crash in which I found that the car had jolted forward and hit the unattended car in front of us.

My first reaction was to vacate the premises immediately, to say the least. Succumbing to hysteria, I shot out into traffic and away from the scene of the crime. At this crucial point, my husband came out of the station with an almost unnoticable lump under his topcoat. His composure was somewhat shaken when he saw that I was about two blocks away, and out in traffic.

I stopped for a red light and he came tearing up the street, arms crossed across his chest.

Finally, he caught me and jumped into the car. To this day he thinks I would have abandoned him to take the "rap" alone. What do you think?

Syracuse, 1958

Principals help teachers, too:

Do you remember Jimmy? Who could help from remembering this irritating, yet endearing youngster. So many times he would bring my blood to the boiling point, only to finish with a punch line that would leave me in helpless laughter. I will never forget this session in my office.

Jimmy at the time was in the first grade. He had been so restless on this particular day that finally Mrs. X, his teacher, brought him in, seated him in the outer office, gave me a hopeless look, and left.

No one paid any attention to Jimmy, except to turn a forbidding eye on him every so often. I expect disapproval, as thick as a tornado's clouds, was written on the faces of every grown person that glanced his way. It would have curdled the soul of most. But not Jimmy; suddenly, clear as a bell, a little voice raised in song. What song? Why "Jesus loves me, this I know."

Teachers write about other things too:

I sat there in the library [ed. note: The room where workshop met] waiting for a chance to escape. There was no way out; nothing I could do to escape from that stale room. And then I began to think why I had called it a stale room, for after all, wasn't it a library filled with many wonderful books which all types of people, young and old, read in order to escape the cold reality of the world in which they lived. Maybe the people who read those books were cold and ruthless and would select books which suited their mood; maybe some were kind and good and selected books full of warmth. Yet, as I sat there, I stared at the books and still could not decide how I wanted to escape. Sitting there my gaze suddenly fell upon a beautifully bound book—a very old story which was called *Cinderella*. And thus I reverted to childhood experiences again and how miserable I had been in my early childhood when other children used to taunt me with, "Hello, fatty, where've you been? Out with dough and rolling pin?" I walked into the book and before my own eyes I became a lovely princess whom everyone admired and thought was very beautiful. I danced through every moment of life and then I woke to reality to discover that I was very old, very ugly, and very tired. My life had been a fantasy and now I was too old to go back.

Johnny Went Home

I worked with foster children at Catholic Charities. It was work that wasn't work for spending time and planning for children who need you affords only pleasure.

One day I drove out to Long Island to pick up a child and return him to a foster home where he had been two years before. His present foster mother was ill so it was decided after talking to Johnny and Mrs. C. that he would be returned to her.

On the way to Mrs. C's, I asked Johnny if he remembered her. He said that he did a little bit; he remembered her kneeling down every night saying her prayers with him. And he remembered Daddy coming in each night and sneaking him a few pennies for the Good Humor man. Johnny's blue eyes seemed to want to remember and with each recollection they became brighter—yet there was still the fear that maybe it couldn't be like that again. I reassured him that she remembered him and was very anxious to see him and have him with her again. I also explained as I had on a previous visit, about Kathy and Kevin, the other two foster children Mrs. C now had and how anxious they were to meet "Johnny-boy," as Mrs. C would always say.

Everything I said he accepted—but Johnny couldn't be totally sure. Only time would tell.

As we approached the gray house, we both saw the early middle-aged woman standing outside visiting her next door neighbor. Johnny stared, as only a hopeful little boy can. We neared the curb, Mrs. C. eyed us and started to run for the car. Johnny jumped over me, fumbled for the handle and was out of the car and into her arms before I had turned the key off.

I left about a half-hour later with tears in my eyes and happiness in my heart. Johnny was home and his Mommy was there.

Undergraduate education majors like to write creatively, too. Here is a piece about a certain feeling during a certain spring.

It's a well worn subject. Poets write about it all the time. Its volumes occupy shelf upon shelf. It's eternal spring with flowers and clouds. It makes my friends so happy. I've dreamed about it all my life—and now that it's here, all it's doing is hurting.

A Pennsylvania State University Undergraduate

Creative Writing Outline

The following is an outline that has proved useful in helping children and adults to write[40]:

1. Teacher makes unusual effort to have the situation free from tension. His voice is low, quiet, serene, yet warm and anticipatory of satisfying and exciting things to come.

2. A pile of new clean paper and new sharp pencils is near or at least readily available, while the teacher reads as interestingly as possible other creative writing. He begins to set a mood.

3. Teacher continues in same vein but suggests that if each child *could* think of a good idea for a story, he would find it very exciting and a lot of fun to write. He reassures the pupils that their spelling and grammar are of less concern that day than getting a good idea. There will be no marking of any kind. In fact, no one will look at any story unless the child desires. He asserts that the only thing he wants to do is help them to write down, as fast as possible, whatever good idea that comes. He will help them spell, or even take dictation if necessary. But the children will be urged to write only when they get this good idea. He will be reassuring if ideas are slow in coming, as sometimes the process takes time.

4. As the mood pattern is well set, the teacher should talk intermittently, allowing much silence for further thought. He will offer ideas that may help initial efforts, such as, "If you were very big, what adventures might you have?" or "If you were something different than what you are, what might happen to you?" He gives general ideas to trigger off a spontaneous thought in each child's mind.

5. As individuals get ideas and so indicate, the teacher bustles them off with a new piece of paper and a new sharp pencil to begin writing.

6. As the majority of the group is writing and only a few are still groping for ideas, he takes them aside (so as not to confuse the rest) and repeats parts of the above procedures. If still some cannot get ideas, he is reassuring and undisturbed and helps them find something to do that will keep them busy while the rest write. If children get ideas at some other time of the day, they can put them on a page in their notebook, awaiting their opportunity.

7. Sharing of finished products or any editing or recopying only occurs at the desire of the child and never at the insistence of the teacher. For an immediate sharing, children need to be encouraged to "practice" reading their work.

8. Ample time is allowed for completion of stories, also for succeed-

40 Adapted from Fleming, *op. cit.*, Chap. 7.

ing sharing time, if desired. But the succeeding activity must be set in such a way that as individual children finish stories they may begin the next activity without disturbing those still unfinished. A sharing lineup is a good way to work. It begins as children are finishing. Then the group is stopped as a whole to hear the results of their efforts.

10. This activity cannot be done too often. Once a week for the whole group is plenty although there should be no restrictions as to other times that individual children might wish to write down stories as their own and the class schedule permits.

Summarizing Writing Activities

In bringing the discussion to a close, another set of directions is presented. As before, they are not intended to be followed verbatim. Each teacher can shift and change to suit the situation. As in all creative activities, however, there are certain constants that accentuate the creativity. The less these constants appear, the less the creativity.

For example:

No marking or grading of any kind.

Mechanics are subordinated to the power of the idea.

The writing must be unique to each child.

The writing is owned by each child.

Emotion is used as motor for writing.

With these directions, then, we move on to the next area of language arts that contributes so much to the reading program.

CRITICAL READING THROUGH CREATIVE DRAMATICS

The final activity in the creative area that needs to be presented is that of creative dramatics. This is another curriculum area that is blessed with many fine sources of the most useful type.[41]

The first concern of the teacher in creative dramatics is to provide a situation in which children enact a real or fictional story in such a way that they lose themselves in the characterization of

---

[41] The name of Winifred Ward is the most notable in creative dramatics. These two books are still classics of the literature: *Playmaking with Children* (2d ed.), New York: Appleton-Century-Crofts, Inc., 1957; *Creative Dramatics*, New York: Appleton-Century-Crofts, Inc., 1930. Other excellent references are: Corrine Brown, *Creative Drama in the Lower School*, New York: D. Appleton, 1929; Isabel Burger, *Creative Play Acting*, New York: A. S. Barnes & Co., Inc., 1950; Ruth Lease and G. B. Siks, *Creative Dramatics in Home, School, and Community*, New York: Harper Bros., Inc., 1952; Peter Slade, *Child Drama*, New York: Philosophical Library, 1955.

Dramatics push reading.

whatever role they play. This is not done by memorizing lines. In the elementary grades there is rarely a time that lines need to be memorized. Nothing is more deadly than the parroting and squirming of a child wrestling to bring forth that which he had learned by heart. Professionals can learn lines. But children shouldn't. Not even their own. It defeats the whole purpose and power of dramatics.

Dramatics Are Life Practice

Dramatics are important in school as they give a child *practice in life* in a safe way. One boy who was a troublemaker for himself and everyone else gleefully volunteered to take the part of King John, the villain in a dramatic play about the Magna Carta. He threw himself into the role with gusto for the two weeks of rehearsals. He swaggered and bragged. He threatened and bullied in his stage role. Two days before the performance in assembly he quit. He said "I don't want to be King John in front of the whole school." He couldn't face the similarity between his own personality and the play's character. Luckily, there were several ready to take over as creative dramatics is built upon acting out what happens—acting out a story—so there is no forgetting of lines to worry about. This boy was assigned to turning pages for the between-acts pianist, to his relief. Another King John was found immediately.

This is an example of how children can practice themselves and then gain insight into their behavior. They can change if they suddenly become aware of what they never knew before. The child could not really face the mirror of himself as the hated King John. It was too close to his own image, *as he saw it.* He quit. The teacher, for the first time, had a way of helping a disturbed and disturbing child.

Dramatics Require Reading

But beyond the benefits of such psychological nature, the benefits of dramatics relate to the act of reading. One must act out a story—or an incident. Thus one must have read stories—or have listened to them. One must have read about incidents in order to know what to do. One of the most powerful experiences the writer observed was in a sixth-grade classroom (average reading about 3.5) enacting an imaginary meeting between Truman and MacArthur the week after Truman fired the General from his post in Korea. Those children may have had limited reading skills, but they had discussed the news event in such a way that they planned a dramatic skit about that major event.

Outlining Plot

Children must be helped to develop the chosen plot and to provide dramatic quality to the action. But they are never told exactly what to do by the teacher. No parts or lines are to be written down, even by the children. But OUTLINES of plots can be written down. In fact, there is hardly a better way to teach outlining!

Keeping the Story Line

Children are continually urged and helped to interpret the character of their choice in their own unique way. However, the story line must never be violated. If the audience laughs in the wrong place, there is something wrong. The action needs to be stopped to see why the audience laughed when the story was not funny. A plot that has been agreed upon by the class before action began must be sustained. There can be many variations—but the story line cannot be touched. The ridiculousness of the sisters of Cinderella may be the way one set of characters interprets them. But another group will make them horrifying and cruel. Little Red Riding Hood must leave for her Grandmother's house with a basket of food on her arm and a warning in her ears about the dangers of the wolf. But how sympathy for Cinderella is engendered, or how Little Red Riding Hood leaves, what she says as she goes, who is with her to say goodbye—none of these change the plot. They are a matter of individual interpretation. The atmosphere must be such that the ingenuity of childhood comes into play.

In one first grade that was dramatizing the scene from Little Red Riding Hood where she is talking to the Wolf in her grandmother's bed, the following was heard by the teacher:

> "Grandma, what big eyes you have!"
> "The better to see you with, my dear."
> "But Grandma, what big ears you have!"
> "The better to hear you with, my dear."
> "But Grandma, what a big head you have."
> —silence—then
> "Oh-h-h-h, such a headache I have!"

They went on then through the usual windup of that story. The child who was the wolf never changed roles. The story was not spoiled.

Structuring the Activity

In terms of structuring, this activity begins when the teacher and the group come to a decision about the material to be enacted. It can be a folktale, an historical event, or an original story from the group. A retelling is usually in order so that everyone knows the version that is going to be developed.

Next the teacher helps the children find the first part of the story. The later parts can come at this time, too, if desired. Sometimes children do not want to act out the first part, but just a certain part of a story. In any case, the action to be worked on is decided ahead of time. The place setting is listed on the board (outlining and paragraphing again). The characters that are in that part of the story are also listed. What happens in that part of the story is discussed orally. If written down it should be a word or phrase only.

Casting the Play

Once these areas are clear to all, the casting can take place. The teacher calls for volunteers for the various characters in succession. He is wise if he casts the most popular character first. The manner of such casting on the part of the teacher must be casual, lest a sense of competitiveness be set up which will eventually spoil the acting. Spontaneity can so be killed.

Jobs for the Shy Ones

For those children who are too shy to volunteer there are other jobs to be performed. Live curtains are a wonderful "breaker-inner" for such children. Light switches need to be manned. Furniture might need to be moved to establish exactly where the stove or the door, or something, might be. Stage hands are important, too.

Perhaps the most important structural element in this activity is the selection of several casts for the same action. This seems to make for increasingly dramatic action as the teacher helps a class evaluate each cast in positive terms only. "What did you particularly like about this cast?" is a fair question.

As children indicate that they liked the way someone glowered at another character, or had a voice that really DID sound like the giant, the path is set for children to imitate, in later casts, those uniquely original actions that make dramatics the fascinating activity that it can be. In this way the several casts perform the same scene in turn before the play moves. Each cast should have time for a brief planning session just before they "go on." But these, too, should be held to a minimum as they can cut spontaneity if overplanned. Repetition of previously spoken lines (with the exception of such time-worn phrases such as "Who has been sitting in MY chair?") is to be discouraged. In as many ways as possible the originality of expression is to be encouraged.

Dramatics may be utilized for the purpose of entertaining the class itself, or to produce full-blown plays, costumes and all. But the elements of spontaneity need not be damaged in any of these cases. One can change a major character at the last minute if everyone knows what is supposed to happen.

If the children wish to climax the various performances with a select cast, such final casting should be done on a basis of consensus of "Who will make the best _____?" Usually, after several sets of characters have performed, there is an obvious choice, apparent to all.

As in Creative Writing, the teacher must resist all temptation to use these dramatic sessions to teach grammar, good usage, or good speech. The quality of talk must be that which comes rather naturally. The teacher will have plenty of other opportunity to eliminate the "he dones" and the "you wases" through writing, through the literature period, and mainly through his own good language. Self-consciousness about the correctness of speech will be the death knell of dramatic action. It will kill spontaneity. If that goes, there is nothing worthwhile keeping from such an activity. For spontaneity carries the power of ideas. It teaches the values of a society. It trains its children to be participants and not spectators. At all cost, the children must end each session satisfied, serene, yet eager for the next one to come.

Creative Dramatics Outline

As in the previous activities, directions are included to shortcut the process for a busy teacher. Again, these are not intended to be sacrosanct. They can be changed and altered, even though certain characteristics guarantee the validity of the creative action. If certain items are omitted or weakened, to that extent is the whole action less creative.

Creative Dramatics

1. A story is chosen that is mutually agreeable to teacher and children. Source: Folk tale, modern tale, original with some child of the group, a news incident, or a poem.
2. Story is retold by teacher or children or both.
3. Group decides what is first part of story.
4. Group lists characters and places setting of that first part of the story.
5. The teacher then chooses each character rapidly, casually, from the group who respond when he asks a question like—"Who wants to be so-and-so?" He is careful to choose only volunteers. If none, the character needs developing a bit. He waits until someone offers.
6. He chooses three or four sets of the same characters in like manner.
7. He then describes the mood of the action as graphically as possible without discussing what the action will be. Each group retires to a corner to talk briefly about what they will do.
8. Each group, in turn, performs. After each one is finished the teacher helps the audience to analyze what they *liked* about the performance. If the actors obviously departed from the story line, rather than allowing negative comments, the teacher explores the atmosphere and setting of the story more deeply. There is no discussion of what was disliked, nor corrections of grammatical errors at this time, only a development in depth of understanding. The teacher works for appreciation of specific actions or phrases that are unique and "right" for the story.
9. If presentation to a larger audience is desired—and the class makes that decision—the teacher selects a single set of characters by

such questioning as follows: "Who do you think should be so-and-so? If there is indecision on a part or character, selection is made by the group after a repeat performance. The teacher makes *no* decisions on casting.

10. In the elementary school lines are not written down, nor memorized. Originality of interpretation of the same characters is encouraged. The teacher is dispensable during action, and enters as an important figure only to promote and to further action.

11. "Prop men" are useful. Shy children can be set on the path of dramatics by acting as "curtains" or "trees" or turning lights on and off.

SUMMARY

This chapter has presented a point of view that the systematic reading period, for itself alone, in the upper grades is a poor use of classroom time. This is not to say that children who have not achieved advance reading levels will not be helped. They will be. But it is to say that those aspects of the language arts program that are open-ended in character and concept will teach reading far more efficiently than any textbook approach, or any content area with a text-centered approach.

This chapter thus contends that reading is best taught, not for itself but in connection with 1) a problem-centered, experience-unit program in the social studies, 2) open-ended discussion with certain specific unique features, 3) independent or creative writing, and 4) creative dramatics dependent upon sociodrama skills, as well as those of role-playing, and performed spontaneously without script or written lines.

The educational assumptions behind these suggestions are based on the fact that all aspects of written and oral language are essentially verbal in character. Those activities that enhance a child's abilities to use words freely, spontaneously, and communicatively will improve reading at surprising rates. These are better *reading* activities than those traditionally labeled as such, as they are vital and dynamic in character.

Although some research supports the point of view of this chapter, more is needed. Nevertheless, these activities will liven up many more classrooms, and will teach a lot more reading skills, than those programs of a question-answering, blank-filling nature. Again, reading is a product of a person's self. To argue, to act, to write stories are all highly personal acts. Thus they lend themselves to the most important tool subject of all—reading.

11

TEACHING SKILLS FOR READING

WORKING IN THE CLASSROOM

Re-evaluation of Phonics

Clymer[1] analyzed a composite list of words from four basal series and the Gates Reading Vocabulary for the Primary Grades with catastrophic results for some time-honored and time-worn "Rules" such as "When two vowels go out walking, etc." Out of 45 generalizations, only 18 were found to be useful. This excellent piece of research is sobering to those who have felt that there were many generalizations worth bothering to teach, even granting the numerous exceptions found in most cases. This study is but the beginning of many that should establish some validity to whatever sequences or progressions, rules or generalizations in the area of phonics are to be taught. More praiseworthy than even that estimable goal is the news that at long last, professionals and not commercial concerns are working at what has always been a professional problem. The field of education is working out its own vexing questions.

However hopeful these re-evaluations might be, we join with Spache in his suggestion that there is a long way to go and the research is too meager to warrant drastic change at this time, as much as we find so much traditional practice in major need of revision. There is a real possibility of "throwing out the baby with the bath," so to speak. What must be taken into account before the disturbing findings of the Clymer study can be applied in actual practice is the process by which words are analyzed. More important, *where do the words come from?*

[1] Theodore Clymer, "The Utility of Phonic Generalizations in the Primary Grades," *The Reading Teacher*, January, 1963, pp. 252 ff.

The Process of Treating Unknown Words

As the process of self-selection demonstrates the reduction of need to teach skills, so the process of writing something valued reduces the need to teach phonics. We insist that the child attacking an unknown word in a basal reader over which he has had no choice is a far different cry from a child trying to figure out a word that he wants to spell in order to write something important. This is the crux of the whole effort in phonic instruction. Where do the words come from? They MUST, we submit, come from the child's need to express himself first, and second, to examine the expressions of others.

Finding Phonic Needs for Written Work

In order to know what to teach each day, the teacher must have several diagnostic tools. There are informal hearing tests. Word analysis skills need to be consistently presented essentially as writing skills. Thus the teacher needs some way of finding out which children need to be taught which phonic element. The individual conference cannot and does not provide enough of this kind of analysis. We must turn to the actual written work of the child.

A teacher needs samples of the interdependence of reading and writing. When the child draws on BOTH areas to help in EITHER area, he has moved through a major developmental stage. But the push to write something that counts is the incentive for the learning of letter sounds or phonics. If the same thing is taught in an abstract situation, it remains just that—abstraction, and devoid of meaning.

Methodology of Teaching Sounds

As we have continually reiterated, the whole of language learning begins with the talking upon topics that count. This is step one. Second, writing and reading reinforce each other. Finally, once the needs are identified, the teacher can take the clues found in both reading and writing and develop a lesson that is the direct teaching of what needs to be known.

The first step is to have the children write independently, with as little help as possible. However, if the teacher has helped in spelling words, he may wish to remember or note the TYPE of category the child needed help in. With such a pile of papers (done once every two weeks should be enough) the teacher finds what needs to be taught. They are not to be graded or "corrected" in the traditional sense.

The second step is to take each paper in turn and look for one or two[2] of the most serious spelling difficulties. For this purpose, errors of usage can be largely overlooked, as we are here concerned with word analysis skills. (For improving written composition, however, such troubles need to be assessed.[3])

The following chart is an example of the worst errors listed beside the children's names. The teacher can now see a panorama of needs and can more easily combine those easily taught together. Grouping follows. Study this list and see how errors fall into categories.

Sample Class Analysis Chart

Names[4]

1.	Mary B.	gril/girl, our/are
2.	George C.	kwort/quart, sint/sing
3.	Tony C.	fel/feel, shell/shall
4.	Mabel D.	fatter/father, beautysiful/beautiful
5.	June E.	prr/purr, frry/furry
6.	Leroy H.	juce/just, wood/would
7.	Sylvia J.	runing/running
8.	Jerry J.	perty/pretty, fell/fall
9.	Beverly K.	whair/where, frands/friends
10.	Sandy L.	haved/had, swan/swam
11.	Virginia L.	huanted/haunted, scret/secret
12.	Beatrice M.	bomped/bumped, triped/tripped
13.	Sam M.	spraned/sprained, finaly/finally
14.	Lisa N.	lighting/lightning, scrieked/screeched
15.	Tim N.	junp/jump, scarery/scarey
16.	Jean N.	gost/ghost, thout/thought
17.	Sally R.	mange/manage, fond/found
18.	Carl S.	dosnt/doesn't, waze/waltz
19.	Earl S.	exersise/exercise, myslef/myself
20.	John T.	habbits/habits, mowths/mouths
21.	Theresa V.	skoot/scoot, to/two
22.	Holly W.	shinning/shining, try'd/tried
23.	Roger W.	berch/birch, minit/minute
24.	Charles W.	arithematic/arithmetic, baterfly/butterfly
25.	Walter Y.	no/on, onely/only

The next step is setting up an overall plan to teach those skills just to those children who need them. As we have emphasized, the rest of the class must be absorbed in independent work. The follow-

[2] If a paper has a dozen errors, the teacher cannot teach the pupil how to correct them all. So why look past one or two on one paper?

[3] Alvina Burrows *et al.*, *They All Want to Write* (rev. ed.), New York: Holt, Rinehart, & Winston, Inc., 1964.

[4] If the teacher would duplicate many sheets with just the class roll, he would save time in applying quickly this pattern of analysis to any area of the curriculum, as handwriting, arithmetic facts, etc.

ing plan sheet indicates who is to work on what. It is written on a separate sheet of paper and is the major reason why no correction *on the children's papers* need be made. Teachers too often operate on the assumption that if they correct each paper, that will teach the children not to make mistakes! Nonsense! The fact is that the teacher gets the exercise the children need. We are suggesting an approach that puts the correction in its proper sphere.[5]

Examination of this plan sheet will show that several children are listed in more than one place. The teacher should use his judgment as to which group should be first. Take Mary, for example. Although she is listed three times, it might be best that she be taught all by herself. On the other hand, she might benefit greatly from sitting in on all three groups. This is a judgmental factor. Machines can't do it. Only flesh and blood teachers.

Teacher's Plan for Group Teaching[6]

Reversals

Mary (gril/girl)
Walter (no/on)
Earl (slef/self)

Doubling of Consonants

Sylvia (runing/running)
John (habbits/habits)
Holly (shinning/shining)
Beatrice (triped/tripped)
Sam (finaly/finally)

Sounding Out of Syllables

Mable (beautysiful/beautiful)
Tim (scarery/scarey)
Charles (Arithematic/arithmetic)
Sally (mange/manage)
Lisa (lighting/lightening)
Virginia (scret/secret)

Vowels Affected by r

Mary (gril/girl)
George (kwort/quart)
June (prr/purr)
Roger (berch/birch)
Jerry (perty/pretty)

Diphthongs

Virginia (huant/haunt)
Jean (thout/thought)
John (mowths/mouths)
Sally (fond/found)

Short Vowel Sounds

Tony (fel/shell)
Jerry (fell/fall)
Beverly (frands/friends)
Beatrice (bomped/bumped)

Word Drill on Hard-To-Remember Words

Mary (our/are)
Leroy (wood/would)
Beverly (whair/where)
Jean (gost/ghost)
Theresa (to, two)
George (kwort/quart)

Middle-of-Word Problems

Mabel (fatter/father)
Sam (spraned/sprained)
Tim (junp/jump)
Carl (dosn't/doesn't)
Holly (tryd/tried)
Roger (minit/minute)
Walter (onely/only)

Endings

George (sint/sing)
Leroy (juse/just)

[5] See also R. Fleming, *Curriculum for Today's Boys and Girls,* Columbus, Ohio: Charles E. Merrill Books, Inc., 1964, p. 183.

[6] There are several other possible ways of grouping these children on their errors.

As discussed in Chapter 7, these groups are specific in their subject matter, their membership being made up of children who know why they are there, what they need to learn to leave the group—all these factors make for brief, ten-minute sessions, as a rule.

The methodology of instruction in the group follows somewhat in this order:

1. Presentation of common problem derived from writing analysis.
2. Presentation of material to appropriate children.
3. Use of discovery technique to find the way to solve the problem.
4. The child (children) tells the teacher *in his own words* what he discovered.
5. (Optional) Follow-up exercise, workbook or teacher-made.

SKILLS: A DISCUSSION

The skills in learning to read are not the same skills as in learning to write. Yet one cannot read without using skills crucial to writing. Nor can one learn to write without using skills crucial to reading. In the broad outline of skills there are two sets, opposite in nature but impossible to separate. The major area of reading skills is known variously as word perception, word recognition, or synthesis. The major writing skills (other than penmanship) are word analysis or spelling skills. Obviously, seeing a word and recognizing as a word is dealing with that word as a whole. Breaking up a word to analyze it, to work out its parts, is a writing—or more specifically, a spelling skill.

Grace Fernald says it well in her still excellent text[7]:

The first step in learning to spell is the development of a distinct perception of the word. . . . In reading he must associate these meanings with the symbols that represent the words. In the first, or perception stage of spelling, he starts with the symbols of the words. It is not enough to merely recognize the word as he does in reading, he must get the word in sufficient detail to make it possible for him to reproduce it correctly. In reading it is only necessary for him to get the meaning of the word when he sees it; in spelling he must get not only the meaning but every detail of the word form.

Durrell[8] makes the same point when he says:

Practice in word analysis is best done in a period separate from reading, preferably in the spelling period. Word analysis is more closely related to

[7] Grace Fernald, *Remedial Techniques in Basic School Subjects*, New York: McGraw-Hill Book Co., Inc., 1943, p. 181.

[8] Donald Durrell, *Improving Reading Instruction*, New York: World Book, Inc., 1956, p. 267.

spelling than to reading. Correlations between the various word-analysis abilities and spelling are always higher than similar correlations with reading at the intermediate grade level . . . spelling itself is a form of word analysis. . . . Several research studies have shown that children make more progress in spelling through word-analysis than through daily instruction in spelling.

The field of reading has greatly confused the issue by not carrying out instructional practices based upon these ideas. Practically all texts on reading instruction make a bow of some kind to spelling and its relationship. Fernald, however, is an exception. She did teach word analysis skills by writing activities. Others, however, do not. Many reading experts state that word analysis is not a reading skill, yet we find little help to the teacher in the majority of reading texts on the matter of teaching word analysis in curriculum areas other than reading.

Perhaps this is due to the current overemphasis on reading itself. It has been cut out of its proper sphere of the language arts and stands alone as a curriculum area. This is not sound, and eventually reading will have to be de-emphasized as a separate kind of instruction and reduced in importance so that it is equal with written composition, oral language, and such related areas.

To compare several texts in reading instruction is to discover a surprising lack of unanimity, a great deal of confusion, extensive or overlapping (often revealing the ignorance of curriculum in non-reading areas on the part of the author), and quite incredible complexity. Most of this, we suspect, is due to the misunderstanding of the complementary nature, the interdependence, the interrelationship of skills needed to master reading and writing. They are like the two sides of a coin, one is heads, and the other tails.

Word Analysis Not a Reading Skill

Teachers have been confused on a basic assumption that word analysis and word perception or recognition are BOTH reading skills. They are not. Reading skills are only those that are used to perceive, to see, to recognize words as wholes, as shapes that have certain meaning. Reading is a "looking-all-across-the-word skill" as one first grader put it. Reading skills are perception skills. They hold a word, a phrase, even a sentence together *by its looks.* Thus synthesizing, crystallizing, bringing unity from vision—these are *reading* skills.

Similarly, all skills needed to break a word apart, to analyze it, to separate such into pieces in order to find out what it is, are spelling or writing skills. The very nature of spelling is to know how to take words apart. One cannot write very much or very well unless one can deal with parts of sentences and phrases and words.

Reading, therefore, is damaged, is slowed, is interfered with when word analysis is applied too much and too soon. Reading is an eye-flowing action hurried up by the pressure of finding out what the message is. The eyes must move as does a "strobe" light in flash photography, or as a flashlight turned on and off in a dark room. It is that flashlight type of action applied to a line of words that makes for the best reading.

Confusion on Skill Identification

Although there are certainly reading skills the numbers of which depend upon the authority being read, the dissection of the act of reading, piece by piece, into "x" numbers of skills is not necessarily a useful exercise. In fact, such dissection can and has atomized a fundamentally automatic operation into "x" numbers of meaningless fragments. Such fragmentation is in opposition to major laws of learning.

As in the story of the centipede who got along just fine until someone asked him which leg he moved first, so have reading experts asked about the act of reading. The centipede collapsed in helpless bewilderment in the ditch. The reading experts have been so lost that development after development has taken place in the field of reading within the current decade without the knowledge of, let alone the assistance of, reading specialists.[9]

To make the point clearer, let us compare reading to the basic acts of talking and walking. We do not show a child where to put his tongue to talk until he is long past the rudimentary stages of learning to talk. Even then we only help a child place his tongue correctly for a very few of the more difficult phonemes. After he is past the making of baby comfort and discomfort sounds does he begin to meet his own native language in conformity with what he hears.[10]

We do not show a child, in walking, that he lifts a certain leg and bends his knee in a certain fashion, then straightens his leg, etc. We merely encourage him to walk toward us. Mother Nature takes care of the rest. Observation of those children whose muscle action needs

[9] Rudolph Flesch, *Why Johnny Can't Read*, New York: Harper & Row, Inc., 1955. Flesch produced a vacuum with the unexpected impact of his book. Almost immediately individualized reading appeared and gained headway. The misapplication of linguistics as phonics is still in vogue as of this writing, but the proper application of linguistic science, priority of spoken language and speech patterns, is moving into view.

[10] See M. M. Lewis, *How Children Learn to Speak*, New York: Basic Books, Inc., 1957, for details on this.

repatterning for medical reasons shows they are cruelly handicapped indeed.

So we have confused the issue in the skill-teaching of learning to read. When the act of reading is properly operating, the NEED of teach skills in an isolated, systematic, drill-type fashion is sharply reduced. There may be a time for such specific instructional attention, but it would largely be subordinate, even incidental, to the whole process of learning to read the given material.

To repeat then, we insist that there are two major areas of skills involved in learning to read—word analysis and word perception. Word analysis is needed in reading but its skills are introduced, are built, and reinforced during the writing activity. They are developed, perfected, and put into practice during writing. Put another way, reading and writing must be taught simultaneously.

The Contribution of Linguistic Science to Reading

Linguistic science has risen in importance and cannot be ignored while describing reading skills. There are at least three major contributions that linguistic science is making to the field of reading instruction. Educators are the experts in the application of knowledge to classroom learning. No other professionals are so trained. We feel that these three elements from a related discipline are of inestimable value. They are:

1. *The priority of spoken language over all other language:*
   I.e., All language is first spoken before it is written or otherwise symbolized. Man learned to speak his own language before he could speak any other language. Spoken language is the building block of all other language learning.
2. *"Sentence" meaning dominates word meaning:*
   I.e., Sentences are speech patterns made up of intonations, inflections, pauses, holders, noises that may or may not have the traditional "sentence" structure. In short, the voice tone is as important in conveying meaning as are the actual words used. Words, therefore, depend on the voice, and are not necessarily determinants for making sentences.
3. *The alphabetic principle:*
   Letters of the alphabet, alone and in combination, are, in large part, useful in reading instruction. (See pages 387–94.)

These concepts will be examined in detail in this chapter. How are they to be used in teaching reading skills—or writing skills, too, for that matter?

The Use of Spoken Language

The remarkable facility of language usage by children coming to school for the first time has been noted in many places. Children can deal competently with approximately ninety per cent of their adult level of speech. This means that most of the time children will make few mistakes in tense, gender, number, and other grammatical constructions (the home speech patterns being considered as one hundred per cent). Studies have shown that the common usage errors of a child tend to be words that are exceptions to some generalization of which he has become aware.

The ability of young children to use language and the extensiveness of their spoken vocabulary provide a most powerful argument for the use of experience charts, particularly the type retaining pupils' speech patterns, although Strickland[11] notes: ". . . evidence is needed whether children would be aided or hindered by the use of sentences in their books (i.e. basal readers) more like the sentences they use in their speech." (See also paragraph 4, page 5.)

While we would agree on the need for research, nevertheless, the logic of transfer of training would suggest that language in speech should be similar to language to be read. Linguistic science has long insisted that spoken language is prior to all other language. Put another way, this means that literate societies learned to *speak* their language before they learned to read and write it. Obviously, ability to speak precedes reading and writing competencies. There is no evidence of any kind that reverses this point of view. Therefore, this text submits that:

1. If learning proceeds from the known to the unknown
2. If transfer of training is best with similar elements
3. If discovery is the best way to find those similar elements in unknown material to those in known material

then it follows that:

1. Spoken language is the best initial resource for reading and writing instruction.
2. Learning to read occurs most easily with materials recorded from the reader's speech.
3. The particular elements of the reader's spoken language provide the means best used to develop any reading skill.

[11] Ruth Strickland, *The Language of Elementary School Children: Its Relationship to the Language of Reading Textbooks and the Quality of Reading of Selected Children,* Bloomington: Indiana University, Bulletin No. 4, 38:106 July, 1962.

Sentences, Phonological Units, Captions, and Written Experience

"Sentence" meaning dominates word meaning. Quotation marks were put around the word "sentence" because linguists and other language specialists differ as to whether or not there is such a thing. The term was used because it has a traditional connotation that was and is helpful. However, the decreasing usefulness of the word "sentence" leads us to substitute another, and more accurate one, "Phonological Unit." The excellent study by Strickland illustrated the reasons. The analysis of spontaneous speech samples of 575 children, grades one through six, showed that children do not speak in sentences in the usual definition of "whole thought with subject, verb, etc." The investigators found this term more useful. ". . . phonological unit—a unit of speech ending with a distinctly falling intonation which signals a terminal point. . . ." (In this study, the term *sentence* will mean a *phonological unit.*)[12]

In any event, it is important for our purposes to realize that children in the early stages of reading see whole units, be they sentences or phonological units. Each line of an experience story or other similar material is a unit and must be so treated.

In the early stages children do not know or find it hard to single out separate words. They see in wholes. Research is needed as to how soon and in what sequence the breakdown of this seeing in whole occurs. Our purpose here is to underline the fact that when children know what they said, they know what to read when their sentences are written down. It is the setting of oral reading pattern upon the recognition pattern that concerns us.

What To Do with Children's Own Language

No teacher will know what to do with the wealth of language children bring to school with them, unless he understands how to fit basic unit of our language, the Alphabet into the instruction. This is rock-bottom knowledge that the teacher can use as a springboard into all of the abilities needed in word analysis. In order for the teacher to understand the use of the alphabet in instruction, he needs to understand what is called the ALPHABETIC PRINCIPLE, which briefly is based on two facts:

1. Spoken language contains words that, in turn, contain the letters, and therefore their sounds, that comprise the language.

[12] Ruth Strickland, *op. cit.*, p. 9.

2. The alphabet, the root of the language, can be used to learn the letter by letter sounds or phonemes of the language.

Thus the idea being presented is that the alphabet is useful. It is a tool. Like all tools it can be misused. It can also lie neglected. But this does not change the fact that it is a most serviceable instrument for teaching. We do not begin with it. Nor do we end with it. But it fits in all along the line to the great advantage of those who know how to use it.

The Alphabetic Principle is based upon as simple an element as can be found. This element deals with and uses the names of the letters and relates these names to their sounds in words.

Beginning the Alphabetic Principle

Children bring thousands of words to school with them. The vast store of spoken language provides all of the material a teacher needs *without cost* to the taxpayer. In addition, most children come to school knowing the alphabet, or knowing that there is such a thing as the alphabet. The Alphabetic Principle takes advantage of this situation that children bring to school, as we will describe shortly.

Of course, the English language is made up of many other languages. That is why it is so hard to organize it into a regular system of rules that can be applied when one wants to spell or read or write. Many have said that English is not a phonetic language. That is not true. It is not entirely a phonetic language. There is no such thing as an one hundred per cent relationship between one letter and one sound or phoneme (which means "indivisible sound"), but there is much of our language that is phonetic. So many letters[13] do have a one-to-one relationship between sound and name that it seems silly not to use what is regular and then memorize what is irregular. There are clearly times in reading and writing that depend *only* on memory or recall. Until we know better we will use generalizations (even with their exceptions) that are helpful and worthwhile to know. Teaching children in the elementary school can be simplified by taking advantage of such knowledge.

Linguistics and Phonics

In concluding this discussion of the contribution of linguistic science to the field of reading, we must bring into focus the erroneous idea that somehow linguistic science is the same as phonics. The

---

[13] In this case, single letters are meant. There are, of course, digraphs, diphthongs, etc., that are made up of more than one letter. But they have no alphabetic name tag.

equation linguistics = phonics is not only wrong, but it denies the most important linguistic fact of all—the priority of spoken language. Faced head-on, no linguist can be called such if he denies this prime rule of that study of language. Yet we have had published certain readers for children called "linguistic" readers. Linguistically speaking, there can never be such a thing. Spoken language is first. Spoken language is prime. Therefore, a published reader is in direct violation of the science's most fundamental precept of all. As we have tried to explain, linguists have given the practice of using children's own language in reading instruction its most significant boost. We propose to take advantage of the situation.

Phonics and Phonetics

Much confusion about the two terms "phonics" and "phonetics" has interfered with the teaching of letter sounds as far as reading and spelling are concerned. Reading instruction dealing with letter sounds requires a unique treatment that differs sharply from that practiced in speech therapy, or recorded by linguistic scientists. Speech specialists work, of course, to prevent and correct problems of distortion of speech patterns. But they tend to isolate letter sounds (the "c" as "cuh" in "cat" sound, for example) in ways that are devastating to word recognition and sentence comprehension. Children being taught in speech classes to say "buh" and "tuh" and "guh" for the letters "B," "T," and "G" are not helped in spelling and reading back in their own class. Speech teachers should be asked to work in other ways that do not distort letter sounds in words. The possibility of confusion is too great.

This is serious because several commercial phonics programs have been developed by speech specialists, who deal with letter sounds in ways that can be detrimental to reading instruction. There is no well designed research in support of any commercial phonics system as of this writing.

There seem to be two types of teacher action that have brought several commercial phonics systems a modicum of success. These are:

1. Those teachers who skip around in the manual or "sneak in," as one second-grade teacher expressed it, some direct application to children's chosen material to relieve the tensions that accumulate when meaning is excluded as recommended by these manuals.
2. Those teachers who have had no, or so little, training in teaching letter sounds that even a poor system of phonics tends to fill a vacuum.

To continue our discussion of the difference in terms, remember that "phonetics" relates primarily to the ear—or hearing—while "phonics" relates primarily to seeing letters before sound is attached to them. When phoneticists try to apply their discipline of hearing to reading, they get into trouble. The following example demonstrates:

Read these two lines silently:

1. Xy xouxxxx xix ox xxee

and

2. Mx cxxntry txs xf thxx.

Most people find the first line difficult if not impossible to read until they puzzle it out. The second line is usually read without trouble after one glance. The difference between the two lines, as you can see, is that the first line has the consonants xx-ed out, while the second line has the vowels xx-ed out. Why does this make No. 2 easier to read than No. 1? Simply because consonants—in English at least—more often preserve the WORD CONFIGURATION, a reading perception skill, more than do vowels. But the consonants must be *seen* to produce this effect. Therefore, reading is geared more closely to sight than to hearing. Therefore, consonants are the first and prime items that must be taught. They are most important in word recognition. Further, eighty per cent of words in English begin with them.

There is at least one popular commercial phonics program[14] that *begins* instruction with the teaching of the sound and the sight long vowels—which are quite unrelated to word recognition *at this stage.* Children are forbidden to read books producing a learning that is clearly abstract. No child who knows the sound of a long "a" will be able to use that sound until he can see a long "a" in its position, usually in the middle of the word. Facts of eye maturation show that he sees the "outsides" of words first. The ability to focus on letters in words should show that connection of sight and sound, as we have been saying continually, must await the child's own developmental pattern. This is one example of how speech specialists have violated basic facts of child development as related to learning.

Pick and Choose from Manual Lessons

There are many fine lessons and good teaching suggestions in all of the commercial phonics systems. But to use them, lesson by les-

[14] "Phonics We Use," Economy Co., Oklahoma City, Okla.

son, as is advocated, is a gross denial of child development. How does an author and a publisher know when a given child is ready to learn a short "i" or the digraph "ch?" No one knows but the teacher of that given child. So if we train teachers to recognize the signals of growth and progress, then they have a quantity of material available to nail down a given needed skill. To teach according to the manual, as we said before, is to say "Here I come, ready or not!" Teachers can become the greatest wasters of classroom time and child eagerness to learn by such tactics. This text is geared to a sequence of perception—or seeing—that is based upon left-to-right direction and the progressive ability of the eyes to converge upon smaller objects closer to the face. One sees wholes before one sees parts.

At this writing there is no proved perfect way to teach the sounds of letters. This text is based upon the theory that spoken language is usable and useful, that spoken language contains words that contain letters. We are proposing to teach all the necessary phonics to children by using their own language (in preference to any adult list, however accurate its claim to be based upon the vocabulary of children.) Any published list, of course, does contain many words that many children in a given classroom would use. But a good teacher must use "teachable moments." He must teach with the high interest that comes every day. Otherwise, a lot of classroom time is wasted in meaningless drill upon vocabulary that did NOT arise on a given day. We have made it hard for teachers to teach with what the child brings.

Talking—The Development of the Verbal Symbol

The drama and excitement in the first grader looking at his first chart as it suddenly dawns on him that those words are his words do not happen overnight. They begin, as does all communication, in the cradle, with wiggles, gurgles, cries, and stretches. A baby's whole body is a study in communication without words. Parents are soon able, in most instances, to tell at a glance, or at one brief sound, what is needed for their offspring.

Parents who enjoy "talking" to their babies, and roar with delight when their reward is a coo or a gurgle or a smile, are the parents that are making verbal communication easier. Each person has a language potential, and such varies enormously from individual to individual. Some people will never be as verbal as others, and that is all right. But parents who help their children to develop to their own highest peak of language expression are those who will find their children getting along in the world at higher levels than would otherwise have been possible.

Talking is an expression of the self. Children work amazingly hard to tell you something. They struggle mightily to put their ideas into words and sentences. There is a reason for this. Psychologists[15] indicate that these vocal, verbal efforts of the child's help him to organize and order his world about him, for to talk is to place in focus those things that puzzle a child. Talking describes his own world, if only to himself (although a child likes confirmation from adults), and so makes life more understandable and manageable.

Talking can be said to be a gift that the child presents to those he loves, his family, his peers. He *must* talk to grow intellectually. Psychological textbooks are full of cases of children who were not encouraged to talk in the early years, and pitiful specimens they are. Talking is truly a creative act on the part of the child. Surely he imitates other's talking, but when words and sentences of his own come forth full bloom, it is a unique expression of individuality. It is creative for that child.

But experience is more than just talking. It is also hearing and seeing. These acts of learning to live in a society cannot be separated, and it is not necessary for our purposes here. Let us say that hearing, seeing, talking are all inextricably intertwined. Some individuals hear more, see more, and say more than do others. They are the ones who live more fully. They are the ones who are better able to contact their fellows and communicate with them (than those less able). Granted that all humans are different—and what a boon that fact is—everyone has a right to the full development of his powers. This sets the stage for the best life possible for each person.

Seeing—The Development of Vision

As a child must learn to talk and walk, so must he learn to see. The retina of the eye is stimulated by the impingement of clear objects. Then the brain interprets what that object is. The eye develops its ability to see—that is, to perceive and interpret in a series of stages. Any trouble or interruption at any level of these developmental stages will damage seeing. If the trouble is not corrected, the damage will increase. The earlier that trouble occurs, the greater the damage, and, more seriously, whatever damage is made cannot be corrected in the sense that the highest potential of seeing will never be realized by the individual that has some interruption dur-

[15] Joseph Church, *Language and the Discovery of Reality*, New York: Random House, Inc., 1961, Chap. 4.

ing these crucial months and years. The damage can be prevented only from deepening, or from getting worse. The course of damage can be stayed, but its stamp will forever be upon the individual.

Parents who leave their child alone and do not urge him to "look at the doggy"—or "look at the ball"—or place something moving, such as a mobile, over the crib, are really not helping their child to learn to see—clearly, distinctly—and thus to know his environment. Vision, then, is just as much a part of the intellectual development of the child as is speech. A child becomes more "human" and less animal by the parents who urge seeing as well as talking upon their offspring. A child who does not gain language and visual experience in living with his family is the damaged child. The sad part is that by the time he gets to school the whole top layer of his potential has been peeled off by the lack of participation with his environment. He must be encouraged to see, to talk, to walk, to share in life itself. This is the family's job.

Eye Convergence

Before we discuss actual classroom practice, the matter of the convergence of the two eyes must be discussed. Contrary to popular opinion, the average ability of the normal 5 and 6 year old to see is not 20-20, but 20-30 and lower. It is not until age 8 that 20-20 vision occurs in average children, although variations occur, of course.

Seeing Must Be Comfortable[16]

Because seeing is comfortable only when the object is clear and not doubled, the eyes must work together, or converge upon an object in order to bring it into focus. Convergence is therefore necessary to clear vision. Immature eyes cannot focus or converge on small objects that are too close to it. They, in effect, see approximately in parallel lines for some distance. And, as the eyes mature, the point of convergence comes closer to the person. It is a natural tendency for most individuals' eyes to converge, turn in, or "cross," but there are some whose eyes naturally diverge—or go apart. When it is difficult for a person to focus on an object, he uses so much energy in order to see, he gets tired, and hence finds such focusing disagreeable. Quite naturally, then, people who have trouble focusing develop a conditioned aversion to that act. They want to avoid the fatigue and its unpleasant aftermath. When the individuals are chil-

[16] The author is indebted to Ward Mould, M.D., F.A.C.S., for his advice in all of the areas pertaining to vision.

dren, we have a ready-made situation for the dislike of the most important "seeing" activity in school—namely, reading. For reading requires clear focusing, and the child who has already been conditioned to dislike and avoid focusing before he meets his first book is already a reading problem—simply because he has a *seeing* problem.

When this conditioned aversion to focusing exists, the only remedy is to UNCONDITION the aversion by means of free choice of attractive materials, of colorful objects, of living creatures in great and abundant variety, preferably with an interested adult. A child who is to choose what he wants to look at is one who will probably move out of his aversion. Later on in this chapter we will discuss the effect of self-choice of reading materials. But for the moment we are referring to objects common to the environment of preschool children.

Left-to-Rightness

Whether or not a child is right-eyed or left-eyed in his "lead" eye has not been proved to be important in itself. What *is* important is that our society expresses itself visually from left to right. However, we do know that we have an inborn trait of *direction* of seeing that is helpful to recognize. Those who are right-eyed (and the majority of the population is right-handed and right-eyed) go from left to right as a natural tendency. They do not need to be vigorously taught to go from left to right. It is natural to them. However, left-eyed people more naturally go from right to left, i.e., in the opposite direction to their right-eyed peers, which happens to be the opposite direction of Western literate culture. Although this innate tendency in left-handed, left-eyed children need not be a serious matter, as left-to-rightness can usually be taught without undue stress and strain, it is nevertheless something to be considered. This is of particular concern to those who work with children who have severe reading problems.

The importance of this inborn trait to see from left to right in the majority of the population is of crucial importance when combined with the ability to focus or converge upon print in the early developmental stages of reading. As we will describe in detail later, the ability of most children to see from left to right more easily than the other way around would seem to make it more natural for them to see the left side of the word, i.e., the initial consonant, when the eyes mature to that degree. However, definitive research is needed as to what a child does see first, when he is able to focus on smaller parts of sentences, phrases, or words.

Many parents and teachers worry about too early focusing in poor light. It is not proved that this is necessarily damaging to the eye mechanism. The damage arises from the conditioned aversion to what is seen. If this conditioning is not corrected before it is time to learn to read, the aversion carries over into reading—even though it began in focusing on ordinary household objects. As the men who run the "Old Shell Game" at fairs and circuses know only too well, the eye can see only one thing at a time, just as a person can *hear* only one conversation at a time.

The Stages of Development in Language Growth

Clear-cut developmental stages are not as arbitrary and regular as a list might make them seem. The wide differences among children, not only in their physical ability, but in their home and neighborhood situation, encourage or discourage talk. There is no guarantee what one child will do at a given time. Many may wander at random through a pattern of progressions that we adults might set up. Some might land at one advanced level and be back at a lesser ability the next day. In short, we know of only gross patterns of development at this time. There are only broad sweeping generalized stages that are certain enough to help us in our work with children. These are[17]:

1. The first few months: vocalizations, crying, nondescript sounds, development of capacity to react to adult voices.
2. The "babbling" stage: random vocalizations using vowels and consonant sounds without pattern sequence to true language—listening develops.
3. The beginnings of language comprehension: understands and recognizes symbolic gestures, phrases, words to relate to people intensely—distinguishes more frequently occurring phonemes.
4. The beginnings of symbolic communication: babblings take on adult language intonations, rhythm, for whole units—single word "sentences" used for many meanings.
5. The beginnings of differentiated speech communication: language experimentation provides variety—lays foundation for true sentence structure.
6. Later stages: age 6—mastery of all grammatical forms and constructions as learned from family, etc., with few exceptions—vocabulary development continues through life.

[17] J. B. Carroll, Language Development," *Encyclopedia of Educational Research*, p. 747; Joseph Church, *op. cit.*, pp. 61; M. M. Lewis, *How Children Learn to Speak*, New York: Basic Books, Inc., 1959.

Just the knowing of these major check points of development is not enough. Certain aspects of classroom management—i.e., self-selection of materials, an individual conference, and task-grouping are psychological aspects that cannot be ignored. In addition, motivation and interest cannot be discussed without mentioning their relationship to the goal that is within reach. Children, or anyone, must know what the next step is for them.

When Is a Skill Teachable? When Is a Skill Learned?

The time element in skill-teaching and learning implicit in these questions cannot be ignored. The range of individual differences is so great, not only in general development of children, but also in the specifics within any given subdivision of general development, that we literally do not know—beyond rather vague guessing—when to teach what.

Carr,[18] after studying six texts written by reading authorities, developed a comprehensive outline of skills or components of the reading process. These are included as a guide to the reader. They, may it be stressed, are an organization of those skills that seem to show agreement. They are, however, inadequate as a display for helping teachers. The entire list is predicated upon a theory, unacceptable to the author of this text, of reading instruction organized around teacher-selected materials. The role of self-selection invalidates much of the usefulness of such a list. It is included more to help the teachers who read these pages to proceed from the known to the unknown than for any other reason. The point is that there is no series of skills that can be ticked off, or checked off, one by one, as a teacher goes through a school year. Learning simply doesn't happen that way.

Skills or Components of "Reading"

1. Ability To Recognize and Analyze Words
   a. Discriminating—auditory, speech, visual
   b. Building a stock of sight words
   c. Using configuration clues
   d. Using context clues—verbal, picture
   e. Analyzing and synthesizing through phonics—consonants, vowel sounds (short and long), sounds in different positions (initial, final, medial, largest known portion)
   f. Analyzing and synthesizing through structural elements—compound words, suffixes, prefixes, syllabication

[18] Constance Carr, *Individual Development of Abilities and Skills in Reading,* unpublished Ed.D. dissertation, Teachers College, Columbia University, 1958, p. 85.

2. Use of Meaning Cues
   a. Use of background experience
   b. Perceiving relationships
   c. Interpreting figures of speech
   d. Using punctuation
   e. Enlarging meanings of words
   f. Grasping sequence of ideas
   g. Seeing details
3. Reading for Different Purposes
   a. To get general import
   b. To generalize
   c. To summarize
   d. To organize
   e. To evaluate critically
   f. To recall or retain
   g. To predict outcomes
   h. To follow directions
   i. To recognize different kinds of material
4. Adapting Rate of Reading
   a. Through skimming
   b. Through rapid-reading
   c. Through rereading for detail
5. Using Reference Material
   a. Knowing how to locate information
   b. Selecting appropriately in materials to suit the purpose
   c. Knowing and using alphabetical order
   d. Using dictionary—guide words, selecting appropriate meaning
   e. Using library
   f. Using special reference materials—encyclopedias, newspapers, and magazines
   g. Utilizing parts of books—titles and authors, tables of contents, index, and special aids
6. Handling Books Properly
7. Reading Orally to Communicate—Voice and Phrasing, Portraying Meaning
8. Sensing Communication of Feeling in Written Material
9. Extending Reading Interests

But this is not all. Imbedded in this list are many skills that, for one reason or another, are not considered important by the six major texts examined by Carr.[19] Of the 26 that follow from one to four of the authorities chose NOT to include them in their books. This is indeed a strange state of affairs when the six most prominent

[19] C. Carr, *ibid.,* p. 110.

—if we are to accept Carr's judgment, even though they are uniden-
tified, in this matter—reading specialists are far from agreement
about what constitutes a skill, let alone how it should be taught.[20]

Carr lists the number of texts that omit discussion of certain of
these skills or components. It would seem to demonstrate the state
of confusion around the hoary problem of skill instruction. The
numbers in parentheses refer to the number of authorities who omit
mention of the particular skill.

> Speech discrimination (2)
> Configuration clues (1)
> Consonants (1)
> Short vowel sounds (1)
> Long vowel sounds (1)
> Sounds in medial position in a word (3)
> Figures of speech (2)
> Punctuation (2)
> Sequence (2)
> Details (1)
> Reading for general import (1)
> Reading to generalize (2)
> Reading to summarize (1)
> Recalling what has been read (1)
> Predicting outcomes (4)
> Rereading for details (2)
> Locating reference information (2)
> Using encyclopedias (1)
> Using newspapers and magazines (2)
> Noting titles and authors (3)
> Using table of contents (1)
> Using index (1)
> Using special aids such as maps and graphs (1)
> Proper handling of books (4)
> Sensing communications of feeling (3)

The major difference between the traditional pattern of teaching
skills in reading and the patterns described in this text is that of
emphasis, purpose, sequence. Rather than learn skills in order to
read, one reads, and *then* learns the skills he needs in order to read
more, read faster, and read more difficult things, and to read for
specific purposes. The ACT of reading must come before the teaching
of reading skills. This is, of course, a fundamental principle of trans-

[20] In this study, those skills upon which there was agreement between all six authors
were found to be taught by the investigator in classrooms in which the teachers were
using an individualized, self-selection approach to reading instruction, rather than a
basal approach.

fer of training. Symonds[21] indicates that skills are best learned, and there are many studies to support him, when they are intrinsic in the reading or any other activity. Skills should not be taught for skills' sake. They are rarely to be taught in isolation and then only if it is clearly to be seen as related to what is to be read.

The Fallacy of Sequential Skills

To those who will ask: "How can children master the basic skills if they're not taught in sequence? How are we going to cover all the subject matter? Won't this lead to confusion?" we reply that one does not read to learn skills, one reads to read. There is a sequence in process, perhaps, but a sequence in content is poor methodology.

In open-ended learning, skills' mastery is made directly, perhaps, but not as ends in themselves. Most reading texts have said the same thing. But where we differ is in use of sequential books. The traditional texts say that skills be learned through basal readers and their ever-present manual and workbook. We insist that skills cannot be taught in sequence when that sequence is in books rather than in the child. We insist that skills be learned in the PUPIL's order, no matter what he chooses to read.

The great problem for teacher-training, in-service or preservice, is to help teachers identify the child's own sequence *regardless* of what he reads. Once identified, then action must follow, to teach the child what he needs to know when he needs to know it.

Stages, Levels, and Groups

In Chapter 7 we insisted that children be aware of what they needed to know in order to belong to a group, and what they needed to know to change to another group. Perhaps another way to say the same thing is to develop a "Flow Chart of Progression or Instruction." Under such a plan, children will be able to stay on one level or in one stage as long as is necessary without the deadly interest-killing repetition of subject matter.

Refer again to the chart on "How We Learn To Swim" page 193. A child has learned to hold his breath under water for ten seconds. He must then work to become comfortable enough in the water to 1) open his eyes under water, or 2) pick up something from the bottom. Both of these activities can be played over and over again without boredom. Open eyes can be done with a buddy, games played with others retrieving broken glass or anything dangerous from the lake bottom, retrieving a thrown object that sinks in the shallow water of a pool, and so on. The point is that it is the STAGE or the LEVEL that is being repeated, and not a body of material that must be "covered." The pupil knows that he must learn to DO whatever it is, and there are dozens of ways in which this can be accomplished. One varies the activities at various levels. One varies the material at various stages even though the pupil has reached a *plateau of ability.* The stages, then, are open-ended.

Thus it can be seen that we don't group children on covering material.[22] We analyze a continuum based upon the best knowledge now available. We help children at each level. This is precisely the message of Chapter 8. In effect, we are now going over that same ground but from the teacher's point of view.

The following is an excerpt written for a presentation to the parents of kindergarten children to help them understand how children do go through these early first-grade stages. The teacher who describes her work was quite conscious of how she must wait—and yet encourage—children ever onward to the goal of satisfying reading in the first grade.

To Coming First Grade Parents[23]

Most children who begin first grade are aware of the fact that learning to read is the important work of this grade. Some children approach reading with eager anticipation, quite confident of success. Other children are fearful because this represents a threat, and they do not face challenge readily. Children should not be led to expect that reading will take place in one day.

It is the task of the first grade teacher to work with children in such a way as to promote continuous growth of *all* children, regardless of their background of readiness, or pre-conceived attitude toward reading or learning in general.

Any adult who works with children knows that to secure attention, he must have the child's interest. Therefore, the first few days of school, the first grade teacher encourages discussion and give and take about things which are of interest to children: their homes, their pets, their toys, their experiences. A child may say at sharing time:

LAST NIGHT I GOT A DOG FROM MY UNCLE.

HE IS A GOOD DOG AND HE DOES TRICKS.

I LIKE MY DOG.

MY DOG IS YELLOW.

The teacher can write this on the board, the children can "read" it together and draw a picture of this child's dog.

[22] Of course, committee work in a social studies unit does require grouping to accomplish a tangible goal. That is not necessarily related to a technical skill.

[23] Presentation to parents of kindergarten children, Mountain Lakes, N.J., by Geneva Hayes, first-grade teacher, Wildwood School.

The first main concept the children grasp, then, is the fact that reading is what someone has said, in written form. In other words, teachers use the verbal ability of the child to begin reading. So:

THE CHILD SPEAKS.

THE TEACHER WRITES IT.

THE WRITING CAN BE READ LATER BY THE TEACHER, AND THE CHILD IF HE REMEMBERS IT.

This may seem like a simple concept to adults but the reading is a mystery to a child, and this basic understanding is very important. These chart stories are called "experience stories" and they may be the story of one individual or a series of sentences contributed by the group. The child will not recognize specific words at first, but he will be learning that reading and writing have a left-to-right progression. He will be understanding that writing and reading are a part of the communication process.

Gestalt psychology tells us children perceive wholes before parts. He sees whole sentences before words, and whole words before the letters in them. Thus the breaking down process goes from sentences to words to letters. Parents are well aware that a child's large back muscles work for him before his smaller hand and finger muscles.

Teachers are more and more realizing that telling is not necessary teaching. Self-discovery on the part of the child has certainly a more meaningful impact on him. If a child sees the word "dog" in each of the sentences in the preceding story, he is using his perceptive powers. The teacher sets the stage and encourages the child to find for himself what he can. The entire process of education is the task of enabling the child to do *without* a teacher and to become self-reliant in learning.

Soon the perceptive child will be seeing words which are repeated again and again of the charts. They begin to build a "sight vocabulary." A sight word is one which a child recognizes instantly by configuration or shape (the way the work looks). *Emotion* packed words seem easy for children to recall. Words which can be represented by a *picture* seem to be not difficult for children. The ones children often do not remember are the abstract words which cannot be illustrated by a picture (mental or otherwise.) These words are of this type: where, was, so, and, from and the like. These words require much repetition between the more concrete important words, such as dog, fire, swimming, Mother, Daddy. These abstract words are sometimes called "glue" or "cement" words as they hold the vital words, the idea words of our language together.

As the children are learning sight words, the teacher begins to teach them to print the letters of the alphabet. Thus, as the sight word vocabulary builds and the ability to recognize and write letters grows, the child becomes aware that "Sally", "so", "soon" and "same" start with the letter "s". The teacher can prepare a chart deliberately pointing up an initial consonant sound, and again the discovery on the part of the child is important. Thus we begin to deal with sounds of letters. Research tells us that if the child can identify a letter sound at the beginning of a word, he probably will know that same letter any place in another word. For example, with "SEE" and "MISS" the child will recognize the sound of "S" at both the beginning and the ending of the words. Consonant sounds which cannot be sustained without distortion (such as "BUH" for "B") should not be isolated sounds. Rather, such letters are better taught in spoken words. The teacher says to the child, Say "Ball". Now shape your mouth like you are going to say "Ball" but say another word that starts the same way. So over a period of time, the child associates sounds and letters through auditory and visual training.

Research tells us children see and hear the beginnings of words, the ends of words before they hear and see the middle sounds of words. A first-grade child who has a good understanding of sounds and letters will soon be able to substitute initial sounds. For example, if he knows "jump" he can figure out "bump", "lump", "dump", etc. Likewise, he will with the teacher's guidance be able to substitute final sounds. If he knows "cat", he can figure out "can", "cap", "cab", etc. The initial letter substitution is easier, of course, because of the rhyming factor as well as the fact that first letters are articulated first when a word is said.

When children have arrived at a point where they know enough words to pick up easy trade books and pre-primers and read them with little help, they are ready for reading independently. Perhaps not all the time, but on an increasingly independent level. Book selection is not always easy for a child. Some cling to too easy books because they lack confidence or initiative. Some pick too difficult books, perhaps because a friend has that one. A teacher must help and guide individual children in selection all during the year. These problems lessen with increased real interest on the part of the child and an adequate supply of books from which to choose.

These independent readers will read their own books, coming to the teacher for an individual conference now and then. During this 5-10 minute period the teacher will question the child about the story, spot check vocabulary, and have the child read orally. As children read, the teacher notes their difficulties and plans to teach small groups of children that have the same needs. At some other time, children who have finished a book may want to have a sharing time—along with other children—before the class. They can have a puppet show, or a demonstration, or a painting or drawing.

The children who are not yet reading independently will need more *direct* guidance from the teacher until they gain confidence and self-initiative. Perhaps, because of various factors, they may not reach this point in first grade. There is much accurate evidence that perfectly normal children delay learning to read until second, third, and even fourth grade.

The reading program is a complex one and difficult to describe in a few words. Perhaps it could be summarized by saying that a first-grade teacher must be part realist—part idealist. Realistic to the point of perceiving a child's needs and guiding him from one level of learning to the next. Idealistic enough to believe that enjoying an experience promotes favorable attitudes and that capitalizing on children's interest combined with the stimulation of self-discovery can result in a child's *liking* to read.

Charting Stages of Development

Stages of development are apparent throughout this presentation to one group of parents. Progression for instruction can be charted, much as can any plan be shown to move from stage to stage. What follows on the next page is such a chart with arrows pointing in the appropriate directions. Then comes the same thing in simplified form, set down in two different ways, with a final production borrowed from another source.

We have already presented the child's view of his own progression. We have described how a teacher would proceed to get talking, writing, recording, back into the reading instructional program. But what is needed now is some background knowledge for the teacher. There are things that the teacher needs to know so that he can be ready to move in any direction that the development of his children might require. This is the knowledge that is needed deep in the heart and mind of the teacher so that he can hop, skip, and jump around any commercial set of materials, through any kind of technique. He must be able to apply this background knowledge as soon as he has diagnosed what is needed.

Through these progressions we hope to have teachers find their way with any child, in any class, at any grade. The stages, the levels, are open horizontally, so to speak. The vertical progression is within the development of the child as he is guided, helped, and even cajoled through a process. It cannot be overemphasized that material must be subordinate to the process, although the latter cannot exist without material, as one does not learn to read in a vacuum. In short form, the above could be condensed as follows:

LIFE EXPERIENCE AS TOLD

+

SPEECH PATTERNS AS RECORDED

+

ANALYSIS OF WRITTEN LANGUAGE

+

COMPREHENSION OF OWN AND OTHER RECORDINGS

=

READING

We might draw an analogy from the field of organic chemistry and note that these items on our progressions are comparable to chemical reactions. Some of these are "reversible reactions," i.e., they can go either way. The teacher can write or the children can write. The teacher can talk, and help, to be sure, but the truth is that there is a major catalytic agent—the child's own speech—his thought units, his inflection, his words, his way of putting words together. All these are crucial when we are teaching reading. They develop in reversible directions.

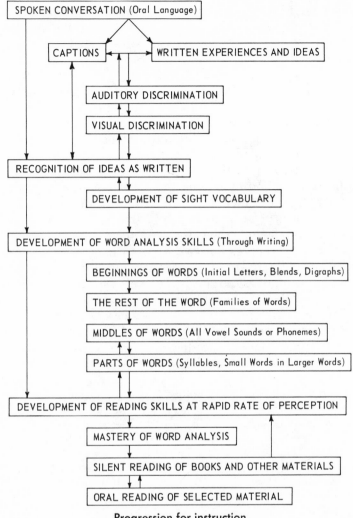

Progression for instruction.

In addition to catalytic agents, there are "bonds" that can be noticed from point to point. Oral language is a bond from the beginning to the end. Hearing is the same. We use our ears over and over in differing ways as we progress in learning to read. The sense of touch is valuable in many spots of our progression. The mental photographic ability starts with the first word that is recognized, and is bonded to the final stage of development, that of rapid reading.

Still another way to indicate the progression of the process of reading is as follows:

THINKING
TO
TALKING
TO
WRITING OWN WORDS
TO
READING OWN WORDS
TO
READING OTHER'S WORDS
TO
READING IN BOOKS

Lee and Van Allen have a more detailed list of similar developmental patterns, as follows[24]:

1. What a child thinks about he can talk about.
2. What he can talk about can be expressed in painting, writing, or some other form.
3. Anything he writes can be read.
4. He can read what he writes and what other people write.
5. As he represents his speech sounds with symbols, he uses the same symbols (letters) over and over.
6. Each letter in the alphabet stands for one or more sounds that he makes when he talks.
7. Every word begins with a sound that he can write down.
8. Most words have an ending sound.
9. Many words have something in between.
10. Some words are used over and over.
11. What he has to say and write is as important to him as what other people have written for him to read.
12. Most of the words he uses are the same ones which are used by other people who write for him to read.

Thus can be seen four different ways to say the same thing. There is a flow of development that must—at one and the same time—be encouraged and yet waited for. This is truly a developmental pattern inside each child. The term "developmental" here refers to that which develops within the child's learning, aided and abetted by the teacher to be sure, but not imbedded with a manual or list without reference to a specific child.

---

[24] *Learning To Read Through Experience*, New York: Appleton-Century-Crofts, Inc., 1964, p. 5. Reprinted with the kind permission of the publisher.

WHAT THE TEACHER SHOULD KNOW

There are many areas of knowledge in our language that teachers should be aware of in order to bring these stages of reading progression to reality. As there is a backdrop on a stage in front of which the action takes place, so, too, is there a backdrop in teachers' minds as they proceed to instruct. We have already shown several ways to look at the development of reading ability, for example, in Chapter 8. We have also discussed in great detail about how to start children talking in order to use their own talk as a basis for reading instruction. Let us now look at another aspect of what teachers should know.

The Usefulness of the Alphabet

Of course, the English language is made up of many other languages. That is why it is so hard to organize into a nice regular system of rules[25] that can be applied when one wants to spell or write or read. Many have said that English is not a phonetic language. That is not quite so. It is about eighty per cent phonetic. However, the remaining twenty per cent has most of the words that we use so much. The verb "to be" for example. Even then, many of the irregular words in that twenty per cent are regularly irregular, if that is a good way to put it! In any event, regular irregularity can be found to the extent that it can be useful when applied to word analysis—taught, we insist, in connection with writing.

Many people have tried and succeeded in finding order and system in English. There are also those who have organized the language in ways that they hoped would help teachers teach reading and spelling.

Sound Articulation

Research has established that certain sounds are articulated more easily than others. This is perhaps why some commercially developed phonics systems begin their lessons with vowels. The origin of speech is the babyhood level of vocalizing comfort and discomfort sounds[26] Robinson[27] reports:

[25] The Roman Augmented Alphabet (I.T.A.) at this writing meets this point head on.
[26] The reader is again referred to M. M. Lewis, *How Children Learn to Speak*, New York: Basic Books, Inc., 1959, in this context.
[27] F. B. Robinson, "Phonetics or Phonics?" *The Reading Teacher*, Vol. 55, No. 3: 84 ff., December, 1955.

The following ages by which children normally are able to articulate effectively the various groups of consonant sounds have been fairly well established:

by 3 ½	the b,p,m,w, and h
by 4 ½	the d,t,n,g,k, and ng
by 5 ½	the f and v
by 6 ½	the sh, th, ch, and l
by 7 ½	the s,z,rm, and wh

. . . Templin concluded that at seven years all consonants, including the blends, are correctly articulated about ninety per cent of the time. That investigator also corroborated what others had found about the inconsistency of articulation with regard to the position in a word in which a sound appears. For example, where a consonant appears at the beginning or in the middle portion of words, accuracy will be attained sooner than when the sound occurs at the end.

Unfortunately, the research is still too meager to warrant any assertion that there is a one hundred per cent perfect way to teach the sound of letters. This text goes upon the assumption that there is logic in teaching children sounds of letters through a left-to-right direction. (That is, the left side of the word is the beginning of the word. Therefore it is best to teach the beginning of the word. Therefore it is best to teach the beginning letters[28] of words, both by sound and sight). Further, in spite of all of the irregularities, there is the alphabet to be considered as a useful tool.

In short, what follows is an attempt to bring order out of this seeming confusion. There should be no real conflict with much of the material existing in commercial systems. There are many fine helps and suggestions in many places. But it is the teacher who must adapt the material to fit the classroom needs, rather than fitting the children in the classroom to any system, as we have stated many times.

Let us repeat the two facts about the alphabet and letter sounds:

1. Spoken language contains words that, in turn, contain the letter sounds of the alphabet.

2. The alphabet, the root of our language, can be used to learn the letter sounds of the language.

The Alphabetic Principle—Part I

The alphabet is a tool. It is useful. Like all tools, it can be misused and misapplied. It can be helpful when it is realized that using it

[28] See also Arthur W. Heilman, *Phonics in Perspective*, Columbus, Ohio: Charles E. Merrill, Inc., 1964, p. 15.

depends upon the simple element that the names of the letters in the alphabet help in learning most of their sounds in words.

Linguists, speech specialists, and others in related fields have given us an extensive analysis of letter sounds with symbols (the International Phonetic Alphabet, for example) to match. These analyses have served the purposes of these specialists. But they have not served the purposes of educators concerned with children's learning. The speech specialist, as we noted earlier, in working to improve the articulation of "c" in "cat," is too often unaware that he is placing real blocks in the reading path of that child by insisting that the child distort the sound of "c" by saying "cuh-at." Those commercial phonics systems, which violate the progression of learning as well as reading in its true sense, have developed because there has been little activity on the part of educators themselves. This omission is rapidly being eliminated. Heilman's *Phonics in Perspective*[29] is a case in point. This present text is similar in theory with a major difference found in its insistence that phonic skill-building is a spelling and writing activity to be transferred to the reading act only as necessary.

To proceed, however, let us forget all the technical terminology such as "plosives" and "fricatives" and the like. These are the kinds of words that will interfere with the background knowledge that the teacher must start with. At a later training stage they perhaps should be studied. But not at first.

The alphabet is our starting point. We begin by saying it slowly. This is where we start with children. They must know it by rote, perhaps in a sing-song way at first, and then gradually slowing up until they can identify the letters, one by one, as they say the whole alphabet.

THE NAMES OF THE LETTERS. Let us begin then with saying the alphabet, letter by letter, with a word—any word—that begins with that letter following it. For example:

A	ATE		N	NO
B	BOY		O	OPEN
C	CAT OR CENT		P	PEPPER
D	DADDY		Q	QUEEN
E	EVENING		R	RAN
F	FALL		S	SIT
G	GO		T	TICKLE
H	HIT		U	UNITED
I	ISLAND		V	VICTORY
J	JAM		W	WIN
K	KIND		X	XRAY
L	LADY		Y	YOU
M	MOTHER		Z	ZOO

[29] *Ibid.*

(Note that in this case we were not concerned with words that could be represented by pictures as we were when we were teaching the alphabet cards to children. With mature people it is not necessary to be so concrete. Not that it is wrong, it is just not a requirement.)

USING THE NAMES OF LETTERS. In order to realize that most of the alphabet conforms to a pattern that is useful we need to discover, each person for himself, the similarity of the names of the letters and the sounds in words. For example: if we were to say:

B BOY

C CENT

M MOTHER

it would be noticed that the mouth is shaped in the same way to say the *name* letters "B," "C," and "M" as it is to say the words that *start* with those letters, "BOY," "CENT," and "MOTHER."

If one starts to say "B" without finishing the word, and then says "BOY," the similarity in feeling on the mouth and the sound in the ear is unmistakable.

Of course, the letter "B" is said as if it were spelled "BEE." But that is not important. What is important is that your mouth went almost the same way to start to say "BOY" as it did to say "B." Thus it is logical to say that there is *enough* similarity between the sound of the letter "B" in a word and its name as said in the alphabet. To be able to recognize it by its sound is the skill we are after when the word cannot be seen and its spelling is unknown.

Put another way, we could say to the teacher (not the child!) that we use only *part* of the name of the letter "B" (said "BEE") when we say "BOY" or "BAT" or any word beginning with that letter. What is involved is pressing the lips together in a characteristic and unique way, used only for the letter "B." It could be described as saying the "consonant" part of the letter name. The parts of the letters that are like their sounds in a word are those *consonant sound parts*, not the *vowel sound parts* (as the "EE" in "BEE"). This is true of many of the letters of the alphabet. (It is not "BEE-OY." Nor is it "BUH-OY."

When asked to state the sound of the letter "B" many teachers incorrectly say "BUH." This is wrong because there literally is no such sound. It is a distortion. To say a group of words beginning with "B" such as: "BILL," "BABY," "BACK," we would have to say "BUH-ILL," "BUH-ABY," and "BUH-ACK." In other words there is no "UH" sound in "B." "UH" is really the sound of a short "U." The only words that have that sound would be those that really had a short "U" in them, as "Buck," "Bump" and the like. There are some words that have that sound called a "schwa." But they are a separate case and will be discussed later. As a matter of fact, "B" is the kind of letter that cannot be sounded accurately by itself—all alone. We teach it by the technique of substitution. More on that later. Let us go on to another letter to illustrate this alphabetic principle further.

Take the word "Cent." When it is pronounced and its first letter, the "C," is repeated right after it, it can be noticed that the mouth goes the same way for the beginning of the word and the name of the letter, just as with the letter "B." The letter "C" sounds as if it were spelled "See." It can also be described as having a "consonant" part and a "vowel" part. We use the "consonant" part to feel the sound of that letter in a word. We don't complicate things by saying "See-ent" for "Cent." The name of the letter and its sound in the word are *enough* alike to be useful. They feel almost the same in the mouth.

There are some letters that sound exactly like their names. If we were to go back and say the alphabet and words that began with each letter as we did above, it would be easy to hear, and understand, that all the long vowels can be pronounced without distortion exactly as said in the alphabet. For example:

A	ATE
E	EVENING
I	IDEA
O	OPEN
U	UNITED

These are so easy that, as most teachers know, even children readily hear them when said in a word.

Let us go on to other and more difficult parts of the alphabetic principle. There are several exceptions to the part just presented above.

The Alphabetic Principle—Part II

Although the sounds of the majority of letters in the alphabet are enough like their names to be helpful, there are others whose names and sounds are not at all alike. Yet they can still be recognized. These letters can also be used to help in spelling a word, even if they do not sound like their name. They are useful simply because they have a sound all of their own. No other letter sounds like them.

For example, if we said "H" and then "HILL," "H" and "HOUSE" or "HOPE," we can hear that the letter "H" is said as if it were spelled "AITCH." Yet no one says "AITCH-ILL" or "AITAH-OUSE" or "AITCH-OPE." There is not the slightest similarity between the sound of the letter and its name.

Here again we have the possibility of distortion. Some teachers say the sound of the letter "W" is "WUH." They are not entirely wrong, as "W" is not like "B." There is a kind of a breathiness when pronouncing a word beginning with "W." If that breathiness is sustained longer than usual, the sound of "W" can be said without distorting it—although what happens to the word is another matter. It is helpful because you can hear the sound of the letter "W" in a word when you hear that breathy type of sound. *No other letter sounds like "W."* It has a sound all of its own. Thus it is hard to confuse it with any other letter. It can be recognized by its sound. It can be heard, even though it is not like its name in the slightest.

There are several letters that also have sounds of their own and so can be learned and then recognized by their sounds. For example, if we went through the alphabet again, searching for letters (and their words) that are not like their names, we would come up with these:

A	APPLE	G	GO
E	ESKIMO	H	HILL
I	INDIAN	W	WAX
O	OCTOPUS	Y	YOYO
U	UMBRELLA		

The letter "Q" is tricky and does not fit easily in either of these categories. We will discuss it in the last part of "The Alphabetic Principle—Part III."

The Alphabetic Principle—Part III

The final step in understanding how useful a tool the alphabet is deals with the sounds of those letters that are not like their names necessarily, but sound *like other letters.* Because this is so, they need be recognized, not only by hearing, but by sight—or memory. When the ears do not help, then the mind's eye must be brought into play. For example: Take the letter "C." If we said "CENT" and then "SENT," it could be felt that the initial letter in each word is similar. The "C" sounds like its name, but it also sounds like the "S"—in both name and sound.

On the other hand, if we said the word "CAR," we would notice that the name of "C" and its sound in "CAR" were not at all alike. In that case, the sound of "C" is like the name and sound of another letter, that of "K."

"C" is one letter you can't tell from its sounds. You must look at the word. You must learn it by heart. It must be committed to memory. Notice the sounds of "C" in these words:

CINDER   CIRCUS   CIRCLE   CERTAIN   CEDAR   CAUCUS

There are other letters that have the same attribute. For example, if we said "GYM" and then "JIM" we would notice that they are the same. When the "G" is "soft," it sounds like its name all right. But it also sounds like the letter "J," in both name and sound. Say these words to see what we mean:

GIGANTIC   GIANT   BRIDGING   DANGER   EDGE

There are other letters and combinations of letters that sound like other letters. For example, what about the "GH" in "COUGH" or the "PH" in "TELEPHONE." Don't both of these have an "F" sound?

We mentioned the "Q" earlier. If we say "QUEEN," "QUICK," "QUIET," we might listen closely and discover that "Q" has a "KW" sound. This letter sounds like two letters, "KW."

THE SCHWA. In Part II we talked about the short "U" sound dealing with letters that did not sound like their name, but had a sound of their own. At that time we mentioned the "schwa," a term used to label the short "U" sound when it is made by *other letters* than "U." It is designated in the dictionary by a sign sometimes called the "upside down e"—thusly, ə.

To show what we mean, say these words:

AROUND   CIGARETTE   SHOVEL   SOFA
TELEVISION   NATION   GALLOP   FASHION

Which symbols have the short "U sound?

AROUND	A		FASHION	IO
CIGARETTE	A		NATION	IO
SOFA	A		GALLOP	O

It is the vowels in the *unaccented* syllables that have a "schwa" sound: Thus, to say these words, we see these letters making a short "U" sound.

This is a very important point because in reading, the unaccented syllables are not the parts of the word that trigger off recognition.

Accented syllables do that. Thus, in READING instruction, emphasis on teaching the "schwa" sound is likely to confuse the child, as word recognition is not furthered by the unaccented syllable. But in spelling or written composition, the student must know all the syllables—accented or no! Thus the schwa must be introduced, taught, understood, and learned in the writing activities rather than during the reading activity.

The "schwa" is the worst offender when working to perceive words. It must be learned by heart in writing before it can be easily transferred into the act of word recognition in reading. The "schwa" can be very much overemphasized because it is usually in an unimportant syllable in a word. Unimportant syllables rarely trigger meaning or comprehension. Unimportant syllables are learned in writing, not in reading.

Summarizing the Alphabetic Principle

The Alphabetic Principle is something you need to understand if you are to learn how to teach children phonics with their own language. You may not teach it to your pupils exactly as you have learned it, but you will know it and thus have a foundation upon which to build.

A teacher might ask: "Do I teach the sounds of letters in their order in the alphabet?" The answer is "No." What must happen is that all letters must be taught to as many children as possible in as short a period of time as possible. How can there be order outside of the sequence of the teaching process? How could letters be taught "A, B, C, etc.," when the words in which they are taught come from the conversations from which dictated stories were derived? What teacher could predict, before it happens, which words would be in a story or experience? Therefore, how can a teacher predict what letters could be taught? It does not matter which letter comes first. But it does matter if a teacher develops a story that has words that can be used to teach a certain letter. The point of making at least two experience charts a day is more than just the encouragement of oral language. They provide the best material by which reading skills can be taught. Just taking down children's dictation is only half of the teaching operation. These stories must be used, and they must be so varied and so frequent that their content never palls upon a class or group.

The alert and trained teacher will wait, even though continually asking questions about a group of captions or words on an experience chart: "What do you see that you can tell me about? or "Is there anything about all of these words that you notice? Eventually there will come the spontaneous recognition of a *part* of a word or several words. This is the payoff for the weeks and months of practice in listening to the alphabetic principle. This is the triumph of instruction. Once such a signal occurs, that teacher should strike while the iron is hot. There will never be a more teachable moment for that skill for that child who recognizes such parts of words. The learning of that letter, or group of letters, must be nailed down *then* in the child's mind.

Some teachers say, "Why bother to wait for this signal? Why not just teach all of the letters of the alphabet regardless of when, or IF, certain words pop up in experience stories?" Many teachers do just that. But it doesn't work well. Some teachers will teach without regard for any such dawning awareness on the part of a pupil. Learning will be more certain, more rapid, more lasting, and more satisfying when brought about by discovery. It brings on the teachable moment without coercion.

The teacher needs to bring sight and sound together in one whole. The Alphabetic Principle, like women's work, is never done and is applied at ever higher levels of learning.

To move on to other areas, let us repeat the three main parts:

1. Most letters sound enough like their names in words to be of help when figuring out unknown words.
2. Some letters, even though they do not sound like their names in the alphabet, still are useful as they have a sound of their own. They cannot be confused with any other letter.
3. Some letters sound like other letters, and thus cannot be learned by sound, but must be taught, recognized, and learned by sight.

The Alphabetic Principle and Individual Differences

As the school days roll by, the teacher will be aware of an ever widening spread in knowledge and achievement within her class. The plan book will show what total class activities entailed, but other methods of keeping track of which child is sure of which skill are necessary for efficient record-keeping.

Check sheets are invaluable to show a quick once-over of how separate pupils are progressing. A check sheet can be developed for any one of a hundred items that a teacher might want to keep track of. In this case, we recommend a general form that would look something like this:

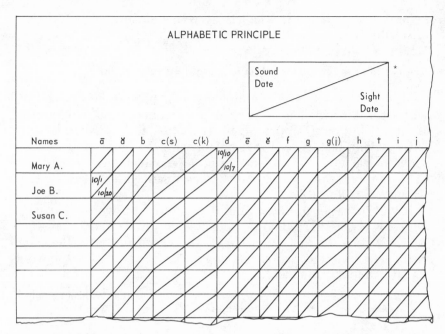

ALPHABETIC PRINCIPLE

Names	ā	ŏ	b	c(s)	c(k)	d	ē	ĕ	f	g	g(j)	h	t	i	j
Mary A.					10/10 10/7										
Joe B.	10/1 10/20														
Susan C.															

*In each square the teacher will put the date upon which the child demonstrated the ability 1) to hear the sound of the particular letter in a word and say another word that begins with the same letter and 2) to see the letter in a word.

With such a sheet in a notebook in hand, the teacher can quickly note the dates upon which the pupils demonstrated the skill indicated. As the teacher plans the next day's schedule, these notes become invaluable as guides to those items that need to be taught to the whole class, to groups, and to individuals.

Teacher's Background for Teaching Sounds of Letters with Children's Own Words

In Chapter 9, there was much discussion of how to get children talking in order to have words that could be used in instruction. Without repeating any more than is necessary, there are some facts that will help a teacher know WHICH words to choose at a given time. These facts are directly related to the alphabet.

You were warned about distorting the sounds of letters, particularly letters that cannot be said in isolation. For example, there is no such sound as "BUH" for "B" or "KUH" for "K," or "GUH" for "G" and even "HUH" for "H." These are distorted sounds. Luckily there are not many letters that can be distorted in this way. Usually such sounds are made with an explosive breath. A special technique is helpful to learn them. It is called, as we noted earlier, the technique of substitution.

Discovering the Letters that Must Be Taught by Substitution

Most of the letters of the alphabet can be sustained in a word without distorting their sounds (although, of course, the word itself is ruined—but more on that later). If we take the alphabet, letter by letter, saying first a word that begins with the letter, and then the sound of the letter in that word, we can see which ones get distorted in the process, and which can be sustained without saying them wrong.

It will be easier to understand if we start with words that begin with vowels, as it is almost impossible to distort them. Say these words. Notice the first letter. See if you can hang on to the sound of the letter without really changing it. Never mind what the words sound like for the moment.

Words	First Letters	Sustained Without Distortion Yes No?
ANGEL	A	Yes
APPLE	A	Yes
EAGLE	E	Yes
ESKIMO	E	Yes
INDIAN	I	Yes
ICE	I	Yes
OATMEAL	O	Yes
OSTRICH	O	Yes
UMBRELLA	U	Yes
UNITED	U	Yes

As can be heard, these vowel sounds can be sustained without spoiling them.

Vowel Sounds in the Middles of Words

A harder exercise is to sustain the vowel sounds in the middles of words. Yet the same thing happens. These sounds can be held (even though the word itself suffers) as long as one has breath. Read these words and note the vowels.

Words	Vowel Sounds	Sustained or Not?
HOPE	O	Yes
SUIT	U (or long double o sound)	Yes
SAP	A	Yes

SAME	A	Yes
SHEEP	E	Yes
RED	E	Yes
NUT	U	Yes
KNIT	I	Yes
SHOP	O	Yes
TIME	I	Yes

To be sure that we are clear on these vowel sounds, let us take the first word, "ANGEL." It should have been said like this: "A-A-A-ANGEL." Or "HOPE" should have been said "HO-O-O-OPE." In "ANGEL" the "A" would come out as a long "A" no matter how long it was held. In "Hope" the "O" would come out as a long "O" no matter how long it was held.

If we can recognize that vowels are easily sustainable and so present no problem in teaching children to hear them in an unknown word they cannot spell, let us move on to consonants. What follows is a list of words and their first letters. Some of them can be said alone without distortion. These can be sustained as long as one has breath. Some cannot. The former are easy to teach. The latter require the use of the substitution technique. They are the hardest of all. Go down this list and see which is which.

Words	First Letters	Sustained or Not?
BAT	B	No
SILLY	S	Yes
DADDY	D	No
LADY	L	Yes
CIRCLE	C	Yes
GIANT	G	No
CANDY	C	No
MOTHER	M	Yes
JAM	J	No
VIOLIN	V	Yes (unless said as "VUH")
FOLLOW	F	Yes
GIRL	G	No
PEPPER	P	No
WIND	W	Yes (unless said as "WUH")
NUT	N	Yes
KETTLE	K	No
QUEEN	QU	No (for "k" sound. Yes for "W")
RAT	R	Yes
YEAR	Y	No
ZOO	Z	Yes
XYLOPHONE	X	Yes (sounds like "Z")

To sum up, those words that begin with vowel sounds and with the consonants soft c, s, f, l, m, n, r, v, w, and z can be taught with the sounds of the letters themselves. All others must be taught by means of substitution. Let us take that up next.

Definition of "Substitution"

This term is defined as that process by which part of one word is substituted for part of another word in order to make a new word that is needed. For example, a child is stuck on the word "BANK." The teacher says:

> It begins like "BOY." What is the first letter?
> *Child:*   "B."
> *Teacher:* Get ready to say ""BOY" and make it rhyme with "THANK."

Children that have learned the initial letters in words, first by sound and then by sight, will be well along the way for the more difficult step of substitution. Children who have participated in a lot of rhyming activities will also be in a better position than those who have had no such experience. Here are some examples of ways in which a teacher may work.

Rhyming Words and the Art of "Substitution"

To change the first letter of the word to make a new word, the teacher can say something like this:

"Get ready to say 'boy' but have it rhyme with 'took.' "

or

"This word begins like 'see' and rhymes with 'think.' "

or

"Can you say 'fat' and make it rhyme with 'sight?' "

In passing, a mention might be made of the common lack of understanding of young children as to what "rhyme" and "rhyming" mean. The teacher—or parent—can say several words that rhyme as:

ring, sing, bring, thing

"When words sound alike we say they rhyme. Do you know your Mother Goose? They are called 'nursery rhymes', as:

> Jack be nimble, Jack be quick
> Jack jump over the candle stick.

or

> Jack and Jill went up the hill
> to fetch a pail of water
> Jack fell down and broke his crown
> and Jill came tumbling after.

If the child still does not understand the meaning of the term, the phrase "Tell me a word that sounds like 'jello,' etc." "Sounds like" can have several different meanings, as we adults well know. But this may be helpful for a child to "catch on" to the meaning of the word "rhyme."

Simplifying the Teaching of "Substitution"

If the child has trouble forming these words that are new to him, the teacher takes him back to the earlier stage where he can practice on the simpler breakdowns of this skill of substitution. For example, let us say a child cannot combine "boy" and "took" to make "book." The following would be such a breakdown.

EXAMPLE 1.

Teacher: This new word begins like "boy." Say "boy." (Child does.) Now say "ball." (Child does and teacher has him repeat several words beginning with the letter "b.") Now get your mouth ready to say "boy" again. Don't say it. Let me see your mouth. Fine. Now can you keep your mouth that way and make a new word that ends like "took?" (Many children can successfully say "book" after this much help. But if not, the teacher can continue with the simplification.)

EXAMPLE 2.

Teacher: You still can't find our new word? Well, let me see if I can find another way to help you. Say "took" again. (Child does.) Now say "cook"—"look." (Teacher has child repeat many words that rhyme with "took.") Now say "boy" again.
Child: "Boy."
Teacher: Can you put "boy" together with "took," "cook," "look?" (This further step is helpful. If the child still is not successful, the teacher can resort to a meaning clue, *even though* this word arose from the child's own language needs).

EXAMPLE 3.

Teacher: Still can't hear it in your head? O.K. Let me see if you can say the two words that we want to put together again. Say "boy" and "took." (child does). I am thinking of something that has two covers that rhymes with "took" and starts like "boy." (If this fails, it might perhaps be best that the teacher demonstrate what he was driving at by saying the word.)

EXAMPLE 4.

Teacher: Well, don't you worry about not getting the word. You will catch on next time. I was trying to get you to hear that "boy" and "took" went together to say "book." Now you follow me and say those words. (Child repeats after the teacher as requested.) (While it would seem obvious to the reader that such a child has a reading disability, that may be no more serious than confusion about isolated sounds of letters. This happens so frequently that it needs the discussion that follows.

Correct and Incorrect Visual and Auditory Images

In the preceding section we made some point of not isolating letters because some letters could not be isolated without corrupting their sound. Put another way, saying "BUH" for the letter "B" is incorrect because there is no such sound (except in such a word as "buck"). As we said, the word "ball" is not "buh-all" as many have pointed out before this text was written. "Buh" is really the sound of "B" with a schwa.

Nonsense syllables are not good teaching. They present incorrect images of words. To separate words into parts or even syllables in early stages of learning is to destroy their proper image. The use of the dictionary at too early levels can be criticized on this basis. Words are wholes. Words are entities that take their meaning from the thought unit in which they are found. Therefore, to divide up a word for a child to look at, before he can see it and PUT IT TOGETHER AGAIN, is to teach an inaccuracy. It is wrong to match letter sounds in succession to various endings of rhyming words. There is no such thing as an "ight" word, or an "ook" word. Yet many teachers will list such families for drill exercises.

> Wrong Type of Example: Add various   ook
>   consonants   ight
>   in front of: ing
>   ump
>   en

Other teachers commit the same errors with cards with slits in them and then long strips of paper with certain consonants on to run through the slit. The idea, of course, is that the first letter and the ending can be combined to make words. This practice is not recommended because it depends upon the destruction of the correct images of words. We cannot properly teach words in this fashion. It is much better to use the principle of substitution. Reading is meaning and nonsense syllables or sounds get in the way of instruction. Most important, they are not necessary.

Isolated Letter Sounds

Words are wholes, and are not a combination of letter sounds *as far as their meaning* is concerned. Although linguists and speech experts with their many technical recording machines can isolate the variety of sounds (especially diphthongs) that make up our words that form our language, they are the first to say that letters have no meaning in themselves. The term "phoneme" means, as we said, a single indivisible sound. For the purpose of reading and spelling, these sounds cannot be said in isolation except where they are not distorted. On the other hand, whatever the linguists may say about any vowel sound, for the purposes of teaching reading and, of course, spelling, vowel sounds can be isolated and used to advantage. For example, although there is no such sound as "buh," there most certainly is the sound of long "a," as in "ate," or short "i" as in "if." To isolate all *consonants* with or without a schwa is to produce a two-syllable word out of a one-syllable word. This is inaccurate and very poor teaching. But sustaining a vowel sound does not produce such distortion of the sound of the vowel.

Isolated Letter Sounds and Those Needing Substitution

It might be fruitful for us to review and then go down the alphabet again and indicate what letters can be taught by holding on or be taught in isolation, and what letter sounds need to be taught by the method of substitution.

Can Be Sustained		*Need Substitution for*
All vowel sounds, regular or irregular, including the schwa.		"B"
Some consonants as:		Hard "C"
Soft "C" (because of similarity to "S")		"D"
"F"	These sounds can be isolated if	Hard "G"
"L"	sounded in continuous fashion,	"H" (harder than some)
"M"	and never terminated with a	"J"
"N"	schwa. The schwa brings distor-	"K"
"R"	tion that prevents comprehen-	"P"
"S"	sion. For example, saying "L" as	"Q"
"W"	"luh" is different than saying in	"T"
"Y"	a continual fashion "l-l-l-l-l."	"V"
"Z"	The latter helps. The former is	"X"
"H" (?)	useless.	

This is a complicated list, it is true, and some teachers might be too confused to use it in its entirety. However, as it is better to resort to substitution in helping children figure out new words, it is not really necessary for teachers to follow the whole list. There is a simplified way to remember it.

Simplifying Which Letters Can Be Sustained or Not

Those letters that can be safely isolated without distortion:

All vowel sounds, long, short, and unaccented

List of letters that need to be taught by substitution:

All consonant sounds

Teachers must remember that letter sounds, then, serve one purpose only—i.e., to trigger off the memory of a known word inside the child's mind. If a child is working on a word that *even after he figures it out* remains unknown to him—and this frequently happens when he is "given a book" to read—he is wasting his and the teacher's time. In such case, he must be told the word, have it explained, perhaps justify his reason for reading material so removed from his experience. Children should work on words they will recognize *after* they have worked them out.

The Teaching of Phonics

With the understanding of the Alphabetic Principle and its use with children's own language, a presentation of steps or sequence in teaching phonics can be made. There is much agreement throughout the literature that teaching sounds of letters should follow a left-to-right progression. Not every child, we feel, needs to know every rule, but every teacher needs to know this or a similar sequence in order to analyze or diagnose at which stage of development a given child might be. Such diagnosis is not the sole activity of the reading specialist. Such personnel should assist teachers in their every-day work in the classroom. Experts work to help teachers and should teach children only in the most extreme of disability cases. Teachers are too prone to banish a slow learner to the nether regions of remedial reading. Specialists are too prone to divorce themselves from the curricular mainstream of the school.

Although some experts differ as to whether or not the initial letters of words, or the rhyming element of words are to be taught first, this text is another that presents the case for going from left to right. Not only is the left side of the word the first sound articulated, but most people are right-handed and therefore see more easily in that direction. In addition, the first word of a sentence or phonological unit is the left side of that sentence. Children must talk before they can read. Therefore, talking forms a foundation for reading skills. Thus, it is consistent that children be taught from left to right—the first part of a word to be heard and then seen is the initial letter.[30] Teachers have long noticed that the last thing that children hear and see is the middles of words.

Previously, on page 384, a *Progression for Instruction* was listed. Beginning with the subhead "Recognition of Ideas as Written," the following deals with that portion of the outline concerned mainly with phonics. As the teaching of phonics needs special attention, we are extracting these subheads from the whole. Of course, phonics is found at all levels of the progression. But what follows is more detailed attention to those areas involving such techniques of word analysis. It is an expansion of that portion of the progression concerned with the skills breaking up a word into parts.

Sequence of Phonics

I. Recognition of Ideas as Written
   A. Sight Vocabulary
      1. Learning words by their shapes as they appear.
      2. Children's experiences first, and then in vicariously oriented material.
II. Development of Word Analysis Skills
   A. Beginnings of Words
      1. Applying the three parts of the Alphabetic Principle as needed in hearing, and eventually seeing, initial letters.
      2. Learning to hear, and eventually see, consonant blends and digraphs.
   B. Endings of Words (or the rest of the word without initial letters)
      1. Ending sounds of words.
      2. Families of words (without small words in them).
   C. Middles of Words (vowel sounds)[31]
      1. Long vowels as learned in initial, final, and middle positions.
      2. Long vowel rules.
         a. E on the end.
         b. Two-vowel rule (sometimes called vowel digraph).
      3. Vowels affected by "R."
         a. "AR" says "ARE."
         b. "ER" rules (er, ir, ur, and sometimes or).
      4. Short vowels.

---

[30] We again refer the reader to Arthur W. Heilman, *op. cit.*, for greater detail. Pages 15 and 19 are especially applicable to the points being raised here.

[31] May we repeat that there is no sacred sequence to be followed for the various rules of vowel sounds. Most teachers find, as we have said, that lone vowels are easily taught as initial letters. Perhaps that is the only rule that is certain.

    a. "A" as in "apple," "e" as in "Eskimo," "i" as in "Indian" or
"igloo," "o" as in "octopus," "u" as in "umbrella."[32]
    5. Vowel diphthongs
       a. "oi" as in "oil," "ou" as in "out," "au" as in "haul," etc.
  D. Parts of Words
    1. Syllables, prefixes, and suffixes.
    2. Small words in bigger words when useful.

Applying the Sequence of Phonics

    I. RECOGNITION OF IDEAS AS WRITTEN—A. Sight Vocabulary. To re-
peat what has been said in detail elsewhere, sight vocabulary is
learned fastest, more surely, and with the least drill when it is com-

Strengthening sight vocabulary.

posed of the children's words that have major emotional impact
upon them. Sylvia Ashton-Warner says in *Teacher*[33]:

---

[32] See page 379 for alphabet cards with pictures.
[33] *Teacher*, New York: Simon & Schuster, Inc., 1964, p. 35. Used with the kind permission of the publisher.

First words must have intense meaning . . . first books must be made of the stuff of the child himself. . . .

. . . the words which I write on large, tough cards and give to the children to read prove to be on-look words. If they are accurately enough chosen, the conversation has to be got if the vocabulary of a child is still inaccessible. One can always begin him on the general KEY vocabulary common to any child in any race, a set of words bound up . . . with the inner world "mommy", "daddy", "kiss", "frightened", "ghost".

"Mohi", I ask a new 5 Maori, "What word do you want?"

"Jet!"

I smile and write it on a strong little card and give it to him. "What is it again?"

"Jet!"

"You can bring it back in the morning. What do you want, Gay?" Gay is the classic, overdisciplined, bullied victim of the respectable mother.

"House" she whispers. So I write that, too, and give it into her eager hand.

"What do you want, Seven?" Seven is a violent Maori.

"Bomb! Bomb! I want Bomb!"

So Seven gets his word "Bomb" and challenges anyone to take it from him.

And so on through the rest of them. They ask for a new word each morning and never have I to repeat to them what it is. And if you saw the condition of these rough little cards the next morning, you'd know why they need to be . . . tough.

Later on she presents some of her maxims about the Key Vocabulary.[34] Among the most important is: "The length of word has no relation to its power content. The Key Vocabulary varies from one locality to another and from one race to another."

She also clearly indicates that this vocabulary varies from one child to another. Thus we see a pattern in which sight vocabulary can be developed with children learning words in four minutes as contrasted to four days or four weeks or four months on words like "come," "look," and "see."

In a study of seven primary reading series by Reeves,[35] 109 words were found to be common to all of the books. Of these 109, about one word in ten could be represented in a concrete way, even to include the "color" words, red, yellow, etc., which still leaves the vast majority of these common words in basal series in the category of abstract words. Many experts have noticed that the most frequent words are the abstract words. They cannot be illustrated mentally or otherwise. They represent nothing in themselves. Often, these types of words are referred to as "glue" or "cement" words. They are almost surely responsible for the excruciating dullness of those books that are written to provide for their extensive repetition. We need to know how to deal with these uninteresting words.

[34] *Ibid.*, p. 42.

[35] Olive Reeves, "The Vocabulary of Seven Primary Reading Series," *Elementary English,* Vol. 35, No. 4: 237–39, April, 1958.

We mainly use them to glue the dynamic, the powerful, the vital words of the child together in a whole—dictated or copies. These words only make sense when they are used to hold together the key words of a child.

> "FLOWERS FOR MOTHER" writes George. (Note "FOR.")
> "KITTENS ARE BEAUTIFUL."
> "HORSES ARE TOO. SO ARE GIRLS."
> "SO ARE FLOWERS."
> "SO IS THE SUN. I LIKE THINGS THAT ARE BEAUTIFUL."
> "I LIKE WHITE HORSES. I DO!" writes another first grader.

Note that there are five "Are's": two "So's," and two "Like's." How much better can we get the cooperation of children in learning these hard-to-teach words than by showing them how well they hold together the important words of their own language—the children's important words.

The blood of young life comes pumping through these ideas that are written down. The whole progression follows the patterns stated in several ways elsewhere. Talk written down and then USED begins the sequence of recognition of words BY SIGHT. The use of power-packed words simplifies the whole process.

To summarize the teaching of sight vocabulary in this "Sequence of Phonics," we reiterate that teachers listen, write down, and begin to talk about how certain words feel the same when you start to say them, about how certain words ryhme, and about how some words belong to the one who says them for that moment. These highly personal words are then to be used. They are to be copied to illustrate stories, to label pictures, to write down a story without a picture, and to be recognized as old friends—*even though the child might not know one letter from the other at this level.* Copying "DEAR MOTHER" means a series of finger movements. Whether or not the child knows the characteristic strokes of "D," "E," "A," "R," etc., is not important yet. He can *copy* it without altering his own unique way of remembering *how a word looks.*

There seems to be no reason then, for children to be drilled on "glue" words IN ISOLATION. Whatever drill might occur would be on those "glue" words extracted from the original writing of each child. He will learn as he should learn—with his own heart and mind—if he is helped to write that which is important to him. And abstractions will fall into their proper place.

E. W. Dolch compiled a list of 220 words and claimed that they make up about fifty to seventy-five per cent of all school reading matter. He argued that these words be learned for instantaneous recognition. These were to be sight words and learned by drill, by repetition. Certainly, children need to have these 220 words and many more at their finger tips, literally! We are not disputing this fact. What we are disputing is the method by which they are to be learned. The abstract nature of most of these words makes it difficult to fit them into any kind of a sensible context. But if the role of meaning is prime in word recognition—and it most emphatically is— then the ONLY way to give contextual clues to children learning any abstract sight word is to have it be learned as a necessary word to WRITE a vital, important, emotionally packed thought. There simply is no other shortcut to the fast, easy learning of these words. They must be learned in their proper context as the cement words of the English language. To do this, teachers will notice that, with most of these words, the application of the Alphabetic Principle, or the use of families or ryhme, will aid the child as he struggles to set down such words in between the more fascinating, easily remembered, powerful one-look words such as "ghost," "thunder," "mommy," "Santa Claus," and the like. Abstract words often lend themselves to whole or partial phonic analysis. Why should children not be trained to take advantage of this fact. Why drill on "THIS" when it can be figured out by listening to it? Why drill on "ONLY" when each letter can be clearly heard as it is pronounced? No reason. Teach children to use their ears whenever possible. It is the fastest way to teach.

Thus we lead into the next stage of learning to use phonics, that of "Beginnings of Words" under the major heading "Development of Word Analysis Skills."

II. DEVELOPMENT OF WORD ANALYSIS SKILLS—A. Beginnings of Words. 1. *Initial Letters.* The background knowledge described previously under the headings of the Alphabetic Principle is essential at this stage in the teacher's repertory of skills. It might be well if the teacher began to assess her class as to who can hear and identify letters, and who cannot. By giving a brief informal hearing test during an independent work period. This test can be made up of any words, of course. But it will be a better test if the words are not those represented by pictures on the alphabet cards displayed in the room; and if the words are not familiar by *sight* to the children. Here is a possible list:

Auditory Discrimination Test

Directions for the Teacher. Explain to the children "This test is only to help me learn how you hear letter sounds. I have tried to find some words you won't know how to spell so I can notice what you can *hear*. Don't worry if you don't know or make mistakes. I will help later. Now, just listen."

As the child responds, record the exact letter (letters) the child says on the line. If he makes two or more responses, record them in order from left to right. Work rapidly, if possible, but allow ample time for thought. Stop when child shows fatigue. When the initial sound is like a different letter, the child should be told.

The teacher asks: "What is the first *letter* that you hear in these words:

		Teacher			Teacher
	Child Says	Answer Key		Child Says	Answer Key
1. alp		a	17. celery		s — c[1]
2. zodiac		z	18. undertow		u
3. xylophone		z — x[1]	19. survive		s
4. wound		w	20. geology		j — g[1]
5. maroon		m	21. nervous		n
6. heather		h	22. canoe		k — c[1]
7. Esther		e	23. kettle		k
8. bilge		b	24. dignity		d
9. quilt		kw — q[1]	25. gallop		g
10. reckon		r	26. juice		j
11. oven		ŭ — o[1]	27. local		l
12. ooze		ŭ — $\overline{oo}$[1]	28. opera		o
13. kosher		k	29. terrier		t
14. fashion		f	30. victory		v
15. injure		i	31. yolk		y
16. particular		p			

[1] "Yes, it sounds like a _____, but is really a _____."

The teacher should go through the class as soon as she is aware that some of the children have reached the ability to see that first letter in the word. As usual, teacher judgment is valuable. As the early days of the first grade go by, the teacher can test child after child as she notices who arrives at that point of seeing initial letter.[36] Perhaps several children would be tested each day until all or most all had been covered.

There are great differences between those children ready for the initial letters and those still in the less mature stage of seeing wholes. For that matter, there may often be children who are ready for far more advanced levels. Once the class is busy with independent work,[37] the teacher is free to inquire, discuss, and test as necessary.

As the teacher records the findings of this informal test, he can pinpoint exactly where the pupils are. With this knowledge, he can group those children who have similar levels and—as part of the continual pattern of development—reveal to them the next stages of growth.

[36] Refer to Chart Record on page 280.
[37] See Chapter 5.

To review the teaching of this initial step in a regular class, let us describe what might be heard between a child and his teacher as he works to apply phonics in his writing.

Child: How do you spell "with?"
Teacher: How does your mouth go when you start to say it?
Child: It goes like this. (Pursing his mouth in characteristic fashion for "w.")
Teacher: What letter is that?
Child: I don't know.
Teacher: Look all long those Alphabet Cards until you find the picture that is the same as the way your mouth is shaped.
Child: (After looking along the series) "Watch." I see watch."
Teacher: Right. What is the letter that goes with "watch?"
Child: "W."

Searching for Help for Beginning Letters

Daily repetition of this kind of scene with child after child alone or in a group soon produces *independent* activity in the same direction. When children are writing something they are committed to, they will search everywhere to get help. The Alphabet Cards are but one resource. Picture dictionaries, experience charts, maps, and books will aid a child when he has something important to say. *That* is the driving power of learning to use resources—something important to say. No drill on flash cards. No wasted time filling out meaningless and unproved educational exercises in workbooks or made by the teacher. Just the need to write a message of significance does the trick.

2. *Blends and digraphs.* Whether or not these terms are to be used is of little concern. But each teacher must recognize that a BLEND is that combination of consonants any place in a word, in which each letter is clearly heard. For example: take the word "clay." The sound of the "c" and the "l" are clearly heard. So, too, are the "b" and "r" in brown." A blend can be remembered if it is noticed that the word "blend" itself begins with a "blend." Both the "b" and "l" can be heard.

A digraph (literally two writings) is also made up of two or more letters, but in this case the letters cannot be heard separately, but combine to have a sound of their own. Many authorities use the term with vowels or consonants. The term, however, is more usually applied to consonants, especially those letter combinations of "sh," "ch," and "th." The words "sheep," "church," and "then" illustrate that in no case can these letters be heard as the word is pronounced. "Sh," "ch," and "th" have sounds that are unique to each set. Note that the word "digraph" has a digraph in it. These sounds are so unique that a card can be made for them, as suggested for the alphabet, to help children when they need to spell a word, as:

In this text, the vowel digraphs of "ea" as in "meat" are put in the section "Middles of Words" and called the "Two-Vowel Rule." This is an arbitrary decision and could just as well, if desired, be considered under digraphs. The reason for this decision is that vowels are usually in the middles of words, rather than at the beginning.

In any event, the teacher proceeds to connect up these sounds that occur in the beginnings of words to the needs of children as they need to write. When there is plenty of dictation, plenty of children's own language on display, plenty of time and intense purpose, these initial letters, blends, and digraphs will become part of the standard writing equipment that the child will carry forever in his mind.

One point of confusion needs to be mentioned, however. Often, in reading back stories and the like, children will recognize—as a *reading act*—any or all of these phonemes. This does not contradict the philosophy behind the suggestion that phonics be introduced, taught, and reinforced as a writing skill. Such recognition may be done in reading activity, but the teacher will pick up whatever the child says, encourage all to notice the same thing, and then state something like this:

Teacher: Tom noticed that his name began like three words in our news today. "Tell," "to," and "take." He is right. Now, when he is writing a letter or a story about his picture and he doesn't know how to spell a word that starts just like these words start, then he can look up and get that first letter.

As described just previously, the push to use the Alphabet Cards is reinforced by the need to write. Children may often see phonemes of various kinds in their dictated material. This is a reading situation. But the necessary repetition for learning cannot continue profitably as an act as reading. It ruins reading! It will be repeated in a far more educative situation when the child must use whatever he notices in writing.

Informal Test for Hearing Blends

There are informal tests that can be used at this stage, too. If the teacher feels that the child is learning to hear blends and digraphs, he can find out rather definitely just where the child stands by giving a test such as this:

Blends Test

The teacher asks: "What *letters* do you hear in the beginning of *these* words? Listen as I say them slowly." (The teacher puts down whatever letter the child says.)

thistle	_____	shamrock	_____
pride	_____	spackle	_____
sweet	_____	fry	_____
sting	_____	sprinkle	_____
brake	_____	floppity	_____
clickety	_____	glamour	_____
grows	_____	quiet	_____
planet	_____	travel	_____
strip	_____	twin	_____
pharmacy	_____	chilly	_____
which	_____		

These, of course, are not usual words for young children to have learned to spell. This is a HEARING[38] test, not a memory of the spelling of words. A teacher of an upper grade can use this test if he notices several children, spelling certain words, have not the slightest idea of sounding. It may be that in the upper grades these children can read quite acceptably. But they might not be able to spell because they cannot hear letters. They have never been taught to identify letters, or phonemes in words. This often happens when children are taught to read only by a sight method. This can be educational deprivation of an opportunity to learn important skills.

[38] Often the term "Auditory Discrimination" is used.

IF a child does not learn letter sounds in reading, there will come, sooner or later, more often than not, spelling deficiencies. Identification of words can come in both areas. They are interdependent.

B. ENDINGS OF WORDS (*or the rest of the word without initial letters*). The seeing of words as wholes in the sight vocabulary stage has been broken down as far as the beginnings of words are concerned. Now we come to the other end of the word, as the Gestalt of seeing a whole breaks down—at least in the early stages—in direction from the outside toward the inside. In the preceding section we followed the left-to-right progression and taught "Blends" and "Digraphs." There is little research to show whether or not most children move in that direction or, instead, hear the last letters, or the rhymes of words before "Blends" and "Digraphs." In any event, it is probably not a major development as all of these come on top of each other, so to speak. The teacher must use his judgment whether to hold off on "Blends" and teach endings first, or the other way around.

Probably the writing the child is doing will be the determining factor. If a child needs to know how to spell "sweet" in describing "candy," he must be helped to hear the "sw" sound in that word. If this is beyond him, as the teacher works with him, then perhaps he might be able to hear the last letter "t" in "sweet." If so, fine. That is what he is taught to HEAR.

Another informal test could be used with as many children as their devlopment indicates. Again we have chosen words that are not common to children, although they may be, as we want to know how much and how well the child HEARS these sounds. Notice words like "love" that have a silent letter on the end. The teacher would record "e" if that is what a child said that "love" ended with. But this would tell the teacher that the child knew how to *spell* "love" and therefore was not tested on his ability, in *this* word, to *hear* that the final letter sound is that of "v."

Final Sound Test

The teacher asks: "What is the last letter that you hear in these words? In the case of "rich," "wish," and "with," ask "What sounds or letters do you hear?" Teacher records exact response.

Ending Sounds	Teacher Answers	Ending Sounds	Teacher Answers
lip	p	buzz	z
rate	t	dray	a
simmer	r	rich	ch
fill	l	true	u
love	v	try	i
yoyo	o	tree	e

fudge	j – g[1]	lamb	m
tax	x	back	k
rub	b	bed	d
wish	sh	with	th
loose	s	win	n

[1] "Yes, it sounds like a _____, but is really a _____."

As far as testing the child's ability to hear rhyming, the reader can refer to the discussion of substitution and ask a series like:

"Tell me what these words rhyme with:

Day rhymes with   _____

Sing rhymes with   _____

Think rhymes with   _____

and the like."

Another way to get at this is to select such words with endings from the dictated experience stories and ask for rhymings or endings of various words in those stories. For example: In the following story, which we used previously, the teacher could ask for words that rhyme with "went," "big," "park," "ride" and "rides," "things," to name but a few.

The Big Pond

We went to Big Pond this summer.

Big Pond is a big park.

Big Pond has lots of rides and things.

Lyle, Bob, and Susan rode the Ferris Wheel.

Susan was scared on the Ferris Wheel.

2. *The teaching of Families of Words.* Picking up on the principle that children are not to be presented with an incorrect aural or visual image, we need to apply this to the necessary stage of helping children use substitution with rhyming or families of words. We have already indicated that word parts should not be presented separately (at least until the later grades). As we said earlier, there is no such thing as an "ook" word, or an "ight" word, or an "ing" word. These simply do not exist, and the teacher that uses such is guilty of teaching nonsense syllables.

How, then, does one take advantage of the hundreds of words that do come in families? The practice of substitution that we have been advocating provides the answer. The teacher's theme song is:

"Get your mouth ready to say ———— and make it rhyme with ————." But in each case the blanks in that sentence must be filled by a *real word.*

"Get your mouth ready to say 'car' and make it rhyme with 'look,' " is a better way to proceed. It could also be stated similarly as: "It rhymes with 'look' but starts like 'car.' "

In addition to this—an essentially oral practice—word families can be taught by sight. Many teachers like to have charts full of "families" hanging up to encourage independent attack on the part of the pupils. If this is the case, and it can be helpful, the families used should be those that have no small words in them.

Wise Use of Families

book	sing	good	light
cook	ring	wood	sight
look	spring	hood	fight
took	string		night
shook	sting		right
brook	wing		bright
etc.	etc.	etc.	etc.

Unnecessary Use of Families

and	old
band	bold
grand	gold
hand	hold
etc.	etc.

The latter group need not be taught as families, as they contain small words. They should be taught in the way we will illustrate with the child that was looking for small words in larger words. There is, perhaps, nothing drastically wrong about including such words as those based upon "all" and "old," etc., on a chart. For that matter, more independent individual learning is encouraged when children are not given the crutch of the chart—for that is what it is —unless really necessary.

The Usability of Families of Words

The general usefulness of these parts of words is not great. There are so many exceptions to families—and if overemphasized, they loom too large in importance in the child skills of word attack. Overemphasis thus leads to so many inaccuracies that will need reteaching and correction that they are frequently not worth the trouble.

When a child comes up short on a word that belongs to a nice, regular, well-behaved family, the teacher can proceed with the process of substitution, as described. But if the word looks like it might belong to a regular family, but really doesn't, then the teacher judgment must come into play. There are a couple of suggestions that might help.

Examples of Unhelpful Families

With the word "brow":

> *Teacher:* That word looks like it might belong to the family of "low," but it doesn't. It sounds like the family of "cow." Get ready to say "brook" and make it rhyme with "cow."

With the word "good":

> I know you think that that word has a vowel sound like "too," but it doesn't. Say the word "took." (Child does.) Now say the sound of the vowel in "took." (Child does.) Now, that is the vowel sound to begin with. Say it again, put on the front letter "g," the last letter "d," and you have "good."

The trouble with the English language is that it is full of word families inherited from all over the earth, and they have so little dependability as to their looks and sounds that they are often less than helpful to struggling children. When this is true, the teacher just as well might tell the child the word and let it go at that.

Thus, we get ready to move into the realm of the middles of words, those vowels and the phonemes that make their unique sounds in that spot.

C. MIDDLES OF WORDS (*vowel sounds*). There is no particular order that seems necessary in teaching children to recognize vowel sounds. However, it is the rare child that does not know that all of the long vowels sound like their name in the alphabet.

To find out where each pupil is, another informal test can be given to get an individual profile—or, for that matter, a class profile—to help decide on task-grouping. The point of this test is to discover whether or not children can hear the middles of words as described earlier under the section on the Alphabetic Principle. Not that it is the reproduction of the vowel in the word, *regardless of what letters make that sound,* that is of primary importance. As vowel sounds can be sustained, the next step is to help the child, by means of this act of sustaining, or holding on, to the sounds in the middle, to identify what letters make those sounds.

In this test, however, the words should be said clearly and distinctly but without undue distortion. Later on, the holding of the sounds for identification purpose will take place. Sample responses are included to help the teacher. There are two answers for each word that must be recorded.

Hearing Vowels in Middles of Words

The teacher asks two questions for each word: (1) "What sound do you hear in the middle of this word?" (2) What letters could make that sound? (Note: In the case of "thirsty" the answer "er, ur"

Short vowels in middle of words.

is acceptable, but the examiner should state, "Yes, those letters do make that sound. But it happens to be 'ir.'")

	Sounds°	Letters	Teacher Answer Key First Answer°·	Second Answer
dark			"ar-r"	ar
foam			ō	oa
sheep			ē	ee
naughty			"aw"	au
sick			"ĭ"	i
rattle			"ă"	a
fruit			"ŭ" or "ōō"	ui
foot			"ōō"	oo

forty	"or"	or
shout	"ow-w"	ou
fine	ī	i
thirst	"r-r-r"	ir
mail	"ā"	a
spoil	"oi"	oi
shop	"ŏ"	o
rug	"ŭ"	u
rest	"ĕ"	e
room	"ōō" or "u"	oo

* The quotation marks indicate the spoken sound. The diacritical marks of long (⁻) and (◡) short indicate the same.

Which Sounds To Teach First?

The writing needs of the pupils should give the teacher the clues as to which vowel rules to teach first, second, and so on. However, the profile of a class, at any grade level, as assessed by the above informal test will be a helpful guide to the teacher. In looking over the results, a series of common difficulties will undoubtedly appear. The most flagrant will be taught first. The teacher will continually draw upon such a lesson *based upon an identified need*, as he helps the pupils write and spell. For example:

Child: How do you spell "farther?"
Teacher: Remember the other day we worked on words that had an "ar" in them? Listen. "Farther." Can you hear it? Say it slowly.
Child: F-f-f-ar-r-r . . . I hear an "f" and "ar."
Teacher: Right! Put it down, and say the rest of the word.

This is an example of how a teacher can draw upon these vowel sounds to help in *spelling*. Suppose we reverse the situation into one of reading.

Child: What is this word? (Points to "farther.")
Teacher: What is in it that you already know?
Child: I see an "ar."
Teacher: Right! Put on the front letter and you have most of it done.

Word Lists for Instructional Use. Let us go back to the "Sequence of Phonics" and begin with II, 1 and 2, Initial Letters, blends and diagraphs. We present those words that most teachers would have difficulty finding in one place.[39] May we repeat that these are to be presented to children after the teacher has identified the need for

[39] The reader is referred to E. W. Dolch, *Psychology and Teaching of Reading*, Scarsdale, N.Y.: Garrard Publishing Co., 1951, or the pamphlet reprinting part of this text, "The Teaching of Sounding" for much help in teaching phonics.

these phonemes and other letter combinations through written, as well as oral, work. They are to be written on the board so the children may see. Their common element is to be discovered by the children, then stated by the children. The follow-up can be through teacher-made or workbook exercises, or by self-assigned tasks by the children themselves. The transfer of the knowledge gained can then take place into other reading and writing situations.

One fourth-grade teacher, after following this kind of pattern to study the weekly spelling list, returned the word analysis skill to the reading sector of the curriculum by saying something like this.

Now you have discovered the letter (letters) that are the same in all these words. You have studied the parts of these words. But that isn't enough. You must put the word back together again. Look at it. Look at it hard. Squint your eyes at it. Now write it. And ask yourself DOES IT LOOK RIGHT?

Words must always "look right" no matter where found. This is a reading perception skill.

Helpful Lists of Words To Teach in Groups

There are many lists of words that are available to teachers in texts, in children's materials published by commercial concerns, and elsewhere. Teachers should use those lists that they can lay their hands on easily. We have already mentioned Dr. Heilman's book. Durrell and Sullivan in *Building Word Power*[40] and *Developing Spelling Power*[41] also have most helpful material. Anything that is helpful is to be used. However, the teacher must skip around and select *that which is needed* at the time that it is needed.

We now will list words, gleaned from so many sources that where they came from originally is a mystery. These are intended to short-cut teachers' preparation time for teaching phonics. Once a "Plan for Teaching Groups" is ready, these, and other sources, may be used. The Clymer investigation is not to be forgotten, but until we know more exactly about the how's of teaching phonics, such lists as this are needed.

Soft "C" ("S" sound)

cent	cereal	center	central
city	certain	circle	cyclone
fancy	cycle	circuit	dance
circus	ceiling	cinder	prince
cement	celery		

[40] D. D. Durrell and H. B. Sullivan, *Building Word Power,* New York: Harcourt, Brace & World, Inc., 1945.
[41] K. V. Russell, N. A. Murphy, and D. D. Durrell, *Developing Spelling Power,* New York: Harcourt, Brace & World, Inc., 1957.

Soft "G" ("J" sound)

giraffe	fudge	orange	change
giant	gentle	page	age
bridge	gem	charge	large
edge	genius	bridge	strange
danger	George	cage	germ

Blends in the Beginnings of Words

clay	grape	fly	crayon
draw	brown	pray	street
tree	black	plan	stripes
smile	spring	gleam	splash
free			

Consonant Digraphs

"CH" Digraph (N. B. cannot be sustained while sounding)

children	chop	ditch	lunch
child	each	patch	inch
chair	much	scratch	rich
chicken	such	chick	which
cherry	catch	change	watch
church	match	teacher	witch
chase	stitch	cheese	teach

"SH" Digraph (N. B. can be sustained)

she	shirt	dish	splash
shall	shell	fish	Oshkosh
sheep	washer	wish	shoot
shine	fishing	wash	English
	lash		

"TH" Consonant Digraphs (N. B. can be sustained)

thing	than	rather	mouth
thank	with	third	mother
think	thick	dearth	father
that	wither	earth	farther
the	bother	this	brother
them	their	those	three
there	throw	these	then
they	thresh		strength

"PH" Consonant Digraphs (taught as an "F" sound, and can be sustained. Must be learned by sight)

phonograph	pheasant	elephant	Philip
phase	Philippines	sphere	telephone
Philadelphia	phone	orphan	Philco

Two Consonant with the First Letter Silent (must be learned by sight)

wreath	wreck	gnarled	knock
wrench	wrote	gnome	knew
write	wrap	gnash	knob
wrinkle	wren	gnaw	know
wrestler	wringer	knee	knot
wrist	wrong	knife	knowledge
written	gnarl	knitting	kneel
wrapper	gnat		

Families of Words

right	low	how	joy
night	bowl	now	boy
slight	row	brown	enjoy
frightened	shallow	cow	toy
midnight	flow	plow	destroy
bright	slow	down	————
tight	grow	flower	
mighty	hollow	crowd	
light	follow	frown	
fright	————	shower	
————		owl	
		————	

saw	new	unkind	caught	sing
draw	knew	behind	taught	bring
paw	news	remind	naughty	string
awful	mew	wind	daughter	going
lawn	blew	blind	haughty	hopping
jaw	threw	find	————	trying
hawk	chew	grind	would	ring
shawl	flew	bind	could	swing
straw	screw	————	should	running
————	————			

day	always	today	may
hay	say	played	lay
playing	pay	ways	gay
away	gray	yesterday	stay
staying	pray	maybe	Sunday
Friday	Tuesday	Monday	Thursday
Saturday	Wednesday	————	————
————			

clock	sick	back	went
tock	trick	sack	sent
sock	brick	tack	bent
knock	click	track	lent
rock	nick	pack	rent
dock	quick	quack	tent
————	————		————

Long Vowels

Initial Place in Word (N. B. can be sustained)

ate	eagle	ice	open	USA
angel	ear	Idaho	oak	UN
aviator	eaves	idea	oasis	uniform

able	eat	idle	oatmeal	united
Abraham	evening	idol	Ohio	union
age	eel	Irene	Oklahoma	unit
ape	equals	Irish	old	Utah
April	erase	iron	oleo	use
	Erie	ivy	over	useful
				usual

End of Words

yoyo	Idaho	oleo	three
Ohio	rodeo	tree	silo

(N.B. All of these final sounds can be sustained, yet many words end in a long vowel *sound*, but there are silent letters that interfere with recognition until memorized. For example, "fry," "day," "sigh," "shoe," "shoot," etc. As so many of these seem to be more easily taught as "Families" of words, they are listed under that heading.)

Middle of Words—"E" on the End rule, which can be stated as: E on the end of a word often makes the (first) vowel long.

The teacher says:

"What is the difference between these rows of words?"

Then

"What is the vowel sound in (at) and (ate)?"

Then

"What makes the difference in sound?"

Short to Long

at—ate	cut—cute	mad—made
hop—hope	mat—mate	pin—pine
can—cane	tub—tube	man—mane
not—note	hat—hate	spin—spine
_____	can—cane	_____
	_____	
rat—rate	slid—slide	
dim—dime	pan—pane	
hid—hide	spit—spite	
rid—ride	strip—stripe	
rob—robe	Sam—same	
_____	_____	

ripe	use	tide	broke	face
brave	gate	hate	wave	made
sale	make	fuse	bite	like
mule	spoke	kite	slave	mine
cute	rise	poke	globe	dime

hope	vine	pole	tube	blade
note	lame	five	cake	came
how	tune	grove	stove	blame
mice	cure	ice	safe	quite
rice	date	same	tribe	wise
————	————	————		————

home	kite	line	bite
hole	ride	knife	rise
bone	time	write	wise
wrote	hide	mile	tie
rope	like	lie	die
toe	fine	wide	life
hope	mine	nine	————
————	————	————	

make	rake	wage	gave
cake	late	ago	race
take	date	cage	case
shake	name	safe	————
bake	game	face	
wake	came	ate	
lake	same	gate	
sake	cave	made	
————	————	————	

Middle of Words—"The Two-Vowel Rule," which can be stated: When two vowel letters occur together in a word or syllable, the first vowel is usually long and the second usually silent. "When two vowels go out walking, the first one does the talking," is the more commonly known statement.

The teacher says:

"What vowel do you hear?"

Then:

"What vowels are really in the word?"

Then:

"How could you say what you notice in these words?"

nail	plain	heat	spear
bait	main	team	leap
main	lain	east	leave
rain	saint	people	lean
paint	————	neither	bean
paid	fear	seize	mean
pain	peak	peat	heal
sail	beat	sea	year
rail	seat	seal	spear
sailor	meat	————	speak
laid	heap	sheaf	————
strain	yeast	seam	died
train	least	sheath	fired

cried	road	board	blue
_____	toad	oat	due
coat	goat	coast	glue
float	boat	foam	_____
toast	roast	oar	
		_____	

quail	each	eat	east
wait	reach	eaten	Easter
maid	reached	heat	least
maiden	reaching	beaten	peanut
paid	peach	seat	pea
afraid	peaches	seated	lead
paint	preach	beat	leave
faint	beaches	meat	sea
raise	_____	_____	_____
raised			
_____			

dream	dear	skies	seem
dreamed	dearest	replied	seed
easy	hear	ties	bee
easier	near	lie	_____
speak	year	dried	keep
speaking	yearly	cries	deep
squeak	nearly	satisfied	deeper
			sleep
_____	_____	_____	sleeping
ear	pie	sea	_____
fear	flies	seen	

sweet	tree	asleep	needle
street	free	sheep	feel
green	knee	between	wheel
feed	teeth	indeed	geese
need	week	meat	cheese
_____	_____	_____	

Middle of Words

Vowels Affected by "r"—"ar" says "are" rule.

The teacher says:

"What sound do you hear in the middle of the words?"

Then:

"What letters make that sound?"

are	bark	farmer	march
arm	barking	part	marching
far	park	party	large
hard	car	star	charge
card	cart	start	mark
garden	barn	starting	market
yard	farm	started	sharp
dark			

Vowels Affected by "r"—"er, ir, ur, and sometimes or" rule. All say "r-r-r."

never	father	letter	thirsty	word	hurt
her	ever	flower	stir	worse	turkey
cover	every	cracker	whirl	world	turn
sister	paper	matter	first	worm	burn
river	afternoon	elder	girl		surprise
mother	butter		third		turtle
other	stranger		dirty		curl
brother	supper		circus		fur
			stir		purple
			bird		burst
			whirling		church
			birthday		furl

Short Vowels

The teacher chooses the appropriate line and says:

If apple begins with "a"

or

Eskimo with "e"

or

Indian with "i"

or

octopus with "o"

or

umbrella with "u"

what letters are to be heard in these?

If there is only one vowel letter in a word or syllable that vowel usually has a short sound.

had	cat	bed	end
bad	at	egg	bell
add	fat	fell	leg
mad	sat	well	tell
pad	fast	men	hen
tag	an	get	den
am	tan	ten	red
jam	can	yes	wet
ham	ran	fed	pet
has	man	elk	set
as	pan	elm	let
back	and	left	
act	lap		
	map		
dig	till	it	not
big	bill	hit	toss
pig	pick	bit	top
in	kick	pin	log
if	miss	tin	hog
is	kiss	win	mop
rip	will	hid	hop
dip	hill	lid	drop

slip	him	fill	dot
ship	six	mill	dog
drip	fix	fit	
hip	sit	pit	

rock	run	but
nod	sun	cut
lot	fun	nut
doll	gun	hut
lock	up	duck
box	cub	us
hot	rug	tub
fox	stub	mud

Vowel Diphthongs.

The teacher says:
"What sound do you hear?"

Then:
"What letters make that sound?"

Long Double O

room	smooth
moon	goose
root	cool
rooster	fool
shoot	soon
stool	noon
caboose	balloon
school	bloom

Short Double O

foot	book
hood	shook
good	hook
wood	cook
look	took
brook	
stood	

OU as in "OUT"

out	round
about	flour
house	south
mouse	pound
loud	ground
mouth	sound
cloud	hour
shout	our

OI as in "OIL"

oil
join
boil
spoil
point
voice

AU as in "HAUL"

caught	taught
saucer	because
naughty	cause
daughter	haul
auditorium	sauce

Parts of Words (syllables, not ending in word families)

In spelling the child says:

"How do you spell _____?"

The teacher says:

"Say the word. Clap or tap the word."

Number of syllables to be discovered by pupils and told in their own ways back to teacher.

or

In reading the teacher says:

"How many vowels do you see?"

Child responds. Teacher "frames" the accented syllables or points to vowel in it. "What is this vowel sound? What is in front? In back?" Then teacher proceeds, left to right until all of word is similarly worked out.

Syllables can then be worked out sequentially from left to right. The clapping, however, clearly indicates the accented syllable. Teachers can help children sound out the accented syllable first. Then the unaccented ones take their usual unimportant place. *Accents* tend to trigger meaning. Too much emphasis on unaccented syllables can kill meaning.

chimney	gasoline	station	nephew
instrument	science	messenger	lovingly
electricity	scientist	special	material
beneath	license	inventor	member
commonest	artificial	inadventure	messenger
material	glycerine	afterward	million
easily	potatoes	arithmetic	neighborhood
picture	probably	factories	loose
returned	usually	diamond	polite
sneezed	protection	government	quilt
collected	minute	health	suddenly
united	beautiful	honest	whether
arranged	pretending	hospital	dynamite
happened	future	ivory	straight
figure	regular	nurse	tornado

Suffixes, Prefixes (on already identified root words)

These lists could well be weekly spelling lists. Saying and then clapping helps here, too, as it does in any multisyllable word.

react	fraction	content	disagreeable
rearrange	inhabit	continue	discuss
rebuild	inherit	contrary	dismal
rebound	injure	control	dismiss
recall	instant	confess	dispatch
recapture	invention	conquer	distance
remove	investigate	contain	distress
repair	infant	container	district
report	inhabit	conversation	dispute
repeat	inland	conscience	disturb
combine	inquire	uncertain	example
compound	decide	understand	exchange

commander	defeat	uneasy	exclaim
committee	defend	unequal	expensive
companion	delight	unfit	explore
compare	depart	unfold	extra
compass	deposit	unless	exhaust
immense	delicious	object	perfect
improve	procession	observe	perfume
imagination	progress	obtain	persuade
immediate	protest	observation	percolater
impatient	provide	obligation	personal
action	promote	dangerous	only
vacation	arctic	famous	fairly
protection	electric	jealous	fully
donation	elastic	joyous	hilly
direction	magic	mountainous	mighty
digestion	energetic	murderous	milky
exception	public	nervous	needy

Small Words Not Always Useful

As most experienced teachers know, there are words that have small words in them. Teachers are cautioned against this when a small word bridges over into another syllable, e.g., "the" in "father." They push the child away from the analytical power we are endeavoring to develop. For example, a child is stuck on the word "father" in the sentence he is reading.

> "Daddy means the same as father."

and, if urged to find a small word there, might well come up with "fat" and "her." It would be better if the teacher might proceed, in this case, by saying:

> Yes, but "fat" and "her" don't make any sense. Listen: "Daddy means the same as fat her." See? It doesn't make sense. Now look at the word again. There is a small word in there, and it sits right in the middle. See it? (If child doesn't, the teacher can frame the word "the" to show the child.)

This example, as can be seen, is one illustrating a reading act. To reverse the process and do the same word as one to be spelled, we would hear:

Child: How do you spell "father?"
Teacher: What is the first letter that you hear?
Child: "F." (He might even say: "And I hear an 'O.'")
Teacher: It does sound like an "O" but it is an "A." What else do you hear as you say the word slowly?
Child: TH sound.
Teacher: Yes, and then on the end is _____?
Child: R-r-r sound. "Er"?
Teacher: Yes. Now, can you write it from your head, or shall I put it on the board for you?

Small Words in Bigger Words (sometimes taught as families of words)

all	and	patch
ball	hand	catch
call	sand	match
fallen	land	kitchen
hall	stand	ditch
tall	grand	itch
wall	handle	witch
small	understand	

dance	corner	told	corn
prince	morning	folder	fork
since	store	gold	horn
pond	forget	sold	wore
chance	hornet	cold	tore
send	short	golden	more
friend	north	bold	born
lend	porch	fold	sort
bend	floor	hold	horse
	storm		

Compound Words

Teacher says, "What do you see that you know?"

because	anywhere	blackberry	newspaper
sunset	undergound	another	whenever
scarecrow	dreamland	without	fisherman
something	understand	kingfish	however
afternoon	goldmine	nobody	everything
bullfrog	seasick	sawmill	outside
gun-powder	houseword	playground	overhead
sidecar	neighborhood	wagonload	snowstorm
become	rainbow	gunfire	newborn
behind	grandfather	nighttime	headfirst
paintbrush	everything	drugstore	headline
watchman	careless	himself	something
	earache	dishwasher	

GAMES, DRILLS, AND EXERCISES WASTE TIME

Many reading texts advocate many types of drills, oral and written, and exercises that are designed to develop skills x, y, and z in order for the pupil to read. Reluctantly, suggestions have even been made herein about such activities. We view such with suspicion. To begin reading with an exercise on discriminating initial letters in words is to deny the basic fact that reading is meaning. Such practices defy the laws of learning by defying the laws of readiness and motivation. Where does the matter of interest come in for such drills?

Looked at from another angle, they do not use transfer of training because the elements of an exercise do not often correspond to the material that the child is supposed to be able to read. Yes, you might say, but children will learn to make generalizations that they can apply in specific situations later on. Not so. Generalizations come from meaningful situations. Even if the drills and exercises are made up as games of chance—word recognition played as bingo, for example—the motivation is still *extrinsic*. Reading, as we have said earlier, is good enough to stand on its own. It simply does not need reward outside of the meaning gained from what is read.

We deny that drills and exercises and games that supposedly prepare for reading really teach much. They simply take up classroom time. More seriously, they get in the way of the systematic and sequential application of life experience to symbols—sentences and words. Now that our progressions are moving into the stages where perception is more and more concerned with details—where the Gestalt of whole sentences, thought units, are breaking down into words and words into their component letters—the need for smaller items for lessons becomes more acute. But there is never a reason for reading being *preceded* by mental calisthenics of this nature.

There is a place for practice. We have already indicated some in Chapter 7. They *follow up* awareness of a need. A child realizes that he has trouble with a certain kind of word. He comes to that realization by its interference with his reading. Then he will benefit from self-drill upon whatever is needed. But it cannot be overemphasized that he READ first, and the need lies directly in that which was read. Cause and effect produce the incentive that drives the child to clear up his self-recognized problem.

Book-Handling

Book-handling is a skill that can be taught in seconds, and rarely needs more than a wordless signal of the teacher to the child that he should 1) hold the book with both hands at the bottom, 2) turn the pages with the right hand (then pages can be turned without the hand covering the print), 3) take care as to use of pencils, crayons, scissors, and the like near books to keep them nicer longer, and 4) know that the backs of books are easily broken.

Even though these are simple matters, they can be viciously violated by the child who has come to hate them. Why do children hate books? Sometimes the hatred stems from a compulsive parent who forces children toward them in such a way that only unpleasant associations are attached. Sometimes the hatred has nothing to do with books *themselves* but only their use as wonderful weapons to get even with an adult. Children learn early those areas in which their adults are sensitive—toilet-training, going to bed, and using books. When children's natural developmental patterns are violated —and no child violates his own unless tremendously motivated—he must get even. So the avenues of aggression are found in those sensitive areas. Children will hold bowel movements, will refuse to go to bed or go to sleep if they are in bed, and will destroy books if given the chance.

But, as Gesell and Ilg pointed out, books easily become loved objects. Books are to be patted, hugged, taken to bed, and mourned over when damage occurs.

In the classroom the child who is "accident-prone" as far as damage to books is concerned needs to be studied for his need to express hostility and aggression. Being coerced and forced into books produces hatred and apathy that can bring explosion and senseless destruction. The principle of self-selection operates to make books objects of affection and love—and one defends his own loved objects. One does not destroy it.

Thus book behavior is more than helping children to handle them in the least damaging manner. It is helping them to love books, and reduce damage by setting the protective devices of love in motion.

How Are Skills Identified?

If we try to analyze the skills of walking, we get into how this and that muscle acts in order to produce this and that result. *But we walk first.* In trying to analyze reading, we submit that the best place to start is with actual reading. If a child is made conscious of what leg to move when, he will be confused in how to walk.[42] We suggest that if a child is made to be conscious of what he does to analyze reading material, he will be confused as to how to read. It is even more certain that teachers are as confused as anybody, and try to bring order out of a chaotic reading world by following some manual, page by page, lesson by lesson—because that is all they know how to do. This text is trying to present a systematic, sequential, developmental plan of reading instruction based on the soundest ground of all—the spoken language, written down.

ORAL READING

The skill of reading orally so that speech patterns are not violated coincides with the increasing complexity of the reading effort. How does a teacher maintain the desired intonations and inflections as children become better able to see single words that make up whole

[42] A second-grader story: "Once there was an octopus that had 2000 legs. He didn't know what to do with them and so he never did!"

sentences? This is a time and level at which it is easy for children to lapse into the stumbling word-by-word reading pattern. They are beginning to recognize sentences word-by-word and the slowness of recognition can make for slowness of oral reading.

As soon as the teacher begins to hear the child's voice take on the normal speech inflections, he relaxes and interrupts no more. Of course, at the end there should be a mighty big pat on the back.

A fine beginning step or in really stubborn cases of word calling and dull oral reading, the teacher should do the same as above with some of the child's own *creative writing*. Understandably, a child's own writing means so much to him that he can lose himself in it—and this is the state of mind that produces good vital, spell-binding oral reading. As one student teacher put it: "When I read their stories over later after school, it wasn't half as exciting as hearing them read their own. It was almost as though part of the story was missing."

Let us repeat a previous example to show how to work:

Our Big Hurricane

We got the tail of the hurricane.

It blew down trees.

There were floods.

It blew windows out.

The wind blew very fast.

It did a lot of damage.

Teacher:	Can we practice reading our story aloud? I want to help you learn to read so it sounds exciting. Lucy, will you start?
Lucy:	OUR—HURRICANE—STORY.
Teacher:	Say it as if you were just telling us. Our Hurricane Story.
Lucy:	Our Hurricane Story.
Teacher:	Fine. Tell us what happened.
Lucy:	We got the tail of the hurricane.
Teacher:	When?
Lucy:	Yesterday.
Teacher:	Well, tell us about it again while you look at the words. (Lucy does.) (Comment: The teacher works to have Lucy HEAR that

each line has a voice inflection that helps tell the story. As one teacher said, "You tell them to ham it up." This is exactly it. If the reader will try telling a joke to friends, and note the ups and downs of his voice, he will note that his normal speech patterns when telling a joke DO "ham it up.")

A teacher may help children perfect this skill by reading aloud and showing how voices do go up and down, soft and loud, slowly and rapidly. The teacher should set an example of good oral reading. He should be the best oral reader in the room.

Reading our own stories aloud.

Some children have trouble learning to read aloud with true natural expression. In difficult cases, teachers can slide in a question in between lines such as:

Child: We got the tail of the hurricane yesterday.
Teacher: (Quickly, with great interest, yet unobtrusively.) What happened?
Child: The wind blew so hard we did not come to school.
Teacher: You didn't?
Child: It rained so hard that there were floods in the streets.

SUMMARY

Certainly, there is no other area in the field of reading that suffers from more confusion than that dealing with the skills. These are some of the questions that have been attacked.

1. What are the skills and abilities? There is notable lack of agreement, or even cohesion in point of view, between text authors.[43] An examination of various texts finds gross differences of opinions and presentations. We have presented a progression for instruction, using oral and written language along with the contribution of the alphabet to recognizing letter sounds.

2. What are the skills that are learned unconsciously? We presented the idea that unconscious learning is inherent in the operation of spontaneous spoken language and pupil self-choice of material.

3. What are the skills that need direct conscious attention and instruction? These are the skills that teachers must make pupils aware of after they have been identified for attention in a group situation following the individual conference or independent writing.

4. What skills are gained as the result of reading teacher-chosen material? If children have *no* part in choosing the stories that they read, their interest and extent of reading are retarded.

5. To what extent do the skill needs of one child coincide in any respect to those of another in the same class at any given time? As children are each unique, they should not all need the identical lesson at the same time. Ways of managing this dilemma lie in the times when needs are similar and therefore taught at the same time.

6. To what extent does the type of material dictate what skills should be taught? Material needs differ, not so much as to the effort required to master it, but as to the purpose for which it should be read. An experience story, a romantic story, a recipe, a newspaper, all strike different pupils differently. A progression has been presented to allow for material to be used effectively.

These are but a few questions to which this chapter has given attention. Let us hope that the chaos presently apparent in reading instruction is somewhat mitigated.

[43] Carr, Constance, *op. cit.*

12

EVALUATION, RECORD-
KEEPING, AND TESTING

Evaluation has many faces. But the one that should be developed and explored the most extensively is that which helps a child look at himself and know where he stands in relation to his school work. To make a child conscious of what he does not know, and what he needs to do in order to improve, is an art. The reader will recall discussion on this point elsewhere, particularly in Chapter 7.

For the purposes of this chapter, however, we choose to suggest those ways by which teachers can show pupils and, in the same vein, show parents the progress or standing of their offspring as far as their learning to read is concerned. There are several systems of making such reports, the best known of which are grades and marks.

These are A, B, or C or those letters that appear on report cards and papers and are designed to communicate a message to all who see them. Grades and marks may or may not help a child to understand his own achievements or show his parents what they need to know about work in school. Whether or not they do has been the topic of many a bloody battle in many a local school system.

How to decide upon a grade is a common question that teachers ask about any system of reading. But they are more insistent and querulous in an individualized approach than in any other. The reasons for this are easy to understand. In a self-selection program each child is reading a different book, at a different pace, and follows up in a different way. Comparison from child to child is most difficult. This, of course, is to be considered a great strength of such a program, but it makes a common base for grading hard to locate.

On the other hand, in a traditional program, children are grouped on ability and each group reads a book assigned by the teacher. Comparison between children is remarkably easier. In addition, "covering the book" is a definite, tangible accomplishment. A common base for a decision about a mark is easy to find.

Grades and marks are easily decided upon when there is a central point from which the best pupils go up, and from which the slower pupils go down. Life is indeed simple when such a midpoint can be established.

Under a basal program, "covering the material" is mistakenly used as a criteria of reading growth. A teacher sees that his pupils "finish a unit" and take a test upon that material. The assumption is that those children who have done so have learned the specified skills allegedly imbedded in that unit. There may be reading growth. But there is no proof that such is the case. Nevertheless, it is so simple to hold a child to this slice of reading and grade him high if he finishes it easily and answers the test questions reasonably correctly, and grade him low if he doesn't. The teacher needs to do little true evaluation. He must know only what has been "covered" and what has not, how accurately, and at what speed.

Under a self-selection program each child is reading a different book; is reading it at his own pace, which is surely different from that of every other child in the room; and is following up his reading with projects and the like that are unique, creative, and personal. Where, then, can the midpoint be set up from whence the talented are graded high and the dull ones are graded low? This is the rub. It is very difficult to find a clear, tangible median from which all marks can be hung.

On the other hand, this very complexity can bring out the best of evaluation practices if the teacher understands what to do. When a grade is not possible—and particularly when an individual conference is an important aspect of the approach—a teacher can discuss with a pupil and help him to see what he needs to do to improve his reading. Does he read well aloud? No? Then he needs to work on it. As noted in Chapter 7, helping children be aware of their difficulties produces a desire to erase them. The point of view in this chapter differs only in that we insist that such awareness pushed children into evaluating their own work. No GRADES ARE NEEDED.

PARENTS HAVE A RIGHT TO KNOW

As sound education as a no-grading system may be, American parents insist on knowing about the school work their children are doing, and they don't feel informed without grades. At least, not yet. As they are paying for their schools, they have a right to know what is going on. Perhaps one reason why so many school bond issues fail passage at election time is the lack of understanding that parents have of what is needed at school. The fault must lie at the teachers' feet. Somehow longer and stronger bridges must be built between teachers and parents. One of the fastest ways to do this is to provide report cards, or conferences, that are clearly communicative. Parents must feel that they know about their child's work. They must come away feeling that nothing is being hidden from them in the depths of the files.[1]

As parents are vocal about being informed, and as the approach to reading instruction presented in this book does not lend itself easily to definite, letter grades, how can teachers be helped to work out their reports to parents on a fair and equitable basis, satisfactory to all, and *still* maintain the important element of child awareness of his own needs in reading?

As is so often said: It is easy when you know how. But certain poor evaluation practices must be laid in the dust and the air cleared for better ways of evaluation.

POOR PRACTICES ERASED BY TEACHER AWARENESS

A first practice to be criticized is certain ways of asking children to do something. A teacher must become aware that his asking children to read (or do anything else in learning) is often an unintentional request for a personal favor. Teachers can be heard to say "I would now like you to do this *for me*" (italics added for emphasis). Or "Will you *please* turn to page thus-and-so." Or the saying of "thank you" when a child has taken his turn to read. "Thank you" for what? For reading? Why? This implies to the child that he does not read for himself, but for the personal wishes of his teacher—nothing else. These kinds of requests are poor practice as they seem to indicate to the child that such learning has little INTRINSIC value. It is not worthwhile to be done for itself. It must be done because teacher wants it done. Reading should need no syrupy "please" or "thank you." It is powerful in itself. (Note: This is not to say that there are not many times during a school day where the social amenities of "please" and "thank you" are not most appropriate. Holding open doors, giving out paper, and the like are proper courtesy situations. But not learning itself.)

A second, poor practice to be questioned is the use of grades and marks, including tests, as a means of discipline and control. Children will not work willingly and eagerly under coercion. But they can be

[1] For a brief and excellent description about reporting, see Ruth Strang, *Reporting to Parents,* "Practical Suggestions for Teaching," No. 10, New York: Bureau of Publications, Teachers College, Columbia University, 1946.

persuaded to work with a semblance of application when they know that a grade or a mark will be the ultimate end by which the teacher, their parents, and others can evaluate them. To use learning as a means of keeping order and control is to corrode its major purpose. The test of a good teacher is how well behaved pupils can be without the whip of a coming test or a grade upon a paper. By simply testing or grading the teacher tacitly suggests, consciously or not, that (1) the work is not good enough to do by itself without a grade—therefore the question arises if it is good enough to do at all, and (2) will the pupils be well controlled if they work without grades?

A third practice needing to be eliminated relates to the frequency with which grades and marks are given. Many situations require that SOME kind of grading be used, usually on the report card at specified intervals during the school term. Grades can be and are used to maintain a kind of control as cited in the paragraph above. The best educational practice would be that of total elimination. Good conferences and narrative reports tell a parent and a child a more complete picture.

But, practically speaking, too many teachers must give a *single* letter grade of some kind, and there is no escape from it. What we are suggesting here is that such grading be reduced to an absolute minimum.

Even when the situation calls for a monthly (or six-week) report card, no grade is needed in between the reporting period. The argument that an "average" is needed does not stand up well. "Average" of what? In reading, would this be how much in the reader is read? Or would it be the correctness with which the "unit" test was filled out? Or the number of errors made in the workbook? The number of errors made in oral reading? All these and more, too, are subject to grades in many school systems. They are artificial measurements, often as a subjective as they can possibly be, and, in any case, demonstrably weak in measuring the attitudes and behavior of the reader toward reading.

It is bad enough that they be used at all. It is worse when such practices are found daily. There are ways in which a teacher may give a letter grade at the end of a reporting period without giving any grades, or, at least very few, in between. We will give some suggestions on this shortly.

Finally, the practice of evaluation that continually misrepresents the act of reading as something one does to answer questions is the most unsound of all. Many school systems, even those priding themselves on not using commercial textbooks, still allow teachers to cover chalkboards with multiple questions (seat work really) on the pretext that children *will not read what they are supposed to read unless they answer questions.*

Reading to answer questions and to get a grade on the answers is a monstrous perversion of the purpose of reading. Reading is a personal act. It is done for personal reasons if it is to have any intrinsic value at all. To place children in this position of reading for the sake of a follow-up exercise or to fill out a sheet after a folder "power-builder" is read is to place that child's interest and love of reading under a Sword of Damocles that will destroy more than it will create—and will destroy BEFORE it creates.

But let us move on to help those teachers with the ever present question: "How do I give a grade on a report card?"

DECIDING UPON A LETTER GRADE

Those teachers who are saddled with antequated report-card systems—regardless of who is at fault for their existence—must come to the major decision of what the symbols of the system mean. For example, when the grades are single letters, with no other symbol provided to indicate grade level or "effort" or some other secondary attribute, a decision must be made as to what each letter means.

What Is an "A" Grade?

Or, for that matter, what is a "B" grade, or an "E," or an "F," or a "C?" Does an "A" mean:

1. The best work of the best reader in the room?

or

2. The best reading that occurs, regardless of whether or not it is the best reading POSSIBLE from any pupil?

or

3. The best reading of a pupil working at his top ability REGARDLESS of how that reading compares—in excellence—with any other pupil?

Which of these does an "A" mean?

Who Makes the Decision?

The best thing to do, short of throwing out the single-grade system entirely, is for all of the teachers in the building, in meeting assembled, to decide which of these alternative meanings for an "A" shall apply for that building. The problem is, however, that few principals see the need or care to (1) steer a staff through such a discussion, and (2) enforce whatever decision is made.

Teachers, however maligned, do have a broad stripe of humanitarianism in them, particularly for those pupils with whom they work daily. Perhaps this affection can be attributed to the teacher's ego, which is necessarily involved when responsibility for a given class is his and his alone. But be that as it may, it is difficult for teachers to be wholly objective, no matter what the decision of a staff in a building might be. To bend a wee bit, or a whole lot, away from whatever an "A" or a "B" is supposed to mean is easy when a teacher is emotionally involved with a child. All sorts of excuses, rationales, and the like are suddenly found to apply in the case of a certain child who has entwined himself around the heart-strings of his teacher.

Similarly, that child that has been a source of irritation for his teacher will be downgraded in proportion to the amount of hostility that he has generated. These may be quite unconscious acts on the part of teachers, but they are nevertheless facts.[2] The upgrading or the downgrading may be a product of racial, religious, or class discrimination and latent in the most conscientious of teachers. The research allows little other interpretation.

However, those teachers who are faced with the report card at specified intervals during the school year must do the best they can to be fair, to be honest, and to face their own prejudices as far as certain children are concerned. The decision of "What does an "A" mean?" cannot be escaped. It is the spectre at the feast.

Let us assume that an "A" is that letter grade to be given to those children who are working reasonably (and what a lot of territory that covers!) near their top level and are above the average for the grade. The question then becomes "What is grade level?" or "What is reading level?"

There are several ways of determining such a level.

DETERMINING READING LEVEL

The use of an interview or conference situation in a program of reading instruction described in this text bears little resemblance to

---

[2] For those readers who wish a more complete picture of marking systems and the research concerning them, the following reference is suggested: A. Z. Smith and J. E. Dobbin, "Marks and Marking Systems," *Encyclopedia of Educational Research* (C. W. Harris, ed.), New York: Macmillan Co., 1960, pp. 783 ff.

the unbelievably complicated procedures usually described under the heading "The Informal Reading Inventory."[3] Every occasion when children read silently or orally in a one-to-one situation offers teachers an opportunity to learn something about pupils' reading abilities. In effect, each individual conference is a chance to perform an informal reading inventory without the complicated questioning suggested in so many texts. What we are about to describe is to be used for purposes of finding a fair grade or mark for the report card, and does not necessarily mean that instruction will follow immediately. Nor does the "inventory" need to be excessively complicated.

The many texts that urge teachers to go through extensive procedures to determine the reading level of each pupil seem to suggest that the reason for such an exercise is to determine reading level for its own sake. If not, then reading level is needed in order for the teacher to meet the children's reading needs *when books are assigned*. In either case, the amount of energy and time to determine a child's reading level is not well used.

The Reason To Determine Reading Level

The major justification for determination of reading level is to decide what letter grade needs to be put on the report card. When children are taught to read with materials they themselves choose, there is little reason for a long and involved operation on the part of the teacher to choose for them. Why bother? A quick glance at the book supply—"Which is well used?," "Which is gathering dust?" —then order more of the former type and ship the latter books back where they came from. Teachers do not need to go through the overly highly structured "Informal Reading Inventory." If they are even slightly aware of what their class is reading—and how can they help it when each child meets frequently with them?—a complicated Informal Reading Inventory (I.R.I.) is too time-consuming for just purposes of changing book supply.

Nevertheless, for those teachers who need to make report-card decisions, there is a simple and uncluttered way to arrive at a *valid enough* determination of reading level. Although admittedly loose, it will help on that awful day when the teacher comes to the conclusion that one child gets an "A" and another is given a "C." What follows, then, is a description of how a teacher might proceed.

[3] For a detailed description on the "Informal Reading Inventory" the reader is referred to Emmet A. Betts, *Foundations of Reading Instruction*, New York: American Book Co., 1957, Chap. XXI, especially pp. 457 ff.

A Truly Informal Inventory

First, a teacher should acquire several graded sets of readers. Perhaps five or six complete sets will do. If the teacher is working at primary levels, or with children severely retarded, each set should contain one or more pre-primers, primer, and so on through the higher grades of the entire series. Each book at each level should be included.

Inasmuch as this evaluation is admittedly a rough measure, the fact that some series do not compare with each other on the matter of graded difficulty is not a matter of serious concern. In the first place, it is good that children be aware of their own growth or lack of it. In the second place, if a teacher has any reason to doubt whatever placement the child's choice seems to indicate, he can be asked to choose from another pile of books, and another, until the teacher is reasonably sure that the child is reading at a certain grade level, insofar as the difficulty levels of the selected basal readers indicate such a measure.

Thus there will be several piles of books within easy access of the place where the teacher will hold an individual conference. Each pile will be a full set of readers from a single publisher. Each publisher should be represented by a complete series. Securing all the books can be done by swapping and sharing within a given building. Surprises may be in store for some. In a traditional program such a collection may be the only time the fast readers in a class see books beyond their grade level.

Beginning the Inventory

The class should be informed of what is about to happen. The teacher might say something like this:

Today I want to find out which book, in any pile up here that you choose, that you can read best. I will ask you to come and go through which ever pile you wish. Choose one you do not know and have not read. Choose a book from your pile that looks just right for you. Read it silently. Then we will talk about it, and you will read some of it aloud to me.

One by one each child follows these suggestions. The teacher encourages and helps, but works to be sure that the child has chosen a book that he can:

1. Read with very little help silently.
2. Read aloud with some ability after reading silently.
3. Answer questions relating to the main thought of the selection.

Recording the Level

When a child and teacher are satisfied that a book[4] is a true measure of level, the teacher will record this book in his notebook along with the date.

Using the Information on the Report Card

Now the teacher has one piece of evidence that is not a grade or a mark. In addition, children can judge their own growth from report period to report period. This, in itself, is a powerful incentive for greater effort. The teacher now has an *approximate* grade-level ability for each child in the class. The notation as to which book each child can read with independence, requiring very little help, should appear after his name. This may be done on one of those single sheets with the total class roll duplicated in full as was suggested elsewhere, as follows:

Name	Book	Publisher's Designation	Date
John A.	Ginn	Easy 3d	11/3
Evelyn C.	Allyn & Bacon	Hard 2d	11/3
Martha J.	American	Hard 4th	11/5
Billy K.	Ginn	2d	11/4
Celia L.	Row Peterson	Hard 5th	11/10
Philip L.	Allyn & Bacon	2d	11/4
Susan M.	Ginn	Hard 3d	11/13

Or it may be listed on the record of the individual conferences as suggested in Chapter 5, page 162.

	I.Q. 112 (1961)		
Mary S.	Test Score 9/15/63 3.6		I.R.I. 11/10/63 Easy 4th
BOOK	DATE	COMMENTS	ASSIGNMENTS

When the teacher has gone through this informal inventory of reading level with these basal readers with each child, he has data from which can be derived a general mid-point for the whole class. If the I.R.I. shows a central tendency around the average for the class that could be expected, then that midpoint can be used as a rough approximation from which good readers will be graded up and poor readers down. For example:

[4] The teacher may not be satisfied with only one book choice. If so, the child is asked to move to another series and proceed in the same way.

The class is the fifth grade.

The time of the school year is December.

Therefore most of the children should be reading at about the midpoint of the fifth or 5.5. This would show when a child could read an easy fifth reader with very little difficulty, or a hard fifth with some difficulty.

But this may not be suitable as most of this class may be retarded below the national norms, even without benefit of a standardized test. Fifth-grade classes may be reading such that the average pupil therein reads most easily from a fourth-grade easy reader. If so, the teacher then needs to go back to the original decision, "What does a letter grade mean?"

If an "A" means reading about national grade level without regard for the ability of the entire class, this is one thing. But if an "A" means reading above the *class* average, this is quite another. Probably most teachers will mix a little bit of both of these decisions together, and thus reserve the "A" grade for those that read above their class level and also above the national norms (whether derived by standardized tests or rough approximations based upon an informal check of reader level).

To sum up, a teacher can use an informal check by drawing a balance, in terms of the grading policy of the school building, between the reader grade level, as designated by the publisher, and whatever other measures might be brought into play.

Using Other Types of Reports

Some teachers who are not bound by such single symbol grades use different types of reports to parents. All of these should, to be useful, help parents to know:

1. The child's reading performance. This should include a sharing of standardized test results with the parent—with careful explanation as to the strengths and weakness of such measures. In addition, the teacher should discuss the child's specific progress and explain any puzzling discrepancies that seem to exist.

2. The child's relationship to others in the class. Where does the child stand in relation to the rest of his world? The teacher is obligated to inform the parent with full explanation. There are always strengths and weaknesses of ability and performance that parents should be made aware of.

3. A general picture of the teacher's methodology in teaching. The report could help parents understand some of the technical aspects

of reading instruction, for example, the relationship of sight vocabulary to the teaching of phonics.

4. The child as a unique individual. Some of the report should deal with those elements of the child that differ from his peers. How is the child's reading unique to him? For example, what are his reading interests? What can be expected in the future?

5. Self-evaluation. Some attention should be given to show the parent how the child can judge his own performance, what he needs to do to improve, and how parents can help in the home situation.

6. Communication. Above all, whatever is discussed should have meaning for the parents; allow them to interact in whatever way might improve their understanding.

Types of Reports

In addition to single-symbol grades as a way to dramatize the teacher's problem in informing parents of their child's progress, there are other ways, several of them far better, some worse, that need to be mentioned. These follow:

1. *Percentage Method.* This system uses the base of 100 as perfect performance, lesser levels are indicated by decreasing numbers, such as 85 or 75.

2. *Five-Point Scale.* A, B, C, D, E, or other single letters, numbers, or symbols are used in a descending scale.

3. *Double Scale or Modification of a Scale.* In this system the meaning of symbol of the five-point scale is explained more fully by the addition of another single symbol (letter or number). For example, "+," or "—," or a check "√" is used to add further meaning, such as "effort," or "ability," etc.

4. *Descriptive Narrative Report.* This is a written account of the teacher to the parent specifically about the child involved and no other. Often a general key is used to guide the teacher in constructing the paragraphs of the report. All aspects of reporting are covered.

5. *The Teacher-Parent Conference.* This is a conference that is planned to bring the parent and teacher together. It is usually scheduled and planned and covers all aspects of reporting with an additional advantage of personal face-to-face communication.

These above patterns, or some combination of two or more, make up the bulk of pupil progress reporting in the nation today. Usually school systems use only one type, changing whenever pressures seem to make a shift advisable. Interestingly, Glencoe, Illinois, as reported in *Nation's Schools*,[5] gives parents an option of the type of report. Other communities might follow suit. Certainly variety in reporting is no unsurmountable difficulty and such free choice is psychologically sound. Perhaps the school's 'image" could be improved by such tactics.

In order to evaluate these patterns, however, the philosophy encouraged by each needs to be examined.

Philosophical Considerations

The point of view of this text is that each child has the right to learn to the limit of his native ability. A school in a democratic society must allow for some success to occur for all, and cannot justify its existence if it allows failure. The fault of failing pupils lies in the school, not the children, thousands of yearly expulsions notwithstanding.[6]

Our compulsory attendance laws give no choice to children about coming to school. This makes those school years under the arbitrary "leaving" age crucial. Unlike the highly professional medical schools, from which those with lesser ability are mercilessly eliminated, the public schools must accept all children. To "weed" out pupils during these years when they are forced to come to school is to deny those children their legal constitutional rights. Thus any reporting system that does not work to allow the success of its pupils, any reporting system that is used as a weapon against children and forces them into a position of failure, is a reporting system that encourages teachers to act against children and their society.

In this connection, a study by Chansky[7] about teacher personality and the types of reporting systems that they prefer is of interest. He found that teachers who, among other things, were mentally alert, had a wide range of interests, mature aspirations, self-esteem, and were free from anxiety and apprehension tended more to choose a report card with the attributes of measuring "the whole child" over the more narrowly based, single-symbol type.

Personality attributes aside, percentage systems of grading, scale and modified scale systems of grading do increase the opportunity of teachers to be punitive agents. These cards have a built-in failure level. A child can flunk. On the other hand, the narrative reports

[5] Margaret Carlson, *Glencoe Parents Can Choose Cards or Conferences*, F. W. Dodge Corp., September, 1963.

[6] The film "The Drop-Out," available from the New York University Film Library, makes some inescapable points on this matter.

[7] Norman M. Chansky, "Report Cards and Teacher Personality," *Journal of Educational Research*, Vol. 57, No. 9, May–June 1964, pp. 492 ff.

and the teacher-parent conferences have no such aspects built-in to their structure. Even though children may need to be considered as working at lesser levels than that of which they are capable, the written narrative and conference include this as only one aspect of a hundred others that need to be mentioned. Focus on failure is reduced.

Parents need to understand school progress in realistic ways. Some reports, for example, allow for two single grades, or symbols, that indicate grade level of the child's reading as well as his performance level. Yet, in a conference, or in a written report, the parent can be told this same information in such a way that he knows far more than the bare facts—if they are facts—of the case.

The problem of pitting child against child or placing a class under competitive conditions is a real one. Competition is a fact of all society, particularly the present one. Competition is based upon the comparison of one child against another. The acceptance of the fact of competition can be made if the goal does not assume more importance than the process by which the goal is attained. The old saying about winning being less important than how the game is played is to the point. The destructive aspects of competition are seen in many ways, notably the early death of American males, more victimized by competitive pressures, as compared to American females. But our concern for report cards suggests those cards that ease child-to-child grade comparison are less desirable than those reports that are difficult to compare.

Over and above philosophical and ethical considerations we see that, legally, parents have no right to know about children other than their own. Yet the demands for just that kind of infomation are inherent in the A, B, C single-symbol, competitive methods of grading. It is easy for parents to compare a single symbol. It is hard for them to compare the contents of a fifteen- to thirty-minute conference.

The psychological devastation brought about by such comparison does not require much imagination. Those teachers who are able to discuss pupil progress in personal terms of a face-to-face conference are fortunate. There is no substitute that is defensible if children and their full development are to be considered important.

The written narrative report or the planned teacher-parent conference is vastly superior to any system of single symbols. The former is superior because it is easier to understand; it gives out more information; and it is more in tune with the principles of the rights of individuals ingrained and built into our governmental structure.

In this context, then, what needs to be done to help teachers use the best of reporting systems?

Getting Ready for the Report to Parents

To assist teachers in getting ready for narrative or conference reports, the following suggestions are offered:

First, the content of each child's work page in the teacher's notebook is the most important source of data.

Second, the content of the several pages in the teacher's notebook, checking off some skill or learning for the whole class, is to be considered.

Third, the content of the child's own evaluation records in his own notebook needs to be included.

Fourth, the findings of formal standardized tests, and informal teacher-made tests over and above the checkoff items of number two above, are important.

Fifth, the collection of samples of tasks performed by each child is to be made and filed (preferably in a folder) for presentation.

Much of the above suggestions calls for a well-organized system of keeping records. The day has passed, if it were ever here, for all evaluations to be noted in symbols, letters, or numbers on one page per class in a "Class Book." The class book can be a summary, surely, but there is much more to be presented.

Once a teacher has a devised system that works for him, then he is ready to prepare a report about any child. There are many ways in which these records can be kept, but the usefulness to each teacher will probably depend upon how practical his system is. Can he find what he wants to find WHEN he wants to find it? The next section presents some suggestions in this direction.

RECORDS MUST BE KEPT

Several chapters have presented certain types of records pertinent to the matter under discussion in the given chapter. For those readers who wish to turn back, the following list is presented:

Chapter	Title
3	Fix a Notebook for Record Keeping
4	Record-Keeping in the Individual Conference
6	Check Sheet for Dates

7	Sample Class Roll
7	Schedule for Individual Conference and Follow-Up Grouping
9	Quality of Contribution
9	Frequency of Contribution
9	Frequency of Daily Participation
9	Quality of Expression
11	Selected Difficulties Class List
11	Possible Grouping for Correction
11	Alphabetic Principle
11	Auditory Discrimination Test—Beginning Sounds
11	Blends Test
11	Final Sounds Test
13	Books I Have Read
13	Child's Record of Individual Conference Book and Sharing Book

This list can be extended almost without limit.[8] But before we give further examples, a look at the checklist used by teachers in P.S. 188, Queens, N.Y., might help the reader to organize his procedures. If "Yes" can be placed after most questions, success in teaching, as well as record-keeping, our concern of the moment, will be assured.

Self-Evaluation Checklist
in Individual Reading[9]

1. Have I examined the reading records in the record card folder?
   1. _____
2. Have I examined the I.Q., reading, and other pertinent test data on the test record card?
   2. _____
3. Have I administered the informal text book text?
   3. _____
4. Have I made written records of each pupil's strengths and weaknesses?
   4. _____
5. Do I have a 5 x 8 card or notebook section for each pupil? 5. _____
6. Does each child have a reading envelope or a reading notebook?
   6. _____
7. Have I established routines for taking and returning books?
   7. _____
8. Have I established routines for indicating when a book is being read?
   8. _____
9. Do I have a way of keeping track of public library or privately owned books that have been brought in by the pupils?   9. _____
10. Do I keep systematic check and written record of the number and rotation of individual conferences?
    10. _____

[8] The reader is also referred to J. Veatch, *Individualizing Your Reading Program*, New York: G. P. Putnam's Sons, 1959, p. 230.

[9] Reprinted with the kind permission of Mortimer Abramowitz, Principal, P.S. 188, Queens.

11. Have I developed a vocabulary for children's comments about books? 11. _____

12. Have I established a method for each child to keep a record of his word growth? 12. _____

13. Do I have records to show which children have read a particular book? 13. _____

14. Have I formed flexible groups based upon common needs? 14. _____

15. Am I developing skills based upon individual, group, and class needs? 15. _____

16. Am I using workbook material *selectively* to eradicate individual, group, and class weaknesses? 16. _____

17. Am I using the reading to integrate the various language arts—writing, discussions, etc.? 17. _____

18. Have I developed a variety of pooling procedures for sharing books? 18. _____

19. Am I guiding pupils' reading so as to widen, elevate, and refine tastes? 19. _____

20. Am I seeking natural ways of integrating reading with other curriculum areas, e.g., science, art, etc.? 20. _____

21. Does my room tastefully reflect a rich reading program—charts, book displays, letters, paintings, stick puppets, etc.? 21. _____

22. Am I familiar with the following basic references? 22. _____

   a. Draper, A *Practical Guide to Individualized Reading*, Publication No. 40, New York: Bureau of Educational Research, New York City Board of Education.

   b. J. Veatch, *Individualizing Your Reading Program.*

   c. W. B. Barbe, Educator's Guide to Personalized Reading Instruction, New York: Prentice Hall, Inc., 1962.

23. Does my plan book show the names of those for whom conferences are planned, ways of pooling for the week, vocabulary work, and group work? 23. _____

24. Does my plan book make provision for specific reading skills I plan to teach each week, and do I list sources I will employ toward this end? 24. _____

25. Have I made an index card for every book furnished by the school for the reading program? 25. _____

26. Have I made a list of publishers and their addresses easily available for each child? 26. _____

Other Suggestions for Record-Keeping

If reports were asked of one hundred teachers who had developed their systems of keeping records, there could well be found one hundred different ways of keeping track of children's efforts. Even so, there is usually a thread of similarity running through the myriad forms. For example, these items, in various sequence, are usually to be found:

1. The date of the conference.
2. The book brought to the conference.
3. Some comment upon the interview as to:
   Comprehension.
   Skills needed.
   Behaviors.
   Attitudes.
4. Some note of future work to be done.

In addition to these common elements, teachers continue to improvise to meet their own needs. For example:

One first-grade teacher, in organizing the plans for the day, asked every child to list his current book, whether or not he was going to bring it to her that day or any day in an individual conference. Thus a quick look at the bulletin board (in this case, but it could have been the chalk board) shows the teacher:

1. If more than one child is reading the same book, and, if so, how their conference can be combined for the sake of efficiency.
2. Something of the scope of the material then being read, largely independently, by the children.
3. Problem cases needing attention.

Another first-grade teacher, in using the idea of "one-look" sight vocabulary words, encouraged each child to record the words of every other child. Interesting problems arose, such as Patrick's word, "camel." Should it be recorded under "P" for Patrick or "C" for "camel"? Toward the end of the school year in May, the children began to see and voluntarily move to bring order out of their enormous mass of words they had accumulated. They were working toward one- and two-letter alphabetizing with little or no help from the teacher by the end of the year, usually during the independent work period.

Balancing the Reading Diet

Many teachers, misguided, we think, are under the illusion that the matter of literary taste can be legislated by fiat. Large "wheels" or "pies" with slices appropriately labeled "Science," "Humor," "Fairy Tales," and the like are used to "balance" literary choice.

Even though it may be well to keep a record of the categories in which pupils tend to choose books, there will probably be little effect on eventual preferences for books. Those teachers that insist that pupils read in every single category in the literary pie are fooling themselves, if they think they are improving "taste." Not that a

NAME	
CATEGORIES OF BOOKS I HAVE READ	
Adventure	
Classic	F
Fairy Tales	I
Humorous	C
Legends	T
Mystery	I
Plays	O
Poetry	N
Science Fiction	
Short Stories	
Family	N
Animal	O
Animal	N
Sports	F
Autobiography	I
Biography	C
Cultural (Music; Art; Hobby)	T
Historical	I
Science	O
Travel (Social Studies)	N

Reprinted with kind permission of Elaine Smiley, Unqua School, Massapequa, N.Y.

teacher might not get extremely tired of, say, horse stories, ad infinitum, from a certain child, and express himself in those terms. But to legislate that such a child stop reading horse stories only dampens the interest in reading, not in choosing horse stories. This, of course, is the age-old tale of forbidden fruit. Once a book is banned, its sales rise sharply. The trick is to get a book banned. Censorship has never worked. Like the little boy who, being scolded by his mother for swearing, was told "Don't let me ever hear you say that word again." She didn't. But he still kept saying the word.

Nevertheless, children can keep track of the categories in which they read with the understanding that such is a public record and, therefore, subject to inquiry on the part of the teacher.[10] The sheet on page 451 comes from one teacher and helped her explore pupils' reading interests during the individual conferences.

The Unusability of "Profile Charts"

Many records are to be found in the literature which list extensive characteristics that supposedly should be evaluated each time a teacher-pupil conference occurs. In general, these "profile charts" are not worth much. For example, we find lists full of items to be checked such as the following:

1. Pointing
2. Substitutions
3. Repetitions
4. Omissions
5. Poor expression
6. Hesitation
7. Too loud
8. Too soft, etc.

First, as can be seen, they are far too complicated to be practical. Second, the minutiae listed are not correctable unless a major reading problem is corrected. Any child evaluated with such a chart and given checks after most of the above items has one major problem. The child is reading something (a) that is too hard for him, and (b) of which he has little understanding and/or interest. If the material were truly at his level, if he liked it and were interested in it, he

10 The reader is referred to an excellent article by Muriel Fisch, "Record Keeping For Individualized Reading," *Grade Teacher*, November, 1958.

would make more of an effort to understand it and reduce his need to point, to substitute, to omit words, to repeat words, to read with poor expression, and so on.

Although research is needed on record-keeping, the impression of the authors, in talking to teachers, is that these types of charts are not only hard to use, they tell very little even when they are used. We do not recommend their use.

The Usability of the Running Log

One of the most popular ways to keep records is that of the log kept on the teacher's notebook. When there are no particular headings to follow, such a log takes on the unique pattern of the individual teacher. An expressive teacher will give way to such phrases as "LOVED his book today," or "cried when he told about the death of Charlotte"; or "MUST find more challenging material for him"; or "check with library for books on snakes." These running logs are veritable gold mines when the time comes for reporting progress to parents or for teacher evaluation sessions with administrators.

The main thing that is needed (see Chapter 2, page 24) is a notebook with a wide-open double page for each child. In a loose-leaf notebook, new sheets can be added, and the used ones removed for filing without interrupting the flow of record-keeping.

Moving into the Teacher-Parent Conference

The preceding are but a few of the many ideas that may be useful to teachers as they prepare for report card time, or for conference time. The great vacuum in the literature seems to be the lack of help and advice to teachers as to how to use the rich material from the many reading instructional conferences that will have occurred prior to the parent conference. Based upon the major headings that were presented in Chapter 6, the following section describes a conference in detail as it might happen.

The Parent-Teacher Conference

What does a teacher say to a parent? There is so much to say about any child that the length of the conference will dictate a picking and a choosing from the total data available. Even though parents have a right to know all there is to know about their own child, to set out to give this amount of information would be impractical. What, then, does a teacher share with each parent from the amount of material at his fingertips?

First, a teacher would have open all of the records of the given child, not that he will be able to go into everything there, but he will hit the high spots. In any event, there should be no attempt at secrecy. The teacher's notebook and other materials will serve as a guide, or an outline, rather than as the detailed basis for a long discourse or speech.

Secondly, how does a teacher begin? Perhaps the best way is to open with a statement about the general ability and activity of the child. For example, each child should keep track of every book that he takes with the sincere purpose of reading. Thus, with the child's listing of these books (probably in his own notebook) in hand, the teacher says something like this:

> As you can see, John has read fifty-seven books since the beginning of the year and twenty-two since our last conference. This is a fine record, because it shows his basic interest in books. It is hard to compare this record with other children as difficulty of these books enters in. Some children are able to read much harder books than others. Sometimes they do not read as many. However, in John's case, I am more than satisfied.

The parent might want to get the teacher to evaluate the child in tems of "is this good? or is this bad?" Then the teacher can go into the information he has gathered about the child's general level of ability. Perhaps something like this would result.

> Last fall all of the children had what we call a standardized reading test. These tests are not absolutely accurate, but they are the best we have. Your child's score showed that he is reading within his grade level. While the score indicates an exact month, we know that too many factors affect it. As his score shows, he is reading in the middle level of this grade. This means we can say that, give or take a few months, we know he is at his grade level.

Thirdly, what other information should a teacher share with a parent? Let us repeat the outline of the individual conference (pages 155 to 158), and then build a sample of conference to illustrate how a teacher might proceed. This outline, of course, is not to be followed verbatim each time a pupil and teacher sit down together. Nevertheless, it has the usual four bases that require attention. From those notes a teacher has recorded on those four points over the weeks, a most adequate parent conference can be conducted.

Sample Parent Conference—Based upon Teacher-Pupil Individual Conference Records

First Area
1. Comprehension Skills
    a. Central thought.
    b. Inferences and critical reading.

  c. Value judgments.
  d. Author purpose.
  e. Necessary plot sequence.

Notes from Child's Record

Five books are listed, approximately one a week, presented to the teacher in an individual conference. These are in addition to a listing of twenty-two in the child's own notebook that were read silently and not presented to the teacher in an individual conference. Of these twenty-two, six were subjects of sharing time projects alone and with a group. Four others were included in a social studies project and noted by the teacher in a special place in his notebook.

What the Teacher Says to the Parent

TEACHER: John has chosen five books to bring to me for instruction. See how he has read twenty-two others since you and I talked the last report time. He has improved a great deal in selecting books that are at his ability level, and is just beginning to realize that reading silently is much easier than reading aloud.

Of these five books two of them are sports stories and three of them are about animals. It doesn't matter what books he chooses, as I can instruct him from any book. He is hard to fool by an author. He is able to read between the lines, so to speak, and get the moral of the story if there is one. This is an important reading skill. John is not ever going to be fooled by what he reads. He understands the main idea of the story and chooses wisely from the supply that we have.

SECOND AREA

  2. Personality Adjustment and Reading Selections
     a. Insight into personal interest in story.
     b. Awareness of peer group reaction.
     c. Insight into possible personality behavior change.

What the Teacher Says to the Parent

TEACHER: John loses himself when he reads. He knows who else in the class likes the same thing that he likes. But they don't read together. I was interested that he chose a book about baseball in which the team was important. I think that hit home with him, as he really likes to play on a team, but isn't willing to give up anything for that team. Not that he should. But this was an example of how a child works through a personal reaction through his reading. He will be a better reader for it. It is personal interest and drive that pushes his reading.

THIRD AREA

  3. The Mechanical Skills
     a. Word definitions.

b. Study skills.

c. Ability to analyze unknown words.

d. Reading for details.

What the Teacher Says to the Parent

TEACHER: I notice that John does not know some words that are common for children his age. We had to work on the meanings of words like these: "demonstration," "average," and "constitution." I am expecting that his ability to learn new and harder words will increase now that he is reading at his top level. I wonder if you could help him learn to use an index faster? Perhaps finding a hymn in church or hunting up a word in the dictionary at home would be helpful. He could use this kind of help. He does rather well in spelling and, of course, can sound out his words. There are very few words that he cannot figure out. The problem is that he can figure them out IF he has them in his vocabulary before he starts. Words jump into your mind when you already know them *in your head*, but do not recognize them when you see them. John is able to read carefully when he needs to. There was a pattern for a dump truck in a book. He was able to follow the directions very well. I don't wish children to read so much for details that they lose sight of the story itself. But there are times when you must read very carefully. He can do that.

FOURTH AREA

4. Ability to Hold Audience Attention

a. Oral reading of selection.

b. Retelling a long story briefly.

What the Teacher Says to the Parent

TEACHER: John needs to work on his voice so that he can charm his audience. This is not a major skill in reading, as we in adult life read aloud very very seldom. Nevertheless, an appreciation of good literature is part of good reading aloud. This is his greatest weakness. Does he have a younger brother or sister he might read to at bedtime? This would be a good exercise for him.

The preceding example of a parent conference based upon the teacher's records of all of the individual conferences could be varied in a number of ways. It depends upon what he has recorded! There is no need to gloss over or avoid the less satisfactory aspects of a child's performance. But it is hard to be punitive and cold when face to face with a parent, too often filled with anxiety about his child. Sometimes there are disarming opening statements that teachers can use that ease the whole effort. Here are several:

Mrs. ————, I know I have no children of my own, but I have tried to learn how to work with other people's children. I want you to know that together we can make a team to make your (John) the finest child of which he is capable.

or

Mrs. ————, you and I have a job. I get paid for mine, but you should know that the pay does not mean that I like your child any less. Would you be interested in some of my reactions about him? Maybe together we can work out a plan, to make him the best boy that he can be.

or

Mrs. ————, I know it must seem as if I don't get around to your child as much as I'd like. I feel guilty about it myself, but I am trying. Would you like to know what I have found out even though there is much more to be known?

or

Mrs. ————, you know that you and your husband and I are really a team. We are all working for the same thing. I know I make mistakes here in school that I am sorry for, but I suppose the same thing happens with you at home. But we don't MEAN to do anything wrong but wish to make your boy (girl) as wonderful a child as it is possible for him (her) to be.

Written Reports Follow Conference Outlines

The preceding suggestions and samples of oral teacher-parent conferences usually follow a kind of outline or planned sequence. For those teachers who prefer or are required to write up narrative reports, these outlines can be the basis for topic sentences of each paragraph. More than one teacher has brought his typewriter to school and, once the pupils are busy, has typed out these letter-type reports, often consulting as he goes.

Scheduling Reports

Most school systems have mandated dates during which parents are informed of their children's progress. When the reports are in the form of a card or letter, teachers often send them all home on the same day. We would like to suggest that a better practice would be to send home no more than TWO or THREE a morning or afternoon, or four to six a full day. There is more incentive for the children to evaluate themselves when they are not just sure when their report is forthcoming. There is far less opportunity to compare from child-to-child in a destructive fashion—although, of course, comparison can never be, nor perhaps should be, entirely eliminated.

If there are forty weeks in a full school year, and four reporting periods, the following weeks could span enough time to fit in each child report.

Weeks 7, 8, and 9   Weeks 23, 24, 25
Weeks 12, 13, and 14   Weeks 32, 33, and 34

Other Helps to Teachers at Reporting Time

The children's book lists kept in their notebooks can be used as one measure of their progress. Of course, these lists can be used competitively and child pitted against child as to the numbers of books listed. The more pressure put on such comparison, though, the more children will find ways of listing books without really reading them, or the more they will dislike the whole activity of reading. Comparing such book lists is not the proper reason to read. One reads because he enjoys the world of books—not to see how many more he can read than his fellows.

Yet these book lists can be used in a noncompetitive way. There should be a time when the teacher looks at every child's lists, and does some random or spot-checking, to weigh the value of those books included. One teacher uses the wearisome Friday afternoon in this fashion once or twice a month. She says something like this:

> This last hour I want to look at your book lists in your notebook. You may have a free reading time, or project time, so long as it is quiet enough for me to talk with each of you about your books that you've not told me about yet. Open your notebook to the list and leave it open on your desk. I will come by and look it over.

Usually, in this situation, the teacher will spot-check one out of every ten books, just to get an idea of how the child recalls those that he lists.

If such a teacher is using an "A, B, C" report card, he must come to some conclusion as to how to weigh (1) the number of books, (2) the degree of their difficulty, (3) the depth of impact they made upon the reader. Somehow a balance must be struck, if a single symbol is to be a grade.

On the other hand, a teacher that is using a narrative report or conference will write or say something like this:

> The books that John lists that he does not bring to me during our individual conference, or during our sharing time, are, in the main, easier than I would expect. He seems to be glad to read without having some kind of direct academic pressure upon him. He remembers what he reads with exceptional clarity.

or

> Mary is reading omnivorously. I feel that in the last month she has become a book lover rather than just a book reader. She has always done well in reading, but I notice her profound absorption with these she has chosen to read to herself. I am pleased her ability is growing so that she needs little or no help in her reading.

or

Harry seems to feel some kind of pressure just to list books without having read them very thoroughly. He is very much concerned about his success in school, and maybe this is the reason. But I must help him to choose more wisely, and choose fewer books. I would like to see him lost to the world in a book. But it hasn't happened yet.

or

Jane is reading about ten books to every one she brings to me in an individual conference. Her tastes are covering the field of literature. I think she could be helped to settle upon some interest in depth, but I am hesitant to push, as I don't want to discourage her in any way. I am sure the major interest will come in due time, if we have enough books to allow wide enough choices.

These are statements that tell a parent a lot about his child's reading. They could be varied infinitely depending upon the circumstances. But these are suggestive of how much more a teacher can tell a parent when the narrative report can be used.

Teacher-Made Tests

As described under the "Sequence of Phonics" in Chapter 11, pages 403 to 404, a test is included on some of the steps in the development of that sequence. Other tests (see below) could be devised on other steps, such as "prefixes and suffixes," or multisyllabic words. The point of the matter here is that there is a fundamental simplicity in these evaluations that even student teachers can perform with very little training.

Similarly a teacher might devise an informal measure to see how well pupils can alphabetize—either on the simplest of levels in the early grades, or the more complicated stages of dictionary drill at older age levels.

Speed of reading, or the teaching of skimming, can be discovered in a one-to-one situation or group or class together. "Let's see how long it will take to find the shortest way to say the meaning of this paragraph."

Teacher-made tests can fit the teaching to what should be learned but they can take far too much time for what they are worth. Our purpose here is mainly to suggest ways in which a teacher can find a midpoint of ability within a class, in order for the fateful decision to be made of "What is an 'A?'"

Making Decisions About What To Report

As in all other measures, the teacher must come to terms with himself about single letter grades. The factors of (1) the child's ability, (2) the child's performance in relation to that ability, and (3) the child's ability in relation to his class must be weighed and balanced. As usual, the narrative and conference method of reporting simplifies the decision of the teacher. When it has to be decided what an "A" means, all sorts of thinking and weighing must be taken into account. But when you can tell the parent what was found out, no such agonizing appraisal needs to be made.

The following are samples of teacher-made tests that have been found to be useful. The first is a repeat of the one on page 408.

Teacher Name ————————————

Class or Grade ————————————

Report on Testing on Hearing Phonemes

1. Child's Name (First Only) ————————————

2. Grade————————————

3. School————————————

Directions for Teacher

"This test is only to help me learn how children hear letter sounds. We have tried to find some words you won't know how to spell so we can notice what you can *hear.* Don't worry if you don't know or make mistakes. I will help later with words you *do* know. Don't look, now, but just listen."

As the child responds, record the exact letter (letters) the child says on the line. If he makes two or more responses record them in order from left to right. Work rapidly, if possible, but allow ample time for thought. Stop when child shows fatigue.

Test 1

The teacher asks: "What is the first letter or sound of these words that you hear?"

1. alp ———————	15. pharmacy ———————
2. zodiac ———————	16. injure ———————
3. xylophone ———————	17. particular ———————
4. wound ———————	18. celery ———————
5. maroon ———————	19. undertow ———————
6. heather ———————	20. survive ———————
7. Esther ———————	21. geology ———————
8. bilge ———————	22. nervous ———————
9. quoit ———————	23. chilly ———————
10. reckon ———————	24. shamrock ———————
11. oven ———————	25. canoe ———————
12. ooze ———————	26. kettle ———————
13. kosher ———————	27. thistle ———————
14. fashion ———————	28. dignity ———————

29. gallop _____   34. terrier _____
30. juice _____   35. victory _____
31. local _____   36. yolk _____
32. opera _____   37. witch _____
33. recipe _____

Test 2

The teacher asks: "What is the last letter that you hear in these words?" For "rich," "wish," and "with" ask "What sounds or letters do you hear? "
Ending Sounds:

lip _____	tax _____	try _____
rate _____	rub _____	tree _____
simmer _____	wish _____	lamb _____
fill _____	loose _____	back _____
love _____	buzz _____	bed _____
yoyo _____	dray _____	with _____
fudge _____	rich _____	win _____
	true _____	

Test 3

The teacher asks: "What letters do you hear in the beginning of these words? Listen as I say them slowly."

pride _____	grow _____	sprinkle _____
tweet _____	planet _____	floppity _____
sting _____	strip _____	glamour _____
brake _____	spackle _____	quiet _____
clickety _____	fry _____	travel _____

Test 4

The teacher asks two questions for each word: (1) "What sound do you hear in the middle of this word?" (2) "What letters could make that sound?" (Note: in the case of "thirsty" the answer "er, ur" is acceptable but the examiner should state, "Yes, those letters do make that sound. But it happens to be ir."

dark _____	fruit _____	mail _____
foam _____	foot _____	spoil _____
sheep _____	forty _____	shop _____
naughty _____	shout _____	rug _____
sick _____	fine _____	mat _____
rattle _____	thirst _____	room _____

Hearing Vowel Sounds

Circle the word that contains the vowel sound, regardless of how it is spelled.

1. Ur as in "fur"—burn, burial, sour, turned
2. Short e as in "elephant"—test, real, stretch, thread
3. Long a as in "angel"—weigh, laid, reins, father
4. Short u as in "umbrella"—fern, rough, good, stuff
5. Long o as in "hope"—broad, loaf, chord, rowed
6. Short i as in "igloo"—tripe, tricky, still, hide
7. Long u as in "use"—guide, suit, room, fool
8. ir as in "sir"—thirsty, heir, tired, flirt
9. Short o as in "ostrich"—foot, opera, flop, float
10. ar as in "arm"—heard, hard, heart, ward

Answer Key

1. burn, turned	5. loaf, rowed	8. thirsty, flirt
2. test, stretch, thread	6. tricky, still	9. opera, flop
3. weigh, laid, reins	7. suit, room, fool	10. hard, heart
4. rough, stuff		

Diagnostic Test of Beginning Sounds:
An Informal Measure [1]

This is an informal test to determine basic knowledge and application of skills. Teachers have reported it to be of value as: one measurement of children's progress; one basis for grouping needs.

Primary grade teachers have used Form I in the spring. Middle grade teachers have used Form I in the beginning of the year; Form II after teaching, usually in the spring.

Directions:

I am going to say some words. Listen to see if you can tell from the sound of the word the letters that begin it.

If you were going to spell the following words, what is the *first* letter you would write?

Form I	Form II	Form III (this space for your words)
bottle	bachelor	
fact	fuselage	
monkey	mellow	
sand	salmon	
table	tapestry	
cough	cavern[2]	
notion	nourish	
gamble	gargle	
kernel[2]	kennel	
jolly[3]	jealous[3]	
hardly	heaven	
desk	davenport	
lamp	linoleum	
painter	percolator	
raisin	rustle	
vase	ventilation	
zebra	zest	
welcome	waddle	
queen	quaint	
yellow	yodel	

[1] Printed with the kind permission of Professor S. W. Shnayer, Chico State College, Chico, Calif. Similar lists of words are developed for the beginning blends: blood, fruit, grass, etc., for primary level and blizzard, frantic, gracious, etc., for middle grades. Development of three-letter blends would include words such as thread, strength, etc.

[2] Accept c or k. Try to get both by saying, "I can think of two letters that give that beginning sound. If you know both write both with a line between them."

[3] Accept g or j. Try to get both as above.

I. Laboratory Notebook	Date			
A. Vocabulary				
B. Capitalization				
C. Punctuation				
D. Spelling				
E. Sentence Structure				
F. Creative Expression				
G. Dictionary				
Comments				

Evaluation sheet for written composition. (Reprinted with kind permission of Elaine Smiley, Unqua School, Massapequa, N.Y.)

Informal Nonreading Measures

Before proceeding to other matters the measures often used by teachers that are not a measure of reading at all, but of the child himself during the reading period, should be suggested. Teachers cannot help but be aware of their need to discipline their class inceasingly, or decreasingly, when such stringent requirements are simply not necessary. To keep track of disciplinary problems during the reading period is not a formal measure of reading ability—or is it? The absorbed child is the one who causes no trouble whatsoever. Some teachers keep track of this.

In the same vein, the child who is rarely absent, and who is dismayed when required to go home when an infection or other illness is noticeable in school, is giving teachers an informal measure of reading. Children who don't like reading won't read, it is true, but neither will they come to school with the same eagerness as they will when they love to read. There is something to the incidence of absenteeism that merits examination when we are looking at our reading program.

The Child Evaluates Himself

The preceding discussion has dealt largely with what the teacher thinks of a child and his progress and how that gets reported to parents. Implicit in this whole discussion, particularly that relating to the content of the records of individual conferences, and those records the teacher and child keeps, is the principle that a child must see where he himself stands. He must see clearly and be able to recognize that which he does not know.

Child Awareness of Own Skill Needs

No child should be taught anything or really can be taught much unless he realizes what it is he does not know. Skills, then, must be so scaled to child-size that they seem possible to each child and *therefore an incentive* to him.

Children are so curious that when a challenge presents itself they must be sick not to respond. They want to walk. They struggle to pull themselves up from anything that offers a handhold. They want to tie their own shoelaces and are furious if not allowed to do so. They want to learn to write "writing"—i.e., cursive—and hound teachers who insist that they should still do manuscript. The drive to learn the possible is one of the healthiest things about the human animal. Thus, in reading instruction, we advise that everything that needs to be learned must be known, in order that it may beckon to the learner. Seeing the goal is the motivating force.

In contrast we can cite the resignation, the lack of enthusiasm on the part of pupils when *they do not know* what they must learn. There is no incentive, no beckoning something to be accomplished. No shoelaces to tie. No buttons to be buttoned. No new dance step to be mastered. No new anything to provide a challenge. Teachers are no different—"Get me out of this rut," some say. Surely the surprising growth of the practice of individualizing reading throughout the nation, in the face of the most violent antagonism and rigorous censorship, attests to the challenge inherent in something "new." Even though it really is not. Remember the discouragement of the children who, knowing they are in the slow "dummy" group, *do not know exactly what to do to get out of it.* Lack of knowledge is a frightening thing. How often we hear "If I just knew what I was facing, I would be O.K.," or "It is this uncertainty that is killing me." Of course. It is no different in teaching skills in the reading program. The point of view of this book is that knowing what it is one *needs to know* is part of the process of learning to read.

It is also part of the process by which a child evaluates himself in order to improve his contribution to his own learning and to society. The child who KNOWS what he does not know is wiser than he who is ignorant of his failings. He who knows his weaknesses becomes the self-directed person. He can stand higher and taller. He can learn.

The first section of this chapter has been designed to help teachers evaluate their pupils in the best way possible considering the kind of reporting system that the given teacher is required to use. There has been little mention of the more formal standardized tests. These omnipresent aspects of the educational scene must come in for their share of discussion. We will limit the discussion to achievement tests in reading.

Formal Testing

A more usual discussion of evaluation includes, in the main, the effectiveness and use of standardized tests. There exist so many references on these topics, written by specialists far more knowledgeable than the writer of this text, that, in view of space limitation, there seems little reason to repeat the same ideas, raise the same questions that can be found elsewhere. Henry S. Dyer, for example, discusses many aspects of testing in an excellent article, "A Psychometrician Views Human Ability."[11]

What tests are best? What are the values of certain types of evaluation instruments as compared to other types? These and other questions need to be answered by those who are specialists in this field.

As far as references on these topics are concerned, there are many to which the reader can refer. Spache[12] raises some cogent questions about formal and informal tests and, in a most helpful section, pre-

---

[11] *Teachers College Record*, 61:394–403, April, 1960.
[12] George D. Spache, *Towards Better Reading*, Champaign, Ill.: Garrard Publishing Co., 1963, pp. 354–75.

sents a "Check List For Test Evaluation." Buros[13] provides the most widely respected listing and evaluation of tests in his five yearbooks. These are of monumental importance. His reviews include the factual data about a test plus his opinion of how well each fulfills its professed intent. Traxler,[14] a major writer in the field of testing, is critical of many tests in that they often appear to emphasize relatively unimportant aspects of the reading process at the expense of other aspects demonstrably more important to the act of reading. Smith and Deschant,[15] in similar fashion to Spache, raise five points about the characteristics of achievement tests that indicate some of their deficiencies.

Austin, Bush, and Huebner[16] provide a brief summary of the use of standardized tests, but focus the majority of their attention to a description of reading-survey techniques. In a short pamphlet, intended for classroom teacher and lay use, Rothney[17] discusses many aspects of the evaluation of pupils. Wrightstone, Justman, and Robbins cover most of the area in their book *Evaluation in Modern Education.*[18]

All of these, as well as writings in major research publications, notably *Encyclopedia of Educational Research,*[19] *Handbook of Research on Teaching,*[20] and the N.S.S.E. 62nd Yearbook, *The Impact and Improvement of School Testing Programs,*[21] provide ample source material for those interested.

Our discussion, therefore, will deal with those questions not frequently raised that seem to be unique to the whole philosophy of this book, centering, as has been shown, on:

[13] Oscar Buros, *The Mental Measurements Yearbooks* (5th ed.), New York: Gryphon Books, Ltd., 1946.

[14] Arthur E. Traxler, "Critical Survey of Tests for Identifying Difficulties in Interpreting What Is Read," *Promoting Growth Toward Maturity in Interpreting What Is Read,* Supplementary Educational Monographs, No. 74, Chicago: University of Chicago Press, 1951, pp. 195–200.

[15] H. P. Smith and E. M. Deschant, *The Psychology in Teaching Reading,* Englewood Cliffs, N. J., Prentice-Hall, Inc., 1961, pp. 410–19.

[16] Mary C. Austin, C. L. Bush, and M. H. Huebner, *Reading Evaluation,* New York: The Ronald Press Co., 1961.

[17] John W. M. Rothney, "Evaluating and Reporting Pupil Progress," No. 7 Series: *What Research Says to the Classroom Teacher,* Washington, D. C.: Department of Classroom Teachers, American Educational Research Association, National Education Association, 1955.

[18] J. W. Wrightstone, Jos. Justman, and I. Robbins, *Evaluation in Modern Education,* New York: American Book Co., 1956.

[19] C. W. Harris (ed.), *Encyclopedia of Educational Research,* New York: Macmillan Co., 1960.

[20] N. L. Gage (ed.), *Handbook of Research on Teaching,* Chicago: Rand McNally & Co., 1963.

[21] N. B. Henry and H. G. Richey (eds.), *N.S.S.E. 62nd Yearbook, The Impact and Improvement of School Testing Programs,* Chicago: University of Chicago Press, 1963.

1. Factors of self-choice and self-assignment on the part of pupils.
2. Factors of classroom and school-wide grouping that are homogeneous in specific task but not in ability level.
3. Factors of individual attention through teacher-pupil conference, and other pacing activities.

This philosophy would seem to change the commonly accepted reasoning behind current testing practice. If children choose their own book, for example, are they properly tested by test material given without regard to the child's own interest or satisfaction? This is quite a different question from those usually raised. Test makers themselves give repeated warning about the misuse of their products, and they are wise to do so. The sins committed in the name of tests are frequently the exact sins that their authors caution users about. Test-makers do their best to analyze the process to be tested, and then develop ways that they feel will best evaluate those elements that they consider to be part of the process.

Spache[22] notes that we are not really certain if reading tests are differentiating between reading and intelligence. Traxler[23] states that no aspect of silent reading can be measured without interrupting the process. Most authorities in the field of reading and testing will agree that the reading process itself is tremendously complex and thus does not lend itself to easy analysis.

Certainly reading is a complex process. But so are walking and talking. But beyond listening to talk and seeing a child walk, what is needed to evaluate walking and talking, *unless something is wrong?* Nothing. Obviously, there are not standardized tests of walking and talking in schools, because such are not considered part of the school curriculum. Thus walking and talking do not need to be measured, except in those rare instances when the child is having trouble walking and talking.

This raises a question about reading tests. Why is so much time spent on them? Could it be that there is a latent fear that, like the walking and talking above, there is a suspicion that something is wrong? Is all of this frenetic testing activity, certainly grossly overemphasized, a defense against some kind of fear that all is not well with the reading world? Why the need for tests, not only in reading, but in every curriculum area?

It is curious that when self-selection approaches are not used, there is a continuing, sometimes formal but usually informal, daily

[22] George D. Spache, *op. cit.*, p. 358.
[23] A. E. Traxler, "Values and Limitations of Standardized Reading Tests," in *Evaluation of Reading*, Supplementary Educational Monographs, No. 88, Chicago: University of Chicago Press, 1958, p. 112.

testing operation by teachers in order to prove that the children *are* reading? The need for constant nagging,[24] the keeping at children to "finish their work," is not only a bulwark against supervisor's visits. Teachers too often feel guilty that *they have not taught* unless they check or test on every single assignment given. It is a curious, and we feel, most unnecessary, activity. Enough is enough. Once in a while. But incessantly? No.

Some questions to be raised about testing would improve the general quality of the instruments. These questions are rather widely accepted among specialists, but are not so widely realized among classroom teachers. Perhaps, if more teachers were aware of these patently doubtful practices, there would be less tendency to overemphasize tests.

For example, some tests can be criticized on the basis of what is called extrapolated scores, so called when children on whom the standardized scores are based were of a different grade or year from the range of scores provided. For example, a test may be standardized with scores from third-grade pupils. From that score those for other grades are then figured upward and downward according to those third-grade scores. A better practice would be to standardize a given test with an adequate sample *at every grade* for which a standardized score is presented.

Similarly, some tests can be questioned when the scores are given that have been derived from a sampling of children of one part of the country, say east of the Mississippi River. Thus, such tests could not be assumed to be accurate for children in the Rocky Mountain areas or beyond.

There are even tests that work to make a school system "look good" as their "standardized" scores are so low that it is easy for children to do "well," i.e., better than the test sample, and thus look good to the non-expert parent of a given community.

These criticisms are not original here but are available in references. Certainly these points of proper sampling practices for standardized scores need to be kept in mind when these instruments are used.

What Can Be Expected of Tests?

At the most we feel that achievement tests can reasonably be expected to yield information that will (1) help the teacher diagnose the reading needs of his pupils and (2) assist the school system in

[24] Roma Gans, *Common Sense in Reading*, Indianapolis: Bobbs Merrill Co., Inc., 1963.

presenting a public face that will justify continuing support. These two areas, however, are extremely limited when compared to what the test-makers themselves, as well as the vast majority of school personnel, expect of formalized tests. As this whole book is based upon a program that differs from the usual instructional reading program, we would suggest that these instruments are overrated and overused, *even when they are demonstrably well-constructed devices.*

For example, most writing about tests is in broad agreement about their general purposes[25] as follows:

1. Standardized tests should provide data that will help the school place the child in a class, or in a group in a class, where he will best learn.
2. Standardized tests must provide a basis upon which diagnosis of reading needs can be made in order that proper instruction can be planned.
3. Standardized tests must provide the material upon which permanent records of pupils, hence public reports to the community, can be based.

We find the first point unnecessary. We see no need for ability or homogeneous grouping whatsoever, and have presented an entire text designed to help schools and teachers avoid such a damaging practice. Second, we question the practicality of expecting tests to be so precise as to plan week-in and week-out teaching. On the third point we agree, as we believe that the public does have a right to know if it is paying for efficient schools. We accept standardized tests as one way for the community to assess value.

Let us take each of these points in greater detail.

Testing for Pupil Placement in Reading Groups

What class is the best for a child? How do we know that a given class is the best? A traditional testing program assumes that all children whose achievement is found to be near a certain grade level will benefit from being placed in the same class with the same teacher. But is this true?

Children who are so considered homogeneous are not necessarily alike. Spache[26] and Smith and Deschant,[27] like many others, point

[25] W. A. Monroe (ed.), *Encyclopedia of Educational Research*, New York: Macmillan Co., 1960, pp. 1461 ff.

[26] George D. Spache, *op. cit.*, Chap. 19, pp. 354–75.

[27] H. P. Smith and E. M. Deschant, *op. cit.*, p. 411.

out that tests, with their "formidable arrays of the subscores," raise serious questions as to reliability. If the children who are found to have a certain grade-level score, say 7.1, are profiled in terms of their sub-scores, and these profiles superimposed upon each other, the results reveal that the homogeneity of the 7.1 is but a myth. On any given sub-score there is wide variation. The following chart illustrates our point.

Names	Totals	Sub-Test 1	Sub-Test 2	Sub-Test 3	Sub-Test 4
Mary	7.1	8.0	6.1	7.5	6.8
John	7.1	8.1	7.2	6.6	6.5
Esther	7.1	6.4	8.3	6.7	7.0
Bill	7.1	7.1	6.6	8.0	6.7

Here are four pupils that have identical scores after all of the sub-test scores have been averaged. Yet these four children are not alike on any sub-test score. Putting these scores on a graph shows even more clearly how different they are, even though their total reading—assuming, of course, the test is a good one—is at the same level.

To so superimpose sub-test scores of several children whose total scores are identical on the same chart is not a new idea. Alice V. Keliher did it first in 1932 in her still important study that evaluated homogeneous grouping critically.[28] Our present purpose, in showing how differently children may perform on tests, is to bring out the same point related to reading.

NARROW RANGE PUPIL PLACEMENT ASSUMES POOR TEACHING. Sins committed in the name of testing are legion. Many have raised important questions beyond the scope of this discussion. Such authorities are correctly concerned about the misuse of tests. However, when tests are the basis upon which decisions are made to put children with this teacher or with that teacher, there are few authorities of any kind that question the practice.

But we are disturbed by this practice and consider it not only a misuse of otherwise useful instruments, but also an indication of a type of education that has some serious deficiencies.

For example, when some kind of measurement indicates that some children are alike in some way, and they are placed together in the same class with the same teacher, this would indicate teaching that is:

[28] A. V. Keliher, *Critical Evaluation of Homogeneous Grouping*, New York: Bureau of Publications, Teachers College, Columbia University, 1932. See also Chap. 7, pages 191–96.

1. Narrow as to the content to be covered. Otherwise, why take so much time and trouble to find out which children are similar in certain ways?

2. Has identical lesson assignments. There is no need to have variety in assignments when the teacher feels all children need to know the same content.

3. Closed in its purposes. Everyone is to learn the same thing. Therefore, nothing new can be added, because what is new will produce differences that cannot be kept identical.

4. Rooted in the past. The past is known and therefore dependable enough to be arranged in bite-sized chunks for easy assignment to the pupils.

5. Conformist in its philosophy. There is no point in having pupils all the same unless they are to be prevented from differing.

Good education is wide in scope. It allows for differing rates of learning. It looks toward the future. It is open-ended in its questioning and grows strong with the unexpected. Variety in learning is to be admired by the good teacher. The above five points, and more, too, illustrate poor teaching. Worse than that. They are SYMBOLS of poor teaching.

NARROW RANGE OF PUPIL PLACEMENT UNNECESSARY. In schools where self-selection, task-grouping, and individual conferences are standard practice, *no tests are needed to decide where to place children.* It is a waste of time and tax money to test for such purposes. No tests are needed because the *range of ability* in a given class does not matter! When children are working at their own rate, on projects of their own, the grade-level differences can assume their normal wide spreads.

Whether or not a test is reliable seems to us important but beside the point. Reliability assumes that we must have standardized tests in order to place pupils in ability groups, or other homogeneous arrangements. Not only does the research defy any scientific effort to prove the worth of homogenizing children,[29] but the philosophical considerations are devastating to the mental hygienic and democratic goals of this society.

A statement by Celia Stendler[30] in a recent *Yearbook of the Department of Elementary School Principles* makes the same point.

[29] Reginald Kierstead, "A Comparison and Evaluation of Two Methods of Organization for the Teaching of Reading," *Journal of Educational Research*, Vol. 56, No. 6, Feb. 1963, pp. 317–321, as an example of how the separation of pupils yielded no significant gains.

[30] National Education Association, *Those First School Years*, September, 1960, p. 156.

"The practice of putting enough faith in results of standardized tests . . . to justify their use for placement purpose . . . is extremely questionable." Any test put to such use should be questioned. No author, no publisher can know a specific group, and any amount of standardization simply misses this point, whatever other values such instruments might have.

Thus we refuse to accept one purpose usually stated by most advocates of a testing program. To say: "Evaluation must provide data that will help the school place the child in the class where he will best learn" is to state a purpose that cannot be defended on sound curriculum grounds.

Put another way, we can say that the formal measurement that leads to ability grouping tends to be poor evaluation practice. We must evaluate. We must evaluate continuously. But evaluation should not be used to set up situations that restrict the learning of children or at best do not provide the most open of educational settings.

Some schools have a better way, and perhaps a less costly way,[31] to diagnose reading difficulties on a daily basis. They use the techniques of the reading clinic, where applicable, in the classroom. Certainly, the reading clinicians do not give diagnostic tests daily, or even weekly. These everyday activities could be used in the classroom. Certainly there are a variety of techniques that would transfer easily. Perhaps the individual conference is one of them. The use of pupil dictation could be another. Informal testing divices would also serve. There are means at hand other than diagnostic tests to help the teacher in his need for daily guidance and planning.

INSTRUCTION SHOULD FOLLOW DIAGNOSIS. A formal diagnostic test should guide teaching. This certainly should be the intent of such a test. But whether or not such good intentions are followed is questionable. How practical is that goal?

For example, many school systems require such a test at the end of the school year. This, in effect, makes such a test a part of the merit-rating system of teachers, obviously a misuse of the instrument. A better plan perhaps for pupil evaluation, which is what everyone is most interested in, would be for teachers to give such tests in the beginning of the year, or even at times throughout the year, in order for the results to be of value in the instructional program. In passing, may it be said that a healthier testing climate is set up when tests are administered by those non-emotionally involved. Teachers, for example, should give tests to those children they have not

[31] I.e., because teachers already are being paid and no new personnel are needed.

taught, i.e., in the beginning of the year. Then teachers have the data *in time* to plan their work. But still there are problems.

Testing for Diagnosis To Guide Instruction

Even though some writers[32] feel many diagnostic tests leave much to be desired when their claims are thoroughly checked, there are some well-made instruments available. But that is not our concern for the moment. We submit that diagnostic tests are impractical for daily teaching, and would be impractical for classroom use no matter how reliable and trustworthy they might be.

DIAGNOSTIC TESTS USUALLY IMPRACTICAL. These instruments are usually impractical for a rather simple reason. First, they cannot be given daily. Nor can they be given weekly. Rarely are they given monthly. Usually they are given once a year. Of course, these tests are not intended to be given daily, as their authors would be the first to insist. But even making such a statement carries within it a hint that a daily test might serve a purpose. Diagnosis is needed daily, of course. But not the kind that comes from a formal type of test.

The need for daily diagnosis is the need for daily planning. A teacher, if he is to meet the needs of his pupils, must know exactly what to teach. Do these tests provide such information on a daily scale? Not often. If they do provide such information, would it be financially worthwhile to spend the amount of money necessary to make daily administration possible? Is this the best way to plan daily instruction? If not, is there as good a way, or better, that is not so expensive?

ARE DIAGNOSTIC TESTS IMMEDIATE ENOUGH? If instruction should follow diagnosis, and no one says that it should not, it would follow that the sooner it follows, the better. Yet the usefulness of tests is not statistically based upon how long after it is given that the follow-up should be made.

Of the many details that might result from diagnosis this is one point not well established. Once a teacher knows the particular difficulty of a child or a group, how soon must that difficulty be included in a lesson? How long can a teacher wait? If instruction follows diagnosis, how long is the period of grace before the need is met? Does it depend on the need? Does it depend upon the lesson that

---

[32] George D. Spache, *op. cit.*, Chap. 19, and H. P. Smith and E. M. Deschant, *op. cit.*, p. 411, provide some material that brings the diagnostic qualities of tests into question.

is devised to meet the need? What is crucial here? Can the need be met with a predigested, planned piece of material? Are there some needs that respond to programming, for example? Are there others that require the tailor-made personalized lesson for the individual child?

We know quite a bit about clinical practice with remedial cases. Is that practice transferable into the classroom with average undamaged pupils? We feel it is. Yet, to what degree? It has always seemed reasonable to assume that the methods used to rehabilitate a remedial case might be methods that could prevent retardation in the first place. A major argument of this text is the insistence that the classroom is the best place to teach reading and that many clinical practices easily transfer.

ARE DIAGNOSTIC TESTS DEFINITIVE ENOUGH? If tests are constructed in such a way that a teacher has difficulty in applying their results quickly, they are often constructed in such a way that the teacher does not see how to proceed to correct the difficulty. This is obviously best met at the preservice training level. But failing that, teachers can be helped at the in-service level plan for needs diagnosed.

As there are reliable and valid diagnostic reading tests, the question is whether or not they are the most useful instruments available. Perhaps they are if used in a carefully prescribed way—i.e., for the early evaluation of a class that will enable the teacher to grasp the profile of his students at the outset of the year. But if the tests are not used immediately, if the teacher knows not how to eradicate the reading needs revealed, then these expenditures can only be classed as something else that costs money, takes up classroom time, and has little educational value.

Testing for Permanent Recording and Reporting

As the public supports the school systems in America at all levels of government, we believe that the public has a right to know whether or not it is getting its money's worth from the schools it pays for. Similarly, parents have the right to know what the school knows about their own children. Thus we have a need to report to the public in two ways, (1) in general terms, and (2) in specific and confidential terms to parents of school children.

In addition, there is need for continuing, cumulative records to be kept on each child that can be used in prescribed professional fashion by the teachers, administrators, and certain community workers in their professional capacities. These records are a necessity if advanced planning, budgeting, construction, and other types of activities are to be carried out.

STANDARDIZED TESTS IN THE PERMANENT RECORD. In this context the use of as objective a measure as possible is necessary. In spite of some serious[33] weaknesses, standardized tests are the best that we have. Much time and expense have been put into the construction of standardized achievement tests. They have values of objectivity and dependability and provide a means by which some kind of comparison can be made to the sample of population used in the standardization process.

There is no magic in them, as Smith and Deschant point out.[34] There are many weaknesses that can be cited. But nevertheless, they have a place in the permanent record of the pupil.

We need not throw the baby out with the bath when we criticize tests. They are the best instruments we have at present. They are continually being improved, checked, and redesigned. They clearly have a place. Their place should be known and understood by those in contact with each child, including the parent.

The Children Speak About Self-Selection

After such a long and academic discussion it might be appropriate for children to speak for themselves. The following statements were solicited by a supervisor among children who had recently been moved from a traditional basal reading program into a literature-based, free-choice operation. The "halo" effect is pronounced, but is presented without apology. The children did have a real opportunity for freedom of speech, although they obviously wished to please their interrogator.[35]

Mrs. R: How do you like your new Reading Program?

Dean: Good, because I like to read. I'm an independent reader. We don't do *Friends & Neighbors*.

Do you like to choose your book or read the same as the others are reading? I don't like to read stories in the same book about the same persons. I like to read books and any book is good for me, just as long as they don't have the same persons every day. I read one story in *Friends and Neighbors*. Then I went to back of book and read *Story Book Friends*. Now I'm reading *What Is It* books and only have a couple more and I'll be finished with them.

[33] W. W. Cook and T. Clymer, "The Impact of Testing on School Organization," N.S.S.E. 62nd Yearbook, *The Impact and Improvement of School Testing Programs*, Chicago: University of Chicago Press, 1963, pp. 75–77.

[34] H. P. Smith and E. M. Deschant, *op. cit.*, p. 411.

[35] Taken from a tape recording made by Mrs. Vivian Rickabaugh, Wellsville, Pa., Elementary School.

Then what will you read?

> We have "appointments." When I finish a book and know all about it and all the words, I go up and tell my teacher about it and am checked.

Have you ever been sent back?

> No, I'm going to make sure I know it. We are going to make scrapbooks on a special subject. I choose presidents. I'm going to gather all the pictures I can. Then we write about each one, like Washington. Get a picture and write the things that go with that picture such as The First President of the United States.

Can you spell all those words?

> Some, but we can get them in the book we read about it.

Can you think of other ways?

> Help one another. Ask our neighbor. If they don't know we could ask the teacher.

Suppose she is too busy to help?

> Oh, I know—we all got one at Christmas time. I have an old one in my desk. A dictionary. Mrs. Smith, that's my teacher, showed us all, that is, in independent reading, how to use it.

Do you think you can read books on presidents? Not many are on second grade level.

> My teacher went over to Mrs. Longwell's room (a fourth-grade room) and got a book about presidents. She said I'm to try it.

Do you think you can read it?

> Yes, it's from fourth but my sister brings home books and I can figure them out. She's in sixth grade. I'm sure I can do them. I want to read about one that came from Pennsylvania. Mothers are coming in tonight after school and our teacher will show our mothers about our new project and how to line our scrapbooks. That's just mothers of us who are independent readers.

Mrs. R: How do you like your reading program?
Cathy: Good. We use different books. We don't have Dick, and Jane and Sally any more.

Why do you like this better than your old way?

> We can read about more people and see what they do. We can read about animals too. Besides this we read library books. In my little book I only have twelve. I get books from the public library and buy in stores too. I like to make scrapbooks and just the independent readers are doing that. Mine is about horses.

Why did you choose horses?

> I like them. My neighbor has a pony and it had a colt. My uncle has two horses and I ride them. I want to find out more about horses. I'll look in magazines for pictures and write about them. I'm reading a

new book now called *The Pony Farm*. When I finish it I'll pick another about horses. I want to read at least five. We must be done with the scrapbook by April.

Mrs. R: I hear you are in a new reading program. Tell me about it.
Wendy: Independent Readers. That's what we are called. I like it better.

Why do you like it better?

Oh—our teacher, Mrs. Smith, gave us a lot of books about things we like to read about. We were to choose something special and I chose presidents. Mommy told me I should have chosen elephants because they call me elephant sometimes.

Why did you choose presidents?

We had a book about presidents on the shelf. It looked good. I did read about animals and Eskimos.

Mrs. R: Why do you like your new Reading Program?
Nancy: It's fun and we don't have to go in the reading circles. I got tired listening to some one else read sometimes. Now I read to myself at my seat.

What do you read?

I pick a book and then make a report. Mostly I pick thick books like *Field and Fences*. I like animal stories. My special book is about horses. I'm going to make a scrapbook all about horses. It's to be finished the first of April. I'll use pictures I get and write about them. I'll read lots of books all about horses for independent reading. I read other books too, not all about horses. They are our library books. I read eleven others.

Mrs. R: I hear you have a new reading program. Can you tell me about it?
Susan: I like to read. I like everything about it. We all read out of different books and read at our seats by ourselves.

What else do you do?

We make book reports on what we read. I reported on four books already. Now I am going to read about something special. Mine is horses.

Why did you choose horses?

I like horses. Dad is thinking about getting me one. We are going to make a scrapbook. I can get pictures from magazines and papers and write stories about them too.

Would you like to be with the other group in reading?

I wouldn't want to go back to Dick and Jane. I like this much better.

Mrs. R: What do you like about your new Reading Program?

Phyllis: I read a little in *More Friends and Neighbors,* but not like the others. We independent readers pick the books we want to read. I like that. I can read a lot more.

What is your special interest to read about?

I choose dogs to read a lot about. I have two dogs at home that are my pets. Their names are Peanuts and Lucky. I'm reading a new book now called *The Dog That Grew Too Much.* I'm going to read all of it. Since I'll just read the parts I want to, and then write down things to put in a scrapbook. I'll get pictures out of magazines to put in it, too.

Mrs. R: Do you have a new reading program?
Patricia: We read in different books. Sometimes you tell about a book, write reports, and sometimes tell about it to the class. After that you can take it back and get a new one.

Do you like it better than the other program you had been following?

Yes. I can pick my own books and they are funny. I pick hard ones sometimes. So I can sound out words. My Dick and Jane book is on the shelf, but I didn't pick it. I didn't think it was funny.

What did you read?

Let's Look Around, Town and Country, Jack, and *Target Ship,* and some others.

What special are you going to read about?

"States" I saw a lot at home in the dictionary. I'm going to look in other books.

Mrs. R: How do you like your new reading program?
Cindy: I like the stories we read. We read about different animals and people. We read more books. We can still read library books. I read about twenty-four.

Did you pick something special to read about?

Yes, I picked horses. They are pretty. I read books I liked about horses. They were *Red Rose* and *Timmy Gets a Horse.* I'll get pictures and put in a scrapbook all about horses. We get new books often. It doesn't seem to take long to read them. Once we are finished we write about it. Then give it to our teacher. Then we can choose another.

Mrs. R: Do you like to read?
Judy: U-huh.

What do you think of your new program?

We have a scrapbook to make for our homework. We are to cut out pictures from magazines and papers about what we are reading and then paste them in and write something about them.

What did you read before you made a scrapbook?

We had a lot of books for the independent readers. Now we are choosing books about one thing.

What did you choose?

Children all over the world.

Why did you choose that?

I'd like to know all about other children. What they eat and what they wear. My mother and father were born in Germany. My grandparents, aunts and uncles, and cousins and friends all are in Germany. My Grandma and Pa came over to visit us three or four years ago. I want to know more about boys and girls over there, and Mrs. Smith said if I want to read only about Germany I can.

Do you like this type of reading better than the basic?

I like extra books. The other boys and girls only have one book about Dick and Jane and Sally. We have a library book on Dick and Jane and Sally. I read it for a library book. When we read one of those my teacher writes the name in a tiny book. Some only read one or two, but I read forty-nine. The more you read the faster you read.

Mrs. R: How do you like your new reading program?
Sally: Fine.

What do you like about it?

What we do and the books we read. We pick our own books now and if we can't find one the teacher helps us. If we don't know a word, for there are some hard ones, she will tell us. We must read close for we must make a report on why we like it and a little long.

Did you like your reading before?

I liked it when I had it but I like this better. Now we can glance through a book and if we don't think we'd like it we don't have to read it, but when we decide or make a choice, we must read it. We have *Think and Do* books. That's our workbook. We do that, too.

Do you take each page as it comes?

No, we go all over it. I don't think it is any harder in the middle or back than it is in the beginning. I don't think it is any harder than the ones we had in first grade. Our teacher tells us where to work sometimes and how to do them. Then later she checks them.

Mrs. R: What do you like about your new reading program?
Eileen: I like to read. We don't read about Dick and Jane and Sally any more. Oh, we can if we want to. Two are on the shelf. We can also borrow a book from Spot or Puppies. Those are other groups in the room. I read seven stories. They were stories I picked.

What are you reading now?

I am reading *Cowboy Sam*. We won't make a report this time. We will have appointments when we are ready and she will ask about the main characters in the book and what they do. Guess that's all.

Are you reading about anything special?

Yes, I'm making a scrapbook on "States." I've it already started.

Do you think you can get a book on your level?

> Yes, Mrs. Smith puts them on the shelf. I have one in my desk already on Alaska. Then I'll read about Arizona, Delaware, Hawaii, Illinois, New Mexico, Washington, Pennsylvania, Mississippi, Massachusetts, Indiana, and Montana. There are about twelve of them. I looked in the encyclopedia and found the flowers, flag, and bird. I'll get pictures and make them for my scrapbook.

Mrs. R: What are you doing these days in the room that you especially like?

Robert: Reading at our seats. I'm going to read about something special. I wanted to read about space. I knew it would be a nice thing to learn about. I want to see how many planets there are.

Do you all have the same reading program as others in the room?

> No. Oh—I like this year's reading better.

Why do you like it better?

> Because of different words and interesting words. I read much more than I used to. That was just about Dick, Jane, and Sally. We still have one on the shelf. I read just one of them to see if they were hard or simple.

Was it hard or simple?

> It was simple. So I'm not going to read it now. I want harder ones. I choose space because I can get books from our library. You know, the ones we have here in town. I'll get pictures from papers and magazines to use in a scrapbook I'm making. We have a telescope at home and have looked at four of the planets. I want to learn more about it. Then we'll get a better one, the best they have.

13

SHARING

When the reading is good, sharing cannot be prevented. A rumor flies around the class about a good book. "Can I have it next?—Can I have it next?" is the recurring question to the proud possessor—owner or not. There is no reason why this latent force cannot be harnessed and used for the proper kind of motivation. This is incentive of the highest order and is reported in many of the studies involving the use of free-choice materials.

Word of mouth is acknowledged—even by Madison Avenue—to be the most potent advertising medium of all. Children (and adults) learn about good books by hearing others talk about their favorites. There are innumerable ways in which stories can be shared. Informal reports, panel discussions, interviews, and book displays are some of the ways in which sharing can take place, and, as important, ways in which the teacher can further evaluate the reading of his class.

The old-fashioned book report is to be viewed dimly. Too often it had the effect of punishing a child for finishing a book. The chore of doing such a write-up dampened even the most ardent reader, and more than one group of educators agree that nothing stultifies reading interest more than a "required reading list" and its accompanying book reports.[1]

When sharing is reporting about books with some fervor, it is a favored activity—something to be looked forward to—a privilege if you will—and not a chore.

Here are two examples of forms that teachers used and did not find particularly discouraging to children's reading. This type of form can be multiplied by the thousand, as many teachers have developed their own. The point is that a record be made, either of all books read or of a select few, by the child who read them.

[1] Jean D. Grambs, *The Development of Lifetime Reading Habits: A Report of a Conference Called by the Committee on Reading Development*, New York: R. R. Bowker National Book Committee, 1954.

NAME_____ DATE _____

BOOK REPORT

TITLE_____

AUTHOR_____

Reason for liking or disliking the book: _____

_____

_____

_____

Something you learned from the book:_____

_____

_____

Favorite character_____

Why?_____

_____

_____

Courtesy of Rita Hamill, Spring Lake Heights School, Spring Lake Heights, N.J.

But there are other ways to tell about a book. A sharing time is one of them. In a very real sense, sharing offers the children a chance to solidify many skills of reading—notably comprehension and inference—by preparing an activity for classmates. In addition, it gives the teacher much insight into talents, thoughts, background, and interests of children that he might not notice at any other time. The child who puts on a skit about the opening scenes of *Treasure Island*, for example, might reveal unsuspected dramatic ability. With such material it is hard to spoil the basic excitement of the story.

"When we love something dearly," says Phyllis Fenner, "we long to share it with someone else."[2] Surely the way the telephone switch-

2 Phyllis R. Fenner, *Something Shared: Children and Books*, New York: John Day Co., Inc., 1955.

BOOKS I HAVE READ IN APRIL	
Name – Theresa	
The Kings Wish	the king alwas wanted to
	go fishing. He wished
	one day, when he went fish-
	ing he got captured then
	the bad men were capered.
	End.
The Curious Cow	Katy is a cow. She was
	alwas curious. She went
	into her neighbors yard
	for some other kind of
	grass. It taste the same.
	One time she got in a
	hole. She got out.

Copy of a child's report—second grade.

boads become hopelessly jammed whenever a major national event occurs testifies to this human need to "tell someone." In using this kind of an activity in the classroom the teacher finds in many cases that enormous amounts of information are transferred. Children, in

BOOKS I HAVE READ IN APRIL Name — Karen	
Benjamin B.	My book tells about a
	little boy who lives with
	his mother and father at
	the end of the st. It
	had a white coat of paint
	on it.
Highlights	I read Highlights. It
	has puzzles to do. games
	to play. pictors to
	color by numbers cross
	word puzzles and other
	things.

Child's record.

effect, teach each other. A peer group is often more interested in what its members say than what the teacher says, even when he is good! Their interest is almost guaranteed, at least at first, or until the person "center-stage" loses his audience. But that is another story to be told later.

An evaluation of these activities can, and perhaps should, be quite informal. But informal or not, the teacher is blind indeed who does not notice the increasing ability of certain children to work better with their fellows, or the rising intellectual curiosity of others, or just plain improved group work in general.

But let us get into the details of planning a sharing time.

SHARING—WHAT, WHEN, AND WHERE

From the bulk of the selected reading of a given child, one book should be presented to the teacher for an intensive private, one-to-one instructional period. As noted in Chapter 6, we urged that children be trained to select an appropriate book for such a conference, and to prepare themselves well for it. While arbitrary figures are always suspect, a child should have such a conference every few days, and should be held responsible for bringing up one book—of his own choice—out of every six to ten he reads. (Remember he lists *every* book he reads in his own notebook or file.)

Ind. Conf X

Sharing X

1. *Heidi* - Spyri
2. *Call It Courage* - Sperry
3. *"What Then, Raman?"* - Arora
4. *Dan Beard: Boy Scout* - Mason
5. *Abe Lincoln Gets His Chance* - Cavanah
6. *Custer's Last Stand* - Reynolds
7. *The Rise and Fall of Adolf Hitler* - Shirer
8. *Three Without Fear* - Du Soe

Aside from that single book for the individual conference, the children should be trained to select another book that will be shared —*in some way*—with the rest of the class (or school). Thus, out of six to ten books, roughly two are to be earmarked for special attention. The remainder are to be enjoyed in old-fashioned, recreational silent reading. The balance between oral and silent reading is maintained as oral reading is too often abused. The diagram on page 485 may give an idea of the ratio and is a way to keep track.

Once the teacher is sure that the children understand the proportion of books that are to be read silently, with one to be presented to the teacher in a conference and another to be used as a basis for some sharing activity, the class is ready to go.

Planning the Sharing Period

Planning for sharing can take various forms. For example, at times the sharing experiences are initiated by a child or children. At other times plans are formulated through teacher-pupil cooperation. In some instances sharing is solely teacher-directed. When this occurs the teacher is obliged to see that "those things planned for" are covered. Usually, however, sharing is an informal type of experience where children volunteer to "share their reading with us"—or "May I tell what I read?" etc. Regardless of how the sharing (or planning for it) is initiated, each child should know the purposes of the sharing sessions, his responsibilities in these sessions, and his role in fulfilling these obligations.

As we noted earlier (see page 72), the first item on the agenda of the independent work period is that of silent reading of a self-chosen book. But before the class settles down to that peaceful task, the teacher must make sure that Job Nos. 2, 3, 4, etc., are all ready when the child has "read himself out."

"What are you going to do when you have finished reading your books," the teacher asks. The responses could well go something like this:

"I'm going to finish my diorama about 'Caddie Woodlawn,' " says one.
"John and Tim and I are getting ready to do an experiment with magnets."
"Well, I found out that Mary and Sue have read the same book I have. So we are going to put on a play about the most exciting part of it."
"Bobby and I like poetry. We want to learn some and say it. Does any one want to join us?"

So it goes. These are ideas the children have thought of, although in the beginning the teacher could help them see the many possibilities of sharing.

If the reader will turn to Chapter 5, long lists of what can be done *during* that period *to get ready* for a sharing time are presented. The self-assignment factor is important, not only because children will push themselves harder when they are working on something they have thought of, but also because their ideas are frequently more creative, more original, and more engrossing for he who thinks them up (and for any audience) than those ideas that come from the teacher.

This is not to say that the teacher cannot enhance a child's ideas. He can, calling upon what should be his more extensive experience in the arts—fine and practical—as well as in the broader based adult world that includes theatre, books, and more advanced types of presentations. More detailed suggestions will be presented shortly.

When Is a Good Sharing Time?

When does sharing take place? A good rule of thumb is that it should be sometime other than the reading period, although some teachers do take a few minutes at the end of that time for a brief run-through on some of the finished tasks. However, the reading period is too short a time for much sharing, because the bulk of it is needed for instruction. Thus we feel that the best recommendation is to place sharing elsewhere on the school-day schedule.

Particularly do we like Friday afternoon. This is so often a bugaboo time for teachers, as they are usually tired and the children are not. As sharing is supposed to be an audience situation, so it is a time that the teacher can sit and be part of the audience (and take whatever notes about performance and growth that seem necessary), and enjoy the show, too.

Where Should Sharing Take Place

The usual place is in the classroom, although there are many times that other classes in the building or an assembly program is a fine forum for the presentations to be made. Sharing can even be done well between schools, although the danger of child exploitation for adult entertainment is very much present. Not so, however, in some of the suggestions coming later such as a pen-pal type of project; a tape-recorded exchange of views on a topic or an exchange of objects in connection with various units in social studies.

Although all of these out-of-the-classroom activities can be made to be educative, non-exploitative, and exciting, the fact remains that most sharing will take place between a teacher and his class in the normal self-contained type of classroom.

TEACHERS AND OTHERS CAN SHARE TOO

Nor is this sharing and reporting limited to students. The teacher who knows and loves books and reading and who reads and shares with children on the slightest occasion can work marvels in promoting good literature to his class. Some teachers take a few minutes during the planning period to "sell" a book—that is, talk briefly about it. Children become interested if teacher is. To read aloud is to expand horizons. The teacher is *supposed* to be the best oral reader in the class. Children's books become common property when presented orally.

Similarly the school librarian can do much to bring books to the attention of children:

There is a time for a librarian to tell a group of children about books, to take a pile of books at random, books that are new and unknown, books that are old and almost forgotten, books that ought to be read, and to tell children about them, picking out without shame, as the children do themselves when trying to sell a book, the part that would most probably be of interest. . . . Sometimes, the librarian tells about the author, how the book happened to be written. Sometimes she tells an anecdote that the illustrator—whatever may help the children remember the book.[3]

Parents, too, can foster love for reading when they love books. They can share and read aloud, and see that children have plenty of books to read for themselves. Parents will often need help and guidance from teachers and librarians. The more all concerned with educating the child act in concert, the more the will to read can be developed.

Wenzel[4] says, "A teacher who wants to help children enjoy literature creatively may need to consider ways to provide an *environment* that encourages creative activity, and experiences through which creative satisfaction can be enjoyed."

She deems these considerations as most important:

1. Provision for a flexible time schedule.
2. Provision for space and quiet and comfort.
3. Provision for a wide variety of materials.
4. Provision for freedom of selection.
5. Provision for many ways of dignifying products.

[3] *Ibid.*, *The Library in the Elementary School*, New York: Hinds, Hayden, and Eldridge, 1945, p. 26.
[4] E. Wenzel, "Extending Creative Experiences Through Literature," *Adventuring In Literature With Children*, Leaflet No. 10, p. 1. Washington, D. C.: Association for Childhood Education International, 1953.

Imposition of adult standards upon children and their work has frequently led to overlooking the rich and/or untapped resources of children's creative powers. The teacher must understand that it is his job to draw out those ideas that each child already possesses in his inner self. There is no prescription, no pat method of doing this. Instead, children are surrounded with many examples of creative work, that is, pictures, objects, writings, etc., that implant ideas and elicit reactions that arouse creative responses. The release of creative potential is triggered when the teacher provides time, encouragement, suggestions, and approval. Honest and sincere praise should be bestowed upon the creator as well as the product created. The product is dignified through sharing with the child's peers.

REAL AUDIENCE SITUATION

When children read aloud—their goal is to communicate with their audience. Expressive use of hands, voice, and face contribute to this communication. This gives pleasure to the audience as well as to the contributor. But when everyone else is silently reading the same material as that being read orally, little incentive exists to read expressively. A true audience situation exists when it (the audience) does not know what is coming next and is eager to find out. Thus, the love of becoming acquainted with stories via the many means available through sharing may be transmitted into a desire to read them.

Audience approval plays a major part in the satisfaction (dignifying the product) that a child gets that results in personal satisfaction, acquiring more poise, confidence, etc. Sometimes the audience will consist of the teacher. Other times it will range from groups within a class, to another class or classes, and finally to a school assembly. Each of these audience situations provides varying degrees of desirable outcomes.

The proof of a good sharing experience lies in the communication between the child(ren) and the audience. There must be understanding between the writer, speaker, painter, actor, dancer, etc., and his audience. Otherwise, no genuine purpose has been given to the child's efforts. The proof of the pudding comes when such remarks are heard: "Gee, that sounds like a good book! May I have it [the book] next, Miss Jones? Did he [the author] write any other books?" Sharing times are extremely valuable, for, when children love their books, they love to promote them.

ACTIVITIES FOR SHARING

Do not be discouraged if, in the beginning, all the reports seem to follow a stereotyped pattern—for example, "This book is about ____," or "The book ____ is about ____," or "This is an educational book and if you want to know what happened read it." First attempts usually seem this forced, but most of this unnaturalness soon fades away. It is amazing to watch the methods of reporting change, improve, and become more diverse and more effective as children gain experience in sharing. The patient teacher will not expect immediate results. Usually, just one original presentation is all that is needed to inspire others. Soon all sorts of original reports will follow. It seems as though the more creative or original the presentation, the more desirable the book will be to other children.

One fine source for ideas for sharing is *A Practical Guide to Individualized Reading.*[5] The organization presented hinges on six aspects of activities and experiences, as follows:

Activities and Experiences

Reading Aloud Activities
    Reading—
        a complete story
        interesting parts of stories
        particularly striking descriptive passages
        provocative conversational passages
        parts which delineate characterizations
        humorous incidents
        important events of a story
        most important facts of informational material
        the child's own book reports, reviews, resumes
        reviews of books in current newspapers

The activities or experiences listed above have important values. They—
    help the child to seek out pertinent materials.
    help the child to make appropriate selections.
    give the child the opportunity to read in a true audience situation.
    provide the listener with suitable "listening" materials.
    help the reader and audience to appreciate the good works of authors.
    help to develop sensitivity to language patterns.

[5] M. K. Draper and L. H. Schwietert, *A Practical Guide to Individualized Reading,* New York: Board of Education of the City of New York, Bureau of Educational Research, Publication No. 40, October, 1960, pp. 46–49. Printed with their kind permission. This publication is the result of a continued plan of experimentation under the direction of May Lazar and J. Wayne Wrightstone.

increase vocabulary.
develop oral reading skills.
furnish an active listening situation.

Oral Reporting Activities—Involving Telling
  Rather Than Reading Aloud

Telling one's opinion about a book; giving valid reasons for liking, disliking, or feeling lukewarm about the book
Preparing a short monologue from a favorite story
Telling humorous incidents
Telling important events of story; main facts of informational material
Giving an oral character sketch
Enumerating important mind pictures which the book conjures up
Choosing other titles for the story; indicating why these titles are appropriate
Giving another ending for the story
Comparing the current book read with a similar one in terms of content, makeup, design
Debating about diverse reactions to the same book
Giving illustrated accounts of informational material; using cartoons, post cards, photographs, slides, one's own drawings or paintings; using blackboard and flannel board as display backgrounds
Giving detailed directions on how to do or make things gleaned from "How-to" books; following through on this by the actual making of demonstrated material
Listening to stories on radio, TV, recordings; reporting back to class
Listening to other people's reviews of books; reporting back to class
Interviewing authors; making oral digests of interviews for the class
Reporting back on interesting books available at the local public library, at book stores; on books suggested on radio, TV
Conducting oral word games; illustrating sentences on blackboard, panel discussions, quiz games

The activities listed above have major values along with those listed under previous categories. They—

help the children to use language as a true form of communication.
help the child to come closer to his audience—with no book to act as a physical barrier.
help to develop increasingly better oral speech patterns.
develop ability to understand importance of building up to a climax.
develop ability to follow and give directions.
help the child to organize his thinking; give him functional practice in outlining, rearranging, organizing ideas in sequential fashion.
develop sensitivity to author's ability to build up a story interesting enough to retell—plot, suspense, movement, character definition.

Activities Involving Writing Experiences—
  Later Used for Audience Presentation

Writing—

an opinion of a book; in prose or poetry form; for class bulletin board,

class or school newspaper; for child's own class or classes on higher
or lower levels
brief biographical accounts of the authors; listing a number of books
written by the author
an advertisement or blurb for a book
two or three sentence comments about a book
original stories stimulated by stories read
simple satires on the stories; character sketches
brief impromptu skits; radio and TV scripts
a more ambitious playlet about a book
new endings to stories; comparing endings; giving reasons why
letters to pen pals in other lands about books read; e.g., comparing English editions of books, comics
notes to friends, past teachers, librarians for recommendations of books
letters to authors
a rebus story; making it large enough for a group of children to see
one's impression of a book by listing descriptive words; e.g., for "Alice
in Wonderland": *amusing, fantastic, amazing*
one's own questions about books; using them for discussions and checks
on comprehension
riddles and playing guessing games with them
original materials on special topics which spontaneously come to children
as they read; e.g., "If I Had Run the Zoo," "If I Lived in Fairyland,"
"If I Had Gone to Mars with Miss Pickerell"

Listing—
interesting, provocative, difficult, dramatic, dynamic words and phrases;
demonstrating meanings through reading or telling parts of the stories
in which they were found; writing one's own story using these words
ideas under special heading as "Things I Didn't Know Till Now"
interesting characters; playing guessing games as to the identity of the
character
the interesting events of a story in sequential order
Making scrapbooks or reference books on themes interesting to children;
using these later as source books for research
Preparing a class newspaper—selecting size, format, types of columns and
ideas to be included; writing, selecting, editing material

The activities and experiences listed above have major values
along with those listed under previous categories. They—

help to recommend books to other children. The child's own reaction to the
book may carry more weight with the other children than publishers'
commercial reviews or reactions.
foster better understanding of other children's contributions.
give functional practice in applying ideas, thinking, and organization to
writing situations.
lead to further communicative arts and other media of expression.
stimulate judgment and critical thinking; provide opportunity for "intelligent guessing."
increase awareness of good ideas and the wonder of words.
add layers of meaning to words; enlarge vocabulary; clarify concepts.
lead to experiences in other curriculum areas.

Dramatizations—

These overlap with the activities in other categories but are listed below because they specifically allow the child to project himself.

Dramatizing stories, poems, special events read about; devising and using props such as frames for TV screen, imitation microphone

Acting out skits, TV scripts, radio scripts, character sketches based on the actual content of the books read or created from the ideas suggested in the books read

Pantomiming persons and events; playing charades

Participating in quizzes patterned after well-known TV quiz programs; e.g., "What's My Name?", "Meet the Author," "The Last Word," Twenty Questions"

Dramatizing through puppets of all different kinds; hand puppets, paper bag, stick figures, shadow plays, string puppets (commercial or self-made)

Participating in impromptu improvisations: "The boy in my story today did something very funny. May I show you?"

The activities and experiences listed above have major values along with those listed under previous categories. They—

give the child opportunity for expressing himself in activities most every child enjoys.

give children opportunity to project themselves into other characters; to understand better the character by identifying with it.

help the child understand better the importance of sequential development of events.

give opportunity to apply evaluative skills in terms of selecting pertinent materials for dramatization; in selecting items or characters to depict.

provide good listening experiences.

Activities Involving Other Expressive Media

Painting and drawing—

favorite characters in books

posters for favorite books

a series of original illustrations for a story

decorative designs for book jackets

favorite scenes

visual pictures for mental images evoked by descriptive words and phrases

maps, graphs, time lines from informational materials

Making—

collage posters; using various kinds of materials such as pipe cleaners, stick figures.

book jackets including illustrations and a written blurb

dioramas, shadow boxes, cardboard stages, and other things with three-dimensional figures

dolls representing favorite storybook characters; dressing them; using cardboard, papier-mâché, plastic, paper, textiles

scrapbooks of various kinds and preparing the written material and drawing the illustrations; making picture files

Collecting appropriate items suggested by informational materials and making suitable display holders for them

Carving out likenesses of favorite characters, historical figures—using soap, clay, wood

The activities and experiences listed above have major values along with those listed under previous categories. They—

give the child opportunity for aesthetic and creative expression; afford stimulation to other children to express their ideas.

supply content for expressive media.

afford innumerable opportunities for conversation and discussion.

afford pleasure to others through the materials on display in the classroom.

afford many opportunities for group dynamics.

develop the child's thinking: gleaning ideas; sorting ideas; selecting ideas; planning type of media; evaluating plans; rejecting, referring, reviewing ideas.

Special Activities—Involving a Large Number
of Books or Special Services

Making tape recordings of stories read aloud; children's book reports; children's ideas about certain books

Holding a class "Book Fair" or grade "Carnival of Books"; organizing categories for books; displaying books; preparing creative materials about the books

Maintaining class and grade libraries; making necessary forms and posters; servicing other classes

Preparing programs for presentation in the assembly

The activities and experiences listed above have major values along with those listed under previous categories. They—

include and reach more children; stimulate their thinking; extend their reading horizon; crystalize interests.

afford opportunity to study style of authors; techniques of illustrating; types of printing.

provide for contacts with a large number of books of many different kinds.

give practice in the arts of organization, making judgments, evaluations.

afford opportunity for leadership; for functional "cooperative" efforts.

An overlapping but nevertheless useful list follows. It was developed from talking with and watching many teachers throughout the nation. Its similarity to the New York City Guide is caused by cross-fertilization of teacher to teacher, some of whom have been exposed to one or both sources. The reader may also look at Chapter 5 for similarly organized activities.

Sharing experiences utilize many practices that stimulate an interest in reading. Below is a listing of the various reporting techniques that have come to the author's attention. This listing is by no means complete.

1. Holding a panel discussion. This means of sharing can be used if several children have read the same book or books of the same type. A variation of this type of discussion is a pro and con panel. A few students who like the book and a like number who do not make up the panel. Both sides present their views before a student (who represents the author) "defends his work." A lively and balanced discussion can be maintained by an impartial moderator.

2. Encouraging students to write letters of appreciation to authors. A response is usually forthcoming from the latter (sometimes photographs, illustrations, etc., are included). These replies can be mounted on a bulletin board or inserted in a scrapbook kept for this purpose. Sometimes "favorite" authors will accept invitations to school assemblies.

3. Making book jackets. Children may decorate "original" book jackets with an appropriate picture for the cover (the title and author of the book should be included). Sometimes the name of the designer is also placed on the cover. A review of the book, an advertisement to accompany it, a teaser, etc., are written on the back. These covers may be fitted over the book itself or they may form a bulletin board display. See suggestion No. 1 above.

4. Dramatizing a story. A variety of methods may be used here.

   a. A student may dress as one of the characters and tell the role he plays in the book.

   b. A number of children may dress as the characters and dramatize part of the book, or present a tableau.

   c. The pupils may create a radio play—using the school's public-address system as the radio station and network.

   d. Tape-recording the play so that the tape can be played to other classes.

   e. Children make paper bag faces (puppets, etc.) of the characters and use these in telling the story.

5. Making murals or friezes. Almost any media can be used—water colors, crayons, charcoal, etc. Cutout characters, collage, cloth, wood, crepe paper, etc., add a three-dimensional effect.

6. Illustrating a scene from a book. Dioramas, drawings, posters, etc., are excellent means for sharing.

7. Reporting in the form of a telegram. Children have to learn to condense the plot. This offers opportunity for teaching main ideas, summarizing, etc.

8. Drawing cartoons or comic strips. This may be done as a means of sharing the plot, interesting facts, caricatures of the characters, etc.

9. Making crossword puzzles for other children to complete. Some children may have to read the book(s) in order to do the puzzle.

10. Constructing puppets, dolls, etc., of story characters and costuming them.

11. Creating an attention-getting advertisement of a book.

12. Writing book reviews. These may be submitted to the school or local newspaper.

13. Constructing three-dimensional models. Table top, sand table scenes, shoeboxes, shadow boxes. cardboard stages, dioramas, etc., can spice up reporting activities.

14. Comparing movies, or radio, or television programs with the books that they are based on. How were they different? How were they the same? Which was better? Why?

15. Making radio or television announcements in which a student prepares a commercial to advertise the book he has read.

16. Lecturing a la "Burton Holmes" type of travelogue using postcards, photographs, pictures, slides, etc., to illustrate a travel book that has been read.

17. Assembling and hanging mobiles. Simple mobiles can be made from clothes hangers. Pictures or drawings of the characters of stories may be hung from these. Mobiles of titles of books read together with the authors' names and short statements about the books may be used.

18. Sharing opinions of books by writing them on file cards or elsewhere and making them available to all.

19. Telling the story to a musical accompaniment (phonograph, tape recording, or done by the child or a classmate on a musical instrument.

20. Encouraging children to comment on illustrations in books they have read. Children will soon become familiar with names and styles of famous illustrators, e.g., Leo Politi, Tony Palazzo, etc.

21. Displaying original illustrations of books on loan from publishers.

22. Presenting the story with the help of the flannel board. Children make the characters from paper. These are colored. A small piece of sandpaper is placed on the back of each cutout so that it sticks to the flannel board. Some children "can operate the characters while others narrate the story."

23. Writing a synopsis of the story. When this is read to the rest of the class, questions arise that often lead to some excellent extemporaneous book talks.

24. Making lists of new, unusual, or interesting words. The student might share his list with the class—using the words in context, or giving synonyms, antonyms, or the derivation. In this way children can get the "feel of the book."

25. Mapping story events is great fun for boys and girls. Children make a map of the real or storied events as they happened in the story. This aids in following relationships or the sequence of events.

26. Using a map in which books concerning the different countries, states, or cities are placed on the map.

27. Making a time line or a map of an historical book.

28. Writing letters in which the pupil pretends he is a minor character and gives a first-person account of the main characters' actions.

29. Constructing the face and feet of a character and attaching these to a wire base so that the book leans between the "face and feet." The character is then placed on the display table.

30. Presenting book reviews to classes of younger children.

31. Making book reports without endings. The pupil gives the plot, however, instead of finishing the report, he stops just before the climax. Other children give their endings. Then the reporter gives the real ending.

32. Using clay, plaster, wood, soap, etc., to carve out models, illustrations, likenesses, etc., of favorite characters found in books.

33. Writing publisher's "blurbs" in which pupils attempt to sell their books in precise and colorful terms. Children may write two or three "blurbs" presenting different aspects of their books.

34. Giving one's opinion of the book: giving valid reasons for liking, disliking, or feeling so-so about the book.

35. Giving detailed directions on how to do or make things learned from "how-to-do" books—a follow-up is the actual attempt at making the item, doing the experiment, following the recipe, etc.

36. Writing or sharing original stories or books stimulated by stories read.

37. Participating in quizzes patterned after well-known television quiz programs such as: "Meet the Author," "The Last Word," etc.

38. Dramatizing through puppets of all types, for example, hand puppet, paperbag puppets, stick figures, commercial or handmade puppets, string puppets, potato puppets, etc.

39. Listing ideas under special headings as "things I didn't know till I read _____."

40. Pantomiming persons or events: playing charades, etc.

41. Writing a letter to a friend, librarian, library board, superintendent, or board of education to recommend a book—an excellent way to share a book.

42. Comparing one book with a similar one or with others written by the same author leads children to do critical analysis of that which is read.

43. Holding a school or class book fair in which categories are organized for books, books are displayed, with creative materials prepared and displayed along with the books.
44. Making models of things read about in stories such as: a house, train, doll, boat, etc.
45. Different schools (or individual classes in them) can make tape-recordings upon books (or topics that are handled in books) and exchange them through the school's delivery system. Teachers could make the contacts through personal or professional channels.
46. Parents could be group chairmen during a Friday Book Discussion period.[6]
47. Crewel, applique, Swedish embroidery, or other types of decorative sewing can be used to dress dolls representing book characters.

SUMMARY

How can sharing be evaluated? How can the time consumed be justified? As mentioned above—such evaluation cannot be obtained from "objective testing." Rather, the authors feel, we must first examine our own objectives—our own values. For example, is it important for children to learn to work with groups of their peers? Are we, as teachers, obligated to guide children's thinking—to help them develop more positive attitudes toward themselves—toward learning—toward school? Is it important in a democracy to be able to stand up—to express oneself—to present one's point of view? How do we learn to consider the rights and privileges of others? Is this important? Should each member of a group—a class—be given equal opportunities? If these and similar outcomes have enough value for children, then we need (as a means to an end) to develop greater skills in the area of sharing thereby justifying any amount of time consumed.

Sharing encourages (as we have seen) children to become active participants, doers, and thinkers—not passive absorbers of entertainment. It is the organizing—the educative meaning and value in the sharing activities of children. Expression through many media is an important aspect of creative expression. As in all creative work, the teacher is less concerned with the product that is made than he is with the growth that is taking place within the child. He is interested in the child's release of tensions, the growing freedom in expression, the emerging sense of power, and the worth of ideas and abilities. Sharing is a means to an end—and the end is a more wholesome and more happy child.

[6] This was done effectively in Valley Stream, Long Island, N. Y., in the fifth-grade class of Grace Palizonti.

14

THE BOUNTIFUL WORLD
OF BOOKS

At no time in the history of the world have there been more books available than now. Books for old and young alike are pouring off the presses in unprecedented quantities. Although some would argue that the quality of books is deteriorating, the charge is not proved, and even were it so, the sheer volume of publishing provides, proportionately, enough good literature to meet the reading needs of American school children.

Children's books traditionally have fallen into two categories, those of trade, or library style, and of texts, or "reader" style. Currently, however, there is an increasing amount of what textbook publishers call "supplementary" books intended for instructional reading programs. These books are neither fish, fowl, nor good red herring. Their existence is an admission of the dull, uninteresting writing so characteristic of their close relatives, children's texts. Supplementary books exist to meet the market of harassed teachers who cannot get their pupils to like to read basal readers. They are a "half-way house" to good literature. On the other hand, there is no doubt that too few tradebooks are available that, although interesting enough, are easy enough for the intended age group to read.

Thus, in an unprecedented state of dismay, we find a multimillion dollar industry responding to a changing market. The existence of basal readers will not be seriously challenged for some time. Yet the demands of the schools for far better books are having their effects.

In order for children to learn to read from good books, there must be enough of them in each classroom. There should be at least three different titles for each child in a class, and even more if possible. This is not intended to be an arbitrary figure, and does not show that the program works better when there are far more than that. Thus one hundred books would seem to be a minimum to begin a program that is based upon the act of self-selection.

The bountiful world of books.

SOME PRINCIPLES BASIC TO BOOK SELECTION

What range in children's reading levels can a teacher expect to find in his class? Children in the same classroom will differ greatly in their ability to read. Betts[1] found that children at the end of first grade will range in ability from the prereading to the third-grade

[1] Emmett A. Betts, "Differences in Readiness for Reading," *Visual Digest*, Vol. VI, No. 1, Summer, 1942, pp. 5–8.

level. Durrell[2] in his classic study found that ability in a typical third-grade class may range from the first- to the eighth-grade level. According to Olsen,[3] children in a typical fifth grade can be reading on nine different levels. The older the grade, the wider the individual differences in the class.

Thus, books are needed on many levels, ranging from a grade or two below the slowest reader to a grade or two above the highest reader as determined by reading test scores. Teachers of first grade, for example, will select books for children with abilities ranging from the picture books of the earliest prereading levels to those of at least third-grade difficulty. Supplies need to be changed as the year goes by, to keep up with the rising levels of ability. The book supply of intermediate-grade teachers will thus span a range of six to nine or ten grades.

Although a bright child can read materials of greater difficulty than the average child, his interests, in general, are about the same. Children in school need books that (1) they like and (2) they can read. Hence, a variety of books on the same topic differing only in level of readability is important. Differences in topics, as well as in readability, however, can be found by the teacher through a continuous survey of the interests of his children.

A great variety of materials are needed if a child is to select a book he can handle with ease and comfort—if he is to progress naturally. When a child is permitted to select his materials, he usually will choose a book he *can* read, or a book so closely allied with his interest that the use of context comes into its full glory. In time, through the individual conference if in no other way, a child will *reject* books that are too easy, too difficult, or lacking in interest. But opportunity and availability of such a book are prerequisites to self-selection.[4]

HOW TO INCREASE THE BOOK SUPPLY

Getting three to five different titles from all the possible sources can be quite an operation. Let us list some suggestions and then go into detail about their implementation:

[2] Donald D. Durrell, *Improvement of Basic Reading Abilities,* New York: World Book Co., 1940, p. 39.

[3] Willard C. Olsen, "Seeking, Self-Selection and Pacing in the Use of Books by Children," *The Packet,* Vol. 7, No. 1, Boston: D. C. Heath and Co., Spring, 1952.

[4] See also E. E. Schatz, *Exploring Independent Reading in the Elementary Grade,* Columbus: Ohio State University Press, 1960.

1. Enlist the school librarian's aid.
2. Seek out public library supplies.
3. Use bookmobiles.
4. Use personal library cards, child and adult.
5. Use the regular book order.
6. Book fairs for new and used books.
7. Teacher representation on school budget committees.
8. Paperback books, newspapers, and magazines.
9. Use basal and supplementary readers.

First, how is the school librarian best used?

1. Enlist the School Librarian's Aid

The book expert of a school building should be the librarian. Taking all of the money[5] that might be available to these unsung heroes and heroines of the book-securing battlefields, teachers should receive lists of books that can be bought for the given amount of money. Whether the amount of money be large or small, the librarian is the advisor and counselor on its spending. Perhaps the teacher makes final decisions as to titles, but the librarian provides the information upon which decisions are based.[6]

2. Seek Out Public Library Supplies

Visit all libraries, local, county, state, within range, and inquire as to how to obtain boxes of books on loan as well as their policy of selling "throw-outs." Now that library service is being used at a greater rate than ever before, librarians are complaining, and being listened to by authorities, about too low inventories to serve their clients. One of the finest problems in reading is developing—that of empty shelves in libraries. Even so, circulation is nowhere near what it should be. Children will become more and more avid book readers if encouraged by good books readily available. For classroom use boxes of books can be secured—usually one for every child. This is not enough, and teachers must develop the art of pressure. Librarians should welcome such pressure and join forces with teachers to demand, for that is the word, more tax support from state legislatures. This is particularly true in states where politicians consider

---

[5] Possible sources of money will be discussed shortly.

[6] In this context can be seen the problem presented by basal and supplementary readers. They are difficult to classify at best, and librarians are not supposed to be classroom instructors. Therefore, as far as such material is concerned, librarians are of little help to teachers.

reading as something that takes place only as a subject. Librarians, whether they know it or not, are often the best teachers of reading in the nation, if only because they put children and books together.

In these days, when it seems as though school districts vie with each other in building elementary schools that have beautiful auditoriums and are equipped with the latest electronic gadgets for intercom systems; when gymnasiums take precedence over well-stocked school library shelves; when communities sacrifice to build Little League stadiums to the neglect of public libraries, school budgets *must* make more provision for the establishment for the type of book collections than they do now.

Reading materials for classroom use are insufficient when supplied largely through central school, county, or state libraries. Although book drives or book-buying campaigns sponsored by Parent-Teachers Associations and community service clubs or by children's contributions from personal libraries are helpful, such practices do tend to reduce the interest of citizens to contribute to support of the school's basic learning aid—namely, its reading matter. The profession, through able leadership from administration, should lead local schoolboards to realize that school budgets must include tradebooks for classroom programs. Only then can we envision those agencies noted above to answer the call for materials to augment class collections. There are means of increasing the number of materials in classroom libraries.

AVAILABILITY OF TRADEBOOKS. What must happen is that tradebooks become as easily available as basal readers are now available. At present this is simply not the case. Any teacher with twenty or thirty dollars to spend has to go through agonies of searching through booklists of hundreds and hundreds of books, or to depend on the librarian (remember there are only 34% of American schools with such personnel) for help. Some kind of a system is patently called for and should be the product of negotiations between the publishing industry and the teaching profession.

However, the push must come from the professional side of the fence as publishers' profits center mainly around text and technical books rather than tradebooks. This is not an insignificant point. Approximately 10% of the black ink comes fom tradebooks. Nevertheless, no publisher would refuse to sell more of any title he has. It is certainly up to an interested group of professional educators and librarians to work out a plan to simplify tradebook procurement in the classroom.

3. Bookmobiles

One community christened its three brand new bookmobiles "Hither," "Thither," and "Yon."[7] While there are many abroad not bequeathed with such charming names, the bookmobile operation is an admirable one indeed. Teachers should request it. Too often a community will not have adequate enough services of this nature. Teachers' insistence upon more and better services (the more vocal the better) again will improve matters. It is the rare politician that will argue against books. It is the rare politician that will argue against anything that the public truly wants. The point is that teachers must be sure to be heard.

Children in classes using the services of a bookmobile can learn to select books wisely when they are made responsible for two book choices: one for themselves and one for the rest of the class. The power of peer approval for a loved book is not to be discounted. One reading skill is that of assessing value of reading material. How can it better be taught than by the act of selecting for yourself and for your friends? Certainly not by a workbook exercise entitled "How to Choose a Book!"

4. Personal Library Cards

When each child in a class has a personal library card, it is not hard to see how the classroom book supply can be upped by the encouragement of their use. Thirty children multiplied by thirty cards can mean one hundred and twenty books. A neighborhood library can be cleaned out of children's books in a week if the school really promoted the use of personal cards. Aside from children's cards, many parents' cards can be brought into use. Thirty children means sixty parents. This could mean sixty books and still leave the family with enough choices within the book-borrowing limit to allow for adequate usage.

A trip to the library can hardly hurt the cause of reading. It is a wonder that teachers do not go more often. "We are too busy," some say. Too busy doing what? What is more valuable than exposing childen to the library once a week, or even a month?

The School Library: A Discussion

The advent of approaches to reading that allow for individual conferences and self-selection of books has presented librarians with the

---

[7] Grand Rapids, Mich.

best argument for increased budgets they have ever had. It will be unfortunate if they do not take advantage of the opportunity. Even though 66%[8] of all elementary schools lack a library, let alone a librarian, the climate has never been better for the use of school library services.

For the first time an agreement between teachers and librarians on how to achieve what has always been their mutual goal, making children book readers and book lovers, is in sight. The library is becoming more and more a vital resource to teachers. Several suggestions would seem in order to smooth the way for even more fruitful mutual help programs.

1. Libraries in schools must be the "holder of learning" and therefore should foster, and keep in motion, a CLASSROOM library for each teacher. Too often, because the library is at a starvation level, librarians are loathe to let their puny supplies be circulated among the classrooms. Nothing has caused more friction between teachers and librarians than this practice, which we consider shortsighted. The shelves of all libraries should be testimony to the scarcity of funds—*they should be empty!*

Each building, then, should have enough money for a centralized library as well as a classroom library for each teacher in the building.

2. As the excellent *Standards for School Library Programs*[9] states: The librarian is an assistant to the teacher. The less the librarian is an instructor, the better. Even story-telling can be overdone, although it seldom so happens. The implications of this statement are apparent at several points. What does a librarian do when a child is at that point of choosing a book? We hope he disappears in order for the child to be alone with himself in a moment of truth. Children attending book fairs or simply going with Mother to the supermarket are encouraged to become lost in the act of selecting a book. This should be standard practice in a school library.

TEACHERS IN CHARGE OF DISCIPLINE. Similarly, if the librarian is to be the assistant to the teacher, the latter must be responsible for the class behavior in the library. Librarians should refuse to discipline children in the library, and for that matter, refuse to accept the class whose teacher disappears immediately.

EXTEND UNSCHEDULED LIBRARY TIME. Further there must be more unscheduled time for investigation and browsing in the library. In

---

[8] This figure is subject to upward revision since 1961, but is still grossly inadequate as a measure of the interest of this society in libraries in schools.

[9] American Library Association, 1960. Chicago, Ill.

Famous Americans in books.

the capacity of assistant to teachers, the librarian can work with individual children who come to track down a specific reference or item. Certainly, in these days of large school buildings, a library schedule is important for optimum use. But once a class has taken over for a period, the librarian can be free to assist such research. More appropriate, however, is the extension of unscheduled time. Teachers and pupils can be restricted to such times if overcrowded conditions exist.

ORGANIZE BOOK SHELVES ON TOPICS, NOT DIFFICULTY. Librarians presume upon the role of instructor too much when they take it upon themselves to ability-group the books and, therefore, the children who use them. To say to a child "That book is too hard for you" is not the business of the librarian. It is the business of the teacher, and even he should tread lightly with such a statement. The little boy who asked for a book on moths, and brought up one entitled "Mothers and Mothers-To-Be" might well pose a problem for a librarian seeking to assist and not teach. The main point, of course, is our suggestion that the shelves of the library should be organized upon TOPICS, not upon the specific reading level of the books. Only the widest range of difficulty should be indicated, as, for example, primary through the fourth grade, and fifth grade through the senior high school. Although it may be presumptuous of nonlibrarians, like the writers of this book, to tread upon the unfamiliar territory of book organization, it must nevertheless be said that poor readers of older ages do not eagerly seek books on the "Easy Book" shelf. There is a stigma about walking over to the "Easy Book" shelf. Browsing need not be furtive, and opportunities for *pupil* assessment of readability and value should be present. If librarians would mix up, under whatever titles, many books of wide-ranging difficulty under each specific heading, children will increase their ability to assess value independently. Then teachers will discover what they must do to facilitate better choosing and evaluating. Spoon-feeding and censorship are not necessary. Adults can help. But the choice is the child's.

Finally, a school library makes the entire collection available to every child in every class. Under any type of instructional program, the school library provides a valuable service, and provides it more economically, for it must cater to the wide ranges of needs, abilities, and interests found within the entire building.

Studies have shown that books first on the list of children's choices are those most readily available to them. It is fair to conclude, then, that accessibility of books will determine in large measure, not only whether a child will read, but what kind of books he will read.

To conclude, what is the librarian's role? She obviously plays a major part in the program. Through frequent conferences with each teacher and through frequent talks with children, she becomes aware of the interests and needs of a particular child. The librarian can often come up with the book or magazine in which she thinks a child may be interested. The cooperation of the librarian helps provide for changes in the classroom libraries as new interests arise and old ones wane.

5. Using the Regular Book Order

Many schools allocate funds on a per teacher basis. Tradebook lists are available (see pages 513–14) from librarians and other sources. Once a teacher knows how much money can be spent, these orders can be made out.

If, as usual, there is not enough money for tradebooks, then teachers can look at the cost of other supplies. Why is it necessary for every child to have a workbook in every subject area? For that matter, why is it necessary for every child to have a workbook in a single area, or even for any workbooks to be used at all (see Chapter 5)? The money spent on such material can be spent on tradebooks. If a workbook costs 90¢ and there are thirty members in the class, that is $27.00 that can be used in other ways. Multiply that by the number of subjects for which workbooks are purchased and it is easy to find upward of $100 for tradebook purchasing.

The use of any books that do not belong to the children themselves brings up the problem of lost books. Whether or not a child takes a book from the library collection, or from a donated supply in the book center, there must be a kind of book accounting. A child librarian can be a most successful appointment.

One suggestion that has worked for the authors when books are lost might be useful to some readers. All teachers face the grim day when a book is missing. Pleas are of no avail. The book is gone. To meet this crisis, as books are valuable, not for their cost so much as for what they represent, the teacher might call the class together for a discussion of the problem.

"What shall we do to find this book—or replace it if we don't find it?"

If, in the beginning of the term, some agreement was made that all lost books would be replaced by the children—as the children are the ones who lost them—the answer to the question resolves itself around: "How much will it cost?" The school librarian can provide the list price. The teacher then can divide that price by the number in the class—or it can be part of the math for the day. The result will be that each child will need to contribute a sum of money. The point is that *every* child will need to contribute. The pressure to find the book is intensified, and often it appears as mysteriously as it disappeared.

Other ways of bringing responsibility to bear upon those children who are too poor to contribute, or those so well off as to make a small sum meaningless, may be necessary. But somehow lost books must be the responsibility of every member of the class. Forbidding the taking of books home is not the answer. Children should take any and all books home that they wish. How better can the love of reading be fostered? So they might come back with a piece of bacon as a bookmark—but that is another problem. Its solution is analogous to others that develop concepts of responsibility and citizenship.

6. Book Fairs

There are book fairs and book fairs. Some are a means of selling the poorest of children's books. But others are a means of selling books of better quality. Help in planning book fairs is available from many sources.[10]

When parents' organizations conduct such events they kill two birds with one stone—book ownership and fatter treasuries. Children buy books that can hardly hurt their reading ability, and the organization makes at least 10% on the purchase price of new books.

A growing practice is that of running a "Used Book Fair." Often families outgrow some of their books and yet find the price of new books prohibitive. A used book fair is a good way to meet the changing needs of all concerned.

7. Teacher Representation upon School Budget Committees

Teachers must be heard on committees that spend the taxpayers' money for schools. A community that spends hundreds of thousands of dollars upon new buildings should ask teachers' representatives about the priority of buying a $15,000 loud-speaker communication system in preference to buying $15,000 worth of books. The priority of an outsize gymnasium over an outsize library needs to be established. Should school buildings have plaster walls and fewer books or the less expensive cement block walls and more books?

Teachers are often the ones who know these things. Although many administrators have their values straight about the wasting of taxpayers' monies, and many teachers have not the vaguest notion about such matters, nevertheless, broadly based professional advisory committees to local schoolboards tend to help in the wiser disbursement of funds, and certainly make graft more difficult.

"What is the most important expenditure?" is the one question that needs to be asked. Then active teachers, librarians, and admin-

[10] Scholastic Magazines, New York, N. Y. *Manual on Book Bazaars;* Children's Book Council, New York, N. Y. , *How to Run A Book Fair.*

istrators can be heard on the matter of more dollars for books—as against reduced dollars for fancy buildings. When such personnel speaks up, the books will be there. It is not hard to convince local citizens that books are important. Of whatever political or religious affiliations, citizens rarely object to more books.

Thus, supplying an extensive variety of tradebooks should not be an insurmountable obstacle. Irene Vite[11] puts the problem in its proper perspective when she states:

> . . . what a veritable treasury of paper-covered pre-primers, hard-covered primers, first, second, and third readers may be purchased for the price that one would pay for many copies of a basic set of readers and one or two supplementary sets.
>
> In a basic and supplementary set a school might perhaps have over two hundred and forty books and still own only about eight titles. In ordering so-called "readers" for use in my individualized reading program I usually request three copies of one title. . . . At this rate of three books per title, approximately eighty different titles can be had for the same price as the eight titles just mentioned.

8. Paperback Books, Newspapers, and Magazines

The increasing numbers of excellent titles from the publishers of paperback books has proved to be a godsend to teachers who are trying to diversify their reading material. Even the semihard-cover books that keep children happily on the floor of supermarkets while their mothers shop are not to be scorned as useless. The fact of the matter is that cheap production methods are frequently being used for books that have been written, selected, or edited by competent editorial boards.[12]

Scholastic Book Services has developed two excellent book clubs for the elementary grades. The Lucky Book Club is geared for second and third graders and has many fine titles. The Arrow Book Club, for fourth to sixth graders, regularly presents titles in fiction and factual material. In addition, the Scholastic Book Service presents a special discount catalogue of five hundred paperback volumes suitable to grades four through twelve, called "Reader's Choice."

As with bookmobiles, there are many heartwarming stories about

[11] Irene Vite, "A Primary Teacher's Experience," *Individualizing Reading Practices*, Miel, A. V. (ed.), New York: Bureau of Publications, Teachers College, Columbia University, 1958, p. 21.

[12] As we go to press two exceptionally well organized and useful references on paperbacks have appeared: Robert E. Newman, "Paperbacks in the School Bookshop and Classroom," *Language Arts of Individual Inquiry*, Unit Two, Chicago: Science Research Associates, November 15, 1965; Max Bogart, *Paperbound Books in New Jersey Public Schools*, Trenton, N. J.: State of New Jersey Department of Education, Division of Curriculum Instruction, 1965.

these book clubs: how teachers and children sacrificed, or had sales of all kinds; how children actually gave up candy money to buy a book of their own. Unhappily, there seem to be some administrators who view these clubs dimly, their reasons being, as should surprise no one, "The skills aren't being taught," or "We take up too many collections anyway." The matter would seem to rest on priority or a sense of values. For children to have paperback books rather than *no* books would seem to be a worthwhile goal. When the pooling of classroom purchases provides for bonus books, as provided by these book clubs, would suggest that the acquisition of *more* books is a good thing. We are critical of these administrators and without a qualm, urge classroom teachers to develop these book clubs.

The education directors of many paperback publishing firms will place a teacher on their mailing list upon request, and thus assure that that teacher will be kept abreast of all new titles. Probably more interesting to a school librarian or elementary supervisory concerned with book purchases, the R. R. Bowker Company[13] will send four issues a year of *Paperbound Books in Print*, the most helpful source of what is available in this type of book. Bowker also publishes *Publisher's Weekly* in which all the paperback news is noted each week.

REFERENCES ON CHILDREN'S MAGAZINES AND NEWSPAPERS. One source of material that is frequently overlooked is the magazine. Magazines and newspapers (along with paperbacks) are relatively inexpensive materials. These definitely have a place in the reading program. Among the more useful references for materials appropriate for the elementary school level may be included:

1. *101 Magazines for Schools; Grades 1-12*, Ruby E. Cundiff, Nashville, Tenn.: Tennessee Book Co., 1959.
2. *Magazines for School Libraries*, Laura K. Martin, New York: H. W. Wilson Co. Annual.
3. *Magazines for Elementary Grades*, Curriculum Division of the Madison Public Schools, Madison, Wis.: 1953.
4. *The Dobler International List for Boys and Girls*, Muriel Fuller,New York, N.Y.

The use of classroom newspapers has become a prevalent practice throughout the nation. The *Weekly Reader* and *Scholastic Magazines* are the best known. However, teachers should not overlook those put out by the Civic Education Press[14] of Washington, D.C.

The way magazines are used, however, leaves much to be desired. Invariably there will be one page of these weekly sheets that is a

13 New York, N. Y.
14 *Young Citizen*, etc.

test. In this case, the publishers cannot be blamed for responding to the market demands of teachers, who in their Friday afternoon state of exhaustion are insistent upon having something "to keep the kids busy." The fallacy of reading in order to answer questions has been dealt with elsewhere. On these "test" pages, the same error is made as in workbooks. It is a flagrant example of what reading instruction should not be.

Teachers need to diversify these newspapers in order to have children choose to read from a variety of material. Particularly if children are paying for subscriptions with their own money, they should have the right of free choice. In any event, the "make-work" aspect of the weekly newspaper test is to be criticized. There are better ways to be sure children understand the week's news. For example, discussion in a round table or panel-type formation. Developing differing points of view is a fine way to bring the outside world into the classroom itself. The standard question-and-answer type of activity indulged in by too many teachers—and often in spite of directions in the teacher's guide for the week—is to be discouraged. (See Chapter 10.)

This regimented manner in which newspapers are used is merely substituting a newspaper for a basal reader. There should be three or four "papers" at various levels of difficulty, as well as three or four different children's newspapers available in the classroom throughout the week.

Although newspapers, paperbacks, and magazines are not suitable for heavy circulation, they are invaluable adjuncts to classroom libraries. They can help children in reading independently, in becoming diversified readers, and in reading for depth.

Paperbacks have additional value. They help develop good readers through ownership of books. Ownership of books is psychologically closely related to enjoyment of books. Ownership makes the book readily available for several readings—no library deadlines have to be met.

Use of newspapers, magazines, and paperbacks will not detract from school or public library programs nor will the advantage of hard-covered tradebooks be ignored.

9. Use Basal and Supplementary Readers

While complete sets of basal readers for a class can be abandoned in favor of tradebooks, soft or hard covers, there is a place for collections of basals, too. One fourth-grade teacher scrounged a few copies each of third-, fourth-, and fifth-grade basals and began allowing her children to choose *any* stories therein.

Teachers can quickly increase the number of different books in their rooms without needing to increase the actual number of books. This is done by exchanging one set of readers for six books of another set of readers with another teacher in the same building. Although more creative and more artistic books are available, this is not to say that basal readers, especially those above the pre-primer and primer level, do not contain stories that attract children. They do, often watered down and emasculated, but nevertheless present. Using these books *hard* will wear them out faster, thus more rapidly releasing book budget money for tradebooks. The money used to buy basals often should have been used for better books anyway. But once spent, there is little that can be done. It is *future* expenditures on basal materials that must be prevented. Thus basals and their close relatives, the supplementary texts, need to be used until they are worn out. Then the argument for their replacement need not be made on the basis of lack of money.

The Use of Book Lists

The current archaic and wasteful methods of procuring tradebooks intended for classroom use are not in harmony with our technological age. There are many fine book lists available. But the sheer volume of book publishing makes most book lists difficult for use by the always overbusy classroom teacher. Approximately two thousand books are coming off the presses these days that are not textbooks. This is a staggering amount. Lists from professional educational organizations try to meet this problem.

> *Adventuring With Books.* National Council of Teachers of English, Champaign, Ill. *Children's Books for $1.25 or Less.* Association for Childhood Education, International, Washington, D. C.

Librarians, who earn their living at book selection, present such excellent sources as:

> *Notable Children's Books.* Children's Services Division, American Library Association, Chicago, Ill.
>
> *School Library Journal.* New York, N.Y. Monthly magazine, September through June, that reviews most children's books.
>
> *The Horn Book* (Boston 16, Mass.). Devoted to children's literature.

Best Books for Children (R. R. Bowker, New York, N.Y. 10036). 2500 books revised annually.

A Basic Book Collection for Elementary Grades (American Library Association). A well-selected list.

Children's Catalog (H. W. Wilson Co., New York). Published yearly, available in all libraries indicates reading difficulty for second and third grade children.

Wisconsin State Reading Circle Board (Wisconsin State Dept. of Public Instruction, Madison). Published yearly, arranges carefully selected books by grade levels, one through eight.

Some references have been found to be helpful to classroom teachers.

1. Larrick, Nancy. *Teacher's Guide to Children's Books.* Columbus, Ohio: Charles E. Merrill Books, Inc., 1960. An excellent source for those teachers who have money to spend or questions to ask about children's books.

2. Barbe, Walter O. *An Educator's Guide to Personalized Reading.* New York: Prentice-Hall, Inc., 1962. Chapter 6 contains many details that are helpful indeed.

3. Arbuthnuot, May Hill. *Children and Books* (rev. ed.). Chicago: Scott, Foresman & Co., 1957. Is still a major text including a comprehensive list and detailed study of books children like.

4. Bowker, R. R., Co. *Best Books for Children.* New York: 1961. Contains a graded, annotated list of 3,300 books for children.

5. Fenner, Phyllis. *Proof of the Pudding: What Children Read.* New York: John Day Co., 1957. A comprehensive list of the best books of all times, why children like them, and interest level. It offers such suggestions as "read-aloud" books and 100 best books for the home library.

6. Giles, Ruth, and Cook, Dorothy. *Children's Catalogue.* New York: H. W. Wilson & Co., 1951. This book contains 3,400 titles—annotated, graded, and categorized as to subject.

7. Larrick, Nancy. *A Parent's Guide to Children's Reading.* New York: Doubleday & Co., 1958. Contains an annotated bibliography—in the main, the book is devoted to answers to parents' questions on reading.

8. Spache, George D. *Good Reading for Poor Readers* (rev. ed.). Champaign, Ill.: Garrard Publishing Co., 1963. Gives both reading and interest levels of tradebooks. Annotated lists of workbooks, games, newspapers, magazines, and periodicals are also presented.

9. Thompson, Jean, *Books for Boys and Girls* (rev. ed.). Toronto: Ryerson Press, 1959. Annotated book list in nineteen broad categories for children of all ages.

10. Tooze, Ruth. *Your Children Want to Read.* New York: Prentice-Hall, Inc. Chaps. 5-8.

11. Tooze, R., and Krone, B. P. *Literature and Music.* Prentice-Hall, Inc., 1955. An excellent resource for social studies.

Information About Children's Books in Newspapers

The Calendar, quarterly bulletin published by the Children's Book Council, New York, New York 10010, provides important information about books for children and adolescents. The November-December issue lists the following book sections, which will appear during Book Week and may be ordered *in advance:*

The Boston Herald. Children's Book Section in November (Stephen Lynch, Promotion Dept., *Boston Herald,* Boston 6, Mass.).

Chicago Tribune. Children's Book Week Supplement in November (W. Bohnsack, *Chicago Tribune,* Chicago, Ill.).

Christian Science Monitor. Children's Book Week Feature of November (Circulation Dept., *Christian Science Monitor,* Boston 15, Mass.).

Cleveland Press. Book Fair Supplement of November (Circulation Department, *Cleveland Press,* Cleveland 14, Ohio).

Courier-Journal. Children's Books in November (Dispatch Room, *The Courier-Journal,* Louisville 2, Ky.).

New York Herald Tribune. Children's Book Section in November (*Herald Tribune,* New York 36, N.Y.).

New York Times. Children's Book Section in November (Mr. Wm. L. Murray, Subscription Manager, *New York Times,* New York 36, New York).

Oakland Tribune. Children's Book Section in November (*Oakland Tribune,* Oakland 4, Calif.).

San Francisco Chronicle. Children's Book Section in November (Book Department, *San Francisco Chronicle,* San Francisco 19, Calif.).

Washington Post. Children's Book Section in November (Circulation Department, *Washington Post,* Washington 5, D. C.).

The teacher who is a science buff may find the science book reviews in the December issue of the *Natural History Magazine* (New York) of great interest.

Many publishing companies offer lists of book reviews recently "off their presses." The authors have found the following to be extremely useful:

1. Benefic Press, Chicago, Ill.
2. Melmont Publishers, Chicago, Ill.
3. Garrard Press, Champaign, Ill.
4. Lippincott Company, Philadelphia 5, Pa.
5. Alfred A. Knopf, New York 22, N.Y.

6. Charles Scribner's Sons, New York 17, N.Y.
7. Globe Book Company, New York 10, N.Y.
8. Franklin Watts Company, New York 21, N.Y.
9. Viking Press, New York 22, N.Y.
10. Harr Wagner Publishing Co., San Francisco 5, Calif.
11. Golden Press, Inc., New York 20, N.Y.
12. Children's Press, Inc., Chicago 7, Ill.
13. Random House, Inc., New York 22, N.Y.
14. Follett Publishing Co., Chicago 7, Ill.
15. F. A. Owen Co., Dansville, N.Y.

Help in Selecting Encyclopedias

The authors include the following references for the teacher, librarian, or administrator who would like help in selecting encyclopedias.

1. "Recommended Sets for Home Libraries: A consensus of library opinion compiled by Library Journal," *Junior Libraries*, 4:9-12, April, 1958. Included are comments by librarians who have used the various sets in "children's libraries." The article contains a listing of statistics and prices on fourteen of the "more popular" sets.

2. *Choosing an Encyclopedia.* Hardy R. Finch. *Scholastic Teacher*, Oct. 6, 1955, ed. 33 West 42nd Street, New York 36, N.Y. Mr. Finch describes in detail the scrutiny that must be employed before an encyclopedea is purchased. A chart accompanies the article in which ten of the more popular sets of reference works are described. The data include such vital statistics as title, publisher, number of volumes in the set, price, evaluation rating, grade-levels, and teaching aids.

3. *A Handbook for Instructional Leaders on the Use of Encyclopedias in Schools.* Single copies issued free from the University of Washington, College of Education, Seattle 5, Wash. This handbook includes criteria for evaluating reference materials, suggestions for use with children.

Getting Reading Materials for the Classroom

. . . if you want children to read, give them books. Buy books, borrow books from the library, surround them with books, and read them books, and listen to them talk about books. Make books such a part of their lives that they will think of reading like breathing—that is, just accept it as naturally as being alive.[14]

In short, hunt everywhere you can think of and reject no book that might be suitable for your children. The main objective is to get books—and lots of them. The books that do not go over so well can be rejected at a later date. Involving children in this quest for books serves to whet their appetites for the reading that is to come.

Provision of classroom materials is step one in introducing children to the joys of reading. Certainly, this thirst for the pleasures of

[14] Phyllis Fenner, *Proof of the Pudding*, New York: John Day Co., Inc., 1957.

reading will not be satisfied by the clasroom book collection. Children will have to be guided beyond the walls of their classrooms—namely, the school and public libraries.[15]

The teacher will do well to convince parents of the importance of a child's personal library. Thus, school, home, and community share the business in alerting children to their cultural heritage through the wonderful world of books.

Arranging the Materials Section of the Classroom

The classroom should be a constant source of invitation to reading. A "reading-oriented" room should have attractive bulletin boards filled with children's murals, book jackets, and pictures they have drawn, reviews they have written, book lists, and other interesting displays. These advertise the library wares. A display case may house exhibits of all types that are frequently changed. Puppets, dolls, or figures of cardboard, paper, or wood dressed as favorite book characters may be placed about the room. A terrarium, an aquarium, and seasonal plants, leaves, and flowers help to make the room brighter and more comfortable and provide new interests and ideas for children.

The book corner should be located in the most attractive section of the room. The following points are important considerations when deciding location of the booknook:

1. It should be housed where the lighting is bright enough for children to read. Glare is to be avoided.
2. It should be the most physically suitable section of the room—out of the way; yet
3. It should be easily accessible—a place where children can read or browse without interfering with passing traffic.

The shelves should be low enough so that children are able to reach all the books. The shelf tops can serve for display purposes. The books should be held in place by bookends. There will be a catalogue case and a file box with student's reactions to various materials that children (even in the later portion of first grade) can learn to use. A magazine rack containing current newspapers, periodicals, or magazines adds to the "corner." A globe, maps, and/or atlases should be available for locating the places read about.

[15] The Elementary and Secondary Education Act of 1965 offers new hope to the culturally deprived, lower socioeconomic areas of the country. The question of Federal aid to education has taken its place among the great debates of the century. Approval or disapproval of Federal aid is not within the purvue of this book. But—for those educators who are interested in children and in books—Titles I, II, and III offer funds for children, programs, and materials.

There is no one best way to arrange the books. Some teachers place books on shelves (covers showing) by categories or subject content; others set them out irrespective of level of readability or subject or interest. The important thing to remember is that books are always arranged for easy access so that children will have freedom in browsing.

Some teachers prefer to have each child sign his own materials in and out. Others prefer to have the materials in charge of student librarian(s) trained in the simple library techniques by the school librarian or teacher. Some teachers rotate the library job among students—others prefer to entrust the responsibility in one or two children. At any rate, children should be given opportunity to learn library techniques. Above all, each child should be imbued with the care and responsibility that goes with using books.

No special furniture is needed for the book corner. Some teachers place a few tables (if the room is large enough) and "comfortable chairs" in the library corner. One school had its windows made into window seats where children could retire with their favorite books. One teacher had some throw rugs that she placed on the floor of the book corner. Here children liked to stretch out on their stomachs a la Sunday comics to enjoy their books. But, truly, it is not the furniture in the library corner, but what happens in it, that really counts.

OTHER MATERIALS CAN BE USEFUL TO SOME

Self-Practice Materials

In addition to the reading materials discussed above, the teacher must have suitable materials of the self-drill, self-practice, self-testing type at his fingertips. These are a must if the student is to be helped to overcome specific difficulties.

These materials, as in the case of the reading books, must be of considerable range in difficulty and varied to meet the children's specific needs. Some of these, such as to the various reading games and puzzles, are commercially prepared. Pages taken from workbooks may be used on occasion. At other times, the teacher-made materials will have to be reproduced and used to fill a specific need. "Whatever the form of practice material, it should be attractive in format, economical of time spent using it, and directly focused on what the child needs to know."[16]

[16] Leland B. Jacobs, "Individualized Reading Is Not a Thing," *Individualizing Reading Practices*, New York: Bureau of Publications, Teachers College, Columbia University, 1958, p. 12.

A comprehensive treatment of most of the field of instructional materials is to be found in Louis Shores' text *Instructional Materials—An Introduction for Teachers.*[17]

Workbooks are used by many teachers for independent seatwork. The authors question the value of the use of these materials when they are used as busy-work for all children. They take issue with teachers who violate good teaching-learning practices when workbooks are misused. For example, when all children get the same workbook assignment, the meaning approach to reading is often sacrificed for mechanics and word recognition. An inordinate amount of time is taken up with material inappropriate for most of the children when they would be better off reading or doing some other activity suitable to their needs and interests.

The authors have discussed the value in workbooks when the teacher selects materials or pages suitable to the needs of a single child, or a particular group and ignores the pages that do not apply. Of course, use would be based upon a need found during the conference or other exploratory teaching act. Publishers could help teachers if work-type materials were offered on perforated tear-out sheets. The teacher would then dole out the materials that are needed. Some teachers take workbooks apart and file the pages according to the type or skill presented.

Making these materials available to children is the first step in the job. It is necessary for the pupils to know how to use them. Reading the directions or telling them "how to do" the exercises may not be enough. Teaching children *the what* and *the how* of working with materials is part of teacher's responsibility in establishing a good learning environment. There is rarely so frustrating an experience as trying to teach amid a constant flow of interruptions. Children get frustrated too when they know not what to do nor how to do it!

The following suggestions are listed when presenting materials for children to use:

1. Make certain that children have received guidance needed to understand how materials are to be used.
   a. Read the directions, or have them read, but remember it will be necessary to explain what is to be done.
   b. Do one or more items with the children. Check these items with the group before leaving to move on to other groups or activities.
   c. Role-play, practice, or run through to see how it goes.

[17] *Instructional Materials—An Introduction for Teachers,* New York: The Ronald Press Co., 1960.

2. Gauge which of the children will need additional help before they will be able to work independently. Supply this help.
3. Go over the material with the group as soon after the work is completed as possible.

While children are busy at their desks the teacher can move on to other groups.

Some of the practice materials will be exploratory in nature, that is, they will help the child discover and understand how a certain skill is related to his effectiveness in reading. Other materials will be evaluative in nature. The latter will enable a child to determine his mastery of the skill being practiced.

Whatever the form of the practice material, the prime purposes governing its use is: first, its worth as a teaching-learning instrument; and second, the motivation it brings to the program.

Free or Inexpensive Materials

Many teachers take advantage of the literally hundreds of free or inexpensive materials that can be had but for the asking.

The section titled *Free or Inexpensive* in each issue of the *NEA Journal* lists many items that teachers can use.

The *Educators Guide to Free Curriculum Materials,* Educators Progress Service, Randolph, Wis., is published annually, containing detailed descriptions by title, subject, and source.

Audiovisual Materials Are Needed

The classroom in which this instructional program is rooted is a bright attractive room—but more important it is an interesting room. Audiovisual aids definitely have a place in the program.

A list of these materials that would meet the needs of all children would be endless. However, it would certainly include such easily available or accessible items as:

1. A 35 mm motion picture projector
2. Motion picture films
3. Opaque projector
4. Film strip projector
5. Film strips
6. Phonograph
7. Phonograph records
8. Radio

9. Television
10. Tape recorder
11. Book jackets
12. Illustrations from books and magazines
13. Picture collections
14. Collections of various materials, e.g., stamps, rocks, leaves, seeds, flowers, etc.
15. Current calendars
16. Display words, phrases, sentences, etc.
17. Aquaria
18. Terraria
19. Blackboards
20. Flannel boards
21. Bulletin boards
22. Classroom visitor or community resource
23. Various dramatic and other creative media.

Teachers have found the following sources of reference for films and filmstrips most helpful:

1. *Educational Film Guide and Filmstrip Guide.* H. W. Wilson Co.,New York 53, N.Y. Published annually.
2. *Children's Reading Service, CRS Audio-Visual Catalog.* Children's Reading Service, Brooklyn, N.Y. Published annually.
3. *Audio-visual Materials for Teaching Reading.* Robert Leestma, Slater's Book Store, Ann Arbor, Mich. 1954.
4. *SVE Filmstrip Catalog.* Society for Visual Education, Chicago, Ill. Published annually.
5. *The Booklist.* Monthly film review column. American Library Association, Chicago, Ill.
6. *Films and Filmstrips.* A weekly column in *Scholastic Teacher,* New York 36, N.Y.
7. Catalogs of universities and colleges, local film libraries, and state departments.

Teachers may rent, buy, or borrow films and filmstrips from the following sources:

1. Audiovisual departments of university or colleges.
2. Public libraries.
3. State education departments.
4. Local commercial distributor (consult the local telephone directory).

References for record lists may be found among the following sources.

1. Annotated lists of records in public libraries.
2. Catalogs from commercial companies.
3. *Landmark Enrichment Records and Filmstrips.* Enrichment Teaching Materials, New York, N.Y.
4. *Picture Book Parade Motion Pictures, Filmstrips and Records.* Weston Woods Studios, Weston, Conn.
5. *Books Bring Adventures Series.* Gloria Chandler Recordings Inc., New York, N.Y.

Records may be obtained from:

1. Public library collections.
2. Commercial recording companies.
3. The American Library Association, Chicago 11, Ill.
4. Children's book departments of publishing houses. Recorded dramatizations of some books are occasionally pressed by the *Calendar.* The Children's Book Council usually lists such recordings.

Teachers can consult local newspapers for television and radio stations for various programs that might stimulate interest and lead to reading.

Visual aids not only offer direct or vicarious experiences to children, but they also serve as sources for ideas. These materials readily address themselves to each child in a different manner and they call for a response in one way or another.

Other Materials Needed

Supplies, tools, and other equipment so necessary for projects or construction work must be available for creative activities of all sorts. A list of such materials could extend *ad infinitum.* Certainly such a list would contain such essentials as:

1. A set of hand tools (perhaps a workbench).
2. A sewing kit
3. Swatches of fabrics, leather, etc.
4. Rolls of unwanted wall paper
5. Assorted color papers
6. Pieces of lumber
7. All types of coloring materials (crayons, paints, chalk, etc.)
8. Paper of all types—writing, drawing, finger painting, murals, etc.
9. Stapler and staples
10. Thumb tacks, nails, screws

11. Scissors
12. Paper punch
13. Mucilage, airplane cement, glue
14. Scotch tape
15. Plasticene, clay
16. Paints, colored chalk

Teachers must remember that noise with decibels at a level that prevents easy communication between teacher and whomever he is working cannot be allowed. But activities that require noise are certainly permissible during a "work period." Materials for project work or other creative activities, then, must be available on the basis of permissible activities.

Community Resources—Field Trips[18]

Resources and resource people help to enrich any instructional program. The school and/or public librarian can play a very important role. They can, through close cooperation with the teacher, learn the interests and abilities of children and thus help be of service. They can also help in providing new materials for the classroom book corner.

Sharing of experiences may be the contribution of the librarian, the principal, other teachers and children, parents, community members, etc. There are times when authors of children's books may be of service through personal visits or through correspondence.

A resource file may be of immense help in planning field trips. Someone on the staff—for example, the librarian, a teacher, or the audiovisual director—should have the responsibility of keeping the files up to date. The list should include municipal organizations, individuals, industrial plants, etc., who have shown a willingness and a desire to work with the schools. Such a list would include:

1. Dairies
2. Bakeries
3. Factories
4. Lumber yards
5. Markets
6. Airports
7. Stores
8. Museums
9. Zoos

[18] See also Chapter 9.

10. Theaters
11. Fire houses
12. Police stations
13. Postoffices
14. Municipal water works
15. Newspaper plants
16. Parks
17. Farms
18. Historical landmarks
19. Sea ports

These are but a few of the easily accessible places for field trips. These provide children with many opportunities to observe, explore, and examine. What a fund of information these excursions provide for discussion, reproduction, role-playing, etc. They can serve as the springboard for initiating study and research; they can be an integral part of the class program; or they can serve as a culminating or follow-up activity. Audiovisual aids, in the form of people, places, or things, are all valuable resources for learning.

The learning child is an active child whose world is no longer bound by the walls of the classroom—no longer limited to the jawbone, blackboard, and textbook. All sources of stimulation are used —many books, many materials, the community outside, and the world at large provide the laboratory in which the children learn.

Thus we come to the end of this text. But we come knowing that nothing is ever really finished, nor ever perfect. Particularly is this true in education. In the future when hindsight will again prove its usual efficacy, we can evaluate how important are the major premises upon which this book was built. Let us rephrase them from the statements early in the book:

> Teaching is a human act, and so we present methodology that puts children and their adult teachers together, not as automatons, but as human beings that grow and strengthen each other.
>
> Beauty is a major force, if not the major force, for good in the world. So we present a way in which the most beautiful of books, the trade books, find their way into the too frequently drab surroundings of classrooms.
>
> Knowledge is crucial in our burgeoning world. It is to be seized, to be shaken, and to be loved, for itself alone, and for what it can do for he who possesses it. We present a means toward its acquisition within the limits only of time, space, and brains.

There are no limits to being human, to loving beauty, to cherishing knowledge. Learning without limitations. Teaching without boundaries. These are the beckoning horizons.

INDEX